WHOLE LANGUAGE, WHOLE LEARNERS

Creating a Literature-Centered Classroom

WHOLE LANGUAGE, WHOLE LEARNERS

Creating a Literature-Centered Classroom

Laura Robb

QUILL

WILLIAM MORROW

New York

Library of Congress Cataloging-in-Publication Data
Robb, Laura.
Whole language, whole learners: creating a literature-centered
classroom/Laura Robb.
p.   cm.
Includes bibliographical references and index.
ISBN 0-688-11956-5
1. Language experience approach in education—United States.   2. Language arts
(Elementary)—United States.   3. Literature—Study and teaching.
(Elementary)—United States.   I. Title.
LB1576.R6   1994   372.6—dc20   93-46444   CIP

Printed in the United States of America

First Quill Edition

1   2   3   4   5   6   7   8   9   10

BOOK DESIGN BY PIXEL PRESS

*For my husband, Lloyd, who has
sustained me throughout my journey.*

*For my students, with deepest thanks
for teaching me.*

CONTENTS

FOREWORD

Here is an exceptional book about whole language and literature-centered teaching that addresses upper grades as well as primary grades. Written by a master teacher who speaks with honesty and integrity, *Whole Language, Whole Learners* rings with truth because it is filled with authentic voices: voices that enchant, voices that sing, and voices that affirm. Many of the voices celebrate children's literacy learning, but others are strident, questioning the new methods used to attain a wholesome literacy. A throng of cheerful voices counterbalances the negative ones, however; they speak passionately about leading a child through the tender early steps or the treacherous adolescent steps to literacy through literature. The combined voices create a chorus of people spread along a continuum from believers to nonbelievers. They represent the actual world of teachers, students, librarians, school administrators, parents, authors, illustrators, and communities interested in children's learning. We learn by listening to them.

The first and primary voice is that of Laura Robb—an advertising copywriter forced to change jobs when she moves to a new part of the country. Laura's husband encourages her to teach school, but, though she herself is an insatiable reader, she fears she doesn't know enough to teach students how to read. She tries her hand at teaching, however, and learns some truths about herself, her beliefs, and her students.

Laura's voice becomes more confident during the second year of teaching, when she moves to a new school district where the administrator's philosophy is closer to her own. She confirms tentative teaching ideas she had tried during her first year and notes with interest that teachers who are avid readers themselves create readers in their classrooms. She finds that the most exciting classrooms are inhabited by readers—teachers who read and have students who read. Laura begins to speak with conviction as she confirms some of her deepest beliefs.

Laura's voice becomes even stronger in ensuing years as she reaches out to work with other teachers in neighboring classrooms. She hones her own beliefs by sharpening them on the edge of others' questions and practices;

she clarifies precisely what she believes and why she believes it as she explains her procedures. Her voice develops courage. She speaks with authority. She becomes passionate about what she believes.

Laura's voice gains even more strength through direct experience with students but also through her independent reading and study. She studies how children learn language, how they respond to literature, and how they learn to write. Her own professional development program is a model for a continuous learner. She not only knows what to do in classrooms but why she does it. She speaks as easily about theory and research as she does about a novel she reads with her students.

Laura discovers that children's book writers and illustrators have goals similar to her own, and that they can contribute to students' and teachers' understanding. She invites them to add their voices to hers, bringing special insights into the process of reading and writing. They talk about why they create books, the messages they want to convey, and the passion that drives them to work hard. Katherine Paterson talks about the need to give children the courage to sail off the edge of a map, to create new worlds, and to explore new horizons. They don't learn this by filling in blanks on work sheets. George Ella Lyon describes the difference between gifts that are freely given and stars that are distant objects to be admired. She argues that we need to nurture gifts in students rather than develop them as stars. Rosemary Wells shows that reading relates to writing because by reading we see how other people use words to get their ideas across. She says that three-quarters of her time is spent revising—nothing is ever good enough the first time.

Illustrators Jerry Pinkney and Steven Kellogg describe creating images and stories through art. Pinkney strives for accuracy by using live models and researching the clothing, buildings, people, and behavior appropriate to the setting and period of his work. Kellogg discusses the care taken to produce a book but says that it remains a frozen tableau on a stage until a teacher, librarian, or parent opens the cover and illuminates the theater by reading to a child.

Teachers' voices sound loud and clear. Some say, "Give me a recipe for whole language." Or, "I will become a whole language teacher if I can learn about it today." These voices are modulated by others who understand the continuous and never-ending learning process characteristic of whole language teachers.

Here are the voices of teachers who work with primary grade students; they help children learn how to read and at the same time learn to love reading. Other teachers work with adolescents concerned with macho behavior, the opposite sex, and maintaining an image among their peers. Whereas many whole language books concentrate on the primary grades alone, one of the unique features of Laura Robb's book is the guidance she gives to intermediate and upper grade teachers.

There are some plaintive voices of students who say, "I'm in big-time trouble . . . because I stood up and said [to a teacher], 'You just ruined this poem for me.'" There are demanding voices of students who yell out, "Stop talkin' and let her begin" because they want to hear what happens to a character in a story the teacher is reading aloud.

There are parents' voices. Some are perfectionists. "Teach my son to diagram sentences and to spell right. I'm sick of messy papers, inserts, and arrows. I want a perfect paper first time round." Other parents describe children who slipped through the cracks of a school system but who have found themselves through reading in Laura's classroom. Laura readily acknowledges and actively seeks parents' help as she guides students toward literate behavior.

The story in this book is really the story of a teacher who finds her voice. We are fortunate because that teacher is Laura Robb and because she speaks eloquently about the thoughtful path she travels to the mountaintop. We join her at the peak as she shouts to the world: Believe in children. Give them literature. Let them choose their own topics to write about. Listen to what students say. Acquaint them with writers and illustrators. For students and teachers who struggle to find their own voices, the rewards are worth the effort.

Bernice E. Cullinan
New York University

ACKNOWLEDGMENTS

This book has been growing within me for thirty years. During that time, several people have provided the encouragement and courage that has nourished my teaching life. My husband, by removing me from New York City and an advertising career, led me into the classroom and never tired of hearing my teaching stories. His listening and probing questions have been a steadfast compass and comfort. He has patiently read and edited each chapter, offering suggestions for revisions and, again, asking those all-important questions that led me to rethink and revise drafts.

To Steven and Helen Kellogg, whom I met in 1964 as parents of fifth grader Melanie—I am grateful for their unflagging belief in the kind of learning community the children and I were building and for prodding me to proceed with the book. I am grateful, too, to Katherine Paterson for trusting me with her stories and spending many supportive mornings and afternoons in my classroom. To Nancy Larrick, thanks for the "gift of doing poetry" and for enthusiastically listening to me rave on about projects: Your ear and joy have always encouraged me to reach for more.

My appreciation and thanks to Donald E. W. Niemann, the headmaster of Powhatan School, who thirty years ago, when textbooks were in vogue, allowed me to construct a program using "real" books. My thanks to Billy Peebles and John Lathrop, recent heads of Powhatan, who have freely permitted me to work with children and teachers, trusting me and the children. And to Carol Chapman, second-grade teacher at Powhatan, my sincere thanks for letting me teach "the younger ones" and for braving the new terrain of writing workshop. I am forever grateful to Powhatan's librarian, Anne Wheeler, who has spent hours sharing and talking about books with me.

How appreciative I am for the trust and support for innovation and change from Superintendent Dennis Kellison and Assistant Superintendent Eleanor Ross of Clarke County Public Schools. Sincere thanks to Mary Anne Biggs, principal of Johnson Williams Middle School, and Paul Jones, principal of Cooley Elementary School, who have always been there for the children and teachers. They have encouraged me to support the transition from basal programs to whole language. A special thanks to second-grade teacher Lorrie Aikens and sixth-grade teacher Cindy Hughes; team teaching with them has been a high point.

Thanks to all the teachers who shared their students' work and enthusiasm, and to the parents who always extended themselves for the children and me.

Bonnie Jacobs, I am forever thankful for your patience and endless energy while photographing the children.

My thanks to Amy Cohn, editor in chief of children's paperbacks at William Morrow, for setting aside time in a full schedule to work with me. And to David Reuther and Ellen Dreyer, my editors, I am grateful for always listening and being there. Ellen, your guidance and our many lengthy telephone discussions have made the revision process exhilarating and joyful.

Heartfelt thanks and appreciation to Bernice Cullinan, who read the manuscript in its early form and offered positive suggestions for improving the book. Her support and interest in the project has been a steadfast, guiding beacon.

Most important, I must recognize my students for allowing me into their lives: You have all taught me well.

And gladly wolde he lerne and gladly teche.

GEOFFREY CHAUCER
PROLOGUE TO *THE CANTERBURY TALES*

PART ONE

TEACHER AS LEARNER

BEGINNINGS

On July 26, 1963, Lloyd accepts the teaching position at Shenandoah Conservatory of Music. A month later, we drive across the George Washington Bridge, headed for Winchester, Virginia.

I wrote that short entry in my journal after I watched the New York skyline disappear from the back window of our green Chevrolet.

I did not want to leave. New York was my home. Friends and family lived there. I wrote copy for a mail-order company and created their magazine advertisements. I enjoyed my work.

But Winchester, a small southern town, had no need for a New York copywriter. My background in English literature, French, and music did not fit any of the want ads I read in the local paper.

"Call some of the area school boards," my husband urged. "Maybe you can teach."

"But I haven't had one education class. They'd never even interview me."

"That's your best qualification—no education classes," he replied. "You're an insatiable reader. You write. That's what the kids should do." Inwardly, I scoffed at his proposal. School starts in two weeks, I thought. There won't be any openings there. Besides, I had never considered elementary or high school teaching as a career option. I ignored his suggestion.

Several days later, filled with envy, I watched my husband drive off to his new job. That afternoon I called the county school board and spoke to the superintendent's secretary. "As a matter of fact, we do have an opening—one of our sixth-grade teachers has taken a year's leave due to illness."

A whirlwind of interviews followed—the superintendent, the instructional director, and finally the principal. The application forms, references. The job was offered, and I accepted.

My inner voice chastened me like a mother scolding an incorrigible child. Come on, Laura. No education classes. No experience. No children of your own. What do you know about sixth graders? About how they learn? About organizing a classroom? Although I liked children, my contact with kids could be described as limited: occasional baby-sitting in high school, two summers assisting with preschool children's play groups at a bungalow colony in the Catskill Mountains, and five piano students during four years of college. I journeyed back in time, rummaging through grade school years, searching for useful images and memories. Two frames consistently reappeared: the daily race to complete workbook pages and snatch time to read library books; and frequent punishments for misbehaving, which meant writing my own words after dutifully copying the teacher's words from the blackboard. Or even worse, not writing about the assigned topic.

My husband believed I could do a terrific job in the classroom. But what did he know, something inside me challenged. "Think like a voice teacher," he counseled. "I have to know how I learn music, how I produce beautiful sounds, in order to coach students. But all the knowledge I share with them means nothing unless they sing. Just let the kids read and write." The words *let the kids read and write* brought a flash of memory of my passion for library books and writing. But with only two days plus a weekend to prepare a classroom for thirty-three boys and girls, I temporarily shelved thinking for action and drove the ten miles to the red brick country school to inspect the room and building. Spacious and sunny with a wall of windows, the room contained thirty-five weathered, nailed-to-the-floor student desks, a wooden table that served as a teacher's desk, a wall of empty bookshelves, a blackboard, an abundance of spiders and crickets on the windowsills, plus half a dozen wasps—all experts at nosediving and circling the new teacher.

I washed. I scrubbed. I covered pock-marked cork bulletin boards with bright colored paper. My share of books consisted of sixth-grade readers and mathematics and social studies textbooks—each with an accompanying workbook. That's all. Tight budgets meant no paper, no paints, no crayons, no real books.

The principal assured me that all students would bring their own pencils and notebooks. "You'll be fine," he said. Would I? I wondered. Thirty-three students ranging from twelve to fifteen. The kids would be mine all day, except when I wasn't on lunch or recess duty.

Assigning seats, collecting lunch money, giving out books, getting to know the children, a schoolwide gathering, and extra-long recesses, I figured, would fill the first day. But what about the other one hundred and seventy-nine days?

Real books and crayons, pencils and paper—that's all I needed to help these kids learn. These words played and replayed in my mind. But I had none of these. The basal reading program contained enough material for one story and several workbook pages per week—boring stories, trivial illustrations, and a guidebook complete with a teacher's script for each selection and a myriad of mindless activities. Since the fourth-grade teacher also served as the school librarian, trips to her classroom, which doubled as the library, would be infrequent. Books. Paper. I needed these for children to become readers, writers.

Three weeks after school started, a telephone call to my mother and father, who were driving to Virginia for a visit, brought cartons of books from my childhood—books to fill empty shelves. I adopted a practice then that continues today: Once a month, my husband and I used our library cards to each check out a dozen books from the local library. Displayed on a special shelf, these books could be read only in school. Letters to magazines and organizations, explaining my needs, brought a windfall of free books and multiple copies of magazines into the classroom.

A local printer donated two overflowing cartons of paper, promising more. And thick rolls of newsprint were mine for the asking—

a telephone call to the office of the local newspaper assured me of a steady supply.

The books and paper comforted me. Fears I had about filling up the long days departed. Each day school opened and closed with my reading aloud from books that were read to me as a child: *Mary Poppins*, *Pinocchio*, *The Wizard of Oz*, *The Secret Garden*, *The Wind in the Willows*, and Grimms' and Andersen's fairy tales. At first the kids snickered comments like "You think we're first graders or something?" and "Just give us our work, we don't need to hear no dumb stories." But I persisted. Mainly because I stubbornly believed that reading stories was infinitely better than copying, as the fourth and fifth graders did, endless paragraphs of information from the board. By mid-October, a small miracle occurred. I had just completed *Mary Poppins* when Rosie Bradley blurted, "Whatcha gonna read us next, Mrs. Robb?"

"Yeah, that was a good story," several voices echoed around the room. Not everyone. But a beginning.

That afternoon I opened the cover of my beloved fairy tales by Hans Christian Andersen and began reading "The Tinder Box." I followed with "The Traveling Companion," "The Little Sea Maid," "Big Claus and Little Claus," and "The Little Match Girl." These tales truly stirred the imaginations of my sixth graders, who sat, attentive, eyes riveted on me.

One warm November morning recess, I watched Debbie and Rosie cajole fifteen-year-old Walter into playing the soldier of fortune from "The Tinder Box." Stunned and speechless, I watched them playact the opening of the story, when the soldier meets the witch and three dogs. Uncooperative Walter, usually sullen and silent, boomed, "What am I to do down under the tree?" Day after day, groups played with stories during recess. I thought that only very young

children dramatized stories and pretended to be characters. My recess observations revealed that imaginative play provided a pathway into the stories, leading the children toward enjoyment and interpretation.

Yes, I dutifully and rapidly completed the three textbooks and workbooks. The children didn't seem to mind, and I had no alternatives. Besides, I didn't know enough about how children learn to march into the principal's office and ask permission to initiate changes. Now, as I recall that first year, I recognize how limiting those children's experiences would have been had I confined them to three texts and three workbooks. Reading aloud and independently, dramatizing, and talking about stories became important ways for the children and me to learn, tapping into our love of, and deeply rooted need for, story.

Never, during that first year, did I assign writing topics. My rebellious memories supported that decision. The class wrote daily. Children chose topics and read work to the class. They progressed, not so much through my guidance, but through continuous use of their abilities.

Teaching claimed me that year, even though I decided not to return to that school district. Criticism from faculty and administration bombarded me—criticism of innovations such as reading real books, permitting children choice in writing topics, and reading aloud. They weren't interested in my observations about the children's stories. The daily encouragement from my husband, and go-for-it letters from my parents, did not relieve the isolation I experienced.

My first evaluation, composed by the director of instruction, described me as "refusing to conform to established instructional and disciplinary routines." That was only partially true. Every student completed the required curriculum—then wrote and read real books.

The persistent irritant was my refusal to accept the whip and paddle. Each time the principal returned these "disciplinary tools" to my classroom, I yanked them off their wall hooks and plunked them on his desk, carefully explaining that fear was not conducive to learning in a democracy. My final evaluation, which I received in April, recommended I be transferred to the high school to teach English. Working with older students, the administration advised, would "better use your knowledge."

In June I accepted a fifth-grade position at Powhatan, a rural independent elementary school snuggled in the Blue Ridge Mountains in Clarke County, Virginia. Though Powhatan was basal- and textbook-driven, as were all area schools, Don Niemann and Billy Peebles, two headmasters I worked under at different times, supported and encouraged change. They allowed me and others to construct a democratic, literature-rich whole language environment. In 1990 I would return to public education to learn with at-risk boys and girls in Clarke County public schools and to mentor teachers who wished to begin the transition to whole language.

During my last full-time year at Powhatan, while browsing through the poetry shelves of the school's library, I heard my name tentatively called. "Betcha don't know who I am." My brain hunted desperately to place the voice. The wide grin and buck teeth resurrected the name. "Steven?" I asked.

"Yup," he said. "Came to install a new coffeepot in the teachers' lounge. Heard some kids say your name and came to see if it was the same Mrs. Robb." Steven had been in that first class. He filled me in on his life and the lives of several classmates, and before he left, he said, "I read to my boys every night.

Learned about reading books in your class. I thought you'd like to know that."

Steven's memories provide a key insight into the reading process. Stories—listened to, read, felt, talked and thought about, and dramatized—provided a memory that time had not buried and squashed. I had not "taught" Steven to love books and reading. Steven remembered books and developed a zest for reading because he *experienced* story.

As I reflect on my teaching journey, I see that two potent beliefs about teachers and learners emerged during my first year. First, that readers and writers develop through choice and authentic experiences; second, that teachers comprehend how children learn by watching students use language. And the exuberant cries of "Eureka, I got it!" empower young and old to continue the quest for knowledge.

Lao-tzu, a Chinese philosopher who lived more than twenty-five hundred years ago, described this philosophy of teaching that has been my personal beacon. Lao-tzu's "leader" is the teacher I aspire to be. For it is in *the doing* that all learning occurs.

A leader is best
When people barely know he exists,
Not so good when people obey and
    acclaim him,
Worst when they despise him.
But of a good leader, who talks little
When his work is done, his aim fulfilled,
They will say "We did this ourselves."[1]

Reference

1. Bynner, Witter, ed. *The Way of Life According to Lao-tzu*. New York: Putnam, 1986.

BREAKING
TRADITIONS

In 1964, during my second year of teaching, I abandoned basal readers and content area textbooks. By November of that year, frustrations mounted as fifth graders and I rushed through basal texts, workbooks, and ditto sheets in order to rob chunks of time to read real books, write, and explore the inviting science laboratory in the woods and meadows that surrounded the school. I mustered up the courage to ask Don Niemann, then headmaster of Powhatan, if I could use literature across the curriculum and initiate a hands-on inquiry science program. Don used real books with his eighth-grade English students; each year his class performed a comedy by Shakespeare and studied Elizabethan England. His personal successes with literature helped my cause, and Don approved my plan. And so folk- and fairy tales from around the world, Greek and Roman mythology, poetry, and free-choice reading replaced the textbooks.

One restriction existed. If standardized test scores dropped significantly, the basals would return. I agreed, too inexperienced to fret about test scores, believing passionately that the percentiles would soar. Spring testing results celebrated our daily fare of reading, talking, and writing: Reading comprehension and vocabulary knowledge rose dramatically; specific language skill scores fluctuated, some up, some down. But I won the right to continue initiating changes. My journey into whole language had begun.

Why did the basal reading programs and textbooks make me feel like a prisoner confined by a ball and chain to a narrow cell? The teacher's guide centered reading around me, providing a script that put words in my mouth and supplied "correct" student responses. The program emphasized silent reading and skill work, neglecting writing and talking. Jeanne Chall aptly describes what I felt when she writes that the teacher who follows the basal program "is virtually enslaved to the program."[1] Though myself a product of traditional education, I rebelled against being told what and how to think and read. I wanted to encourage independence in thinking and come to know why some children loved to read and write and others didn't. In my classes, I observed, children turned to library books, not basal texts, for pleasure and entertainment.

The basal instructional series, which influenced education during the 1950s, 1960s, and 1970s, were sequentially structured programs. These series, with accompanying workbooks, ditto sheets, readers, charts, tests, reteaching and enrichment dittos, and teachers' guidebooks, formed the backbone of the traditional transmission model of teaching. The programs, written cooperatively by teams of specialists, had a senior author who coordinated the entire project. The selection and ordering of skills did not necessarily emerge from research on how children learned to read. Basal authors selected skills based on the premise that learning to read is sequential, and the placement of skills bowed to the need to design, grade by grade, a logical series of lessons for the school year.

Traditional reading instruction supported the notion of reading as a separate subject. Teachers directed students, grouped by ability, to master a series of subskills. Sets of accompanying tests measured students' mastery of the particular program, testing knowledge of subskills such as phonics, syllabication, word identification, synonyms, antonyms, dictionary use, and even comprehension skills. Connections relating isolated skills to reading continuous texts were nonexistent. In fact, workbook and ditto exercises had little or no relation to the stories in the readers. And these stories, written by committee, controlled vocabulary and lacked a strong author's voice.

This structure confines and narrows thinking. It assumes that all children will learn the same set of facts in the same way and from the same materials. Though most basal authors agree that programs should not be all-inclusive and that children should read library books, the overwhelming amount of material to be covered eliminates time for free-choice reading during the school day.

Getting into a book during sustained silent reading.

A power pyramid develops that directs learning. Curricula control and restrict teachers, and putting children through the paces becomes the measure of effective teaching. Teachers and curricula control and restrict children, and the measure of students' progress consists of completing the program and giving "correct" answers. These controls and restrictions disempower teachers and students. Debate, divergent thinking, and decision making disappear in this quiet teacher-centered classroom where the answer key, not inquiry and thinking, judges students' responses right or wrong.

Even the revised literature-based basals of the 1980s, which include stories by outstanding authors, still supply teachers with a sequential, total reading program that, according to the National Council of Teachers of English (NCTE) Commission on Reading, has constructed "a gap between how reading is learned and how it is taught and assessed" in the majority of American classrooms.[2] Many teachers successfully use the stories and selected activities from these updated programs as part of a reading-rich program that also incorporates real books. The point is that talking and writing about stories are central to classroom life. However, those teachers who carefully follow all elements of basal programs often focus on prescribed answers and cease to encourage divergent thinking.

During a children's literature class I taught in 1985, a group of teachers discussed reasons why the lady in Natalie Babbitt's "The Very Pretty Lady" found happiness after she turned ugly. Using the story to support ideas, the group compiled this list of possible reasons:

- She found a man who loved her.

- She was loved for who she was, not for her beauty.

- She married and had a baby and wasn't alone anymore.

- Her beauty no longer posed a problem.

- She was able to give love and not worry about why she was loved.

- Instead of teasing men, she had a relationship that was meaningful—husband, child.

- She felt the fulfillment of having a family.

- She learned that giving to others was more important than taking.

One teacher raised her hand and in a timid voice asked, "But which is the right answer?"

"All of them," I replied.

"How would I grade a work sheet or test?" she asked. Unfortunately, the guides and answer keys had narrowed her thinking to expect a predetermined set of right answers.

In the traditional classroom, mandates to cover more and more information have created product-driven curricula that focus on mastery of facts and students' final work, both easy to measure and grade. In this environment, both teacher and child stop inquiring, stop thinking, stop storying—using stories to make sense of their world. Arrival is more important than the learning process itself.

That's why, in 1964, I turned my back on basal instruction, for I disliked being controlled and told what to say and what to accept as right or wrong. Students' responses to workbook exercises, though judged incorrect by the answer key, made perfectly good sense—especially when they explained the reasoning behind a choice. There seemed little to model my teaching practices on except those wonderful teachers who read aloud. The high school teacher whom I can still vividly picture is Mr. Ames, my American studies teacher. Tall and reedy, in baggy corduroy slacks and loud plaid flannel shirts, he read us Mark Twain, Stephen Crane, Edith Wharton, Tillie Olsen, and Willa Cather. His passion for those authors became our passion, and I remember rereading every book he shared. Those powerful memories and my passion for reading supported the decision to integrate long and short read-aloud sessions throughout the school day.

The children were my first whole language teachers. I listened to their conversations, I observed, I asked them questions about their reading and writing and why they devoted endless amounts of time to some projects and minimum energy to others. Their message was simple: interest. A burning curiosity about a particular subject motivated the children to read and research, to write and construct elaborate projects that satisfied their quest for answers. And I asked myself a question then that I continue to ask teachers today: Why shouldn't children read and write in ways that adults read and write?

Even with choices in reading and writing, even with pairs and small groups talking and researching topics they selected, life wasn't perfect. Those first two years and thereafter, I had some students who were uninterested in reading and writing. But they didn't relish learning with workbooks and textbooks either. However, reading aloud each day and hearing classmates and me talk about books we read and loved did more for many reluctant readers than a multitude of threats and bribes. When a resistant reader checked out a book, it was his or her choice to risk investing time in a novel or story. Choice made the difference, for desire backs choice.

The teaching lessons from those early years still ring true today: Watch and listen to kids, talk to kids about their process, read their work, and take copious notes for reflection.

Working alone often opened the door to voices that chided my beliefs; I yearned for support. In the mid-1970s, I joined a local and state reading council, attended annual conferences, and heard about educators such as Frank Smith, Louise Rosenblatt, Donald Murray, Ken and Yetta Goodman, and Gordon Wells. Their books and articles confirmed so much of what I had observed in my classroom, and they all greatly influenced my own literacy learning model. I embraced a democratic philosophy with a solid historical tradition, based in research on how children learn to read, write, think, and speak: whole language.

The years 1938 and 1939 produced works by three major educators who provided the rationale for key whole language views. John Dewey emphasized the importance of constructing curricula centered around learners' needs and the power of reflective teaching; Alvina Burrows called for teachers to allow

Sixth graders confer about a story they are writing together.

children to write about their own experiences in their own voices; and Louise Rosenblatt, in her revolutionary work *Literature as Exploration*, destroyed the concept of texts, written or spoken, transmitting uniform meanings. She described the complex and active relationship between reader and text as a transaction, with each reader creating an original "poem" from the text.

Psychologists and linguists like Jean Piaget, Lev Vygotsky, and Michael Halliday influenced whole language beliefs by emphasizing that learning language and solving problems are social and active, and that learners comprehend how language works by using it.

Donald Graves and Lucy Calkins popularized the writing process, using the classroom as a laboratory to understand how and why children write. Ken Goodman and Frank Smith offered insights into the reading process along with ways to apply research findings to the teaching of reading. Don Holdaway, working in New Zealand, developed the shared book experience, demonstrating how oversized books prepared by teachers and parents engage children in reading. Brian Cambourne logged hundreds of hours in Australian classrooms conducting research on literacy learning. A wealth of books about literacy and language acquisition by master classroom teachers and university researchers is available today to help teachers understand classroom practices and to support the development of the teacher as researcher, decision maker, thinker, and observer.

Whole language, as the Goodmans point out in *The Whole Language Catalog*, is a grass-roots revolution in education. Teachers, influenced by what they observe in classrooms, form the backbone of whole language theory. Their research, observation, stories, debate, communication, and continuous inquiry into how children learn ensure a dynamic evolutionary philosophy that continuously responds to the search for a greater understanding about learners and learning, teachers and teaching.

This ever-evolving democratic learning model defines the classroom as a place where students and teacher work together, governed by a set of rules they have established. While teachers and their students work daily, negotiating and building a learning society in the classroom, school administrators provide opportunities for teachers to build community. A supportive network develops when a school makes time within the day for teachers to learn and share together. Learning is social for kids and adults. Young and old exchange stories, share decision making, celebrate triumphs, grow from errors, collaborate, take risks, speak out, listen, and nurture. And a by-product of this exhilarating process is community.

Through individual enterprise, by working with students and communicating with

Second graders listening to Jan Brett's Annie and the Wild Animals.

colleagues, whole language teachers constantly grow and change as learners and thinkers. To know each child and understand how that child learns, to evaluate that child in ways that reflect individual progress, takes time and dedication. Perhaps the most difficult task of whole language teachers is to admit that studying and reading and researching never stop.

In the larger community of town or city, groups of teachers, parents, and administrators read and write and reflect the same way that students and teachers work in the smaller community called classrooms. Authors and illustrators create stories and art that bring young and old together. Whole language philosophy provides the framework for a lifetime learning model that encourages collaboration and personal involvement in literacy in school and beyond.

Periodic reflection on classroom practices and educational philosophy should lead to a questioning of daily experiences in terms of whole language and traditional models. The context of one's teaching and learning life should reflect one's philosophy. The chart below compares some of the basic premises of the traditional transmission learning model with the active, democratic whole language model in terms of teacher and student roles and classroom practices.

Traditional	Whole Language
Decision making is autocratic.	Decision making is collaborative and democratic.
Students are grouped by ability.	Students are grouped heterogeneously.
Teacher transmits a body of knowledge to students who passively receive it.	Teacher is coach/ co-learner who provides a variety of resources.

Traditional	Whole Language
Teacher talk dominates.	Students talk and think about reading and writing.
Language is divided into subskills; learning moves from parts to whole.	Language is kept whole: integration of reading, writing, listening, and speaking across the curriculum.
Learning consists of mastering skills and memorizing facts.	Learning consists of developing strategies for independent problem solving.
Curriculum is the same for all learners.	Curriculum meets the developmental needs of individual learners.
Basal- and textbook-driven.	Literature-centered, print-rich, writing-rich, inquiry-rich.
Product-driven.	Emphasizes process.
Learning is competitive.	Learning is collaborative.
Objective testing.	Evaluation of process.

Breaking with tradition is difficult and comes slowly. Start where you are—with what you know—and build on that unique foundation. Sure, you'll make mistakes; sure, you'll move back and forth between both models, and that's okay. You'll learn about whole language teaching as you learn about language—through use.

Whole language teachers listen to and watch children learn. They view learning as a very personal thing and recognize that teaching must respond to children's individual developmental needs. Together, teacher and children construct meaning by talking, by reading, by writing, by observing, by inquiring; both negotiate curriculum and choose topics of interest to research. In the process, teacher and students refine their concepts about oral and written language. The teacher hypothesizes how children learn, confirming and adjusting theories through observation and reflection.

Whole language teaching calls for courage, grit, and personal commitment. Moving beyond the guidebooks requires taking control of your own learning. You'll need to lobby for more effective use of faculty meeting time and invite colleagues to explore their teaching assumptions.

For years I watched colleagues at Powhatan secretly grade papers or design tests during weekly faculty meetings they called "boring." Just like the children, we passed notes back and forth, shuttling personal comments. A typical meeting agenda included such items as sports events and snow day schedule changes that could have been circulated among faculty on a weekly information sheet.

When I asked several teachers if they would like to meet bimonthly before school or in the evening, most replied, "Don't ask me to do another thing!" At first, I resented their lack of zeal and desire to learn—for some faculty these were the very traits they often complained about in their students while chatting in the teachers' lounge. But I moved beyond those first feelings, realizing how difficult it was for teachers to learn about whole language in schools where the traditional teaching model prevailed.

For weeks I lobbied for two hours of unstruc-

Recording a dictated story based on Jill Bennett's Teeny Tiny, *illustrated by Tomie De Paola.*

tured faculty meeting time per month. Billy Peebles, headmaster of Powhatan, will tell you that I wore him down. And it's true—I persisted, feeding him articles and books I wanted to share with colleagues. After one early morning administrative meeting, heaving a huge sigh, he agreed to one hour every other month—on a trial basis.

As the year went on, our meetings looked like a whole language classroom as small groups and pairs read, discussed, and finally shared with the entire group. Some even took notes, and a few checked out journals and books to take home! Our reading connected to classroom practices and student issues, and I observed teachers using planning time to help each other solve problems. Best of all, many teachers were taking the time to visit each other's classrooms.

Part of the commitment in adopting whole language philosophy involves redefining the meanings of learning and learners. I spent the month of August 1985 training the faculty at Powhatan School in writing workshop. Everyone voluntarily read *The Art of Teaching Writing*, by Lucy Calkins, and Donald Murray's *Write to Learn*. During those hot summer days, teachers agonized about their ability to cope with change. "There's a voice inside my head," confessed Carol Chapman, "that says I can't write myself. How can I get the children to write?" Carol, like all teachers who are breaking with traditions, must fight her inner voice—the voice that challenges change and capitalizes on fears.

Writing workshop opened the door to whole language teaching for Carol. One day, after dismissal, she came running to my classroom, excited and out of breath, pulling me to her second-grade room. "The kids didn't want to get ready to go home," she told me. "They said 'We're writing and can't stop.' When I told them they'd miss their bus, I hardly got a reaction." And Carol described her class to me: Pairs and groups read to each other in small groups under desks and in corners. Several students, lying on their stomachs, alternately wrote and drew pictures. All were so absorbed in their work that she felt guilty insisting they clean up and pack for dismissal.

One year later, Carol shelved her basal readers to create a literature-centered program. "I'm learning as much as my children," she observed. "And I watch them and listen to them instead of parroting teaching scripts."

Carol, like other whole language teachers, now recognizes the language variations within her classroom, and she works to integrate reading, writing, thinking, and talking into every lesson. By becoming an active contributor in the community of her second graders, Carol has created a supportive environment where children and teacher learn through observation, collaboration, talking, reading, and writing.

Though I've been teaching for more than thirty years, I'm still becoming a whole language teacher. Day in and day out I revise past observations and thinking, combining them with what I see and know today, in order to meet the present needs of my students. Each year newly discovered books mingle with old favorites as students and I adjust themes and meet new authors and illustrators through our reading. Sometimes it's lonely work, but it's never boring. And the best part is the new challenge waiting to be explored.

References

1. Chall, Jeanne. *Learning to Read: The Great Debate.* New York: McGraw-Hill, 1967, page 218.

2. The Commission on Reading, National Council of Teachers of English. "Basal Readers and the State of American Reading Instruction: A Call for Action." *Language Arts.* Vol. 66, No. 8, December 1989, pages 896–898.

AS I SEE IT

Katherine Paterson

Those of you who know me well are wondering how I dare make a speech about courage. Well, this isn't the first time. I made a speech which was sort of about courage nine years ago in Boston. As you might suspect, I had nothing to do with choosing the topic of my speech, which was a quotation from T. S. Eliot: "Do I Dare Disturb the Universe?" My answer at that time was no, I hardly dared disturb my springer spaniel, who was a creampuff of a dog if there ever was one. Now Blossom, the springer, is long gone, and I am no more eager to dare the universe than I was nine years ago in Boston.

Yet when Laura asked me to speak to you today, it seemed to me that the single quality needed by both teachers and writers today was courage. People are always asking me about talent. How do I know if I'm good enough? they ask. Well, you don't know. Nobody knows. There's no guarantee when you start this business that you'll succeed. There's no knowing in advance if you *ought* to succeed. We all know stories about people who were told by a teacher or a great writer that they had no talent. That they should give up writing and get a real job. They were discouraged, but they somehow didn't give up and years later they were rich and famous—or at least famous.

So talent is an iffy commodity. A lot of people have it. But the courage to keep at it— sheer donkey endurance—that is rare, and without it you might as well give up and get a real job.

In this business you need all kinds of courage. Courage to keep going, courage in the slough of failure, and courage in the fishbowl of success.

Some years ago a friend asked me about another writer who had written one wonderful book and was never heard of again. "What happened to her?" my friend asked. "She had such great talent, so much to say. How could she just quit?"

"Loss of nerve," I muttered. Of course, I have no idea why that writer stopped writing. I think I was engaged in something psychologists call projection. I know all about loss of nerve. A lot more about loss of nerve than I do about courage. But my subject today is not loss of nerve but courage. So let me, like the storyteller I am, begin with a story.

The story is told that in the fourth century B.C., Alexander the Great, fresh from his conquest of Persia, began a march eastward toward the fabled treasures of India. His army fought its way through what is now Afghanistan and Pakistan, moving through the mountain passage in the Hindu Kush into India proper, across the Indus River and the plains, and beyond even the Ganges River, when suddenly, one day his men looked up and saw before them a gigantic wall of snowcapped mountains blocking their path. They consulted their maps. There must be some mistake. There were no mountains on this route. Slowly it dawned on them. They had marched right off the map.

Now, whatever you may think of Alexander, or Columbus, for that matter, it takes a great deal of courage to march or sail right off the map.

What do you do in life when all the charts let you down? Recently I heard about Max Wartburg, a bright, happy eleven-year-old boy who suddenly learned that he had a rare form of leukemia. Eleven-year-old boys are not supposed to contract chronic myelogenous leukemia. There's no chart on how to live such a life. You can retreat into yourself, into fear and self-pity, but Max chose instead to march right off the map. Instead of living out his days in absorbed self-pity, Max organized a drive to get bone marrow donors not only for himself but for all the victims of his disease.

Teachers, I thought, know about marching off the map. It takes a lot of courage simply to face the unknown of every morning in a classroom of children, coming as they do from such varied and often deeply troubled families. I suggest the geography of most classrooms is off the map, and every day brave teachers march forward, not knowing where they will be going.

Last night Laura was speaking of your courage—those of you who have decided to venture out into new ways of teaching. There are no charts for what to do at 8:45–9:15–10:10. You remember *Raiders of the Lost Ark*. Harrison Ford says to Karen Allen, "Go to Cairo and I'll meet you there."

"But what are you going to do?"

"I don't know. I'll make it up as I go along."

Some of you must be feeling like Karen Allen this week—what do we do next? Believe me, it can be scary to launch out over the edge of the map.

Let me tell you another story. Vermont, like too many states in our country, has a large illiterate population. For the last decade, great efforts have been made to tackle this problem in my state, as in yours. Seven or eight years ago, a couple of the tutors for adult basic education began talking about how they might do a better job, and they decided that adults who were just beginning to read needed to know the full joy of books. Their concern blossomed into the Vermont Reading Project. This is a book discussion program for new adult literates using children's literature.

This is the way it works: A series of discussions is set up on a single theme: home—friendship—courage—history. It will run for three months, meeting once a month, usually in a public library. Adult students are invited to attend with their tutors. Each night three books will be discussed that relate to the theme. One is a picture book, one a beginning reader, and the third a novel. The idea was that each student would be given all three books, and then he or she could choose a book on his or her own level and still be able to enter into the discussion of the theme. The idea broke down, however, when it became apparent that every student was determined to read all three books. The students who could not handle the novel simply bullied their tutors into reading it aloud or helping them get through it word by laborious word.

In 1989 new literates in Rutland had a wonderful idea. Through book discussion, they had come to love books. "Let's have a celebration," they said. "Let's invite the students from all over the state, choose a book that everyone will read, and discuss."

The book they chose was *The Great Gilly Hopkins,* and because the author just happened to live in the state, and Barbara Bush wasn't available, they asked me to speak at the celebration.

The Vermont Council on the Humanities, IBM, and, of course, that company that always helps, Ben and Jerry's, were enlisted to provide money for the event. The owner of a ski resort motel offered his beautiful facilities. But would anyone come?

More than three hundred students and tutors did, from all over the state, even though for many it meant missing a day's wages, taking a bus at dawn to meet with strangers, and, not incidentally, to reveal to three hundred other people that they had just learned to read.

When the invitation to speak was passed on to me by Sally Anderson, the state director of the Reading Project, she said: "Um, Katherine, I think I'd better warn you. Most of these people have never heard a formal speech in their lives."

"I think you're saying I shouldn't have a speech written out the way I always do."

"I'm afraid so," she said.

A librarian friend drove me to the Cortina Inn near Rutland, over the mountains, along curved back roads by the river. I am not given to motion sickness, but believe me, I was near death from fright. And it was not Grace's driving. An hour and a half to fill and no prepared manuscript, not even any real notes. I don't memorize well anymore. My gray cells have blanched out. I alternated during that long early morning drive between nervous giggles and intense if silent prayer. "Oh God, let me get through this speech without making a fool of myself!" Now, I have not in my long Presbyterian life had many experiences when I could truly say that I heard the voice of God. But I seemed to that morning. And God said: "Shut up. This is not your day."

And when I shut up and forgot about myself and my own fear, I had one of the most amazing days of my life. It was an audience a politician would die for. They hung on every syllable. They laughed at every joke. If I asked a theoretical question, someone was sure to answer. The leaders had to bully us to stop at the end of the hour and a half while the audience was still giving their testimonies to life and the power of books to challenge and to heal. These people gave me themselves, because they had read Gilly's story and they identified with her hurt and anger. They loved her, and by extension, they loved me because I had somehow given her to them. How rich we writers are to be allowed to share so deeply in the lives of readers!

As I turned back to the story I was trying to write, set in the Vermont of the nineteenth century, of course my growing friendships with adults just coming into the joy of reading were very much on my mind. Lyddie, like many of my new friends, had to take on the responsibilities of adulthood when still a child. She, like they, had to struggle against terrible odds and, despite her lack of schooling, determined to read for herself a book a friend had read to her and that she loved.

Still, even as I wrote, I felt sad that the book was too difficult. It would be inaccessible to the very people who had inspired much of its writing, but I believe strongly that a book teaches you how it ought to be written, and I was trying to obey the dictates of this particular story. I would wreck it if I tried to scissor it down to fit a particular audience.

As it turned out, I was wrong about the inaccessibility of *Lyddie*. For this, the third year of celebration of People and Books, *Lyddie* was one of five books relating to Vermont history that participants might choose to read and discuss. In honor of Vermont's bicentennial, the Shelburne Museum (which is our answer to Williamsburg) provided elegantly written and printed study guides to each book, relating the contents of the book to what participants would see as they toured the various buildings and exhibits on the Shelburne grounds. More than five hundred people came, and of those, more than one hundred new readers chose to read and discuss *Lyddie*.

One of the participants, Delphia Lupien, has said I might share some of her reflections on that wonderful day.

[My teacher, Barbara Ploof,] is the one who encouraged me to read *Lyddie*, and I'm glad that she did. . . . Lyddie is a lot like me because I don't know how to read very well, and Lyddie had a hard time, too. But Lyddie is more like I would like to be. . . . I really did have such a wonderful time that day at the Shelburne Museum. The museum brought *Lyddie* to life. . . . I want to thank you for spending the day with us and writing and autographing such a wonderful book. I really had a great day. I can't remember when I had such a wonderful day. I didn't want the day to end.

That is what Delphia wrote about her reading adventure. And thinking of new readers like Delphia, this is what I wrote:

The next day in the mill, the noise was just as jarring and her feet in Triphena's old boots swelled just as large, but now and again she caught herself humming. *Why am I suddenly happy? What wonderful thing is about to happen to me?* And then she remembered. Tonight after supper, Betsy would read to her again. She was, of course, afraid for Oliver, who was all mixed up in her mind with Charlie. But there was a delicious anticipation, like molded sugar on her tongue. She had to know what would happen to him, how his story would unfold.

Diana noticed the change. "You're settling in faster than I thought," she said. But Lyddie didn't tell her. She didn't quite know how to explain to anyone, that it wasn't so much that she had gotten used to the mill, but she had found a way to escape its grasp. The pasted sheets of poetry or Scripture in the window frames, the geraniums on the sill, those must be some other girl's way, she decided. But hers was a story.

That is our work, isn't it—yours and mine? To, like Betsy, give stories—to provide the nourishment and healing and joy of books—to those who need them for the spirit as they need food and drink and shelter for the body. It's too daring a business for me and I often lose my nerve. But readers like Delphia make me ashamed of my cowardice. I see the courage of ordinary men, women, and children living out their lives in a harsh and frightening world, and I pull myself together and, once again, head off toward the edge of the map.

SELECTED BOOKS BY
KATHERINE PATERSON

Angels and Other Strangers: Family Christmas Stories. New York: Crowell, 1979.

Bridge to Terabithia. Illustrated by Donna Diamond. New York: Crowell, 1977.

Come Sing, Jimmy Jo. New York: Lodestar, 1985.

The Crane Wife. Translated by Katherine Paterson. Illustrated by Suekichi Akaba. New York: Morrow, 1981.

Flip-Flop Girl. New York: Lodestar, 1994.

Gates of Excellence: On Reading and Writing Books for Children. New York: Elsevier/Nelson, 1981.

The Great Gilly Hopkins. New York: Crowell, 1978.

Jacob Have I Loved. New York: Crowell, 1980.

The King's Equal. Illustrated by Vladimir Vagin. New York: HarperCollins, 1992.

Lyddie. New York: Lodestar, 1991.

The Master Puppeteer. Illustrated by Haru Wells. New York: Crowell, 1975.

Of Nightingales That Weep. Illustrated by Haru Wells. New York: Crowell, 1974.

Park's Quest. New York: Lodestar, 1988.

Rebels of the Heavenly Kingdom. New York: Lodestar, 1983.

The Sign of the Chrysanthemum. New York: Harper & Row, 1973.

The Smallest Cow in the World. Illustrated by Jane Brown. New York: HarperCollins, 1991.

The Spying Heart: More Thoughts on Reading and Writing Books for Children. New York: Lodestar, 1989.

The Tale of the Mandarin Ducks. Illustrated by Leo and Diane Dillon. New York: Lodestar, 1990.

A SOLID FOUNDATION

- "Don't you have whole language lesson plans?"

- "I just want to know how to do whole language an hour a day. That's all I have time for."

- "Can you show teachers how to do whole language in a two-hour in-service?"

- "I don't want all this theory, just tell me how to teach whole language."

Requests and comments like these worry me. Teachers and administrators searching for microwave whole language recipes. Not surprising, though. Basal programs stocked with workbooks, reproducible dittos, and elaborate teachers' manuals have raised a set of expectations about teaching that just don't exist in whole language classrooms, expectations that stem from ready-to-deliver programs.

Too many school districts have directed teachers to implement whole language philosophy with little or no support. Other schools want teachers to "do" whole language in addition to using basal reading programs and texts. Adding some literature to the curriculum and eliminating ability grouping for whole group instruction is what they consider whole language. Tests and evaluation follow the traditional teaching model, and when scores drop, whole language philosophy frequently shoulders the blame. Teachers feel frustrated, overwhelmed, and unsupported. "I've lost my way—I'm floundering," a teacher told me. "Maybe the basal wasn't so bad."

Unfortunately, without a solid theoretical base, whole language strategies become gimmicks, daily activities offered to fill stretches of time formerly consumed with workbooks and ditto sheets. When a strategy doesn't work, the teacher without a theoretical foundation can't make informed revisions and decisions.

Uninformed classroom practices can confuse and stress teachers and parents, leading to myths about whole language. Teachers, administrators, and parents not grounded in solid theoretical knowledge often assume that spelling, phonics, and writing conventions don't matter. The process of revising and reconstructing your literacy learning model should, therefore, include daily observations of how students learn. By reading the theories, observations, and research of others, you can validate your philosophy as well as rethink and innovate daily practices.

Gordon Wells's research redefined the role of stories in the learning process and created new roles for parents, children, and teachers. For fifteen years, Gordon Wells and his team of researchers studied children of different socioeconomic backgrounds, from their first words through the end of elementary education. His book *The Meaning Makers* offers examples of the children's recorded oral and written language, at home and in the classroom, and reveals how children actively construct language. Wells describes the results as "absolutely clear-cut." His research clearly associated only one activity with literacy acquisition: listening to stories. Children who have listened to thousands of stories and engaged in meaningful conversations with adults at home are more successful learners than children who are language- and story-deprived. But Wells carries the importance of reading to children and exchanging stories one step further. He suggests that *storying*, the ability to construct stories in the mind, is basic to thinking and learning across the curriculum.

> When storying becomes overt and is given expression in words, the resulting stories are one of the most effective ways of making one's own interpretation of events and ideas available to others. Through the exchange of stories, therefore, teachers and students can share their understandings of a topic and bring their mental model of the world in closer alignment.[1]

Wells's study also offers three noteworthy observations on family reading and writing patterns. These observations have implications for home and school, parents and teachers.

- The number of books parents owned and the amount of reading they did provided an adult model for children to imitate.

- Children in the study who were the most accomplished writers by eight or nine had parents who frequently wrote lists, notes, and memos.

- Parents noted that the child's interest in all forms of written language—signs, ads, labels, newspapers, and so on—was an important factor in learning to read and write, as was the child's desire and ability to spend chunks of time on literacy activities.

Wells makes the crucial point that literacy develops in environments where others continually model reading and writing. Parents, teachers, and children become proficient readers and writers by using language in meaningful, authentic contexts.

Three conclusions become apparent from *The Meaning Makers*—conclusions that support whole language philosophy and a revision of traditional classroom practices:

- Wells defines learning as "the guided reinvention of knowledge." It's the *active doing* and not the passive receiving that creates opportunities for bridging what we already know to what we desire to understand and make our own.

- Wells calls for partnerships between learners; partnerships that change roles for teachers, students, parents, and administrators. Learning becomes a collaboration. The interactions and joint ventures of various partnerships contribute to the ongoing growth of all members.

- Stories connect what learners know to new concepts and information. Stories are bridges to deeper meanings, to remembering, and to making seemingly impossible visions realities.

Stories include written and oral texts that emerge from talk about stories, from personal experiences, and from family traditions. Undoubtedly, reading and trading stories enriches a child's life in a multitude of ways. Unfortunately, too many parents stop reading to their children once the children can read, and too many middle school teachers don't read to students for the same reason. At an in-service workshop for elementary and middle school teachers, I was asked to review whole language philosophy. To involve teachers in the process, I gave small groups index cards. On each card I wrote a word or phrase associated with whole language. None of the twenty middle school teachers associated the phrase *reading aloud* with themselves. Only kindergarten and first-grade teachers consistently read aloud each day to their students.

Evaluating picture books.

Every benefit of reading aloud to young children applies to all children and adults. Reading aloud is as satisfying and beneficial for the reader as it is for the listener. Reader and listener collaborate with the writer, the listener receiving the gift of story from the reader and writer. The shared experience nourishes and sustains all three, bridging the narrow world of self to the greater world.

Whole language partnerships affirm the human passion for story and need for social interactions. Partnerships nurture individuals' gifts and provide support for each other's emerging learning process. Partnerships recognize that stories and the learning process are provisions for a lifetime of learning. The stories we gather about self, others, and the physical world propel this ongoing quest for self-awareness.

Brian Cambourne, an Australian researcher, documented what he observed in classrooms where young children successfully engaged in literacy learning. From his observations, Cambourne developed a set of seven conditions he believed were necessary for successful language acquisition. Cambourne's seven conditions are for both children and adults. They operate every day in the whole language classroom, the entire school community, and the home and surrounding neighborhoods, identifying a variety of learning partnerships.

Immersion. Children must be surrounded by all kinds of print.

Demonstration. Students learn when teachers and peers demonstrate or model the structure and use of texts for reading and writing.

Expectation. The strong bond that develops between teacher and student has the power to facilitate learning. Teacher expectations dramatically affect student performance.

Responsibility. Children learn best when they make decisions about when, how, and what to learn. Many responsibilities that belonged to the teachers have become shared responsibilities.

Use. Learners need time to practice and use their new knowledge in realistic and natural ways.

Approximation. Mistakes are necessary for learning to take place. A safe atmosphere allows for mistakes as a natural way to know and understand.

Response. Feedback from, and exchanges with, more knowledgeable learners helps children make meaning.[2]

Engagement of the learner by doing is central to Cambourne's model, and that is why all conditions must be present for students to be actively involved in reading, writing, speaking, and thinking events that foster responsibility and independence. In such classrooms, Cambourne maintains, the teacher helps learners make decisions that further their language development. This sensitivity to how children learn and to those key "teachable moments" transforms teaching into an art.

FOUR ADDITIONAL CONDITIONS

Based on classroom experience, I have added four additional conditions to my whole language learning model.

Literature. Books and wall charts with songs and poems fill classrooms. Only when chil-

dren handle, read, and talk about real books will they experience the transforming power of story and use their imaginations as they enter other worlds and lives. They create their own stories and connections as they replay and revisit texts, combining the story with their life experiences and knowledge. Louise Rosenblatt described this process as a transaction between the reader and the story; the story lives as the reader creates a unique version based on the author's words.[3]

Multiple Texts. School libraries and classrooms offer learners a range of books and magazines on a topic or theme, so every learner finds texts to read and enjoy independently. Furthermore, when the entire class reads and discusses many books on a topic, learning possibilities expand, unlike relying on one textbook or one novel, which limits the range of learning. Textbooks can become one of many learning resources—they should not be the only source.

Sixth graders browse through books in their classroom library.

Drama and Elements of Play. Drama, simulations, storytelling, and play are ways children learn before they come to school. Shirley Brice Heath documented ways children dramatize stories and assimilate traits and actions of characters into their own lives. Drama and pretend play offer children opportunities to live their way into stories and concepts and supply the framework for making connections to their own lives.

Reflection. Learners remember and begin to make connections to experiences and other stories when there's time to re-create, contemplate, talk, and write about stories and information. According to Rosenblatt, "The reader seeks to participate in another's vision—to reap knowledge of the world . . . to gain insights that will make his own world more comprehensible."[4] Teachers who pace children, marching them from one story and activity to the next, never "stopping by the woods" to savor, to ponder, to wonder, discourage meaningful transactions and move children away from choosing to read books for personal pleasure.

An important aspect of reflection is self-evaluation. Teachers and students who pause to reflect on their process come to understand "how I learn." Self-evaluation is the driving force that aids teachers and pupils to develop a thriving, democratic community where everyone has the freedom to learn and set reasonable goals.

LEARNING CONDITIONS FOR ADULTS

The eleven conditions necessary to literacy acquisition for children also apply to the adult community of learners. Young and old band together as a network of learners who honor each other's journey and process.

Immersion. To be an effective decision maker and guide learning, each whole language teacher must make a personal commitment to study, learn, communicate, and share ideas and texts. Groups of teachers from different grades need to read and discuss professional books, journal articles, and children's literature to obtain and continually update their knowledge of literacy theory and practices. In this way, whole language teaching is alive and vital, changing with our knowledge of learning and learners.

Demonstration. Teachers must also demonstrate, for colleagues and parents, reading-writing connections and strategies, and how they model them for students. Shared teacher mini-lessons afford glimpses into colleagues' processes and augment experiences with strategic demonstrations.

Expectation. As teachers, we need to recognize that our own peer group will be as varied as a class of students. Responsibility rests with teachers who know more about implementing whole language philosophy to exchange teaching stories and project positive expectations. "I'm an advanced whole language teacher, and I don't want to be with novices," a woman confided at a summer seminar. Unaware that such terms as "advanced" and "novice" whole language teachers existed, I asked her to explain the difference. "I've done whole language for a few years, and I'm ready for some advanced methods. I can't learn anything from teachers who are just starting." Notions of "advanced" versus "novice" whole language teachers are myths that attempt to establish an elite within a democratic community.

Responsibility. In child-centered classrooms, teachers negotiate curriculum and classroom rules with students. The teachers, not manuals, are responsible for guiding and evaluating curriculum and learning. Relinquishing preplanned schemes calls for reading, studying, and talking about classroom practices and anecdotal student stories. That's how teachers grow as professionals and make informed decisions.

Use. Teachers who read and write get acquainted with their own process and are better equipped to guide children's reading and writing. Eyes focused on her desk, a teacher handed me her journal of classroom observations. A strip of yellow paper marked the section for reading. "Last night *Bridge to Terabithia* made me abandon my early-to-bed schedule. At 2:00 A.M. I finished the book. I cried for Jesse and Leslie, but I cried for me, too. I never gave my students a chance to read a book through. Always questions and exercises and never enough time to really feel the story. Today will be different."

Recommendations and encouragements to abandon chapter questions and allow more time for natural reading did not click until a story compelled her to read without stopping. Reading and trading stories hold the potential for change. If writing helps us discover and comprehend these changes, then we cannot afford to deprive ourselves and our students of these transforming activities.

Approximation. The move from relying on guides and teaching formulas to individual and shared professional judgments means taking risks and making mistakes. One evening Kathy Eichler called me from Atlanta and told me that her kids called her room a "reading and writing shelter." Kathy teaches at-risk children, and she strives to help them feel safe in her room—safe so they can make as many approximations as they need to learn and progress.

Like Kathy's children, we teachers need to build our own safe shelters so we can celebrate successes and support approximations. There is no one way to become a whole language teacher. We need to tune into each learning situation so carefully that when the moment arises, we're brave enough to try a strategy. The very worst that can happen is it won't work. But we can try again and make adjustments, especially if we can turn to support groups for bolstering courage. The classroom then becomes a vital place for teacher and students to approximate, adjust, discover, and change.

Response. The skepticism and criticism of parents, colleagues, and administrators often counteract positive feedback whole language teachers receive from pupils. Commitment to change can flag as negative remarks feed shaky inner voices. Forming study and support groups with colleagues and parents, attending conferences, and reading articles by other teachers validate change and innovation as teachers explore beliefs about learners and learning.

Literature. If teachers want students to read, then they themselves must read and write, inside and outside the classroom, to demonstrate the importance of literacy. Groups of teachers who discuss adult and children's literature apprehend the power of story and the pleasure in exchanging ideas and feelings. What we do in our own lives affects how we view literacy learning in our classrooms. Donald Graves has noted a key point in speeches and in his book *Discover Your Own Literacy*: Unless reading is part of the teacher's necessary diet as a literate person, little or nothing of significance will happen for the children.

Multiple Texts. A variety of books and articles by different authors addresses various levels of comprehension and differences in knowledge and interpretation of the subject. Multiple texts offer multiple opportunities to read a range of viewpoints on a particular subject, expanding the readers' experiences and knowledge. Multiple sources reinforce the spirit of research, for opposing statements urge the reader to further explorations in order to sort information and know what is reasonable to accept.

An effective method of allowing adults to "discover" multiple texts is to form a study group where members research a topic by reading different materials. Imprinted in my memory forever is the day a teacher study group, researching portfolio assessment, polarized two members. One insisted that portfolios should only reflect a child's reading and writing. The other took a more holistic view, arguing that portfolios should represent all aspects of a child's life. Each advocated the position presented in two different articles. Finally, a teacher pointed out that perhaps there wasn't one hard-and-fast point of view. It might be better to wait until everyone had the opportunity to discuss the articles and benefit from reflection and visiting classrooms that employed portfolio assessment.

Coming to terms with diverse information is a natural result of inquiry and research. Over time, the study group connected the value of their multiple and diverse experiences to classroom learning opportunities. Members voiced the notion that relying on one book or text restricts learning and shrinks the horizon of new experiences and new knowledge.

Drama and Elements of Play. Adults play with stories in fantasies, dreams, and meditations, pretending to be a character, re-creating events to suit personal dreams and interpretations. Stories can capture our imaginations and penetrate our inner lives in mysterious and exciting ways. Dick Bell, who was teaching eighth-grade humanities with me, appeared at my desk at 4:00 P.M. "We can't let them read this book!" he shouted, shaking *My Brother Sam Is Dead* under my nose. I looked up, startled, choking back my immediate thought of how could I not let them read the book. Red eyes damp with tears confronted me. "Sam died—they let him die—I can't handle it—how can the kids?" Halting, emotion-laden words pleaded with me. "I could barely get through my classes. . . . Sam—he haunted me all day." Dick had entered the story so deeply that Sam's public hanging caused him anguish and pain. That's okay. The books that haunt us are the books worth reading.

Reflection. Reflection guides decisions. It's the foundation of innovation based on a review of data that leads to rethinking, revision, and evaluation. Reflective teachers read, write, discuss, research, and correspond with their literacy process and patterns. Knowing yourself as a learner will heighten your sensitivity to how students learn and to daily classroom events. Logging reactions to, and observations of, teaching in a journal provides notes for reflection and self-evaluation. Your journal and students' work are the tools of contemplation.

Before you move on to initiating a transition from the traditional to whole language teaching model or assessing your present classroom practices, take some time to review the chart that compares some basic beliefs of both philosophies (page 12). Reread the conditions for adults and children presented in this chapter. Consider your own teaching model and philosophy by thinking about the following questions. The process will move you toward becoming a reflective, self-evaluative practitioner.

• What does my classroom look like?

• What materials and resources do I use?

• What are my teaching practices?

• What are students' roles?

• What kinds of talk do I hear?

• How do I evaluate students?

• Is there meaningful interaction and negotiation between me and students?

Knowing yourself as teacher will assist you in taking those initial steps that lead to change. As you implement whole language philosophy, revisit the questions, review the comparative chart, and update your list. You'll be able to place yourself in "teaching space" as you evaluate and revise your goals.

By adopting the eleven conditions, you will use language to learn information, to think, and to better understand how language works. Throughout the process, you will gain insights into teaching and how children learn.

References

1. Wells, Gordon. *The Meaning Makers: Children Learning Language and Using Language to Learn*. Portsmouth, NH: Heinemann, 1986, page 219.

2. Cambourne, Brian. *The Whole Story: Natural Learning and the Acquisition of Literacy in the Classroom*. Auckland, New Zealand: Ashton Scholastic, 1988, pages 32–42.

3. Rosenblatt, Louise M. *Literature as Exploration*. 4th ed. New York: The Modern Language Association of America, 1983, page 7.

4. ———. *The Reader, the Text, the Poem: The Transactional Theory of the Literary Work*. Carbondale, IL: Southern Illinois University Press, 1978, pages 16–21.

AS I SEE IT

George Ella Lyon

I want to tell,
a person can't help if they're not so pretty as the next.

All of us are given different things
and the gift God give to some of us
ain't always lookin'
like we just come out of a beauty shop.

Now, I don't mind.
I got what I want.

But I always told my mother
that teasing me about always lookin' so awful
was goin' to make me mean. . . .
And it did.

This East Tennessee woman, whose opinion Jo Carson collected and honed in *Stories I Ain't Told Nobody Yet* (Orchard), is speaking out to teach us something: All of us are given different things. That's obvious, you say. Yes, but like many of the truths offered in the book, it's so obvious people have ignored it—or so democratic that they don't believe it. Ours is a culture that would rather make stars than nurture gifts. For one thing, stars can be sold or used to sell things, whereas gifts tend to be given away. No profit margin there. Star-worship, while generating ever-escalating performance pressure in the few, also generates a dissatisfaction with self expressed by consumerism in the many. It is in the interest of a market economy, then, to create stars. It is not in *our* interests.

Nurturing gifts requires belief in the goodness of the self unfolding, related to but not competing with others. Thus, where star is about scarcity—only a few places at the top—gift is about abundance; star leads to the surfeit (not the nourishment) of the few and the starvation of the many. Star isolates, gift weaves; star dominates, gift emanates; stars are pinned on the breasts of generals—and mothers whose children have been devoured by war. Stars we follow into battle; gifts we share on common ground like the baskets of loaves and fishes. And the circulation of what sustains us is in itself a source of peace. As Lewis Hyde says in his book *The Gift*, "When the gift moves in a circle its motion is beyond the control of the personal ego, and so [it] is an act of social faith." And again, "The gift leaves all boundary and circles into mystery." And finally, "With the gift, as in love, our satisfaction sets us at ease because we know that somehow its use at once assures its plenty."

Hyde says that one of the artist's dilemmas is to negotiate between the natural medium of gift exchange and the necessities of survival in a market economy. One of my methods of negotiation is to earn part of my living talking to kids about writing. But when I visit schools, I find myself thrown back into this conflict of gifts and stars by the questions kids ask: "Did you come in a limousine?" is one of my favorites. No, I say. I came in a dirty Dodge. "Do you have a bodyguard?" No, I say. Though our society is becoming more violent by the minute, picture-book authors do not require bodyguards. "Are you famous?" No, writing is not about being famous. "Are you rich?"

That last question stumped me for a while. I know in the child's terms—which is to say the culture's—the answer is no. But I have a quarrel with those terms. I'm not wealthy, but I feel rich: I get to do what I love and to share it—even make a substantial portion of my living by it. I have a wonderful husband; two healthy, funny kids; a house to contain us all. A newspaper article described the house as modest. I was shocked. I think it's grand. The boys each have a bedroom; I have a writing room; Steve has a music studio—it's grand, I tell you. But I was also relieved to read that it was modest. I felt worried about having so grand a house. You can see I'm double-minded about these things.

What makes a successful person, a successful life? Gifts discovered, nurtured, given, and received. I think that's it. In that model are community (discovering, nurturing), continuity (giving, receiving), and contentment. "Now, I don't mind," says the speaker in Jo's poem. "I got what I want."

Do you hear how radical that is? How many people do you know who have what they want and realize it? This would not be good news in a recession, but if people have what they want, the mall is going to be a lot less crowded; the real estate ads and therapy suites likewise. If you've got what you want, the life-style escalator ratchets to a halt. You don't climb up but dig in. Not ascending but nesting.

How often have you seen a bird sitting on her nest? They're there all the time, but who would notice? It's the bird against the sky who becomes an icon; it's the one above us. I'm here to speak for looking in the backyard, in the tree next to us, in our own nest.

A few months ago I went in to wake up my son Joey, who was not quite five. "I can't get up," he said. "I'm an Apatosaurus."

"But Apatosauruses get up, too," I told him.

"Yeah, but I'm laying eggs."

I reflected on this a moment. I liked it much better than the night before, when the bed was a fighter plane and he was dropping bombs.

"Okay," I said. "You finish laying your eggs while I dry my hair."

In five minutes I was back.

"Have you finished?"

"Uh-huh."

"Up you get, then."

"Not yet!" he exclaimed. "First we've got to stand back and admire."

I laughed at that, too, thinking, Well, you can tell he's the child of artists. Has to have an audience. But then I realized he was expressing something more universal: the need to take pride in what we do and to have it appreciated. Not set apart and bronzed (the eggs wouldn't hatch); not judged and ranked and awarded some sort of prize; just appreciated. As in, "Wow! Those are some eggs! Are they always that color?"

In a sonnet called "As Kingfishers Catch Fire," Gerard Manley Hopkins tells us:

Each mortal thing does one thing and the same:
Deals out that being indoors each one dwells;
Selves—goes itself; *myself* it speaks and spells,
Crying, *What I do is me: for that I came.*

St. Paul, in I Corinthians, puts it this way: "Now there are varieties of gifts, but the same Spirit. And there are varieties of service, but the same Lord."

In the natural order of things, we each express our essence; we "selve"—are capable of living out our inner nature as sure as the oak tree manifests its oakness. But imagine an oak which had spent its life, itself, trying to be a redbud, despising its height, the weight of its branches, its girth. Imagine a bear trying to be a bass, dwelling as much as possible in the water, expecting to change that fur to fins. Misery! And underneath that, anger. Ultimately no peace within, no peace to act from. But if there were a teacher, a parent, an uncle, a friend, who recognized and confirmed the oak tree's nature, who said to the bear, "Forget gills, let me tell you about grizzlies"—in other words, if the child were nurtured in the direction of her gifts—what a transformation that would be!

Hopkins goes on:

I say more: the just man justices;
Keeps grace: that keeps all his goings graces.

In other words, the bear bears gifts to the world as bear that it can never discover in its sojourn as fake fish. And in that congruence of inner and outer comes peace, the only peace we can build on, that which is rooted in our own deepest selves. Selving, to extend Hopkins's verb, isn't just "doing your own thing"; it isn't selfish. Unself-conscious, done for the joy of the process, it always bears gifts.

Ours is a culture, however, that has very little interest in process. We want products. A star is a product, glittering with two of our obsessions: fame and money. And how do we get stars? We label the gifts of the few, enroll them in competitions, and let the system of judgment, ranking, and image making do the rest. Not only does this leave most children out, their gifts undeveloped, it creates frustration in those who make it partway, and isolation and sometimes self-destruction in those few hauled up above the horizon.

In the first grade, just about every child sings, hangs from the jungle gym, colors, does math, observes the turtle, talks at show-and-tell. By high school, only a few sing, draw, play ball, are math whizzes, budding naturalists, and writers. But, you may ask, isn't this because their gifts have been identified or have sorted themselves out? I don't think so, for several reasons. Most important, a lot of children are excluded in this sorting. They're in the *miscellaneous* or *dud* pile. Not in chorus, not on a ball team, not in the band, in the gifted class, on the paper staff, or on the academic team. Even with these essential programs, many children's gifts go undetected. The result is kids who slide through halls, classes, and hours expressionless—or with a defiant disguise of clothing and attitude—because no one has helped them find a way to express themselves. No one commented on one child's mechanical dexterity, another child's sense of design, still another's ability to empathize. Not "star" material in the few categories legitimized by their world, these youngsters feel themselves to be nothing.

Think for a minute about the last time you were in a group of people who were asked to sing. Maybe it was at church or before a game, maybe a reunion. How many people sang? Eighty percent, sixty percent? Of those who did, how many sang audibly? How many indicated by expression or posture that they had a voice and the right to use it? Twenty percent? Fifteen percent? Six percent?

How did those first graders who stood up and sang straight as rain falling become this crowd of tall people who barely open their mouths?

Well, you say, they grew up.

They grew up.

Found out what's what.

Who could sing and who couldn't.

Learned not to embarrass themselves.

Learned to keep their mouths shut.

Lost their voice.

That's only one of many doors that get slammed or closed silently by our relentless focus on product. If the product is not outstanding—and for much schoolwork, that product is the grade, not the learning—then the process is worthless. The process exists to create a product. Writing is to produce papers or A's or books; running is to break records, win ribbons, scholarships; music is to cause applause, make records, get on television. Many children, realizing that they'll never play first-string high school basketball, much less start for the NBA, lose all joy in the game. Or have that joy shadowed by a sense of inferiority, failure. No one taught them that a pickup game can bring people together; that basketball can keep you stronger, healthier; that the gift is having something you'll enjoy all your life.

Bernice Johnson Reagon, founder of the singing group Sweet Honey in the Rock and consultant in ethnomusicology at the Library of Congress, asserts that songs "are a way to get to singing." A way to get to the process of running sound through your body, integrating emotion and memory, finding yourself as music maker. Let's look for a minute at the difference between process and product, between gifts and stars.

Process is about exploration, going deeper. Product is about "More! More! Higher! Higher!" Process asks the writer, "What are you working on?" Product says, as someone said to me, "I don't think your new book could top that last one." Process is about growing, a year-round venture; product is about harvesting, which is only possible in some seasons. Peace is a process—of responding to diversity and conflict with tolerance, imagination, and flexibility; war is a product of our intent to stamp out diversity and conflict when we give up on the process of peace.

One of the traps of product-vision is that we don't value a person's work until it reaches a critical mass. I know this from my own experience, since it took eleven years of rejection before I published my first book. Not a children's book, by the way. A chapbook of poems called *Mountain*. During that time, I knew I was a writer, but few other people thought so, and this made it harder to justify taking time away from family and jobs to write.

Another way to look at this is as the difference between inward and outward. The gift expresses what is inner, what is unique; the giver becomes self-forgetful, and the gift exists for itself. By contrast, the star is outwardly perceived, the result of competition, and has to be self-aware because it exists for effect.

We've seen something of the destruction that the star syndrome creates for nonstars. What happens to the gifted person turned into a star? What happens to process in the wake of "More! More! Higher! Higher!"? Nearly one hundred and fifty years ago, Charles Dodgson's headmaster warned the parents of the future Lewis Carroll of this danger in the first report he sent home:

> The love of excellence is far beyond the love of excelling; and if he should once be bewitched into a mere ambition to surpass others I need not urge that the very quality of his knowledge would be materially injured, and that his character would receive a stain of a more serious description still.

Blinded by the rays of outward perception and expectation—by klieg lights—the star can reach a state where she can no longer follow or even feel the inner light. And when the public light goes off, or just shifts elsewhere for a while, the star is left in immense darkness. Set down in a desert that was stage, with nothing to glamorize the gulf between her and the world, the star is likely to self-destruct. With no one there to claim the product, the process seems worthless—and unattainable.

Writers, musicians, actors, athletes—anybody to whom culture offers the addiction of those lights—all are in peril. For their souls. Because if you try to measure, time, package, clone, buy, or sell the soul, it dies. Just as the soul that never knows its gifts shrivels. Even the speaker in Jo's poem, the rare person who can say, "I got what I want," pays a price: "I always told my mother," she says:

> that teasing me about always lookin' so awful
> was goin' to make me mean. . . .
> And it did.

Gifts, not stars.

SELECTED BOOKS BY GEORGE ELLA LYON

A B Cedar: An Alphabet of Trees. Illustrated by Tom Parker. New York: Orchard, 1989.

Basket. Illustrated by Mary Szilagyi. New York: Orchard, 1990.

Borrowed Children. New York: Orchard, 1988.

Cecil's Story. Illustrated by Peter Catalanotto. New York: Orchard, 1991.

Come a Tide. Illustrated by Stephen Gammell. New York: Orchard, 1990.

Dreamplace. Illustrated by Peter Catalanotto. New York: Orchard, 1993.

Five Live Bongos. Illustrated by Jacqueline Rogers. New York: Scholastic, 1994.

Mama Is a Miner. Illustrated by Peter Catalanotto. New York: Orchard, 1991.

The Outside Inn. Illustrated by Vera Rosenberry. New York: Orchard, 1991.

Red Rover, Red Rover. New York: Orchard, 1989.

A Regular Rolling Noah. Illustrated by Stephen Gammell. New York: Bradbury, 1986.

Together. Illustrated by Vera Rosenberry. New York: Orchard, 1989.

Who Came Down That Road? Illustrated by Peter Catalanotto. New York: Orchard, 1992.

GETTING STARTED

I used to tell teachers that it takes five to eight years to become a whole language teacher. But now I know that it takes five to eight years to reach what I call a comfort zone—a point where a teacher can honestly say, "I'll never arrive, and that's what's so great about whole language." Whole language teaching is like living—each day we write and rewrite the script of our life's story. Each day we teach, we rehearse, write, revise, and rewrite our understanding of how we and our students learn. Informed change and informed decisions lead to renewal and growth, and that's the great challenge of whole language philosophy.

I asked several teachers I've mentored and trained to reflect on their experiences and offer some guidelines to teachers just getting started. Suggestions varied. But at some point, each teacher wrote, "Tell them they'll never go back to the old ways." Their recommendations, which follow, can provide support as you make the transition.

- Find someone to talk to. Talking about your feelings and what's happening in the classroom will help you guide your students and will boost your confidence.

- Read Calkins, Graves, Atwell, Murray, Hansen, Wells, Clay, the Goodmans, and journals published by the International Reading Association and the National Council of Teachers of English. Join a whole language support group or start a group if none exists in your community. Attend professional conferences. It's great to learn you're not alone in that room!

- Give parents articles to read and talk to them. Parents need to know and understand as much as we and our students do.

- You'll feel scared and lonely lots of times. It's okay when you understand we all feel that way. It doesn't go away. That's what makes us improve.

- Keep a journal about what you see in the classroom and about your reading. Don't worry about being a "great" writer, just write what you see and think. Be very specific. Your journal is a ticket to growth.

- Voices of your teaching past will challenge and shout. Talk to others when you're shaky. Writing about it helps, too.

- Read aloud and use the books you love. And read lots of children's literature so you can suggest books to your students.

- Take chances the same way you encourage your kids to take risks. Think about errors and grow from them. It takes time for us, as it takes time for the kids.

- Listen to your students, and ask them questions about their reading and writing process—the kids know a lot more than I ever realized.

- If you want your kids to read and write, then you'll have to read and write. This will help you understand your students' process.

- Get to know your librarian and your library—two great resources and sources of support.

- The hardest thing is making mistakes— but you can always change. I think I grow more from my mistakes than my successes.

The teachers I've mentored have journeyed into whole language in different ways because, believing in choices, I always discuss and offer several options. There's no one right or perfect place to begin the transition from textbooks and basal readers to a literature-rich whole language environment. Schools with strong support systems and commitment to whole language philosophy ease teachers' transitions away from basals and textbooks. You might feel more comfortable beginning your transition by exploring oral and written responses to story with the literature in your basal and incorporating a themed study that extends the basal unit with trade books. The pivotal change has more to do with the shift you will make in teacher-student roles and interactions than in specific materials. Not only will teaching become a joint venture between you and students, but each child will inform your knowledge of how language works; each child will raise questions about the learning process for you to reflect on. As a co-learner and the most experienced language user in your room, you will share your knowledge and process with students.

Teachers who have just taken the plunge into whole language suggest the following ways to involve students in reading, writing, and speaking:

Learning Events. When children can inquire and learn for real and significant purposes, when their learning at school connects as much as possible with the ways young and old learn outside school, then reading, writing, talking, thinking, and problem solving gain authenticity. To grasp the nature of authentic learning experiences, you will begin to read stories composed by other teachers, by students, and by published educators. Your learning stories will be the bridges to others' stories. As you make these literacy stories your own, you will shape them into choices and invitations to offer your students, who will, in turn, use their stories to modify the process. You will become a collector of stories that will inform your teaching practices and increase your knowledge of how each child uses language to think and communicate.

Reading Aloud. All elementary grades benefit from teacher read-alouds. A simple way to introduce you and your students to a variety of genres and authors, reading aloud cultivates an interest in books, develops listening capacity, broadens experience and vocabulary, and encourages children to create mental images. Don't confine read-alouds to daily ten- to fifteen-minute sessions; sprinkle poetry and short tales throughout the day, using them as a transition to different events, to change classroom mood, as a lunch dessert, and for sheer enjoyment. Select books you love and you'll transmit that love to students.

Read-aloud guidebooks like Jim Trelease's *Read-Aloud Handbook* and Judy Freeman's *Books Kids Will Sit Still For* offer tried-and-true titles children love.

Reader's Chair. A relief from tiresome written book reports, reader's chair invites children and teacher to talk about books completed and books-in-progress. With the child

Second graders reading a retold book.

sitting in a special reader's chair, the brief presentation is not a retelling of the plot but involves personal connections to, and evaluations of, the story and observations about characters, events, setting, or theme. The class questions the reader, who calls upon peers. Schedule several weekly sessions; students reserve share time on a sign-up sheet or make reservations with the teacher. Reader's chair motivates talking and thinking about reading and trading favorite titles, and extends kids' knowledge of what's out there to read.

Journals. "This is my book," first grader Shelly says as she clasps her journal to her chest. "I can write anything in here." Journals are safe places to toy with ideas and plans, write with pictures, words, or pictures *and* words. In journals, children can express a wide range of personal feelings, attitudes, and reactions to school, home, friends, vacations, illness, and books. And initiating journal writing is so easy; simply say "Write." Reserve time for writing and share sessions that honor authors and illustrate a variety of entries. Keep a journal along with your students, for teachers who write in journals understand their value and discover infinite uses to pass on to students.

Curriculum will consist of components planned by you, those jointly planned with students, and investigations that are a natural outgrowth of classroom inquiry. As you reorganize learning, you will notice changes in your teaching process, the nature of literacy experiences students actively engage in, and the methods of evaluation you employ. In addition, room arrangement and changes in student behavior will create inner conflicts that conversations with supportive colleagues can help subdue.

The Teaching Process. The minilesson will enable you to model and share your process. These strategic demonstrations, recorded on large chart paper, afford students countless opportunities to observe how language works. Instead of practicing isolated skills, students discover strategies that enable them to solve reading and writing problems independently. Brief and focused, minilessons permit you to demonstrate, by thinking aloud, how a reading, writing, or thinking strategy works.

The real benefit of a minilesson is in the student participation that follows. Demonstrations raise questions among students and prompt some to explain how the technique or strategy works for them. Summarize students' suggestions on the chart and display it for them to reread. It's their recorded voices that make the chart a powerful resource. Help the kids understand their roles during minilessons: listen and watch, and save questions for the end of the demonstration.

Invite students to take notes during the minilesson. There will be times when students interrupt a demonstration; their questions and/or observations compel them to speak. Let them, before they forget a significant observation that could help them and others. Below are students' ideas recorded after a minilesson on *setting the scene* in a sixth-grade class.

- I draw a picture first, then I think of the words.

- I talk to a friend and describe the place and see what they think, then I write.

- I list all the words I can think of that I might use.

This sharing of techniques opens up more choices for children who have not yet reflected on their process. The talk and trading of "how I do it" can clarify ideas and motivate children to risk trying something new.

Use the opening weeks of school to discover students' interests and history. Trade stories about family, friends, experiences, hobbies, and dreams. Such exchanges build community, understanding, and cooperation. Besides, the more you and your students know about each other, the easier it is to be supportive as you learn and plan together.

As you build community, ask students to write about their strengths as learners and feelings toward reading and writing. Harold, a sixth grader, wrote this at the beginning of school: "I never write anything, I got nothing to say." His honesty assisted me in making the decision to give Harold the space he needed to grow during workshop. In his final and lengthy end-of-year self-evaluation, Harold wrote: "This year I learned to write. I wrote three books and five stories that everyone liked."

Written interviews can also shed light on reading and writing attitudes of children. Work collaboratively to design reading, writing, and interest interviews. Pose questions such as: What should I ask to learn about you as readers, writers? To learn about your interests? You'll find that the questions children ask provide a history of their past and present experiences (see appendix). Information gathered from trading stories and from interviews can inform the planning of a theme cycle. You'll quickly experience the difference between a themed unit and a theme cycle. Units are preplanned and teacher-directed. Cycles are responsive to students' interests and developmental needs. Your role will be co-learner and guide as you include students in the planning process.

Establish whole class gatherings to build community and responsibility in self-contained and departmentalized classes. Assemble all members each morning and afternoon or at the outset and end of a time block. Preview the day's schedule; discuss special issues; celebrate class and student events; anticipate upcoming field trips, parties, holidays, and guests. At closing gatherings summarize all the terrific things that transpired that day, saying, "I noticed how partners helped each other," or "I appreciated the responsibility you demonstrated during choice time—everyone was involved and pitched in at clean-up."

Gathering is an opportunity to model writing and maintain records for genuine purposes. Primary teachers can compile, in an oversized notebook, a dated log of morning gatherings throughout the year. In middle schools, a rotating class secretary can log key items raised during gathering and be responsible for invitations, thank-you notes, telephone calls, and messages.

Think about the experiences you offer students in terms of effective grouping. Create situations where children can construct meaning in a variety of social contexts similar to the diverse social interactions beyond school. Organize a mix of groupings: Whole groups build community and the democratic process; talk-focused small group and paired activities permit students to practice collaborative problem solving. Make sure you reserve time for independent work to foster self-directed learning.

Evaluation. Supporting the concept of strategic demonstrations is reflecting on and writing about process: yours and your students'. As a reflective teacher, you will constantly think about the classroom community in order to assess individual and group needs. Kid watching, taking anecdotal notes, and self-evaluation will focus you on how student and teacher make meaning. An effective kid watcher, as Yetta Goodman points out, must not only know what, how, and when to observe but also know how children learn to read and write. Reading professional books and journals, sharing your stories with students, colleagues, and parents will fine-tune the watching and noting. Taking anecdotal notes can resurrect those angry inner voices: "Who has the time? I can't write anything worthwhile. I don't even know what to write!" The basic principle of learning and gaining proficiency—"doing it"—applies to taking anecdotal records. The more you consistently write, review, and share, the easier the process, the richer the detail.

To monitor my teaching process, I created a list of questions that I review and revise twice each year. The list, taped to the inside cover of my journal and clipboard, is a constant reminder of the need to reflect on students, parents, administrators, and teaching practices. Below are some key questions that yearly make the list.

- Am I a good listener?

- Have I made reading aloud a daily priority?

- Is the feedback I offer students positive and specific so they can build on strengths?

- Am I writing regularly in my journal?

- Do students have enough choices?

- Are classroom experiences authentic?

- Do I communicate with colleagues, parents, administrators?

- Do students solve their problems and take ownership of learning?

- Do I foster inquiry?

The questions you pose and revise can reveal where you are in "teaching space" and guide your journal reflections. As you watch, reflect, write, and contemplate, you will change and grow as a whole language teacher.

Room Arrangement. Whole language classrooms don't look like traditional classrooms. I remember Bernice Cullinan telling me that when she steps into a classroom "I can tell immediately if whole language philosophy is in practice." Although there is no specific way to arrange your room, there are changes that encourage an atmosphere of inquiry and celebrate children as users of language.

Establish a classroom library with an inviting and comfortable space for reading. Include individual books as well as class books made by the children. Since school funds for classroom libraries rarely exist, you might try some of these suggestions: Collect bonus points offered by book clubs such as Trumpet and Scholastic. Invite parents to donate books and organize a fund-raising event for additional titles. PTAs will often funnel money to teachers for books. Also, many schools permit teachers who no longer purchase workbooks to use workbook dollars for libraries.

Set up a listening center with a tape recorder and several earphones. Here, small groups of children can listen to a story and follow along

Third graders enjoy Beverly Cleary's Ramona Quimby, Age 8 *at the listening center.*

in the book. Supplement your collection with tapes made by the children, parents, and teachers as well as tapes of authors talking about their books and writing experiences.

Create a writing center chock-full of materials writers use. Maintain a good supply of pencils, erasers, crayons, marker pens, staplers, tape, scissors, drafting paper, colored paper, and deadline or final draft paper. Store the children's work in two large boxes filled with individual writing folders. Mark one box Work in Progress and the other Deadline Drafts.

Identify a quiet space for a conference area and furnish it with a table, desk, and three chairs. Here you will privately confer with students about learning and behavior; students will also confer with each other.

Strive for flexibility with the arrangement of desks and tables, for the physical appearance of your room depends on the nature of learning experiences. Desks can be arranged in small neighborhoods, in a large semicircle, in pairs, or stacked against the wall to make room for storytelling, creative drama, movement, and poetry. "Removing those rows," a teacher confided, "was like tearing down a wall that prevented any kind of interaction."

Shelve those teacher-made and prefab bulletin boards. Display children's work and the large charts filled with students' ideas and collaborative stories. Immerse the children in the language they construct.

You'll need to carefully explain how to use and care for centers before extending invitations to students. No matter what age group you work with, periodic review of the guidelines governing centers can avoid confusion and set a positive tone for choice and independence. I find it wise to limit choices at first. Once daily routines run smoothly, you can slowly increase the number of choices offered to students.

Managing the Students. Children who actively use language behave differently. It's helpful to know the changes that will occur, so you don't feel that you're the only teacher experiencing them. Moreover, anticipating these changes gives you time to think about ways to assist children in setting reasonable behavior guidelines and creating a positive atmosphere for learning. Take the time to periodically review behavioral expectations as learning experiences change. Help your students understand when it's appropriate and beneficial to talk or quietly concentrate on projects. The difficulties that many teachers new to whole language encounter can be avoided by carefully explaining and practicing classroom procedures.

Noise Levels. Reading and writing are social activities, and children will naturally talk about favorite books and share writing. Work with your students to establish acceptable noise levels and times when quiet is appropriate. Involved and invested children produce harmonious noise that I call "whole language music." You and your students will easily differentiate between the sounds of productive and unproductive talk.

Movement. Changing partners, flexible groupings, and student choice create movement in your classroom. Students leave the room more frequently to visit the school library and use the entire school community as a learning resource. When you offer students options in selecting work space, activities, and materials, they move more freely around the classroom and school as they cope with choice and responsibility. To avoid mayhem, limit the number of choices, especially when you're getting started! Also, too many choices confuse younger children. Be sure behavior guidelines include bathroom procedures, when it's okay to obtain peer assistance, and when it's okay to interrupt the teacher.

Different Work Clocks. Children engaged in reading-writing workshops and research complete tasks at different times. Teachers comforted by the structure and control of traditional learning tasks can be easily frustrated. There will be children who take more time to become involved in their learning, those who fear taking risks and elect not to try. You will also notice differences among a group of children due to varying levels of competency. By negotiating deadline dates and the quantity of work expected, you can empower each child to set and attain goals.

Your first challenge as a whole language teacher will be to include your pupils in negotiating and constructing new classroom rules. Most children arrive at school with enough social experiences to discuss the issues of noise and movement and to construct reasonable guidelines. Allow pairs or small groups to brainstorm suggestions and gather these on a chart for a whole class discussion. Help them understand that these first ideas will change, and should change, as they read, write, and research together.

So many children who have had rules imposed on them think negatively. Remember to talk about positive statements, and how to turn a negative comment into a positive one. So "Don't run," for example, becomes "Walk from place to place."

Your list will change several times as the children gain more insight into the conditions that fuel learning. Their final list will reflect personal experiences with reading and writing workshop and celebrate their developing cooperative spirit, sense of community, and respect for individual needs. Here's an end-of-the-year sample from one second grade.

- Quiet or very small noise helps us read.

- Talk softly so we can all hear and think.

- Do your share of the work.

- Take time to help others in your group.

- It's okay to have different ideas.

- Say things that make a person feel good.

- Listen and ask questions at the end.

- Take notes so you remember your question.

- Help your group clean up.

- Quiet when lights flick.

Finding Support. The many changes you initiate will rekindle those inner voices that challenge and scold. Self-doubts can build to a crescendo if you work alone in a traditional school, where colleagues feel threatened by changes in your classroom and pass cutting remarks to you and students. A sixth-grade class told me that one teacher asked them daily, "Why are you noisy in Mrs. Robb's class and silent in mine?" Never satisfied with students' explanations, the teacher continued to subtly undermine me even after a joint meeting. Such conditions breed emotional stress and feelings of isolation.

Most negative attitudes toward whole language theory and practice result from lack of information and clinging to personal experiences. One technique that works well is to invite supervisors and colleagues into your room again and again and actively involve them in your community. Their direct experiences with students' energy and enthusiasm for reading, writing, and inquiry might pave the way for meaningful dialogue.

The affirmation and validation you need and

deserve can come from joining or starting an area TAWL (Teachers Applying Whole Language) group, support group, or Teachers as Readers group. Attend local reading council meetings to find others who believe in whole language. You can increase parental support by regularly communicating classroom news via correspondence written by students and by you. Some teachers send home a weekly or monthly newsletter (see appendix).

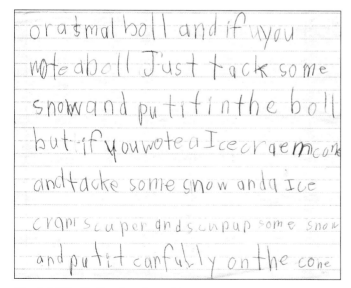

Fig. 1 Mildred's directions for making snow cones.

Sometimes it's the children and not the adults who resist change. Mid-January, Lorrie Aikens and I box the second-grade basal readers and initiate a reading-writing workshop. The last basal story the children read is "Keep the Lights Burning, Abbie," by Peter Roop. Lorrie and I decide we'll move the children away from the workbook and introduce drama. Convinced that the children would clamor to dramatize parts of the story and compose discussion questions, we plunge into the activities. No such reaction. "Acting out is for babies," says Tish. Most of the group agrees. "Use the workbook," shouts Kirstin, when I ask for questions. We meet similar resistance the first few days of writing workshop. "I've got nothing to write" and "I'm not even going to draw" are typical comments from many students. Mildred saves the day. On a blustery and snowy Tuesday morning, she writes a story and stands up and reads it (figure 1).

Mildred opened the door of possibilities, and that morning all but two of the children wrote. I tell this story because it's crucial to recognize that children new to whole language have fears and concerns just like those of teachers, administrators, and parents.

"They've had such limited book experiences. I want books to surround them," Lorrie tells me. We both agree that bookmaking should form the nucleus of our first workshops. The children assemble informal books based on topics they suggest:

- math
- retellings
- character
- story structure

- settings
- favorite parts
- what I learned
- copying books

Many in my group of reluctant readers copy a story from a favorite book and add original illustrations. Adults sometimes associate recopying a book with cheating. However, I believe children copy a text in order to comprehend its structure and organization; in time they write original stories, taking greater risks with bookmaking (figures 2, 3, 4).

By the end of March, bookmaking, writing, and reading define the workshop in Lorrie's group and my group. I interview the students, asking them how they feel about reading trade books and bookmaking. Their comments show progress but also illustrate struggles with writing.

STEFAN: I like to write and make books now. When I draw pictures I always write about them.

KIRSTIN: I like real books better because I get to hold my book. I like making my own books better than the workbook. I like drawing pictures and writing my book.

TISH: I like books better. I like how they have pictures and stories and covers. I can hold the book and read the dedication.

JAMES: Writing is hard. Sometimes I don't like it still when I don't have an idea. Drawing pictures is hard and sometimes dumb. I like the books.

ROSIE: I like drawing better than writing. The writing part is hard. I love author's chair.

KERI: The writing's not my favorite. I like drawing. Reading real books is the best. Making books is hard and fun.

A child from another class, visiting during recess, told me, "They're lucky because you get to make your own books. I come and read them and I like them. Will you tell my teacher to let us make books?"

Parents may also be reluctant to move from the traditional classroom structure. But parents who understand the reasons for change will be more likely to support it. The more knowledge you offer to parents, the more equipped they will be to break with their own educational traditions. To enlist parental support during the year, Lorrie held several after-school meetings with parents to explain the reading-writing workshop and to allow them to participate in whole language learning. Several times each year, I hold lunch-hour workshops. Brown bag in hand, parents join student groups to read, write, and talk about books.

Parents want to be involved and tuned in to their child's progress. With most parents working, we need to invite them to participate and learn before or after school or during lunch. I always recommend that teachers communicate with parents and form a learning partnership with them. Here are some easy ways to open this communication:

Parent Education Sessions. Reserve time during monthly PTA meetings to discuss changes and to celebrate children's work.

Hands-on Workshops. Two to three times a year, invite parents to learn with you the same way their children learn. As with all of us, parents' "doing" will lead to greater understanding.

Correspond. Children and parents write letters to each other about projects and theme studies, keeping parents informed about new ways of learning (see appendix).

Reading Buddies. Children and parents read and talk about books at home. The children introduce parents to reading and discussion strategies they practice at school.

Extend Invitations. Invite parents into your room to assist with a theme study or read to

Fig. 2 *Retelling of Kevin Henkes's* Chrysanthemum.

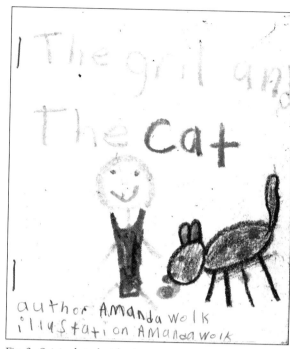

Fig. 3 *Original student book.*

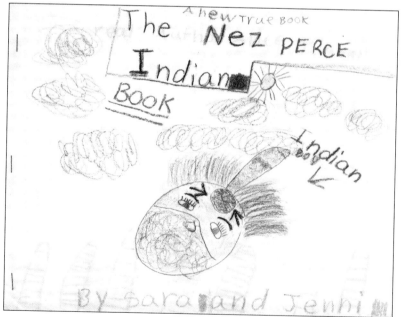

Fig. 4 *Collaborative book based on research about the Nez Perce.*

individuals or groups. Observing the children's enthusiasm and working with them will open parents' minds to change. Working parents can type writing for publication or, with training, read and respond to students' writing.

Parent Conferences. Meet with parents and review children's work. Assist them in understanding your emphasis on process and problem solving; share anecdotal stories and inventories.

Whatever modes you select, information and meaningful inclusion in classroom life can build support from parents, making them part of your school community while constructing powerful partnerships.

When I think about getting started, I always recall third-grade teacher Liz Davies. Three months after Liz began the transition to whole language, we both sat in her empty classroom discussing response journals. "Laura, I've got to say this to you." Liz's voice is serious, thoughtful. "Some days I get scared—clammy scared. Those manuals and dittos were my security. *They* made the decisions. Now it's Liz and the children." Silence. "But I've grown more these past three months than in three years of teaching. . . . I'll never stop growing and changing."

As you get started, like Liz, your first and most important step is to alter your view of learning. Once you accept that children and adults learn by actively constructing knowledge and that both groups need to make responsible choices, you will have begun your journey.

Be reasonable with your personal goals and expectations, and recognize that change arrives slowly, thoughtfully, as you strive to learn from new experiences and reading. If you bite off too much, don't worry—you can always pull back. All you can ask of yourself is to begin the transition where you are and travel as far as you can.

AS I SEE IT

Ed Young

TAKE TIME FOR 8 MATTERS OF THE HEART

 Take time for repose
it is the germ of creation

 Take time to read
it is the foundation of wisdom

 Take time to think
it is the source of strength

 Take time to work
it is the path to patience and success

 Take time to play
it is the secret of youth and constancy

 Take time to be cheerful
it is the appreciation of life that brings happiness

 Take time to share
it is in fellowship and sound relationships one finds meaning

 Take time to rejoice
for joy is the music of the soul

The above is an excerpt from an illustrated lecture on Chinese characters delivered by Ed Young upon his acceptance, for *Lon Po Po: A Red Riding Hood Story from China* (Philomel), of the 1990 *Boston Globe*–Horn Book Award for picture books. The award was given in Sturbridge, Massachusetts, on October 1, 1990, at the annual meeting of the New England Library Association. Mr. Young keeps these eight points over his desk as he works.

SELECTED BOOKS WRITTEN
AND ILLUSTRATED BY ED YOUNG

Little Plum. New York: Philomel, 1994.

Lon Po Po: A Red Riding Hood Story from China. New York: Philomel, 1989.

Moon Mother. New York: HarperCollins, 1993.

The Other Bone. New York: Harper & Row, 1984.

Red Thread. New York: Philomel, 1993.

Seven Blind Mice. New York: Philomel, 1992.

Up a Tree. New York: Harper & Row, 1983.

SELECTED BOOKS ILLUSTRATED
BY ED YOUNG

Calhoun, Mary. *While I Sleep*. New York: Morrow, 1992.

Carlstrom, Nancy White. *Goodbye Geese*. New York: Philomel, 1991.

Coerr, Eleanor. *Sadako*. New York: Putnam, 1993.

Coleridge, Samuel Taylor. *The Rime of the Ancient Mariner*. New York: Atheneum, 1992.

Horton, Barbara Savadge. *What Comes in Spring?* New York: Knopf, 1992.

Larrick, Nancy, ed. *Cats Are Cats*. New York: Philomel, 1989.

———. *Mice Are Nice*. New York: Philomel, 1990.

Lewis, Richard. *All of You Was Singing*. New York: Atheneum, 1991.

Osofsky, Audrey. *Dreamcatcher*. New York: Orchard, 1992.

Shulamith and Oppenheim. *Eblis*. San Diego: Harcourt Brace, 1994.

Taquith, Priscilla. *Tall Tales of the Gullah*. New York: Philomel, 1993.

Yolen, Jane. *The Girl Who Loved the Wind*. New York: Crowell, 1972.

PART TWO

BUILDING A FOUNDATION

PREPARATION

One day I watched Lorrie Aikens introduce a science lesson about pond life. Using large chart paper, Lorrie recorded all the information the second graders offered: Polliwogs live there, plants, little fish, salamanders, lots of flies. Jerry raised his hand, and I noticed his puzzled expression. "What's a pond?" he asked. And I held my breath, hoping the other children wouldn't leap on Jerry with negative comments. "It's like a little lake," explained Della. "But what's a lake?" questioned Jerry. Lorrie stepped in and helped Jerry imagine a pond by telling him it was a huge puddle with fish and tadpoles and plants and mud. Then James brought Jerry a book with an illustration of a pond, and the two of them pored over the picture and talked about it. I breathed a sigh of relief as the class returned to completing the chart. Their support made it possible for Jerry to ask his questions.

Imagine how confusing a chapter on pond life would be if you had never seen a pond. Because Lorrie asked the class to exchange knowledge about pond life, all the children, including Jerry, had a framework of information to guide them through the chapter.

Moreover, the preparation strategy enhanced Lorrie's perception of each child's previous experiences, so she could identify the child who required additional support and monitoring *before* reading and research.

Lorrie's experience demonstrates the relationship that exists between the preparation students receive prior to reading and their ability to comprehend print.

In 1938, Louise Rosenblatt wrote prophetic observations about readers and texts. A word on a page is simply a set of marks and is read as a word only when the child links it to personal experiences and knowledge. *Bus* becomes a yellow-and-black vehicle the child rides daily to and from school; *beach*, the sandy shore of the ocean where the child builds roadways and castles and runs from the crashing waves.[1] The child who has never been to the ocean or read about beaches will not be able to connect meanings to this word. Rosenblatt notes:

> The reader's fund of relevant memories makes possible any reading at all. Without linkage with the past experi-

ences and present interests of the reader, the work will not "come alive" for him, or rather he will not be prepared to bring it to life.[2]

Researchers like Marvin Minsky and Richard Anderson developed a theory that explained how readers go about creating their unique responses to text. They called their hypothesis schema theory.

According to schema theory, from birth our minds store all experiences and knowledge gained from daily living, books, and other sources in frameworks called schemata. Schemata (plural of schema) are the mental scaffolds we use to make sense of print and of our real environment. Our minds constantly modify, adjust, and enlarge existing schemata as we examine, rethink, revise, and compare new knowledge and experiences to the mind's storehouse of knowledge. And so we use our schemata for feeling ill and weak to understand the word *enervate*; we use our schemata for eating to behave one way at a picnic and another way at a formal dinner party; we use our schemata to identify different literary genres.

Since most written texts and statements are never completely explicit, our schemata fill in the implied meanings.

When a four-year-old tells his father, "Everybody sang when I blew out the candles," Daddy knows his child is talking about a birthday party. I asked several second graders to tell me what that statement meant.

STEFAN: They sang "Happy Birthday," and he blew out all the candles on the chocolate birthday cake.
KIRSTIN: It's a big birthday party and a cake with lots of lit candles and everybody singing "Happy Birthday to You."

ZACH: It's his birthday, and he's having a big party with lots of friends and balloons and a giant cake with lit candles to blow.

Nowhere does the statement talk about a cake or a birthday party or the name of the song everybody sang. The children's stored experiences, or schemata, for birthday parties enabled them to infer meaning from the statement. Without the schemata for birthday parties, the statement can take on different meanings based on an individual's experiences. To children living in cultures where birthday celebrations are different, this sentence would signal a different set of meanings.

Schema theory implies that children bring a different set of experiences or schemata to events, and their level of comprehension and interpretations will differ. Teachers who know the culture, values, beliefs, and experiences of their students can assist them in building experience bridges.

Although Rosenblatt never uses the term *schema,* she discusses the importance of what the reader brings to make sense out of printed texts: "personality traits, memories of past events, present needs and preoccupation, a particular mood of the moment, and a particular physical condition."[3]

Rosenblatt, in *The Reader, the Text, the Poem,* clearly supports her theory using studies conducted on her students. As students read passages unidentified by author or genre, they noted inner comments and thoughts. Readers actively groped for a framework, based on their knowledge of literature and life, to create a response to the text. During the process, students selected, rejected, and clarified prior experiences in their effort to comprehend and identify the genre.[4]

Rosenblatt suggests that the reader's interpretations of the text depends on the feelings, thoughts, memories, and images the text evokes within the reader. The words exist only when they are read and reinterpreted through the associations, experiences, and feelings of the reader. What the reader brings to the text affects his or her ability to comprehend the author's words. The work of Rosenblatt and other reading researchers offers insights into what successful readers do as they transact with texts.

1. As good readers interact with a story, they integrate their experiences, knowledge, and emotions with the story and reinterpret the text in highly personal terms.

2. Good readers use what they already know to make predictions about a text. They read to confirm their hypotheses and continually adjust their guesses based on new information and reasonable inferences.

3. Good readers ask questions to assess what they already know and to set guidelines for what they need to learn in order to enlarge their knowledge.

These three characteristics argue for the necessity of teachers initiating getting-ready-to-read strategies as well as modeling the strategies good readers employ. You may already prepare your students for field trips with discussions, brochures, pictures, and stories. It's equally essential that you provide time for them to talk and think about their perceptions before reading. But that's only a beginning. It's crucial that the children share in the discussion of why preparation activities improve their reading.

After several weeks of school, when my class has completed many different prereading strategies, I begin explaining why we engage in these activities. Even very young children are capable of absorbing the rationale behind such preparation. Once a child recognizes the importance of getting ready to read, that child has real reasons for adopting and using the strategy during independent reading.

To emphasize the importance of preparation, I have children work with partners when they visit the library to check out reading books. Not only does it make browsing for books more enjoyable, but the pair must talk about the title, cover illustration, and any text on the back cover or the inside flap of the book jacket. Paired library visits permit the social interactions children crave and utilize these interactions to reinforce prereading strategies.

Whether you teach kindergarten or eighth grade, it's important to gather your students' prereading ideas on a large chart or an overhead transparency. Reflect on what pupils know about a topic, theme, or genre. Based on this record, you may decide to build in additional background knowledge or skip elementary introductions with children who have a rich knowledge base.

Before any writing or collecting of students' ideas, allow pairs or small groups to talk in

Two students discuss poetry books during a workshop.

order to reclaim stored ideas and stimulate connections. Circulate among groups and join in the discussions. If I ask students to record their thoughts in journals, I also record my ideas and share one or two with the entire class. The list of management tips that follows comes from my classroom experience.

- Fashion a safe atmosphere for freely sharing ideas. Accept all ideas without judging. Allow students to say "Pass" if they don't want to share or if all of their ideas are already on the collective list.

- Avoid student complaints about other students "taking all the ideas." Rotate the group that initiates share sessions.

- Have students use the collaborative list of statements to ask questions, formulate hypotheses, and set reading and research purposes.

- Return to the original chart during and after completing the book or theme to refine and adjust statements.

- Research chart statements not confirmed during reading. Small groups, pairs, or individuals conduct research and report findings to the class.

- Have students separate their independent preparation notes from notes added during whole class share sessions by drawing a line underneath their original list. This way you can easily scan a journal page to reflect on each child's previous experiences.

Incorporate the written record of a preparation strategy into class studies, returning to it during and at the close of your studies.

Reflecting upon and discussing collective ideas honors the value of the exercise as students affirm and adjust their original ideas. Such visits furnish students with concrete evidence of newly acquired knowledge.

Here are some tried-and-true suggestions for prereading activities to use with both fiction and nonfiction, or to introduce a themed cycle:

Predicting the Story. Ask your students to describe what a story is about from its title, cover illustrations, title page, and/or the opening page or paragraphs. Accept and record all predictions, but ask that they be supported by available information. Supporting statements will demonstrate students' attention to the meaning of the title and clues in the cover illustration and opening paragraphs. To maintain a safe atmosphere and insure that students will risk sharing hypotheses, explain that all predictions will not mirror the story's outcome.

On chart paper, record five or six predictions with supporting ideas. I always tell a class the amount of predictions I'll be recording, but that over a period of two weeks, everyone will have a turn. Notes on a quick checklist keep tabs on students who have responded (figure 1).

Storing individual predictions in journals supplies teachers with a written record to review during reading conferences.

When everyone is reading a different book or when small groups or pairs are each reading different titles, students can record their predictions in journals. Younger children might draw predictions and explain them in a reading conference. When second grader Adam drew predictions for Steven Kellogg's *Pinkerton, Behave!* (figure 2), he explained that Pinkerton is so bad he bites people, jumps out of windows, and raids the refrigerator.

Name	November–December 1989 Pre-Read-Char All Subjects		
Melly A.	11/1 11/9 11/20		
Ryan A.	11/8 12/7		
Jason C.	11/7 11/29		
Roger C.	11/9 12/11		
Linda F.	11/15 11/29		
Jennie F.	11/20 12/15		
Cate H.	11/8 12/7		
Carl J.	11/29 12/7 12/15		
Carl J.	11/1 12/11		
Melissa N.	11/15 11/20 12/7		
Billy P.	11/7 12/15		
Bob P.	11/9 12/7		
Richard P.	11/20 12/11		
Tina S.	11/1 12/7		
Joyce S.	11/7 12/15		
Roslyn S.	11/9 12/11		
Larry T.	11/7 12/15		
Alan V.	11/20		
James W.	11/7 11/29		
Sallie Y.	11/1 12/15		

Fig. 1 A record of student participation in prereading activities.

Reading the Pictures. Don Holdaway's introduction of the shared reading experience and the use of big books, and reading research conducted by Marie Clay, support the "reading" of pictures as a group in order to activate and build upon prior knowledge. I find that children who have just begun to read tend to jump up and point to words they can read instead of focusing on the story the illustrations tell. Covering the print on each page with construction paper draws attention to the illustrations. A group of at-risk second graders picture-read *Teeny Tiny*, by Jill Bennett, and a transcription of their "reading" illustrates how this strategy introduces characters and portions of the plot. Beginning with the cover, children took turns telling the story through the pictures.

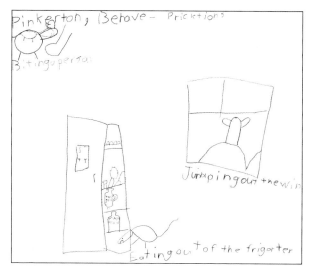

Fig. 2 A second grader's predictions for Pinkerton, Behave!, *by Steven Kellogg.*

DELIA: It's about a teeny woman and she has a tiny dog and cat and great big flowers. Oh, oh. Look at the ghost [picture opposite title page].

JAMES: She lives in a little house that's got a fence. Then she puts her hat on. That's her all dressed with the dog and cat.

ROBB: Where is she going?

JAMES: Out.

TISH: Look at the ghosts.

JAMES: Yeah, I see them.

TISH: There's a gate with a bird. There's the ghost and two sheep. Now she's in a place with graves. The cat is on top of the grave.

ROBB: Where do you think they are?

ZACH: A graveyard.

KERI: No. A churchyard.

JAMES: That don't look like no church. It's a castle.

STEFAN: They see a bone. Now there's three ghosts. It's getting spooky now. [Pause] The dog and cat want to eat the bone, and the ghost's eyes are popping out.

MONICA: Now there's seven ghosts and they're plenty mad.
JERRY: Look at them slanty eyes.
ROBB: Why are their eyes slanty now?
MANDY: It's their bone.
ROBB: How do you know?
MANDY: She stoled it from their grave.

By focusing on the pictures before I read the text, the group observed the role of the ghosts in creating a scary atmosphere and furnished clues to the changes in mood. I asked the group to predict what the teeny tiny woman would do with the bone. The three predictions they offered were logical because they had anticipated the text via the illustrations.

• Give it back to the ghosts.

• Put it back in the graveyard.

• Cook it.

Picture reading instilled a strong desire to see if the written text matched their "story." Before the second reading of the written text, we studied and discussed illustrations the children did not include in their "picture-story"; these furnished support for extending their vocabulary: sunflowers, village, thatched roof, shawl, and cupboard.

Book Browsing. Browsing through books in the classroom or the library introduces children to new information and augments their schemata for a topic. I find browsing can effectively provide much-needed background knowledge in science, mathematics, and social studies, especially where children have little or limited information. Poring over illustrations and photographs stimulates curiosity and conversations among children.

Small groups can discuss what they've grasped while browsing, and then share their insights with the entire class.

To help second graders expand their concept of natural disasters and natural phenomena, the class spent two hours browsing through fifty books, compiled a list of topics, and then decided what to study. Before browsing, their suggestions filled half a sheet of chart paper; after browsing, they filled an additional sheet.

Before Browsing	*After Browsing*
• earthquakes	• volcanoes
• Venus's-flytraps	• blizzards
• Tasmanian devils	• hurricanes
• storms	• lightning, thunder
	• forest fires
	• planets, solar system
	• gales
	• fossils
	• tornadoes
	• how rocks form
	• space
	• life cycles
	• galaxies
	• life and death
	• tidal waves
	• phases of the moon
	• atmosphere
	• meteors
	• shooting stars

Brainstorming. In this activity, students and teacher work separately or in small groups. Everyone writes down all the ideas that come to mind about a topic, key word, or concept. Encourage students to record all associations and not censor any thoughts. Brainstorming is an effective way for the teacher to learn what

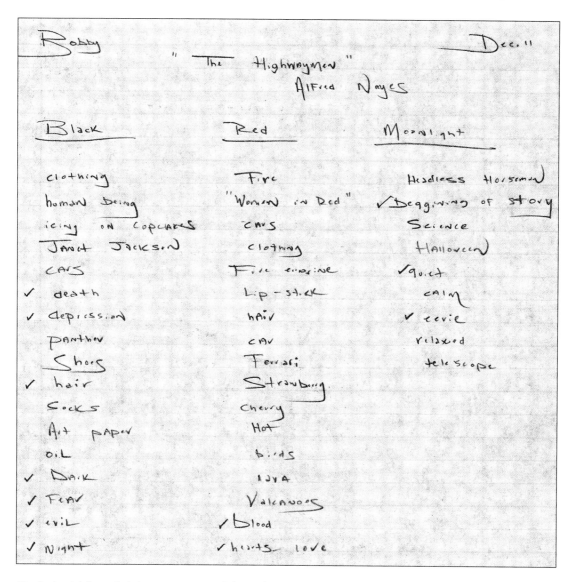

Fig. 3 An eighth grader's brainstorming on "The Highwayman."

students know about a topic such as the American Revolution, the concept of peer pressure, or symbolic words such as *black, red, moonlight* that might lead them to a deeper understanding of Alfred Noyes's narrative poem "The Highwayman" (figure 3). Allow students several minutes to write down their ideas, then collect and record them on a master list.

Clustering. Like brainstorming, clustering is a free-association activity that grows from a central word or phrase that represents a topic or a concept. Gabriele Rico developed this strategy for prewriting, but it works beautifully for prereading. Students write the word or phrase in the center of a page and circle the word. Then they record all the associations that come to mind without selecting or

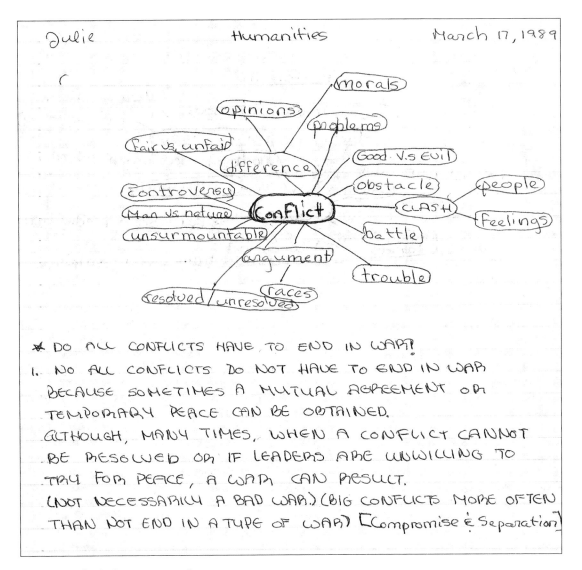

Fig. 4 A student's clustering on conflict.

judging their value. Write and circle the associations that radiate outward from the central word, clustering together connected ideas. After one to two minutes, the teacher collects students' associations and records them on a chart. The discussion among students that follows clarifies vocabulary and new ideas and offers possibilities for many connections. Older students can add new ideas to their journal during this whole class exchange. As a co-learner, you may wish to participate by sharing one or two ideas from your own journal (figure 4).

Asking Questions. The questions students pose before reading give specific reasons for reading a text. I find that students readily generate questions after they've brainstormed or clustered a topic or concept, listened to part of a story, or previewed illustrations in books. Eighth graders listen attentively to Eve Bunting's *The Wall,* then browse through books on Vietnam, studying photographs and reading the captions. Students collaborate in twos and threes and write questions they have about the war (figure 5). Fifteen minutes later I list these questions, which steer their reading and research.

My second-grade at-risk group brainstorms a list of ideas for the phrase *hurt feelings* to set a purpose for reading Kevin Henkes's *Chrysanthemum.*

1. What do hurt feelings feel like?

2. Why do you want to hurt others?

3. What things do you get picked on for?

4. How can you stop it?

5. Who can hurt your feelings?

6. How can you make the hurt go away?

7. Why do kids tease?

Questions built so much anticipation that the group begged to read the book immediately. Far superior to any questions I could write, theirs pointed to issues relevant to the children's lives.

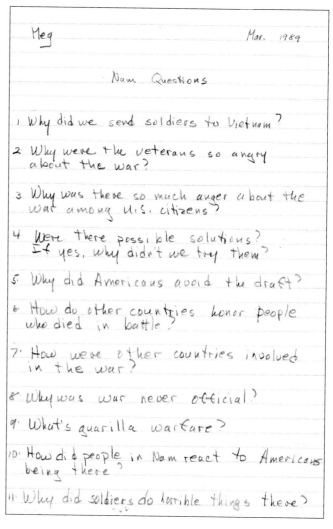

Fig. 5 Eighth-grade students' questions about Vietnam after having listened to The Wall, *by Eve Bunting.*

Skimming. Skimming through the chapter of a text or through an illustrated nonfiction book builds familiarity with a new subject and sets purposes for reading through the questions students pose. Pause to read captions, charts, boldface headings, and words. In place of questions, students can set purposes for reading by listing several things they hope to learn. In content area subjects, children must often cope with topics they know little about. Skimming strategies familiarize children with book structures and information prior to reading.

To introduce a seventh-grade class to a unit on geometry, Harry Holloway asked the group to skim through the chapter and then illustrate some of its contents. He encouraged students to return to the text to draw unfamiliar shapes. Returning to the chapter made students more familiar with its contents and encouraged many to illustrate new as well as familiar shapes. The class first shared their illustrations, using them to discuss things they already knew and what they hoped to digest (figure 6).

Concept Question. Sometimes I want students to be sensitive to an important or complex theme in a story, and to discuss the theme and its implications before reading a book. For Milton Meltzer's *Rescue: The Story of How Gentiles Saved Jews in the Holocaust,* I ask sixth graders, "Why do you think Gentiles endangered their lives to save Jews?" Eighth graders discuss what they know about the democratic and totalitarian models of government before reading *The Island of the Skog,*

by Steven Kellogg. Seventh graders argue the point "Would you have an operation that made you extremely intelligent for a short period of time?" before reading *Flowers for Algernon,* by Daniel Keyes. Concept questions stimulate lively and thought-provoking discussions around powerful issues.

Before I read Katherine Paterson's *The Tale of the Mandarin Ducks* to a sixth-grade class, the students considered the concept question "Is there a difference between evil thoughts and fantasies and acting upon these thoughts?" The question so intrigued boys and girls that the issue remained alive way beyond heated arguments over Shozo's guilt or innocence. Their ideas spilled into discussions of Unferth's thoughts and deeds in Robert Nye's retelling of *Beowulf* and the thoughts of Shabanu in *Shabanu: Daughter of the Wind,* as she struggled to maintain her identity.

Collaborative Murals. Painting what you know about a subject translates thought and experiences into visual images. Collaboration calls for group communication, preplanning, decision making, and shared responsibility for explaining the illustrations. The second graders studying natural phenomena planned and painted murals that reflected what they knew. "This is fun, but very hard work" was a frequent comment. Hang murals on classroom walls; each group conveys the stories in their mural to the class. Collaborative murals are a wonderful way to initiate content area theme cycles and explore nonfiction.

FINDING TIME

Many teachers tell me they don't have time, in an already rushed day, to prepare children for reading and learning new information. Those hurried, pressured feelings exist for sev-

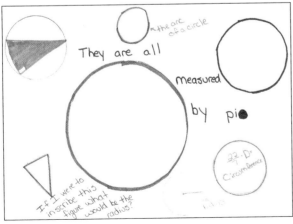

Fig. 6

A second-grade team presents their prereading mural on tornadoes.

eral reasons. In the last decade, schools have added computer studies, drug, alcohol, and sex education, and whole language teaching to curricula without eliminating subjects. Many administrators remove teacher guides, basals, and workbooks and legislate that teachers will adopt whole language philosophy. Often little or no training, and no budget for books, is supplied. The sense of no time breeds anger and frustration, and like the Red Queen in *Through the Looking Glass*, keeps us furiously running—in the same place!

Research in the reading process calls for teachers to incorporate strategies that activate and broaden children's prior experiences. Moreover, we honor and value the cultural and developmental diversity in our classrooms when we allow children to approach literature through their unique perspectives. According to Louise Rosenblatt, a complete experience with a work of art depends on two factors: the work itself, and the reader's capacity and *readiness* to receive the work.[5]

References

1. Rosenblatt, Louise M. *Literature as Exploration*, page 26.
2. Ibid., page 81.
3. Ibid., page 30.
4. Rosenblatt, Louise M. *The Reader, the Text, the Poem*, pages 6–12.
5. ———. *Literature as Exploration*, page 81.

AS I SEE IT

Lois Lowry

"A writer is, after all, only half his book. The other half is the reader."

When P. L. Travers said that in a *New York Times* interview in 1978, I read it with a sense of recognition; I had been her other half back in the 1940s every time I curled up with *Mary Poppins*. Reading about the charmed nanny in the London town house, I had in my mind transported her to Pennsylvania and brought her in, umbrella and all, for a tasteful landing on my own front sidewalk on College Street. She lived there in my heart and imagination and in my own fictional world, half written by P. L. Travers and the other half a private book that was only mine, a gift from P. L. Travers to the child that was me.

Many years later I tried to acknowledge that process—the paired creation of fiction—in a book of my own called *Rabble Starkey*. Twelve-year-old Rabble, listening to *The Red Pony* read aloud, ponders Steinbeck's description of a one-eared dog named Smasher: "So we could all picture Smasher in our minds, just the way he was supposed to be, but at the same time each of us had our own private Smasher, built out of all the dogs we had ever known."

I hear it all the time, in letters from the kids who read my books. They bring their own lives—and all the dogs they've ever known—to my fiction; and in doing so they write the other, more personal half of each book they read. And so the books that I write are never, really, the books that the children read. They create their own, out of their own needs, in the same way that I—a lonely nine-year-old—created a prim and magical companion for myself and made her story into ours.

"I really like the book you wrote about Anastasia Krupnik and her family because it makes me laugh every time I read it," a child wrote me from Kentucky. "I especially like when it says that she doesn't want to have a baby brother because she has to clean up after him every time and change his diaper when her mother and father aren't home, and she doesn't like to give him a bath and watch him all the time and put him to sleep every night when her mother goes to work."

I reread that letter several times, amused but also somewhat puzzled by it at first. *None of that happens in the book*, I said to myself. Yes, Anastasia has a baby brother. But she doesn't have to take care of him. Her mom doesn't go to work. She doesn't— Then I smiled in recognition. *Oh yes*, I thought, remembering the way it works. It does happen—for that child. That's the half that child wrote. It's the half that came from her own life.

Every time I finish writing a book—every time I type THE END on the final page—I know that it is still incomplete. Its real, and most important, completion will take place when a child holds it in his or her hands.

SELECTED BOOKS BY LOIS LOWRY

All about Sam. Illustrated by Diane de Groat. Boston: Houghton Mifflin, 1988.

Anastasia Again! Boston: Houghton Mifflin, 1981.

Anastasia, Ask Your Analyst. Boston: Houghton Mifflin, 1984.

Anastasia at This Address. Boston: Houghton Mifflin, 1992.

Anastasia at Your Service. Boston: Houghton Mifflin, 1982.

Anastasia Has the Answers. Boston: Houghton Mifflin, 1986.

Anastasia Krupnik. Boston: Houghton Mifflin, 1979.

Anastasia on Her Own. Boston: Houghton Mifflin, 1985.

Anastasia's Chosen Career. Boston: Houghton Mifflin, 1987.

Attaboy, Sam! Illustrated by Diane de Groat. Boston: Houghton Mifflin, 1992.

Autumn Street. Boston: Houghton Mifflin, 1980.

Find a Stranger, Say Goodbye. Boston: Houghton Mifflin, 1978.

The Giver. Boston: Houghton Mifflin, 1993.

Number the Stars. Boston: Houghton Mifflin, 1989.

Rabble Starkey. Boston: Houghton Mifflin, 1987.

A Summer to Die. Illustrated by Jenni Oliver. Boston: Houghton Mifflin, 1977.

Switcharound. Boston: Houghton Mifflin, 1985.

Taking Care of Terrific. Boston: Houghton Mifflin, 1983.

Us and Uncle Fraud. Boston: Houghton Mifflin, 1984.

Your Move, J.P.! Boston: Houghton Mifflin, 1991.

EARLY RESPONSES
TO LITERATURE

Twenty-two eighth graders and I sit in a circle on the classroom floor. Myra Cohn Livingston's book *There Was a Place and Other Poems* slowly journeys around our circle. Pairs study the front and back cover and reflect on the title and illustrations. Then the kids and I take turns reading aloud. As the poems travel the circle, words ring upon a backdrop of silence that develops after "Olive Street" and continues until our ritual ends. Tearstained faces, knowing nods, gentle pats on backs are the reactions of young adults who hear their own voices and painful voices of friends. Sara read the last poem:

Seashell,
  I will take you home
  where you will sing to me
  of waves you rode in an angry storm,
  fighting the wild sea.

And I will sing to you,
  seashell,
  the dreams of a child tossed
  over the waves of another storm;
  both of us blown and lost.

One by one, students silently return to their desks. Some write in their journals, others talk; a few sit alone on the floor, and one girl gazes out the window at the back of the classroom. The choice is theirs. The choice has to be in the hands of the students. Once their imagination connected to the poems and stirred feelings and memories, they selected the method of dealing with emotions. One student wrote, "The hurt came back like it was the night my father left. I haven't told anyone at school. He's gone."

"Stop talkin' and let her begin," shouts Keysha. I open Katherine Paterson's *The Great Gilly Hopkins* to "Homecoming," the last chapter, and start. A choking sob echoes through the room after I read, "She hadn't come because she wanted to. She'd come because Nonnie had paid her to." My eyes scan the class of sixteen at-risk seventh and eighth graders. Tears roll down Lisa's face; her hands fidget. I struggle to complete the chapter and take a deep, comforting breath when I finally close the book. Silence. It's the middle of January and the first time this class has been silent. A few minutes pass this way. Then I gently remind students that they can write responses, talk in pairs, or just sit and think. Lisa heads her paper and writes furiously. Her letter (figure 1) is to Gilly.

These two events and so many others celebrate the transforming power of stories as they merge with our experiences and feelings to clarify what appeared incomprehensible, to confront what we preferred to hide, and to imagine and know what we did not know. But these two events also demonstrate the students' personal responses to story, responses that occur when the reader connects with the potential of the writer's words and steps inside the book. At the moment the story engages mind and heart, the characters spring to life. We talk to them, we imagine how they look and speak, we relive, reshape, and reconstruct their story lives in ways that are personally meaningful and satisfying to us.

According to Louise Rosenblatt, reading is a nonlinear, recursive process. As readers shuttle back and forth within the text, they revise, adjust, question, and sort in order to construct meanings. Rosenblatt described reading as a series of transactions with the author's words. Each reader transacts, or "activates the text," producing a unique literary work as experiences, knowledge, emotions, and present mood mingle with the written text. Through transactions, the reader becomes author-artist, merging self with the author's text. The reader transforms the author's words into his or her version, which Rosenblatt calls a "poem."

One fifth grader, William, talking about the first few chapters of *Bridge to Terabithia* with his discussion group, said:

> I know how Jesse feels. My dad's just like his. [Pause] He wants me to play soccer. I'm no good at it. When he catches me

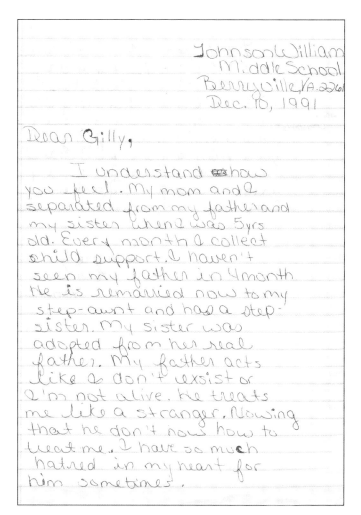

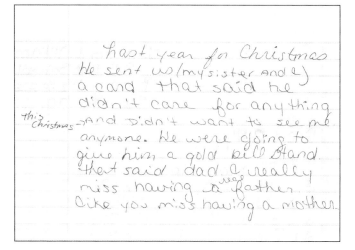

Fig. 1

drawing he gets mad. Thinks I'm a sissy and hardly talks to me.

Tony, the only boy in a family with four girls, sits in another group and talks about the same opening chapters.

Boy, I know how Jesse feels with those sisters. All I ever see at home is girls, bossy, yacky girls.

Both boys read the same words, but the story sparks a different connection within each. Since each reader comes to stories with a unique set of experiences, emotions, and dreams, it is no surprise that personal reactions to texts differ widely. And these variations appear among children and adults of similar or diverse backgrounds.

This reshaping, this re-creation of story, not only is different for every reader, but undergoes metamorphosis with each rereading. Knowing this, we teachers must encourage those initial, sometimes invalid, personal responses that can bond readers to story. Once they are bonded, we can offer them strategies that eventually lead to more valid interpretations of the author's words.

One Friday Wally asked to borrow Andersen's fairy tales so he could reread his beloved "Traveling Companion." Wally returned to the book daily for several weeks, rereading the story, but never talking about it. Monday morning Wally, who arrived on the first bus, placed the book on my desk. "You know," he told me, "I think I understand the story now. Magic is really hard work, and John risked his life to get his reward. At first I thought it said that all you had to do was be good and a good thing would happen. Now I understand." Each rereading revised Wally's thinking, and he reread until he arrived at a satisfactory interpretation.

Literature—poetry, story, drama—transfixes and transforms the reader who journeys into the lives of the characters. "The text is merely an object of paper and ink," notes Rosenblatt, "until some reader responds to the marks on the page as verbal symbols."[1] Rosenblatt's transactional view of reading, which she presents in *The Reader, the Text, the Poem*, translates into these whole language concepts:

- Personal, aesthetic responses to literature precede analysis.

- Read the finest literature to generate diverse views and interpretations.

- Emphasize interpretation with essay-type answers instead of asking questions that seek factual knowledge.

- Interpretations of texts can and should change through rereadings and reflections.

- The text is the source of valid interpretation.

How teachers permit students to respond to literature often determines children's attitudes toward reading literature. Responses confined to answering a set of factual questions deprive the reader of forming a personal relationship with the story. Workbooks and end-of-chapter questions to determine the "correct" response diminish the emotional impact of the story. Such activities encourage readers to bury spontaneous reactions to comply with classroom practices. Factual and technical questions trivialize stories and often turn children away from books, for reading becomes a frustrating and unsatisfying experience. As a result, many students develop a school reading life that satisfies their teachers and a secret reading life away from school. Melanie Larson, a teacher in California, has recognized this double reading life in her own children. "Answering the questions at the end of each chapter has ruined books studied at school for my girls. Thank goodness," she adds, "they still love to read at home." But not all children continue to read independently.

Rosenblatt presents two ways of reacting to texts: aesthetic and efferent. Aesthetic readings result in personal reactions, for the reader willingly submits to the magic of the author's imagery, metaphors, and language rhythms. Efferent, or factual, readings concentrate on gaining information from the text, focusing attention on gathering a body of facts or studying form and structure. Rosenblatt notes that efferent readings often mingle with aesthetic readings. Teachers of literature, in order to help students intimately explore story, must value aesthetic reader responses and comprehend that there is, then, no one generic reading of a literary work. Emphasizing information and testing for facts prevent students from experiencing literature and often bar personal reactions.

Recently, an eighth grader arrived in my office with a troubled and angry look. She gave me a poem by Emily Dickinson that her teacher had carefully marked for figurative language. Frustrated, she blurted, "We never once talked about how the poem made us feel or what we saw and thought when we read it. And I'm in big-time trouble," she added, "because I stood up and said 'You just ruined this poem for me.'" The teacher felt both "put-down and put on the spot." But the student believed that by emphasizing a technical analysis of the poem, the teacher had sent an unspoken message that devalued the student's personal responses. According to Rosenblatt, the teacher's job is "to help the student realize that the most important thing is what literature means to him and does for him."[2]

Rosenblatt's research supports the following literature response model, which promotes personal reactions and the right of children to formulate opinions about and interpretations of stories:

1. preparation

2. transactions and interactions with story

3. personal responses

4. reflection

5. valid interpretations

While readers usually experience the first three steps, they do not necessarily reflect on and interpret every story read in class or independently. Literature-centered curricula that use this model respect the reader's right to find his or her own way into stories—"to realize," in Rosenblatt's words, "what literature means to him and does for him."

To achieve this goal, teachers must assist students in discovering *their reactions*, not use the classroom as a forum for dictating meaning. Once the teacher states "the interpretation," students refrain from grappling with their own reactions, recognizing, all too quickly, that the teacher's interpretations will be solicited on the test or in the essay. Instead, students need a safe atmosphere that values spontaneous personal responses. It should be clear to students that there is no grade, no preconceived standard. Choice is another key element. For students to freely respond to a literary work, they should be able to select the mode of response.

Offer situations for students to share initial responses, but point out that working in pairs or groups is optional; students who wish to deal with their feelings alone should have that

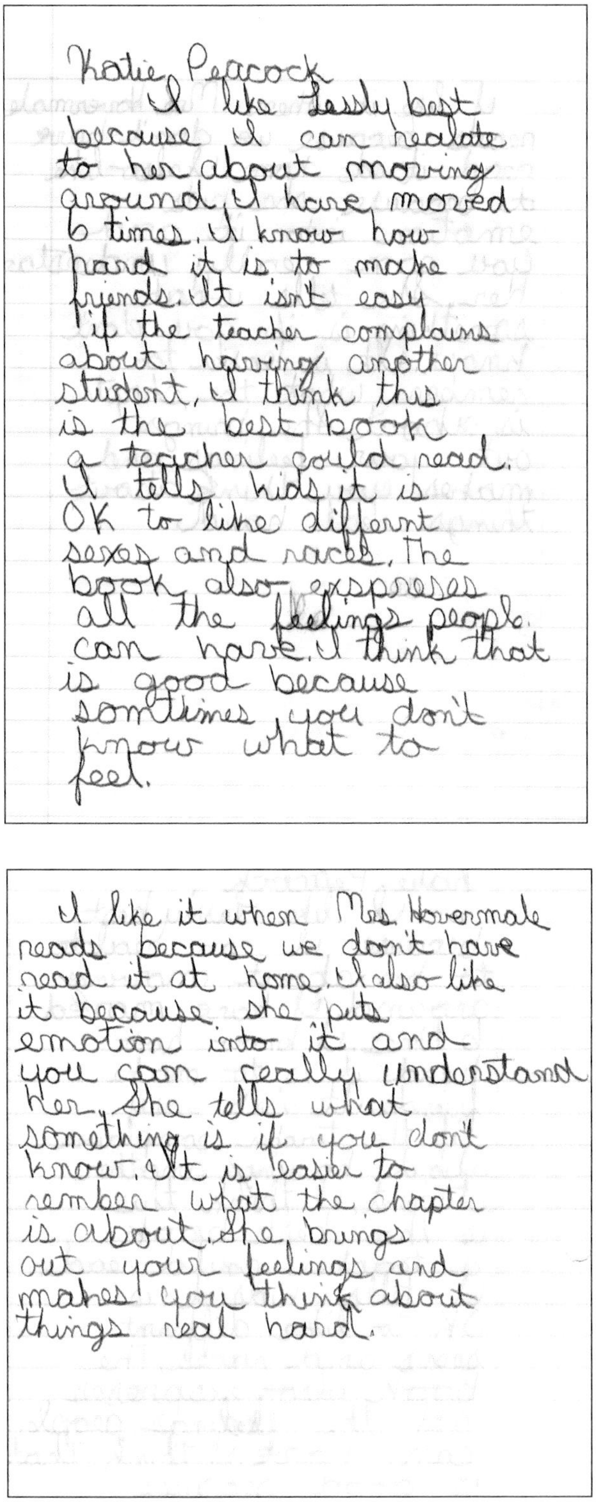

> Katie Peacock
> I like Leslie best because I can relate to her about moving around. I have moved 6 times. I know how hard it is to make friends. It isn't easy if the teacher complains about having another student. I think this is the best book a teacher could read. It tells kids it is OK to like different sexes and races. The book also exspreses all the feelings people can have. I think that is good because somtimes you don't know what to feel.

> I like it when Mrs. Hovermale reads because we don't have read it at home. I also like it because she puts emotion into it and you can really understand her. She tells what something is if you don't know. It is easier to rember what the chapter is about. She brings out your feelings and makes you think about things real hard.

Fig. 2

choice. Each literary work affects students differently, and some students will share little while others respond more openly. The teacher accepts all responses, even ones that appear negative. Keep in mind that fledgling responses are beginnings, and as students explore and reread a story, they reshape and revise initial reactions. Only through unprompted responses can students determine how a text affects them and teachers gain insights into students' relationship with the author's words. Such an approach, according to Louise Rosenblatt, is "essential to the survival of the reading of literature as an active part of our American culture."[3]

SOME SUGGESTED STRATEGIES

Unprompted Written Response. Students confront their own feelings after reading a book by writing lists, free associations, or phrases. The term *free* means students should not be inhibited by structures such as summarizing, finding themes or author purposes, discussing characters, plot, or setting. Few readers, after completing a text, have sorted out their own connections enough to begin an analysis. Students can review all responses in a notebook and periodically review their written reactions. Later on, these reactions play an important role in developing valid interpretive responses. A fifth grader in Sally Hovermale's class connects Katherine Paterson's *Bridge to Terabithia* to her own experiences and feelings (figure 2).

Informal Discussions. Students *decide* what to talk about; pairs and groups speak freely about feelings and attitudes toward a literary work. Students might want to record portions of these exploratory discussions in notebooks. This should not be mandatory. The transcription below is of a conversation between two sixth graders after completing *Walkabout,* by James Vance Marshall. The story connects one to death and the other to the book's ending; both talk about the story from a personal perspective.

STUDENT 1: I hated that the bush boy died.

STUDENT 2: It's weird how Mary's looks made him believe he'd die. He just accepted it.

STUDENT 1: Death. [Pause] I hate to think of it. It scares me. I have nightmares about my grandma's body in the coffin. [Pause] I didn't want to go in the room.

STUDENT 2: I've never seen a dead body—I mean, yeah, in movies—but not a real one.

STUDENT 1: You think Peter and Mary will go back [to South Carolina]?

STUDENT 2: Mary wants to. She still remembers her old life. Maybe not Peter.

STUDENT 1: I don't know what I'd do. I hate when I have to decide what happens.

STUDENT 2: I don't. I can think about them [Peter and Mary] and plan endings.

STUDENT 1: But I like to know what the author thinks.

STUDENT 2: Maybe he [the author] doesn't know.

STUDENT 1: I'm gonna look at the photos.

The pair look at the photographs in the book for a few minutes.

Drawing; Drawing and Writing. Through pictures, children can express feelings about a story. Reserve time for students to talk about their drawings, in pairs and small groups, only if they wish to confer. Drawing appeals to all age groups; middle school students tell me that it's frequently easier to confront feelings with pictures. Grayson, a kindergartner in Nancy Chambers's class, adds a golden fairy to his illustration of Marianna Mayer's *The Unicorn and the Lake.* There is no fairy in the story; Grayson's "fere" is there to assist the unicorn in its battle against the serpent (figure 3).

Jaime, a first grader, tells me as she draws, "The picture [hers] makes me feel I'm in the story." Her reactions to Steven Kellogg's *Chicken Little* link the story to her life (figure 4).

Jaime loved *Chicken Little* so much that she slept with the book for a week and wrote a

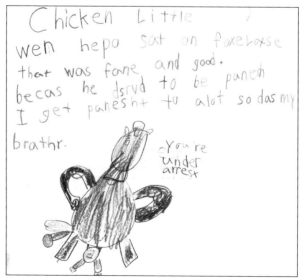

Fig. 3 Top. Fig. 4 Below.

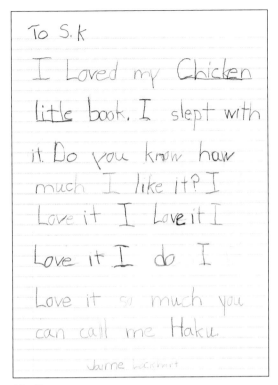

Fig. 5

letter to Steven Kellogg, granting him permission to call her by her pretend-princess name (figure 5).

Impromptu Dramatizations. Children turn to the costume, prop, or puppet center and pretend favorite parts. Students design stick or bag puppets of characters in the story for improvised dramas. Occasionally, reserve time for groups who wish to present dramas to the entire class.

Second-grade at-risk students and I have completed a third reading of Mary Ann Hoberman's *A House Is a House for Me*. Working in twos and threes, eleven children improvise dramas. One group molds clay characters, another fashions stick puppets, and one pair designs props. Two groups want to present to everyone. I notice each drama

is short and centers around one character and its home: a lost pony searching for a barn, a boy whose tree house is destroyed, whales singing in their watery home. First reactions revolved around story, not retelling textual information. Sam and Max's stick-puppet drama, transcribed below, is about a spider.

SAM: Once upon a time there was a spider named Robert.
MAX: I'm weaving my web. It's perfect.
SAM: A farmer came by and knocked the web down. The spider was angry.
MAX: I'll find a better place.
SAM: The spider found a horse barn.
MAX: I'm building my new web near the roof.
SAM AND MAX: And the spider lived happily ever after in his web.

Max and Sam are developing a sense of story structure; their knowledge of fairy tales has entered the drama. Early, unprompted responses often afford insights into children's knowledge of how stories work and the connections they're making between observation and experience.

Paired Reading. Partners read and react during and after completion of a text. Use Jerome Harste's "Say Something"; pairs pause at mutually agreed-upon places in the story and spontaneously comment on what they've read. Or you might wish to introduce Susan Lytle's think-aloud procedures, which ask students to read and comment on a story, sentence by sentence. Lytle's research points out that students comment on what they understand and try to verbally relate their own prior knowledge and experiences to the story.

To introduce a study of World War II, I ask pairs of eighth graders to read poems to each

Second graders use puppets to dramatize "The Three Billy Goats Gruff."

other from *I Never Saw Another Butterfly . . .* , poems written by children interned in Terezin concentration camp. Pairs each select one poem to read and think-aloud to their partner. The transcription below is of an eighth-grade girl's think-aloud of the first stanza of "Birdsong."

Birdsong

1. He doesn't know the world at all
2. Who stays in his nest and doesn't go out
3. He doesn't know what birds know best
4. Nor what I want to sing about
5. That the world is full of loveliness.

Lines 1 and 2: I think the kid is saying that if all you do is stay in a nest and never fly, you're never free, then you'll never know anything about living. It's like when I'm grounded, and I know my friends are doing things I can't. It's like jail.

Lines 3 and 4: If you never have friends and go places and see things, then you don't have much to talk about or write about. It's like being born but never being allowed to go places and live a life.

Line 5: It makes me cry to think that you could live a short life in a prison camp and not know anything about how great the world is. It makes my complaints seem so ridiculous.

Paired reading during a sixth-grade workshop.

Throughout the think-aloud, this girl makes connections to personal experiences. The process begins to clarify the poem for her.

In *The Call of Stories*, Robert Coles explains the task of those who teach literature:

> To engage a student's growing intelligence with any number of tempestuous emotions with the line of a story in such a way that the reader's imagination gets absorbed into the novelist's.[4]

Unprompted personal responses open the doors of readers' imaginations as they travel into stories, providing reasons for revisiting and reflecting again and again. Journeys into stories commence with personal responses, which connect stories to our imagined inner world so that we can begin to identify with people, places, and events alien to the limitations of our daily existence.

References

1. Rosenblatt, Louise M. *The Reader, the Text, the Poem*, page 23.

2. ———. *Literature as Exploration*, page 67.

3. ———. "Retrospect." In *Transactions with Literature*. Urbana, IL: National Council of Teachers of English, 1990, page 104.

4. Coles, Robert. *The Call of Stories: Teaching and the Moral Imagination*. Boston: Houghton Mifflin, 1989, page 63.

AS I SEE IT

Myra Cohn Livingston

We know that in literature is the power to stimulate, to strengthen the imaginations of our young people, to arouse curiosity, to develop creativity; and yet do we offer it, really offer it, at all? Indeed we categorize it, label it, make lists of it; our minds have logically arranged all this. But what we have often failed to do is to recognize that the mind and logic do not, in themselves, insure successful use of the books, the words. "The mind alone cannot make sense of images," Archibald MacLeish tells us of poetry, "but emotions can—feelings can."

I am suggesting that we have become so consumed with the technicalities of the literature we offer that we often fail to read, really read, the text to understand with our hearts what it is saying. We have obliterated entire areas of exploration and substituted, when we speak of originality and creativity, mass-produced feelings and responses. Worse still, we have mistaken the tools and techniques, the forms, those things that should serve as the utensils and dishes for serving the food, the books, for the food itself. We have shied away from developing original thought and stretching the imagination; we have been fearful of emotions, of feelings; and the result is masses of so-called creative writing done by our children without the slightest glimmer of real creation.

In Randall Jarrell's *The Bat-Poet*, you will remember that the bat admires the songs of the mockingbird. The mockingbird has consented to listen to a poem that the bat has written about an owl who almost killed him. The bat eagerly awaits the mockingbird's response to the poem.

> "Why, I like it," said the mockingbird. "Technically, it's quite accomplished. The way you change the rhyme-scheme's particularly effective."
>
> The bat said, "It is?"
>
> "Oh, yes," said the mockingbird. "And it was clever of you to have that last line two feet short."
>
> The bat said blankly: "Two feet short?"

"It's two feet short," said the mockingbird a little impatiently. "The next-to-the-last-line's iambic pentameter, and the last line's iambic trimeter."

The bat looked so bewildered that the mockingbird said in a kind voice: "An iambic foot has one weak syllable and one strong syllable; the weak one comes first. That last line of yours has six syllables and the one before it has ten: when you shorten the last line like that it gets the effect of the night holding its breath."

"I didn't know that," said the bat. "I just made it like holding your breath."

"To be sure, to be sure!" said the mockingbird. "I enjoyed your poem very much. When you've made up some more do come round and say me another."

The bat said that he would, and fluttered home to his rafter. Partly he felt very good—the mockingbird had liked his poem—and partly he felt just terrible. He thought: "Why, I might as well have said it to the bats. What do I care about how many feet it has? The owl nearly killed me, and he says he liked the rhyme-scheme!"

Later, the bat has occasion to say the poem to a chipmunk, hoping to interest him in his own portrait in verse "for only six crickets."

A shadow is floating through the moonlight.
Its wings don't make a sound.
Its claws are long, its beak is bright.
Its eyes try all the corners of the night.

It calls and calls: all the air swells and heaves
And washes up and down like water.
The ear that listens to the owl believes
In death. The bat beneath the eaves,

The mouse beside the stone are still as death—
The owl's air washes them like water.
The owl goes back and forth inside the night,
And the night holds its breath.

He said his poem and the chipmunk listened attentively; when the poem was over, the chipmunk gave a big shiver and said, "It's terrible, just terrible! Is there really something like that at night?"

Later, the bat starts on his portrait in verse about the chipmunk.

But somehow he kept coming back to the poem about the owl, and what the chipmunk had said, and how he'd looked. "He didn't say any of that two-feet short stuff," the bat thought triumphantly; "he was scared."

How many mockingbirds failed to be scared—to sense the force that elicits emotion and imagination? How many teachers, so concerned with the rhyme scheme, the rhythm, accept these tools as substitutes for the meaning? How many little bats, how many children, must keep their poems and flights of imagination to themselves because there is a mockingbird so puffed up with his own song, his own dictates, that the real stuff of creation never gets through? I am reminded of any number of articles written by well-meaning teachers who pay lip service to the idea that poetry is made up of all the elements of life, yet who painstakingly elaborate on "themes" (nature, picnics, pets, holidays) they feel "suitable" for poetry. Heaven forbid that their students should venture off into realms that depart from the teacher's prescribed ideas of "Beauty" and "Truth"!

How many teachers have taken to their hearts a volume of children's poems called *Miracles*? It is very pleasant to read, for the beauties of nature are extolled on every page; it is what adults want to hear. But in how many other children do there burn more important, urgent things to feel and say? How many teachers have seized upon the haiku, with its apt nature symbols, as a sop for counting out seventeen syllables (which is only a little better than an exercise in mathematics), never concerned with the meaning of the word *haiku*, or *beginning phrase*, which is the essence of the poem? How many more have set the children to busily turning out language arts cinquains, another syllable-counting exercise? How many have misunderstood Mary O'Neill's *Hailstones and Halibut Bones* as an exercise in having children write out red is a fire engine, blue is the ocean, green is the tree, ad infinitum? How many have spent endless hours praising such drivel as "The cat ate the fat bat and slept in a hat and that was that"?

None of this is creativity and imagination. It is but a mass-produced easy way out; and it concentrates on the form, the techniques, rather than on the force that burns in the child's mind and imagination and will never, at this rate, find a way to express itself.

Creativity and imagination are not built and fostered by these gimmicks. It is emotion and feeling that release creativity. To encourage in our children these qualities requires the sort of commitment made by an individual teacher who is willing to ferret out that which may be meaningful to each individual child. Such a commitment is made by encouraging different varieties of expression, by the recognition that each child will approach that which is read differently; it is built by the trust between child and teacher that nothing is alien to the emotions and imagination and that children will not be turned away because they have written something "unsuitable" in the teacher's judgment.

For some children, who, like the little bat, are born with the acute sensitivity that separates them from their peers, the release may be Randall Jarrell's *The Bat-Poet*; for this book will say to them that they are different, that such sensitivities do often alienate one in the beginning and such a person is inclined to be dubious and doubtful about the technicalities.

For another it may be such a book as Maurice Sendak's *Higgledy Piggledy Pop!*, for children may well put themselves into the role of the dog, Jennie, bored by material comforts, alienated by immaturity and lack of experience, yearning to become a Leading

Lady, and plunging, therefore, into the perils of the world and Castle Yonder. Yet for another, it may be the very real story of Micucu, in Elizabeth Bishop's *Ballad of the Burglar of Babylon*, running from the police, a man alienated because he has flouted the rules of society.

Without dwelling on the various aspects of personal and social awareness within these books, I would only point out that there is, in all three, the potential for identification. The bat, the dog, the man all wish to be part of their world; yet each is alienated, each faces the fears of his society—a bat-eating owl, a lion, and a gun. Is it the mind alone—reason, logic—or is it creativity and imagination that make the bat turn his fear of death into a poem, that inspire the words that Jennie uses to save Baby from the lion, and that cause Micucu to settle for ninety hours on the hills of Babylon although his death is certain? For each the experience is different.

I should like to interject here that lack of experience, which we presume to be common to all children, just starting in life, is one of the most germinal factors one can think of for creativity and imagination. A young mind, unhampered by clichés, by staid and oftentimes outmoded rules, can put into new relationships the stuff of the world he sees. Yet how often is this fresh approach squelched; how often is the child's imagination made subservient to techniques, forms?

Let me add quickly that I am far from opposed to forms, to the proper training and use of the tools of the craft, but I feel they come second to the content, the meaning, the force. At the risk of repeating myself for the thousandth time, I should like to offer that one does not teach a child imagination or originality or how to write creatively. One only establishes the climate, the relationship with the world through literature, that helps children develop their sensitivity and introduces them gradually to the forms and craft in which imagination will find expression. The trouble, as I see it today, is that too many teachers are willing to accept the tools and techniques of creative writing for the real thing. They will dig no deeper than insisting a haiku have seventeen syllables—not fifteen, not nineteen—and making certain that cat rhymes with hat, and that whatever thoughts or words come in between be correctly spelled and legibly written on neatly lined paper.

What, then, if we discard the gimmicks and turn back to the box of literature? What, then, if we commit ourselves to the imagination of each individual child who enters our classroom or library? "It is," says George Steiner, "a matter of seriousness and emotional risk, a recognition that the teaching of literature, if it can be done at all, is an extraordinarily complex and dangerous business, of knowing that one takes in hand the quick of another human being."

We must find new ways, new methods by which we may bring literature to our young people. For me, poetry, as the literature of heightened consciousness, is one way of touching the individual child, finding the poem that sings in the child's own rhythm, offering, in Stephen Spender's words, "an event individually experienced" but with the knowledge that "this uniqueness is the universal mode of experiencing all events. Poetry makes one realize that one is alone, and complex; and that to be alone is universal."

For you, there will be hundreds of ways, based on your own feelings as to what a piece of literature strikes in you, as an individual, and therefore, one hopes, in the individual child. With this approach there can be no room for gimmicks and gimcracks, no mass-produced exercises in creativity and futility.

SELECTED BOOKS BY
MYRA COHN LIVINGSTON

Abraham Lincoln, A Man for All the People. Illustrated by Samuel Byrd. New York: Holiday House, 1994.

Birthday Poems. Illustrated by Margot Tomes. New York: Holiday House, 1989.

Celebrations. Illustrated by Leonard Everett Fisher. New York: Holiday House, 1985.

A Circle of Seasons. Illustrated by Leonard Everett Fisher. New York: Holiday House, 1982.

Earth Songs. Illustrated by Leonard Everett Fisher. New York: Holiday House, 1986.

I Never Told and Other Poems. New York: Margaret K. McElderry, 1992.

Let Freedom Ring: A Ballad of Martin Luther King. Illustrated by Samuel Byrd. New York: Holiday House, 1992.

Light & Shadow. Illustrated by Barbara Rogasky. New York: Holiday House, 1992.

Monkey Puzzle and Other Poems. Illustrated by Antonio Frasconi. New York: Atheneum, 1984.

My Head Is Red and Other Riddle Rhymes. Illustrated by Tere LoPrete. New York: Holiday House, 1990.

Poem-Making: Ways to Begin Writing Poetry. New York: HarperCollins, 1991.

Poems for Brothers, Poems for Sisters. Illustrated by Jean Zallinger. New York: Holiday House, 1991.

Remembering and Other Poems. New York: Margaret K. McElderry, 1989.

Roll Along: Poems on Wheels. New York: Margaret K. McElderry, 1993.

Sea Songs. Illustrated by Leonard Everett Fisher. New York: Holiday House, 1986.

Sky Songs. Illustrated by Leonard Everett Fisher. New York: Holiday House, 1984.

Space Songs. Illustrated by Leonard Everett Fisher. New York: Holiday House, 1988.

There Was a Place and Other Poems. New York: Margaret K. McElderry, 1988.

Up in the Air. Illustrated by Leonard Everett Fisher. New York: Holiday House, 1989.

Worlds I Know and Other Poems. Illustrated by Tim Arnold. New York: Margaret K. McElderry, 1985.

READING EXPERIENCES IN A WHOLE LANGUAGE CLASSROOM

Second grader Cory and I sit side by side at the conference table. School has been in session six weeks, and this is Cory's first scheduled reading conference. Cory, an avid reader and researcher, makes some key observations about reading and learning at the close of the conference. The dialogue that follows has been transcribed from my notes:

CORY: So far I like school this year.

ROBB: What do you like about it?

CORY: This year I read books. Lots. Like this one [points to his copy of *Big Cats*, by Seymour Simon]. Last year I got teached.

ROBB: What do you mean you "got teached"?

CORY: The teacher told us what to read— we hardly picked our own.

ROBB: Is that what you mean by "got teached"?

CORY: Every book had sheets to do [nodding]. I guess the sheets teached us.

ROBB: Who teaches you now?

CORY: Me. I'm the guy who reads and writes.

This literacy story celebrates the elements of choice and authenticity in whole language classrooms. Though Cory read literature during first grade, he recalls the lack of choice and the work sheets instead of meaningful stories. Now that Cory selects books he relishes, reading and writing have real significance. Reading in a whole language classroom should be an empowering experience for both teacher and students. Every member of such a learning community can choose books and find their own meaning as they respond to stories in their own words.

Whole language teachers strive to incorporate books naturally, inviting children to read the way young and old read in the real world. Reading is no longer a "subject" confined to one special period. Children read throughout the day for pleasure and enjoyment, to satisfy their questions, to test hypotheses, and to learn to think and connect new information to what they already know. The finest literature, magazines, newspapers, and charts form the basis for learning in science, social studies, mathematics, the fine arts, and sports. And certainly selected unabridged and unadapted stories from basals and anthologies can be included.

Daily read-alouds and sustained silent reading periods—with pairs and groups of children reading and discussing books, reading fiction and wonderful informational books, regularly checking out library books, and choosing books and topics to research—mean children have countless enriching experiences with books across the curriculum. These experiences can develop a passion for reading and offer students opportunities to discover how authors use language.

In whole language classrooms, the teacher's goal is to provide powerful and meaningful encounters with literature. Teachers and children reread stories and poems and live their way into the text and illustrations. Such teachers recognize the importance of silent reading and honor the social aspects of reading. They reserve time for pairs, small groups, or the entire class to talk about stories, so children can explore and discover meaning for themselves. Rather than turn powerful stories into skill lessons, these teachers help children understand language through the children's writing and minilessons, which model problem solving strategies.

During daily shared reading experiences, teachers actively engage children with print and pictures. Shared reading is a partnership that acknowledges the importance of teachers reading with children. Such shared involvement includes encouraging students to participate during read-alouds, permitting

children to answer their own questions, joining informal discussions as a co-learner, reading silently with the class during sustained silent reading (SSR), jointly negotiating topics to investigate, and together identifying areas of literacy learning that require additional practice. Reading with children demonstrates:

- Language and reading are fun!

- Reading is an activity everyone can enjoy.

- Deeper meaning comes from rereading.

- Literary genres and their structure.

- An appreciation of illustrations.

- The parts of a book: title, author/illustrator, endpapers, front and back covers, and the title, copyright, and dedication pages.

- How language works: words, spaces, letters, and punctuation.

- How books enlarge our knowledge of the world and people.

- That reading validates our experiences and feelings.

You, the teacher, hold the power to broadcast to students positive messages about reading. Talk about a book you couldn't put down at night. Or hand a newly completed book to a student, saying, "I think you'll love *Interstellar Pig* because you're really into science fiction; I can't wait to talk about the ending with you." Or "Yesterday my teacher reading group discussed *Bridge to Terabithia*, and I told them about your journal entry,

Dave, where you wrote how you returned to that book to help you through your best friend's fatal car accident. We wept."

Yes, you hold the key to building lifetime readers. The disheartening news is that 60 percent of all Americans who have completed their formal schooling never read another book; the other 40 percent read, on average, only one book per year.[1] And that last statistic, unfortunately, does include many teachers.

Children learn by imitating adult behaviors. It's unfair to expect children to love reading and choose reading for pleasure and enjoyment when their teachers don't read aloud or independently. "Do as I say, not as I do" just doesn't work with children or adults.

An easy way to lure children into books and metamorphose them into readers is to schedule a regular read-aloud period for fifteen to twenty minutes once or several times a day. Unfortunately, too many parents and administrators have made teachers feel that reading aloud is a frivolous activity, and that the amount of work sheets and completed workbooks is the real measure of learning. During my visits to schools, teachers talk about those awful moments when they're "caught" reading aloud or reading silently with students. Comments such as "Reading aloud isn't teaching" or "The kids can read on their own—at home" or "I came to observe teaching" intimidate teachers and hurl them back to filling children's work folders with piles of meaningless reproducibles.

Upper elementary teachers in a departmentalized schedule have the most difficulty reserving read-aloud time. I faced that problem. Compelled to share stories with students, I robbed time from the schedule: five to ten minutes from homeroom and ten minutes from workshop time. If no flexibility exists, read poems, folktales, and short, short stories during mini-read-aloud breaks. The point is the benefits are so great. And once children leave elementary school, it's almost too late to develop that passion for books that nurtures them throughout their lives.

Teachers who read aloud daily breathe life into an author's words and provide students with a good oral reading model. Ashley Bryan, an author and illustrator, always urges teachers and students to play with poems and stories, to find the song in the words. Practice until the rhythms and words merge with the reader's voice, and the sharing communicates meaning through the beauty of spoken language.

Second grader reads from The Weirdest Teacher on Earth, *a big book she and her classmates composed.*

SOME READ-ALOUD TIPS

- Read the book before you share it with your class to make sure it's appropriate for your students. Reading in advance familiarizes you with the language and offers time to think about expression and making the author's words live.

- Be dramatic; find your voice and become a ham. Kids love to hear you adopt the voices of different characters and move from whispers to forte. Remember, you're modeling good read-aloud techniques!

- Use your librarian for read-aloud suggestions. Librarians know children's books and can also direct you to outstanding read-aloud resource books.

- Select a variety of literary genres and authors throughout the year.

- Share books you love, and you'll transmit your enthusiasm to students.

- Read picture books and chapter books to all age groups.

- Invite students to gather close to you or settle in a comfortable niche. One year a parent donated a rug for our classroom library area, and the kids called it "The Magic Reading Carpet." We used it for read-aloud time and for independent reading.

- After completing a read-aloud, make the book available to students. Many will want to reread sections, look at illustrations, or read the entire book.

Of course, the potential to influence children's reading attitudes resides not only in teachers but in all school community members. Students, school administrators

Sixth graders reading poems from Space Songs, *by Myra Cohn Livingston.*

and staff, parents, and others can cultivate a passion for story by reading aloud. Once you're comfortable with a classroom read-aloud program, you might want to introduce your school to some of these variations:

Cross Grade. When older students regularly read aloud to "reading buddies" in the primary grades, great friendships form. Some teachers regularly schedule weekly periods where older students read aloud to younger buddies. Self-esteem increases among both groups, and books play a prominent role in the relationship. Older students often pass up a recess to fulfill a child's request to read a book together. "Couldn't hurt the little guy's feelings," I heard James explaining to his peers. "He asked me to read [James Marshall's] *Fox at School*, and I couldn't say no."

Community. "Dad's reading to my class all week," my eight-year-old nephew Douglas tells me on the phone. "And I get to pick the book!" he proudly adds. Douglas attends school in West Lafayette, Indiana, where parents and members of the community read aloud to classes. Many schools have organized similar programs to promote reading and to demonstrate that reading is a pleasurable lifelong activity. In addition to parents, they invite men and women from factories, offices, hospitals, retail shops, restaurants, and so on to read aloud to children at school. One father told me that he enjoyed reading aloud in the schools so much that now, when his family takes long car trips, he and his wife take turns reading to their children.

Take-home Stories. Many teachers, especially those in primary grades, have begun "Take-home Story Programs" whose goal is to connect books, children, and families. Teachers prepare a folder and a large brown envelope for each child, containing a library book and a chart with directions (see appendix). Parents, grandparents, older siblings, or any adult in the home can participate. The chart encourages talking about the book and recording a child's comments, reinforcing the importance of talking about books in social situations. Not only does this extend a child's knowledge of language, as Wells, in *The Meaning Makers*, points out, but it also sends the important message that talking about books and learning from books is fun for the entire family.

The book remains at home, to be read and reread many times. Then the family returns the folder and envelope to the teacher and receives another title.

When families share books at home, they develop their own traditions for reading aloud. In fifth grader Paul's family, Mom and Dad read stories around the dinner table and at bedtime. Second grader Jaimie can't wait for weekends, when she cuddles in her parents' bed to hear a before-breakfast story. It's these traditions that make family read-aloud times magical and memorable moments. Denny Taylor and Dorothy S. Strickland document the value of family reading in *Family Storybook Reading*, noting how creative the process of shared reading is. "Sharing storybooks enables parents and children to create their own family story."[2] Moreover, children grow up with story traditions to bring to their own families, ensuring that traditions pass to future generations.

Read-aloud Partnerships. Principals and school supervisors, custodial and administrative staff read aloud to the children. Some visit classrooms on a regular basis; others gather students, a class or several grades, in the library or school auditorium to read stories. The point is to sustain the program throughout the year, sending a powerful message about the pleasure and importance of reading.

Middle school principal Mary Ann Biggs reads aloud to students sent to her office for misbehaving. "Sometimes they arrive so angry that talking feels impossible. So I whip out a picture book and we read and chat and laugh side by side. Then I can begin counseling."

Though most parents work, many are willing to read aloud to children during their lunch hour and early in the morning, prior to the start of classes. Such partnerships are rewarding for parents, children, and teachers.

At Powhatan, I organized a lap-reading program in first grade, staffed by working parent volunteers who provided one-on-one reading experiences. First-grade teacher Robin Northrup and I led three training sessions that concentrated on book orientation and effective lap-reading strategies; each session concluded with parents asking questions. Parents read to their first-grade partner twice each week. The program began in January, and we met as a group, during lunch, every four weeks to exchange experiences and respond to questions. Four years later, Mary Carter, a supportive parent volunteer, wrote this about the lap-reading program:

> One thing remains vivid in my mind, and that is the look in a child's eyes when he recognizes a word he has stumbled over many times. The eyes speak in a split second, before the child does. They become bright, they twinkle and even laugh and say, "Hey, I know this, I remember." I hope that memory remains with me. It is one that always causes me to smile.

An educated parent body celebrates rather than challenges new ways of learning. Once you know the type of support you require, extend invitations that offer choices to parents. Provide training sessions in reading aloud and give parent volunteers positive feedback after they've read to individuals or small groups. Schedule some meetings to respond to questions and encourage volunteers to exchange literacy stories. Invite parents to class celebrations so they see the benefits of their efforts. Meaningful parent involvement can provide you with a corps of staunch supporters in the classroom and the community.

Family Reading Nights. Educating parents about the value and enjoyment of family reading is a crucial job of schools and public libraries. Genevieve Patt, a remarkable French librarian, told me how she linked books and families. Discouraged by the poor attendance at family story hours, Genevieve and her team of associates piled large wicker baskets with inviting picture books and peddled titles door-to-door. "First we bring books to the families," Genevieve says, "and then the families slowly begin to visit the library."

Family reading nights reach out to tired working parents, inviting them to the school to read with their children. A camaraderie and support system build when families band together to read. The hope is that families continue to read to children at home. An abundance of books and a relaxed environment help foster a pleasurable evening for moms and dads, siblings, and grandparents. As one dad pointed out, the event "is free and fun."

At Clarke County, Lorrie Aikens and I instituted a family reading program that began with one grade level; each month we added another. Children wrote letters inviting parents to attend; parents responded on the child's letter, and teachers displayed these in classrooms and hallways. Primary grades composed a collaborative letter that teachers typed and children delivered. All meetings began with a read-aloud to the entire group; new-comers observed demonstrations of how to read and talk about a book. Teachers displayed books everywhere; parents and children selected a book and found comfortable spaces in the library, a hall, or a classroom. For forty-five minutes, pairs and groups read, reread, chose new titles, and talked about books. The evening concluded with punch, cookies, a whole group discussion, and time to check out library books.

Fifty-six parents and children attended the first family reading night at Cooley Elementary; eighty arrived the following month, and one hundred seventy came three months later. Comments of parents and children celebrated the time together without interruptions from the telephone or other siblings. Kenny, a second grader, told me, "I never believed anyone liked to read in spare time. I changed my mind tonight." Kenny left with a book about Mars and one about dinosaurs. "Reading with other people is more fun than reading alone at home" was a remark made by several adults and children.

Many parents were anxious to learn more about joining the public library. Their questions sparked the idea of inviting a public librarian to family readings to discuss community library membership and permit busy parents to fill out library card forms. As the year progressed, we organized an "indoor picnic" on a windy March evening. Families set up blankets and baskets on the floor of the multipurpose room, feasted, exchanged stories, and read books!

Reader's Chair. Weekly reader's chair sessions honor the books children select to read. Reader's chair builds community through sharing, values free-choice reading, and sends this powerful message to each child: "What you read is so important to me

and your classmates that we want to hear about it." Posted on a bulletin board is a reader's chair sign-up sheet, and when that's full and another isn't readily available, use the blackboard.

By mid-October, whether in second grade or middle school, students have agreed not to retell their book at share time. "That's boring!" noted second grader Christie. "Why bother to read it after you've heard it all," comments seventh grader Angela. To provide a model for students and reinforce the concept of reading with them, I initiate the first five to ten share sessions and discuss genres, a character I related to or disliked, or why I chose a "fast-read" novel. My book shares also relate to reading and writing minilessons, and I incorporate literary techniques such as flash-back and foreshadowing.

Book-share sessions are powerful reading motivators because children speak to each other. The transcriptions of sixth- and eighth-grade reader's shares illustrate how students avoid retelling and focus on new information and personal reactions to theme and events.

The Kestrel is a story that will make you hate war. It's a combination of adventure in a make-believe kingdom. It's strange how the weapons were old, like muskets and sabers, but the book deals with guerrilla warfare that we hear about on the news. Theo goes from a printer's devil in Westmark, which is an apprentice, to a devil of a killing machine. I looked up *kestrel* in the dictionary, and it's a predator, a fighting bird, and that's what war can do to a person. (Sixth grader)

Foreshadowing helped me deal with the horrible events in *Wolf of Shadows*. Strieber works to prepare you for the effects of the nuclear winter after the bomb drops on Minneapolis. Each disaster—the geese losing their feathers, the destruction of the plane, the death of the baby—all prepare you for what Wolf of Shadows and the mother and daughter face. You'll learn about a literary technique, but you'll also have to deal with your feelings about nuclear holocaust. (Eighth grader)

Each reader's chair session concludes with students clamoring to check out titles. Some books grow a waiting list of four to five. As others read a title, groups discuss the story during lunch and class. Relishing one book by an author leads some to search out and read the complete works of that author.

Carol Chapman's second graders broadened the scope of reader's chair and established their own methods for sharing books. They incorporated music, puppets, costumes, clay characters, charts, and murals. Some children read exciting or humorous passages aloud; others imitated a character's speech and actions, or created commercials. "Talk slow and with expression and *Don't Tell All*" were guidelines they agreed upon and published on a reminder chart.

Reservations for books increased. Children furiously traded titles, and many willingly forfeited morning and lunch recess to read a classmate's book rather than wait a few days. The two second-grade transcriptions that follow reflect the children's desire to invite classmates to savor both fiction and nonfiction.

Jim tapes two huge ears on either side of his head and begins:

You'll need these when you take a listening walk. I read *The Listening Walk* by Paul Showers to my dad and we did it

Talking about Steven Kellogg's The Island of the Skog *during reader's share.*

together. I never knew there were so many sounds like a red bird singing, bikes riding, and my own footsteps. Start listening and have fun!

Andrew portrays Bouncer from Steven Kellogg's *The Island of the Skog*. A large piece of construction paper covers his torso, leaving only face and feet in view as he speaks:

I didn't think I'd like this book, but I stuck to our class bargain that I'd read the first two pages before returning it. I read it five times already! The mice and skog were the same 'cause they were afraid of things they didn't know. It made me think about my fear of not being able to write at the beginning of the year. Now I write a lot of words, but I like to draw pictures best. I stayed up until 9:30 doing this picture. My mom said, "Go to bed, Andrew. It's late." But I stayed to finish the sailboat. I tried to give my picture lots of details like

Steven Kellogg. I need to read it once more and then some of you can read it.

Many, like Andrew, found solace and comfort in books they read and unabashedly shared their feelings. Knowing pats on the back as students returned to seats and comments such as "I used to not be able to read lots of words like you" helped children accept that learners develop at different rates.

In addition to reader's chair, ask children to keep a record of all free reading in a book-log folder. Log entries keep you informed of their choices and reactions, and students periodically review and reflect upon their logs during reading conferences.

My middle school students keep a reading log where they record book titles read in and out of school, the date completed, and a brief comment. Comments are unprompted, and the content improves as they dialogue in journals, discuss literature, and exchange responses in small group share sessions (figure 1).

Nancy Roche's third graders log in titles and comments and compile a list of "Books I'm Dying to Read." Reader's chair and group discussions uncover books students just have to read. They record these in their log folders and check off completed titles (figure 2).

DEMONSTRATING READING STRATEGIES

The purpose of strategic reading is to develop children who are self-monitoring readers. Teachers model the strategies and

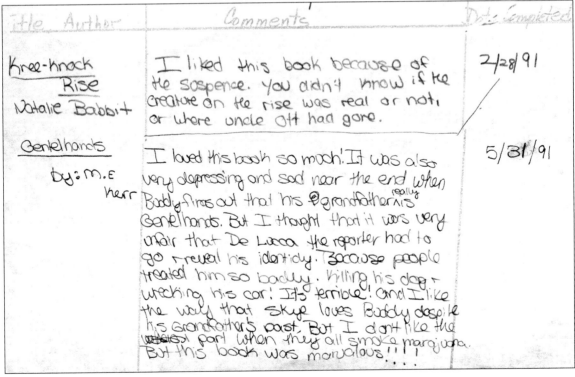

Fig. 1 Sixth-grade book log entries for February and May.

behaviors successful readers employ, inviting the reader to actively use what she or he already knows to learn something new. Accompanying demonstrations are teacher think-alouds, which reveal the inner thoughts, questions, and possible solutions teachers rely on when reading. Think-alouds send the reassuring message that adults and children require support and use the same reading strategies. During the talk that follows my demonstrations, I invite students to model how they solve a reading problem. After all, the point is not to find one way but to uncover as many ways as possible to help children become strategic learners.

Teachers new to whole language, and middle school teachers who function within forty-five- to fifty-minute time blocks, may feel more comfortable conducting strategic demonstrations with the entire class, rather than conducting several small group demonstrations. It does take time for children to be able to work independently at a few choice activities, which frees the teacher to work with groups. You'll also find that periodic reviews of the steps to obtaining assistance with reading problems can foster independence in reading. First students try to use what they already know, then they can ask a peer for help, and finally they can ask the teacher.

14 Reading Log Title and Author	Name annie Give a REACTION, RESPONSE, FEELINGS or SHARE your book in your own way if you choose	Date Completed
Animals can talk	it is a sints Book of animals can talk it was felly interesting becaus they Comunicate in sounds	
screamer	it is a very Good Boot and it is about acogel.	
the gost of wind hill	it is about a scary story and they is some other Boks obot the	
Antarctica By Helen Coucher	Its about some unr like poiquin sels and other skuces and peopel.	
Jamestoun in Virinia	it's abot a long ago story and I LIKE it.	
smal Wolf	it's like Jame tone whow sow the indens and the stog ar teling	
Love is a speshel angel	it was a litle book and it talk about how yoe feel about some	
Earth Calender folling	it is a sinte book men and I thik it wil make you fell nacher too.	

Fig. 2 A third grader's book log entries.

Sustained silent reading in kindergarten.

List strategies on large chart paper and place in a highly visible area so children can reread and review the strategies. Some teachers believe that only younger children require teacher demonstrations of reading strategies. My experiences reveal the opposite.

After demonstrations, children practice the strategy as they read alone or with partners. Keep practice sessions short; students who successfully employ the strategy should pursue a choice activity. Permitting pairs and small groups to support and assist each other affords many opportunities to observe how others internalize and modify a strategy. It's also comforting to know that other students struggle with aspects of making meaning from print.

Independence in reading and self-monitoring readers develop when children

and teachers have opportunities to use and evaluate strategies that enable them to gain control over reading. Third grader Bobby is able to explain how he copes with a difficult word or phrase; Bobby has also identified a classmate who can assist (figure 3).

Periodic review of data collected from reading conferences, kid watching, and anecdotal notes inform teachers about the reading strategies students do and do not employ. Information you gather will suggest many possible minilessons to present to the whole class, small groups, pairs, or individuals. Here are some reading strategies that have been successfully employed in many whole language classrooms:

Book Orientation. Talk about the parts of a book: front and back covers, endpapers, title, copyright, and dedication pages, table of contents, and index. Gather reactions to the illustrations, the dedication, and the endpapers. The endpapers in Richard Egielski's *Hey, Al* change from dull, ordinary beige at the front to bright yellow at the end. Children are quick to point out that the color change represents a future change in the lives of Eddie and Al. Ask children to study and discuss endpapers by illustrators such as Susan Jeffers and Steven Kellogg, who use their endpapers to create a mood, set the scene, and support the story.

Approximations and Guesses. Both beginning and skilled readers use approximations and guesses to make sense out of new and unfamiliar words in texts. Guessing—based on story clues, previous knowledge, and illustrations—can assist readers as they construct meaning. You can prepare for a lesson on coping with unfamiliar words by writing a section of a text that posed problems for students. Then demonstrate the strategy by reading to the end of the sentence, using

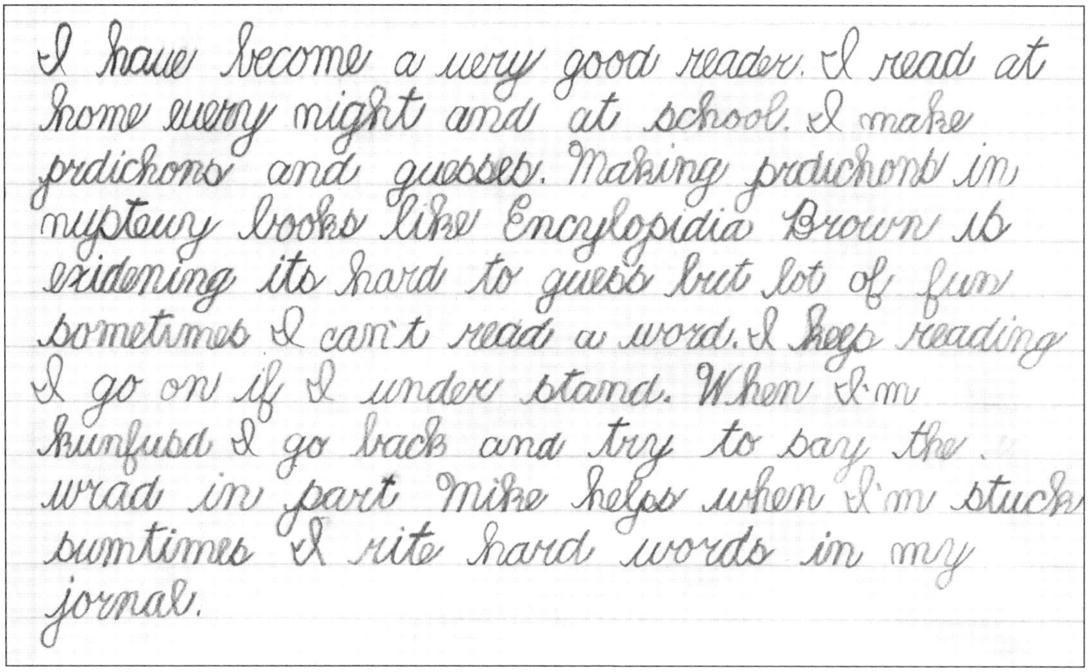

> I have become a very good reader. I read at home every night and at school. I make prdichons and guesses. Making prdichons in mystery books like Encylopidia Brown is exidening its hard to guess but lot of fun sometimes I can't read a word. I keep reading I go on if I under stand. When I'm kunfusd I go back and try to say the wrad in part Mike helps when I'm stuck sumtimes I rite hard words in my jornal.

Fig. 3 Bobby evaluates himself as a reader.

picture clues, finding familiar segments of words within a word, or saying individual syllables to guess the meaning of the unfamiliar words. If the meaning remains unclear, try rereading the paragraph to discover contextual clues that can help tackle the new word. Explain, during the minilesson, that comprehension is possible even though every word is not completely understood. Remind children that classmates are available for assistance.

To prepare for whole class study, invite children to write new words they want to explore in depth either in response journals or on scratch paper. A group of sixth graders wrote words they wanted to know more about on our message bulletin board; vocabulary building lessons evolved from student-selected words. Borrowing the sixth graders' idea, I established a word chart for at-risk second graders, and small or whole groups analyzed words. Student vocabulary collections stimulated an interest in unfamiliar words, and we referred to the dictionary to satisfy the children's curiosity to know more about these new words.

Teachers always ask if they should send children to the dictionary when they don't know a word. By the time a child retrieves the dictionary, finds the word, and deciphers the definition, she or he has lost interest in the text. Immediate help provides the best support.

Predictions. Successful readers make predictions before and during reading. Stauffer developed the process (the Directed Reading Thinking Activity) of predicting and confirming as a way for teachers to use the strategy with literature. Explain that predicting, then reading to confirm or adjust predictions, improves comprehension, for it causes the reader to pause and think about the text. Ask students to periodically pause and ask themselves, "And what will happen next?" Then read on to test predictions and confirm or adjust them.

Questions. Model questions readers pose and attempt to answer: "Does this passage make sense?" or "Are there words or phrases that confuse me?" Questions that focus on "Do I understand?" lead readers to pinpoint confusing sections of a book. Write on a chart or overhead transparency a passage from a book that posed difficulties; point to the confusing words and phrases. Share the questions that led you to identify the passage and the strategies that clarified meaning. Middle school students always register amazement during such a minilesson, convinced that adults never experience difficulties with reading.

Read On, Then Reread. Once students identify troublesome parts of texts, they require strategies to unravel meaning. Reading on and rereading are two helpful strategies. Think aloud the process you employ when you confront a confusing phrase, sentence, or paragraph, offering students these strategies: Read to the end of the sentence or paragraph and see if continued reading offers clues; reread the difficult section, sometimes several times.

Second graders reread the chart the class created for Jan Brett's Annie and the Wild Animals.

During minilessons I inform the class that frequently I require assistance from my husband or a friend. Suggest your students seek peer support when they are unable to solve the problem. Organizing class reading buddies or small reading teams, which change frequently throughout the year, fosters peer support. Children should seek your help only when they are unable to solve the problem, for your goal is to quickly develop self-monitoring readers who work together to solve problems.

Pause, Think, and Retell. Use a think-aloud to demonstrate reflecting on and recalling passages. Encourage children to pause after chapters rather than in the middle of a story. Children reading picture books should only pause once or twice during the reading or they will disrupt the flow of the story. Tell students the benefits of "pause, think, summarize": Thinking and summarizing reinforces memory of the text and encourages contemplation. Self-directed readers draw conclusions about what they recall and determine whether or not to reread.

Multiple Readings and Retellings. The more story details students recall, the richer their discussions, and the more information they've accumulated for critical thinking. Illustrate the benefits of rereading; ask students to read a passage once and retell, then reread and retell again. Students can practice orally with partners and discuss the differences observed between retellings, or each student can write several retellings of one story and compare first with later retellings.

"My kids whine when I ask them to reread," said third-grade teacher Liz Davies. "And many go through the motions, but don't reread." I encouraged Liz to persist and plan a series of rereads and retells, ending with student self-evaluation of the strategy. Liz hooked the kids

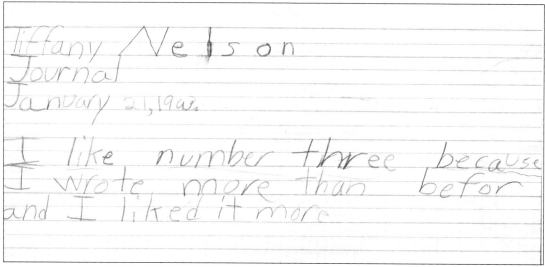

Fig. 4

with the self-evaluation aspect, and several said, "That'll show we don't have to reread." Third graders read and retold Barbara Cooney's *Miss Rumphius* three times; the evaluations unanimously confirmed the benefits for the children of rereading and retelling (figure 4).

Think-alouds. This strategy invites students to verbalize their thoughts, questions, and connections as they read a text line by line. Model the think-aloud process with a student partner because the listener can support the speaker, who reads one sentence at a time and verbalizes meaning and personal associations. Children can do a think-aloud with pairs reading the same or different books. When someone gets "stuck," the partner suggests a strategy such as "reread" or "read on." Second graders Jeremy and Jerry were reading *Chrysanthemum,* by Kevin Henkes, and neither child could decode this sentence: " 'And envious and begrudging and discontented and jaundiced,' said her father." None of the strategies helped them comprehend the unfamiliar words. "Let's ask Steven,"

suggested Jeremy. "He can read anything." Steven willingly assisted the pair but also asked for a return favor. Jerry, the class artist, promised to help Steven solve an illustration problem. Peer support systems build a room full of potential "teachers."

Reading Rate. Through demonstrations, children begin to understand that reading rate changes with a reader's purpose. Skimming requires a faster rate than reading for deep meaning or researching new information. Help your students understand that finishing fast and first should not be equated with good reading. Unfortunately, many students believe the myth that a fast reader equals a competent reader. Savoring and enjoying words, images, and illustrations all contribute to enjoyable reading experiences. Speed takes away the possibility of playing with words and story. Sixth grader Emilia, during a student-teacher conference, said, "I like to take my time with a book I'm loving. I mark my favorite parts and reread them until I feel satisfied. I keep the book with me and think about it most of the time."

Mental Imaging. Anthony Fredericks, in his article on mental imaging (*The Reading Teacher,* October 1986), explains how the ability to imagine and draw mental pictures of characters, settings, events, poems, and scenes from plays not only increases comprehension, but makes reading a highly individualized adventure. Use minilessons to explain the connection between comprehension and mental imaging, then demonstrate imaging with words or drawings. Ask students to translate their mental images to a partner, through talk, drawing, or by writing detailed descriptions of what they imagine. The TV and video era we live in serves the same images to all children, and those children who don't read soon cease to imagine and conjure unique mental pictures. Fredericks carefully cautions teachers that mental imaging takes time and practice. Children who learn to film their own movies can realize one of the great pleasures of reading as they play with the story.

The K-W-L. A predictive approach to nonfiction, the K-W-L (Ogle) consists of three questions that actively engage readers: What do I know? What do I want to know? What have I learned? Before reading, ask your students to brainstorm a list of ideas that answer: What do I know about the topic? Then invite students to set purposes for reading by creating a list of what they would like to find out. Teachers can participate in the process by adding a few questions. After reading, have students assess what they've learned by discussing their questions and affirming and adjusting what they thought they knew. Students can research unanswered questions and extend their knowledge of information that interests them. Once students understand the K-W-L, they can use the strategy to support independent reading and research.

Bookmarks—Interacting with Stories. Bookmarks are a self-monitoring strategy that encourages readers to interact with texts: predicting, questioning, agreeing, disagreeing, and linking previous life and reading experiences. The idea for bookmarks comes from Dorothy Watson; Linda K. Crafton describes the strategy in *Whole Language: Getting Started . . . Moving Forward.* Crafton recommends that students have many opportunities to discuss responses to literature before initiating the strategy. Fold notebook paper or unlined standard size copier paper in half. Cut ten to twelve strips and staple them together. On the bookmark, students note their name, the title and author of the book, and the page or pages they're responding to.

Teachers carefully model the process before students begin, pointing out that responses can be questions, predictions, confusing sections, emotions aroused, unfamiliar words or information, connections to other books, word pictures of characters and settings, or evaluations of events and characters. Reading student bookmarks provides teachers with information about how students interact with texts and which students would benefit from additional modeling.

Cindy Hughes and I introduced sixth graders who were reluctant readers to bookmarks. Reading inventories revealed that out of eighty students, two-thirds disliked reading, rated themselves poor readers, and only checked out books when required. Most acknowledged that they didn't read the required book because it was too difficult. Anxious to monitor students' reading and involve them with story, we introduced bookmarks and quickly identified students who were reading books too difficult for them. Jake wrote, for example, "I don't understand how they talk," referring to Mildred Taylor's *Mississippi Bridge.*

Students used the bookmarks three times during the school year. Bookmarks were a springboard for group discussions, as students shared in small groups comments they wrote. Trading bookmark notes, several remarked, "helped see other things to write about to help us read better." Students could elect not to share; by the third round, all shared.

Cindy and I read all the bookmarks, discussed them, and celebrated students' growth by reading unidentified responses to the class. We wrote positive comments on Post-it notes, not wishing to write on the bookmarks. Gradually, students incorporated suggestions, based on whole group demonstrations, of ways to react to stories and improve comprehension. Following are notes and bookmarks from two sixth graders participating in their second round of the strategy (figures 5, 6).

Both students ask questions, form hypotheses about characters' actions, connect their lives to the story, and recall specific details. There is always an integration of response to story with strategies such as predicting and questioning. In her end-of-the-year self-evaluation Karen wrote, "Bookmarks got me into the book and made me think more about how to read. I can tell if a book is too hard with a bookmark and exchange it for one I can read."

Making Inferences and Connections and Drawing Conclusions. Your demonstrations can clarify the inferring process when you analyze real-life situations and then move to literature that simulates life. In a minilesson, I make children aware of the way they auto-

Students discuss their Betsy Byars books after sharing bookmark comments.

Jennie

31/36 = I think Sara is a little weird, because she thinks her sister is everythink. If I was her and anyone will ageer nobody thinks her sister is everything.

37/41 = I wonder why charlie can't speak. Sometimes it seems like he can't speak either. Do you think he can read?

44/48 = Sara has change a little bit, so has her sister. They're communicateing more eachother than Her sister. Her sara's sister doesn't worry about herself so much anymore.

49/53 = I think that sara and her sister wanta are coming closer and closer together. Her sister is going to ee a nuse.

54/58 = I think nobody cares about charlie anymore. Sara was the one he can count on, But not anymore. Everyone thinks hes annoying. Poor charlie

59/63 = Charlie is outside running with the wind. I think charlie is like me a little Because when nobody talks to me I feel like talking to myself.

64/68 = charlie is lost in the woods he even don't know how he got there.

69/73 = Charles ran away from home. I would to if my feelings were hurt like his was

I noticed how you followed through on your opening comment about Sara + her sister. You also made connections to yourself when Charlie ran away from home + showing how you and Charlie are alike. Do you think Charlie can read? Thanks for numbering. Keep up the fine observations + Connections. Mrs. Robb

Fig. 5 Bookmark excerpts and teacher's response for Summer of the Swans, *by Betsy Byars.*

matically draw conclusions based on the actions and words of others. I might ask a child to yawn and put her head on the desk. From these actions I infer reasons such as she's tired, ill, bored, upset, or angry. Then groups dramatize situations that emerge from classroom life, such as ignoring a peer, falling asleep in class, hiding books, or tripping a student. I then ask groups to collaborate and draw conclusions from these impromptu minidramas.

Once students make the connection that inferring is a part of daily living, I demonstrate the process using a character's words and actions, then invite groups to practice. All children can gain access to this type of critical analysis and eventually begin to make connections between books. Bobby, a member of my at-risk seventh- and eighth-grade class, explained the personality of Mrs. Mason, the foster mother in *The Pinballs,* by connecting her to Trotter, the foster mother in *The Great Gilly Hopkins*, a book I had read to the group earlier in the year. "They both love their foster kids, and they knew enough to not boss them into thinking and feeling like perfect prisses. You gotta feel strong about what you do and trust kids to let them be."

> You really identify with Kate and question her computer ability. I'll be curious to see what you conclude. I like the way you speculate about Frank and decide to wait to figure out the problem. Sometimes early predictions are tough. You're very involved with the story. It helps if you number the pages.
> *Mrs. Robb*

> 1) I dont think Kate should answer the alein, I would t.
> 2) This book makes me wonder how good she is on the computer.
> 3) If I was Kate I wouldnt tell my father.
> 4) I think Kates parents are nice, I mean it seams like that.
> 5) I think two people that met in McDonalds are kind of weird, I mean they hardly knew each other.
> 6) I dont think Frank sent her that message because I think its an alein.
> 7) I wouldnt try to figure out who it is yet I would wait until I had more information

Fig. 6 Bookmark excerpts and teacher's response for The Computer Nut, *by Betsy Byars.*

I have included a sample strategic minilesson presented to seventh and eighth graders using the opening pages of "The Swan," by Roald Dahl, from *The Wonderful Story of Henry Sugar and Six More*, in order to illustrate the teacher's process and students' responses.

Today we're going to practice creating mental images based on the first two pages of "The Swan," by Roald Dahl. I want you to close your eyes and imagine pictures as I read. What do family members look like? What do they wear? Can you envision their surroundings? When I finish reading, think about your impressions and reread any part of the first two pages. Then decide if you want to draw, write a description of your impressions, or do both. Take your time. If you finish your project before the end of the period, you can complete reading the story for response groups tomorrow or work on writing your research project or dialogue journal.

I remind students of options for using time, since I know they will all be at different points, and some will decide to complete their work at home.

Groups make decisions quickly; some reread the passage silently, others select a reader and listen. Students exchange images of Ernie, his parents, the sofa, their clothes; some try to imitate their speech, how they might walk. By talking, miming, and comparing images, students work to get inside this family, using the clues in the first two pages.

Below are a seventh grader's drawing and an eighth grader's word picture illustrating the inferences about the family that both students have begun to make. After completing the story, I always invite students to share their work with pairs or small groups. At this time students confirm or adjust their original images and hypotheses (figures 7, 8).

The best way to observe how children adapt and modify reading strategies is through one-on-one reading conferences. Once a reading-writing workshop develops a rhythm, I reserve time for conferencing students. Four to five weekly conferences are all I can manage in a class that meets an hour and a half daily. You might want to conference younger children in two ten-minute sessions. Older students can concentrate for fifteen minutes. Once you've identified students with special needs, conference them more frequently.

Select appropriate areas from the following suggestions to observe and conference. Your choices will depend on grade and developmental level. Students arrive at a conference with reading log, response and/or dialogue journal, and free-choice book.

Fig. 7 Illustration of Ernie and his parents in "The Swan," by Roald Dahl.

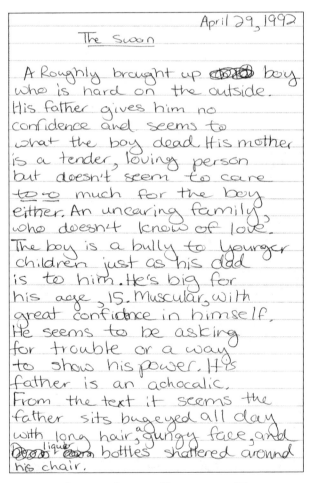

Fig. 8 Word picture of Ernie and his parents in "The Swan."

Nonprompted Student Comments

- Offers personal reactions and opinions.

- Connects story to own life.

Teacher Observations

- Holds book correctly.

- Moves eye/finger from left to right.

- Spends workshop time reading.

- Demonstrates pleasure in reading books.

- Shares with classmates in reader's chair.

- Reads a variety of topics and genres.

- Reads silently or subvocalizes.

Book and Print Awareness

- Knows the parts of a book.

- Able to point to specific words in big books and small books.

- Aware of spaces between words.

- Points to print and knows words tell story.

- Recognizes lower- and uppercase letters of alphabet.

- Understands page sequence and knows print moves from left to right.

Oral Retelling Features

- Recalls characters' names and problems each faced.

- Retells events in sequence.

- Discusses setting.

- Relates setting to theme.

- Retelling moves from story line to personal responses and to connecting ideas to self, others, and life experiences.

- Connects characters and themes to other books.

Comprehension of Entire Text

- Uses pictures to tell story.

- Retells stories with rich details.

- Retells stories in correct sequence.

- Knows main characters, setting.

- Identifies beginning, middle, end.

- Understands characteristics of specific genres.

- Identifies problems main character faces.

- Describes changes in character from beginning to end.

- Identifies themes.

- Relates story to other books and experiences.

- Identifies minor characters and their significance.

Reading Aloud: Student Selects Passage to Read

Teacher tapes a running record on an audio-cassette when necessary.

- Holds book correctly.

- Reads fluently.

- Reads with expression.

- Makes frequent repetitions.

- Makes frequent hesitations.

- Makes word substitutions.

- Reads through punctuation.

- Reads word to word.

- Needs frequent prompting on words.

- Aware of letter-sound relationships.

- Understands vocabulary in context.

- Connects selections to the entire story.

- Reads from left to right.

- Moves finger under text as reads.

Students' Reading Strategies

- Self-corrects errors that do not make sense.

- Rereads to self-correct.

- Rereads to clarify meaning.

- Knows rereading increases comprehension.

- Reads in meaningful chunks.

- Asks questions and reads to confirm or adjust.

- Pauses to summarize reading.

- Makes logical predictions based on text.

- Uses familiar syllables or small words to decode larger words.

- Uses prior knowledge to make predictions.

- Uses prior knowledge to comprehend.

- Uses clues such as pictures, charts, diagrams to comprehend.

- Creates mental images.

- Seeks peer assistance.

- Sets purposes for reading.

- Understands reading is comprehending meaning.

Self-Evaluation

- Do I read a variety of themes and genres?

- What are my strengths as a reader?

- Do I predict and ask questions?

- Do I set purposes for my reading?

- Do I pause to think about and review what I've read?

- Do I read for pleasure in and out of school?

- How much do I read at home?

- Why don't I choose to read outside of school assignments?

- How can I improve my reading?

Teacher-Student Recommendations

Record suggestions to improve self-monitoring strategies, fluency, word recognition, print awareness, book orientation, and sight vocabulary.

Student-Teacher Goals:

Next Conference Date:

Like strategic demonstrations, the purpose of conferences is to develop self-monitoring readers. The comment I hear most frequently from students is "I learn so much about my own reading and writing and math when I help others. I have to think about how I do it, and how to explain how I do it." It's the same for teachers: We learn from our students and from each other. Below are some guidelines that can help you with your conferencing techniques.

- Create a relaxed, informal atmosphere.

- Allow time for the student to make unprompted remarks.

- Make students aware of your support.

- Help students identify their strengths and progress.

- Guide students from where they are to where they can reasonably go. Review and evaluate past goals.

- Listen, allowing the student to help you understand more about his or her reading/writing process.

- Ask questions that encourage the student to reflect on process and strategies.

- Keep conferences short and focus them on one point.

- Prevent interruptions. This is a student's special time with you.

- Take notes during the conference.

- Conclude the conference by setting joint goals and a future conference date.

- Make a copy of the conference for your files; have the student place the original in his or her reading log folder.

Conferences can foster the development of self-monitoring and self-correcting strategies. Periodically, ask students to contemplate themselves as readers, reflecting on the strategies they use. The concepts under the headings Self-Evaluation and Students' Reading Strategies can provide

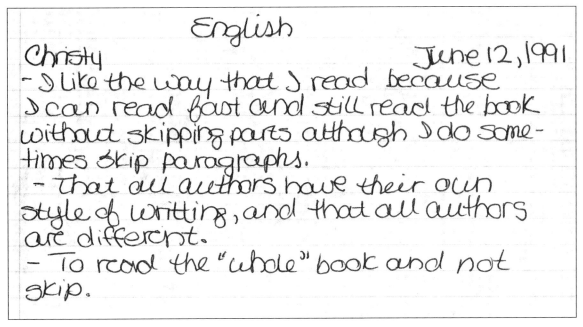

English

Christy   June 12, 1991
- I like the way that I read because
I can read fast and still read the book
without skipping parts although I do sometimes skip paragraphs.
- That all authors have their own
style of writting, and that all authors
are different.
- To read the "whole" book and not
skip.

Fig. 9 Sixth grader's self-evaluation of reading and skipping sections of text.

students with reflective guidelines for self-evaluation. When students write about the reading process and how they construct meaning from print, they identify strengths and clarify needs.

Christy wrote about her tendency to skip passages and pages and what she discovered by discussing her habit with peers and me (figure 9).

NURTURING THE INDEPENDENT READING LIFE

Nurturing the independent reading life means offering children choices, so children read books *they discover*, not titles adults select. Here's what kids say about choosing books:

• I learn what I like and don't like.

• I get to look through books and find ones I never knew.

• I feel you trust me when I can choose.

• I read more when I choose.

• I can get into a topic I love.

Browsing is a way for students to discover which books they want to read. But browsing takes time—time to wander through bookshelves, read titles, pull books, leaf through pages, and linger over illustrations. Students give browsing high ratings. "You get to read parts and show your friends. I find books I never knew existed." The bonus is teachers can browse with students and explore the pleasures of anticipating new books to read.

JAMES AND ROBBIE: TWO DIFFERENT READERS

James and Robbie were unusual students. I first met them in the sixth grade and tell their story here because it reveals so much about nurturing independent readers.

James stored several books in his desk and snatched every free moment to read during the school day. Consistently unprepared for class, James devoured books at home, rarely completed or even thought about his assignments, and was in deep trouble with many teachers. He relished the reading in English class and always contributed to discussions, whether whole class or small group. James's writing folder was noteworthy for its absence of writing. His frustrated mother called school weekly about incomplete work notes in science and history. "He reads every free moment—he even rereads books three and four times. As long as he passes, I guess he'll be all right," James's mom said, as if she was trying to convince herself.

During that year I learned that James's father had died of a lingering illness and James, always a reader, buried himself in books, reading aloud to his dad during the final months of his life, or reading alone in his room. "They were my refuge . . . my hope," he told me. When a good story captured his waking thoughts, James explained, "I have to read. I can't put the book aside."

Frequently, I found myself getting angry with James, especially when I received piles of notes from annoyed teachers who constantly complained about incomplete assignments or low test grades. As if I could do anything about it! My attempts to open discussions with James about meeting minimum requirements were always detoured by a breathless comment like, "Have you read Howard Pyle's *Story of King Arthur and His Knights*? Let's talk about that." And then he would read the passages he'd carefully marked, and we'd study the illustrations, forgetting about assignments.

James did, however, learn to balance his passion for reading with school responsibilities. Now a research doctor at a university, James avoided all the doom-and-gloom predictions announced by those who believed he would never graduate high school. James recently visited me; we reminisced and laughed about his middle school years. "I still love to read. I read to my family; I read for myself." He paused and chuckled. "I've always got a book with me just in case I can snatch a few minutes." And from his briefcase James pulled out a copy of Tillie Olsen's *Tell Me a Riddle*. "Have you read this?" he asked. I nodded. And it felt like old times, with James reading the passages he marked, and the two of us talking about personal connections to these touching stories.

Teachers dream of having a class of students like Robbie. Cooperative and responsible, Robbie worked diligently, completed assignments on time, had many friends, and was academically successful. But Robbie, in his own words during an early reading conference, told me, "I don't like to read. I only read what I have to and not one book more." His words haunted and distressed me. The successful student, the student I expected to enjoy reading, found no pleasure in books. Robbie was never able to verbally express reasons for negative reading attitudes. Near the end of the year, however, an angry journal entry shed some light on Robbie's resistance to books (figure 10).

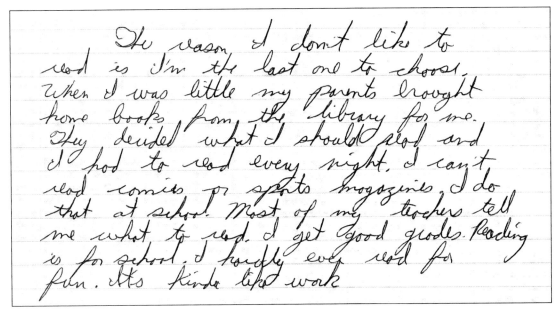

Fig. 10

Robbie had never entered a story to the extent that he and the characters became one; he'd never yielded his imagination to the author's text. Reading became a necessity for school achievement. James, by contrast, stepped inside a character's soul and lived that character's life so deeply, he could not tear himself away from a story, compelled to revisit favorites again and again.

Banners wave at local, state, and national conferences urging us to develop "lifetime readers." That should be the goal of all education: Reading aloud and providing children with opportunities to read books they choose develops literary appetites. I know many teachers and parents like Robbie's mother, who censor choices and force books on children. The message here is that we don't trust your choices, so we'll tell you what to read. Not only do such actions discourage independent reading, but they remove the joy of pulling several books from a library shelf, browsing through them, and checking out those that tempt and invite us to read. Our job is to help children discover books that illuminate their imagination and inspire a lifelong passion for reading.

References

1. Coffin, Tristram, ed. *The Washington Spectator*. April 15, 1992, Vol. 18, No. 8.

2. Taylor, Denny, and Dorothy Strickland. *Family Storybook Reading*. Portsmouth, NH: Heinemann, 1986, page 31.

AS I SEE IT

Steven Kellogg

In a celebrated poem by Robert Frost called "A Tuft of Flowers," a worker mentally sends a message to a colleague who has labored earlier that day on the same task with which the narrator is concerned, and he says: "Men work together, I told him from the heart, whether they work together or apart." And that's the way we work, as librarians and teachers of reading on one hand, and authors and illustrators on the other. We are colleagues and co-conspirators who put our energies separately, but together, into the very important and exciting work of turning kids on to books, giving them a passion for their written and spoken language, and opening them up to its vast communicative and artistic range.

As creative partners, we depend upon each other to do our work with care and sensitivity. You rightfully expect authors and illustrators to put into your hands books whose words and images can be effective tools for reaching, inspiring, and moving the children in your care. Happily, that expectation is being validated by a surge of interest in literature-based reading programs throughout the country. It seems to be fueled by the growing conviction that children don't become particularly excited about basal readers, workbooks, or ditto sheets, nor do they file into libraries to check them out. They *do* become excited about stories and pictures that capture their imaginations. Like all of us, they are drawn to works that communicate in the language of feeling, which is the way that elusive thing called art so effectively reaches us. And the communicative power of art, as it is utilized in its varied means of creative expression (from architecture to painting to literature to drama), has been a compelling outlet for every culture and civilization since man's beginnings.

An increased emphasis on the role of children's literature is a challenge to librarians and teachers as well as to their partners in publishing. Your role in our collaboration is to share the books with care, enthusiasm, creativity, and love so they have the maximum opportunity to reach their audience as effectively as possible. Although authors, illustrators, editors, art directors, designers, and printers all work together to produce a book, it's not until the book is actually read and looked at that it really comes to life. Until that moment, it's a darkened theater—a tableau frozen on a stage in a vacant auditorium. But when the teacher, librarian, parent, or friend opens the cover and shares the book with a child, the theater is illuminated, and, as the pages turn, the curtain rises and falls on successive acts and scenes. Through that reading and sharing the words come to life, and the illustrations move and flow with action, feeling, and vitality.

Of course, each book must stand on its own merits and earn applause and approval from whoever experiences it. But if you bring a child and a book together with a sensitive understanding of that particular child and a knowledge of, and quality of excitement about, that particular book—if you recommend and share and read the book aloud as if you were a part of its creative life—then that book has a much greater chance of being special to that child. And you will be remembered as being part of that book, and part of that gift, as surely as if your name were engraved on the jacket and the title page: a colleague, a co-conspirator, a creative partner.

I have loved picture books since my childhood, and I recall with deep gratitude the relatives who were sensitive enough to give me books as gifts, and to share both the books and themselves in magical read-aloud sessions. I had a passion for drawing as a child, and I used to make up my own tales and illustrate them for my two younger sisters, Patti and Martha, in a ritual we called "telling stories on paper." On a rainy Saturday afternoon, or just before bed, I would sit between them with a stack of paper in my lap and a pencil in my hand, and I'd spin some kind of a bizarre yarn while scribbling illustrations to accompany the narrative, passing them first to one of the girls and then to the other. I found the process of "telling stories on paper" enormously compelling, and during those early days, before the blessings of editorial intercession were available to me, I would rattle onward with interminable enthusiasm until my dutifully attentive sisters were each buried under piles of pictures or comatose with boredom.

My childhood fascination with illustrated storytelling persisted into young adulthood, and shortly after graduating from college I began sending manuscripts with accompanying sketches to major publishing houses. When I was offered a contract to illustrate George Mendoza's stories "The Hunter," "The Snake," and "The Hairy Toe" in a forty-eight-page book entitled *GWOT! Horribly Funny Hairticklers*, I was ecstatic.

I had a wonderful time putting the book together, and I sent copies off to various friends, particularly those who had encouraged me to make the leap into publishing. Among these was a couple who lived in New York with their precocious but rather shy four-year-old daughter named Helen. They were concerned that exposure to stories like "The Hunter," "The Snake," and "The Hairy Toe" that were assembled in a book entitled *GWOT!* might prove to be a traumatizing experience for her. But because I had illustrated the book and inscribed it to their Helen, they dutifully read it to her at bedtime. Several nights later, my wife and I were invited to their apartment for dinner, and in response to my knock the door swung open and there stood tiny Helen in a ruffled party dress. For a moment she remained poised with a sweet hostess smile on her face. Suddenly, it transformed itself into a jubilant mischievous leer, and she screeched: "GWOT! I Love

You!" It was obvious that the book had not traumatized her in the least, and indeed her parents, to their ultimate despair, had to reread the stories night after dreary night for many, many months.

Helen and her family moved to the West Coast, but I continued to send her my books as they were published. A few years ago, the second oldest of my stepdaughters was married, and Helen, now a young woman and an established television actress, flew east with her parents to attend the wedding. I had not seen her in quite a few years, and, as the reception in our backyard was nearing its end, Helen and I strolled along the edge of the woods together, and she brought me up-to-date on all that had been happening in her life. And then she proceeded to tell me that among her treasures are the battered, dog-eared copies of my books, which are still on her bedside shelf. She told me that whenever she opens them, the words and the pictures are a magic carpet to her childhood. She feels that she is once again a little girl snuggled against her parents as they read the stories aloud, and she happily loses herself in the illustrations that were once spread across their laps.

In reflecting on Helen's involvement with her books, I realize I had known something intuitively when beginning my career that I am convinced, thirty years later, is indeed true. Too often, I think, we define children as a bland herd, and we do not adequately recognize the complicated variety of personalities that they, as a group, represent.

There should be made available to kids, as well as to adults, a delicious smorgasbord selection of books that deal with many facets of human experience. We should provide books that present an opportunity to explore a great range of emotions, exposing children to stories and images that inspire laughter, tears, shivery-spooky feelings, flashes of glowing, loving warmth, and insight. They should be acquainted with books that contain the creative approaches of many different authors and illustrators so that each young reader can find the ones that speak to him or her with particular clarity and poignance.

Helen's recollection of the way in which her parents shared books with her is also revealing. I believe that the picture book's finest hour occurs during a read-aloud session when the book is bridging two laps and uniting the reader and the audience. The reading adult's voice unlocks the magic of the story, inviting the child to enter the lives of the characters and to explore the landscapes that are delineated in the illustrations. There is a special warm and personal quality to the participation in that shared experience that is not duplicated while seated in front of a television set in a darkened room, and it is important for all of us who love children and books to continually express the value of reading aloud.

SELECTED BOOKS WRITTEN
AND ILLUSTRATED BY STEVEN KELLOGG

Aster Aardvark's Alphabet Adventures. New York: Morrow, 1987.
Best Friends. New York: Dial, 1986.
Can I Keep Him? New York: Dial, 1971.
Chicken Little. New York: Morrow, 1985.

The Christmas Witch. New York: Dial, 1992.

The Island of the Skog. New York: Dial, 1973.

Jack and the Beanstalk. New York: Morrow, 1991.

Johnny Appleseed: A Tall Tale. New York: Morrow, 1988.

Mike Fink: A Tall Tale. New York: Morrow, 1992.

The Mysterious Tadpole. New York: Dial, 1977.

The Mystery of the Flying Orange Pumpkin. New York: Dial, 1980.

The Mystery of the Missing Red Mitten. New York: Dial, 1974.

The Mystery of the Stolen Blue Paint. New York: Dial, 1982.

Paul Bunyan: A Tall Tale. New York: Morrow, 1984.

Pecos Bill: A Tall Tale. New York: Morrow, 1986.

Pinkerton, Behave! New York: Dial, 1979.

Prehistoric Pinkerton. New York: Dial, 1987.

Ralph's Secret Weapon. New York: Dial, 1983.

A Rose for Pinkerton. New York: Dial, 1981.

Tallyho, Pinkerton. New York: Dial, 1982.

SELECTED BOOKS ILLUSTRATED
BY STEVEN KELLOGG

Bayer, Jane. *A My Name Is Alice*. New York: Dial, 1984.

Ehrlich, Amy. *Parents in the Pigpen, Pigs in the Tub*. New York: Dial, 1993.

Glassman, Peter. *The Wizard Next Door*. New York: Morrow, 1993.

Mahy, Margaret. *The Boy Who Was Followed Home*. New York: Dial, 1983.

———. *The Rattlebang Picnic*. New York: Dial, 1994.

Noble, Trinka Hakes. *Jimmy's Boa Bounces Back*. New York: Dial, 1984.

Paxton, Tom. *Englebert the Elephant*. New York: Morrow, 1990.

Schwartz, David M. *How Much Is a Million?* New York: Lothrop, Lee & Shepard, 1985.

———. *If You Made a Million*. New York: Lothrop, Lee & Shepard, 1989.

Thurber, James. *The Great Quillow*. San Diego: Harcourt Brace, 1994.

Twain, Mark. *The Adventures of Huckleberry Finn*. New York: Morrow, 1994.

WRITING PROCESS IN A WHOLE LANGUAGE CLASSROOM

"I wish you'd teach my son how to diagram Joseph Conrad's *Lord Jim* instead of all this writing workshop stuff," an agitated parent shouted at me before I began a process writing workshop for parents. "I'm sick of messy papers, inserts, arrows. I want a perfect paper first time round." Each year, parents and teachers express anxieties about process writing and insist that diagraming and completing grammar exercises develop writers. And each year I invite parents to write, first the old way, assigning a topic and expecting a perfect piece in twenty minutes. Grumbles and growls fill the room as writing begins. "I've paid my dues," one mother announced. "It's my kid's turn now." Once I've reclaimed a barrel of negative writing associations, I put them through the process of talking to find topics, brainstorming for ideas, focusing, and drafting. They compare these process experiences with their schooling. Most depart less hostile, a recommended reading list in hand, and invitations from their children to help with writing workshop during the year.

In time, parents come to understand that writing is a craft that improves with practice. No one would dare recommend that to play tennis successfully all one need do is memorize the rules and draw a tennis court. It's no different for writers, who must read to better understand their craft and then write every day to progress. Writing workshop, based on professional writers' process, is not rigid and sequential, like a factory assembly line. It's recursive, with writers omitting and shuttling between parts of the process. And it's different each time.

Through minilessons, teachers introduce elements of process writing but allow students to practice, synthesize, and adapt the information, constructing a unique writing model. Teacher demonstrations present a menu of writing resources where selection depends on the writer's needs. Don't insist that students complete every identified step in the process. Differentiate between practicing to understand a strategy and rigid adoption.

A sixth-grade student presents a minilesson on the use of direct quotations.

Teachers complain to me, time and again, that students omit steps in the process: They refuse to generate a list of topics or revise three times or write enough during class. Andy, a member of my reading-writing workshop during three years of middle school, frustrated content area teachers who incorporated writing process into their subjects. Frequently criticized for "staring into space" while others busily brainstormed and drafted, Andy listened to his own voice. One teacher told me "He [Andy] is setting a poor example for other students who need to brainstorm." Reflecting on his writing process during his senior year of high school, Andy wrote about brainstorming: "This first step is often necessary to work out ideas and to get them down on paper, but after writing for several years, ideas have begun to come freely without the need to cluster."

Andy's final words address how writers find their way into the process and make it their own: "Beginning writers should experiment with various ways of writing until they are comfortable with a pattern and organization. All writers are unique individuals, making their own contribution to the creative arts."

To standardize a creative process is to peel away its unique qualities and make creativity fizzle out into stale seltzer. *Recursive* means that the parts, the activities zigzag, preventing us from isolating a reproducible pattern to follow. Donald Murray, in *Write to Learn*, explains that his writing model is only one approach and advises us to carefully monitor our own writing, especially when it goes well.

> You should know what you did, how you did it, the order in which you did it, and how you felt before, during, and after you did it. You should develop your own models of the writing process so that when the writing doesn't go well you'll have those positive experiences to look back on.[1]

Teachers who write can verbalize experiences and explain how they transformed the model. I write a journal on teaching, observations of students, transcriptions of students' discussions, stories I discover in and out of school, comments on my reading, and conversations with other teachers.

During workshop, I try to reserve time to write with the class. The trick is to find a balance between satisfying students' requests and modeling by doing. Some days I have a large chunk of writing time; other days none at all. Unless we write and struggle through barren periods of "nothing to say," unless we wrestle with words, groping to shape our inner vision, how can we understand and assist students?

My friend Helen Kellogg once told me how taking a shower can be frustrating for her. "I do my best composing in the shower," she said, "and the words and feelings seem so perfect. But when I'm dried and powdered and dressed and try to write my recollections down, it's a poor version of what was in my mind."

Teachers must write in and out of class to understand this eternal battle between the inner vision and the harsh reality of composing. Only then can they accept a classroom where each day some students can't write and some students appear to be "wasting time," while others are productive and successful.

THE STAGES OF THE WRITING PROCESS: AN OVERVIEW

Pulitzer Prize–winning author Donald Murray describes five stages of the writing process: collecting, focusing, ordering, drafting, and revising. By the end of the first week of workshop, students will be at different points in the process, yet they will always interact with all or some of the five parts as they move from stage to stage.

Collecting. Drawing on sensory input, our brains collect and store information and sensations; writing reclaims these memories. The collecting stage, often called prewriting, includes finding a topic, freely generating ideas, and discovering what you know and don't know about that topic. Thinking and talking assist recall. Jot ideas down during and after talking. Hearing a list of ideas read aloud to another person often jogs recollections.

Introduce some of these strategies to generate ideas and stimulate recall:

- whole class discussion

- paired or small group discussions

- writing lists, jottings, pictures, charts

- students reading through journals, learning logs, and diaries independently, in pairs, or in small groups

- asking questions about a topic

- free-writing, letting ideas flow

- brainstorming

- cluster

- web

- taking detailed, objective notes

- browsing through books and magazines

- interviewing others

Focusing. Identifying the topic or part of a topic you want to explore in a first draft can be as elusive as grasping a slimy, wriggling fish. Focusing a topic, reviewing and studying information, deciding "What do I want to write about?" and "What am I trying to say?" often frighten young writers who hide behind "I have nothing to write about" statements. A characteristic of collecting is to gather more than you'll need in your piece. Some children seem to know exactly what their purpose is and immediately narrow their ideas. Most don't. And that's why we teachers need to demonstrate ways to focus a rich inventory of information.

The list below represents some questions and activities to model. Post a list in your classroom and add students' suggestions; what works for one student might help another.

- Reread your list. Circle the ideas you want to write about.

- Discuss your topic with a peer; sometimes talking leads writers to discover what they're trying to say.

- Do I need more information? Where can I find it?

- Who am I writing this for? What do I need to include to help them understand the topic?

- What questions do I want my piece to answer?

- What genre do I want to use? Is the information appropriate to the genre?

- What do I want to tell my readers?

Most primary grade children, unlike older children, aren't ready to generate and focus lists of information independently. Through collaboration, they can participate in and observe the process. As Jason said, "We kinda feel how it works together."

A class of second graders had been asked to submit a collaborative poem about wishes and dreams for a school-wide grandparents' magazine. Small groups of children discussed their ideas, then individuals offered suggestions, which I recorded on chart paper. We studied and reread, and students told me which ideas to circle. Here's part of their list of twenty-four ideas.

- Fly to a volcano.

- Live in a land of trolls and elfin creatures.

- Save the rain forests.

- Fly to and slide down a rainbow.

- I wish my mom's sister was alive.

- To be an airplane pilot and fly.

- Give the homeless people homes.

- For my own puppy.

- Fly to the moon.

- I wish I was a body builder.

After copious rereadings, groups discussed choices, searching for a topic to pursue. Two topics surfaced: flying and a visit with elfin creatures. Still no consensus. More discussion. The class narrowed the topic to "I Wish I Could Fly." Once again groups brainstormed; then I wrote ideas on a chart. After John read the chart, reproduced below, to the class, he announced, "That's a lot of great ideas we all collected. I think we'll get a good poem."

• soar	• bees
• fly like a bird	• clouds move
• squirrels fly	• orange sunset
• up in the air	• dragonfly
• go high in the sky	• wasps
• glide	• stars

- hover like a helicopter

- airplane

- hovercraft

- clouds like a big umbrella

- bats fly

- flies as fast as a bullet

Ordering. Before drafting, professional writers order information into a plan. Note cards, maps, and lists of what may be included are some techniques writers employ. I use the term *may* because most drafts depart from the original outline. View the outline like a series of sketches the artist completes before painting. Murray says that "most of us write too soon, and run into problems that could have been solved in advance, and waste time starting over again and again. . . ."[2]

Show students how you organize information and design a writing plan, then practice these together. First second graders and I reviewed the list and placed a dot next to ideas all agreed should be eliminated. We discussed the remaining ideas and decided to circle four. Next I rewrote the four ideas on a new sheet of chart paper. Children carefully reviewed the culled and master lists and decided to reinstate "clouds move." This is the cluster of ideas the second grade thought they'd like to include in their collaborative poem "I Wish I Could Fly":

> like a bird
> hover like a helicopter
> an airplane up in the air
> fly as fast as a bullet
> clouds move

Introduce your students to various writing plans. Expect students to adapt plans to their needs. A plan for an article will differ from a plan for a story, fairy tale, poem, essay, or chapter book. In minilessons offer a varied menu of strategies for students to adapt to their individual writing needs.

- cluster

- note cards

- web

- story map: setting, character, problem, solution

- title: establishes purpose

- beginning, middle, end notes

- informal map with topic headings for non-fiction piece

- thumbnail character sketches

- chapter plans and titles

Writing plans, like trip itineraries, uncover final destinations. Plans disclose the necessity for additional information and research; they're invaluable tools for middle school students required to write reports and essays and complete research projects. Plans can be simple, like seventh grader Mary Beth's map (figure 1), or complex and detailed, like third grader Gabe's (figure 2). Writing plans change throughout the writing process. As authors compose, they will adjust their original guidelines.

Drafting. Starting a first draft is an imposing task. Some students plunge right in, concentrating and maintaining momentum. All of us have wished for a classroom of these students.

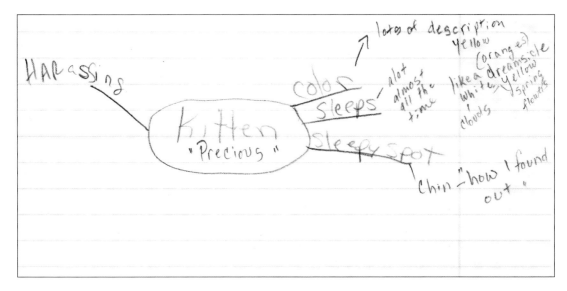

Fig. 1 Above.

Fig. 2 At left.

Reality, however, deals us a different kind of hand, filling our classes with students who "can't write" during class time, those who prefer to socialize or appear to avoid writing. Professional writers experience similar feelings, only there is no teacher to chastise them. However, writing deadlines eventually place an end to avoidance.

Students and I negotiate the number of first drafts to be completed during four-week time blocks. I post deadline dates in the classroom, and students always have the option of negotiating changes. Adjustments are frequently necessary, and students lobby for additional time when problems arise. Use of time in class and home is a topic we repeatedly discuss.

Class Inventory: Writing Workshop
Abbreviations

C: collecting
R: researching
F: focusing, organizing
MP: making a plan
D: drafting (1, 2, 3...)
PC: peer conference - content or edit
Rev: revising

SGC: small group conference - content or edit
TC: teacher conference - content or edit
DD: deadline draft
Self-C: self-conference - content or edit

Grade 8

Class List	9/13	9/17	9/24	10/1	10/6	10/11	10/15	10/22
Rachel	R, C	R, C	R, C MP	D1	D1 PC-Content	Rev. TC-Content	D2 C -new piece	D2 PC-Edit
Anne	C, F	D1	D1 - Self-C - Content	PC-Cont. Rev.	Rev. TC-Edit	Rev.	DD	DP C
Liz	C MP	D1	D1	D1	PC-content	TC-Content	Rev. PC-Edit	Rev. TC-Edit
Ashton	C F	MP D1	D1	C F	Rev.	D1	D1	Self-C Cont. D2
Clare	C MP	C, R	Adj. Plan D1	D1	D1 PC-Cont.	Rev. D2	D2	D2 TC-Cont.
Grandin	C, R	C, R	C, R PC notes	D1	D1 TC-focus cont.	Rev. D2	D2	D2 Self-C edit

Fig. 3

Individual responsibility affects the entire workshop community, for students with no work can't interact productively with a partner or group.

Meeting deadlines requires support from the teacher. I've adapted Nancie Atwell's "Status-of-the-Class" checklist to quickly determine where students are in their writing (see appendix). Once or twice a week I take an inventory of students during workshop to quickly gather information that I record on the chart (figure 3).

You can collect this data during the first five minutes of gathering for, or prior to, a scheduled writing workshop. With younger children, you might prefer to circulate among students, pausing for brief miniconferences, then jotting down inventory notes.

This system identifies students who might require either support to meet a deadline or a teacher-requested conference during the process. Most important, the inventory chart can keep you abreast of a child's progress. As you review several entries, questions about students and their specific needs can arise. For example, I wonder why Ashton has not conferred while composing two different drafts. I query why Liz has opted to bring her first piece to final draft rather than developing several early drafts. My questions can initiate short dialogues that help me to understand a student's choices, or offer me a chance to present alternate viewpoints or make helpful suggestions.

Write several collaborative first drafts, permitting children to consider the nature of a first draft, that it's an imperfect experiment. It may or may not follow the group's plan, or it may follow only part of their plan, or it might have too much or too little information. Collaboration is nonthreatening because students elect to participate, and the teacher accepts all responses without editing. Help students understand that drafting is like a journey into the unknown. The beginning place is secure; the destination murky. Here is the first draft of the poem the second grade wrote.

I Wish I Could Fly

I wish I could fly and
be like a helicopter
And hover over open blossoms
I'll drink their sweet nectar
Then fly like a speeding bullet
To a different flower

Demonstrate and discuss these strategies that can help writers break the "blank paper barrier" and get started with first drafts.

- Talk to someone about your idea.

- Review your notes and writing plan.

- Start where you're comfortable—in the middle or even at the end.

- Write without rereading. Revising at the drafting stage slows down the flow of ideas, for the censoring voice inhibits and judges.

- Dictate your piece into a cassette and transcribe it.

- Draw pictures about what you want to write, then write about them.

- Write a summary of what you want your piece to contain.

- Discuss experiences of professional writers.

- Drafting is like talking on paper.

Producing several first drafts during those first weeks of school, and continuing to draft throughout the year, allows students to choose which piece to revise and edit. Student choice invests children in tasks that demand self-evaluation and hard work. Bringing every piece to final draft regiments the spirit of the workshop and focuses students more on product than process.

Revising. Taped above Katherine Paterson's wooden desk is a three-by-five-inch card. On that card she's printed, in large letters, a Greek saying borrowed from an Edith Hamilton book:

BEFORE THE GATES
OF EXCELLENCE
THE HIGH GODS
HAVE PLACED SWEAT

Sweat and hard work surround revision. Revision clarifies and refines, and during that process the writer assumes the dual role of writer and reader. Tedium and frustration often accompany revision, yet the shaping

A student thinks about her draft in a sixth-grade reading-writing workshop.

also brings great rewards as the words and images coalesce with the writer's inner vision.

Revision materials spill out of containers in my classroom writing center: staplers, tape, white-out, pencils, paper clips, scissors, and scrap paper. The children, through demonstrations, learn how to use these materials. Tape, staple, or clip the revised section over the draft, or number the section to be rewritten and number the new version the same way, writing at the end of the first draft or other paper. "I can write lots of revisers and read them and then decide," second grader Willie told me during a conference. Willie had written three leads to his story on dinosaurs. "I'll read them to my group," he told me when we finished. "But I'll decide." The right to decide should always rest with the author, to insure that the writing belongs to the student.

The second grade and I revise the first draft of our class poem "I Wish I Could Fly." Several children take turns reading the draft aloud to listen to the language and imagine the word pictures. Hearing the words highlights the need for revisions such as repetitions, unclear sentences, and omitted words. After the third reading Jill says, "Something's wrong. [Pause] We're flying like birds, and then we talk about a helicopter."

"Are there birds that hover?" I ask.

A group choruses, "Hummingbirds." We change helicopter to hummingbird. I remind the class about previous lessons on being more specific. "Let's find phrases that could be more specific," I suggest. They identify "blossoms," "speeding bullet," and "another flower." I leave all their suggestions on the chart in the room for them to review. They make decisions three days later. Like professional writers, students put work aside to gain distance from it and time to consider choices. Below is the revised poem, which the class reread, thought about, and discussed over several days.

I Wish I Could Fly

I wish I could fly
and be like a bird
And hover over newly opened blossoms
I'll sip their honeylike nectar
Then fly like a speeding bullet
To another flower.

Each year, your children's writing and your own writing will supply topics for revision minilessons. Ask children to revise portions of their writing, and focus on one revision technique at a time. Consider the following suggestions for revision:

- Read aloud to self, to a partner, group, or class.

- Learn how to use writing center revision materials.

- Focus on leads, endings.

- Make transitions.

- Show with details, don't tell: Instead of writing that the tree is beautiful, describe the tree using details that help the reader discover its beauty.

- Think about introduction, conclusion.

- Be specific, instead of general, for images gain clarity when the reader knows the type of flower, airplane, fish, and so on.

- Sequence: Are events and details in the best order?

- Is there too much information?

- Is there not enough information?

- Revise poems: shaping a poem, figurative language, economy of words.

Content revisions precede technical editing. What good are perfect punctuation, spelling, and syntax if the text fails to communicate with the author's voice?

Before arriving at a final draft of the second-grade poem, students argued about which word was the best choice. After printing many versions, the class collectively decided to publish the poem that follows in the school booklet for grandparents.

I Wish I Could Fly
by the second grade

I wish I could fly
Like a hummingbird
And hover over honeysuckle blossoms.
I'll sip the honeylike nectar
Then flap my wings like a speeding brass bullet
To a dark red tulip.

Second graders' collaborative writing stimulated discussions about words and what the group really wanted to say. The children thought more about words and figurative language. Amy, quite exasperated during one discussion, stood up, placed her hands firmly on her hips, and asked, "Well, what kind of bird can you be if you're hovering? Robins just don't hover." And down she sat, a victorious expression on her face.

A seventh-grade teacher confessed at one of our meetings, "My hands always want to correct everything they [her students] write. I mark their papers and then they recopy. They never catch all their errors, and I dislike seeing errors." But if we correct students' work, we not only, as Murray points out, take authorship away, we destroy their motivation to edit. In junior high and high school, when I received a paper all corrected with red ink, my face would burn with anger. Soon, however, I developed a crasser outlook. If the teacher wants to do all the work, so be it, I thought. Recopying a fully corrected essay took less time. I could read and write what I was interested in during the time I had gained.

Writing takes time. I fear that administrators and parents pressure teachers to fill folders with student products. Teachers who have lost touch with their own literacy fall prey to these pressures and labor long hours over correcting students' papers. "I can't keep up with grading," said one middle school teacher. "That's why I don't have them [her students] write that much. They despise recopying every paper, but that's how they learn."

The reality is that we don't have to read and grade everything a child writes. Nor, with peer helpers, do we have to read and edit every stage of writing. Edit for one thing only: first spelling, then capitalization, then usage, and so on. Minilessons establish editing standards; these change and expand during the year. Like an editor at a publishing house, you can have final editing conferences with students before publication in a class magazine, book, or on a bulletin board.

You can view the technical errors in students' drafts with dismay or joy. I prefer the joyful stance. Students' errors teach me what they are ready to learn. When they try to use a convention, that's a signal for a class minilesson or a conference. The day a second grader asked me, "Is this how you make those tiny squiggles—you know, the ones that tell people are talking?" I knew she was ready for a lesson on direct quotations. As I read students' papers, I make a list of errors (figure 4).

Error lists are a treasure box of possible minilessons that reflect children's development and experiences with language. The day my seventh and eighth graders turn in writing with subordinate clauses marked as complete sentences, I dance and hum, for I know they're ready to absorb minilessons demonstrating the difference between independent and subordinate clauses. Moreover, they'll be able to revise from their own writing instead of mindlessly underlining clauses in a workbook. "Underlining clauses in sentences never improved my writing," an eighth grader told me at an editing conference. "Doing it, that's how I see how it works."

Minilessons for all elementary grades can effectively present editing and writing options that children may or may not be ready to adopt. Repeatedly meeting and reflecting on ways writers use language gives children access to strategies they can experiment with. Strategies observed during minilessons might be vaguely understood at first; repeated modeling, over time, can catch a child's attention, revealing benefits and spurring on use.

Too often we teachers take it for granted that students arrive in our rooms automatically knowing how to write narratives, reports, leads, or endings. We simply assign a writing task without modeling the thinking, the steps, and the struggles.

You can help students read texts as writers do. Bring in passages that illustrate a particular writing technique. Invite students

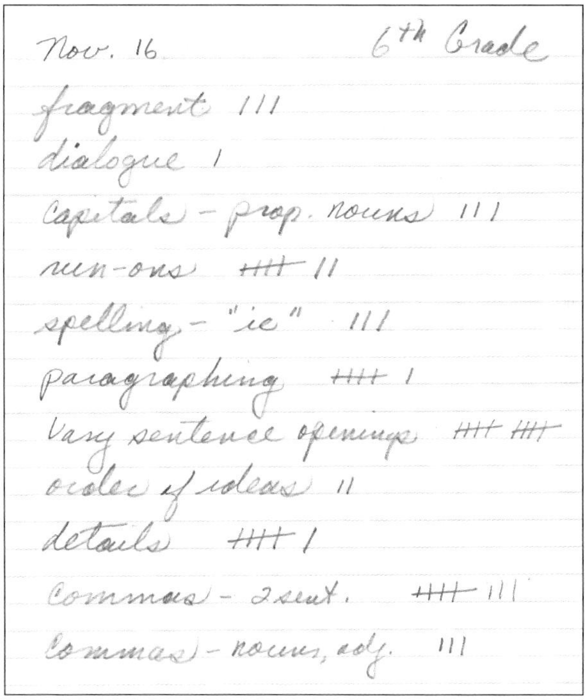

Nov. 16   6th Grade
fragment ///
dialogue /
Capitals – prop. nouns ///
run-ons ++++ //
spelling – "ie" ///
paragraphing ++++ /
Vary sentence openings ++++ ++++
order of ideas //
details ++++ /
Commas – 2 sent. ++++ ///
Commas – nouns, adj. ///

Fig. 4

to reread until they can discover how the writer created suspense, set a scene, used dialogue to build character or create conflict or emotion, foreshadowed, and so on. Discuss students' observations; offer your perspectives.

By analyzing authors' writing, students gain invaluable insights into the art of consciously crafting a piece of writing. Then have students practice techniques as writing exercises. During minilessons and conferences you can begin to discuss the effort and fine-tuning that go into revisions. Help your students understand that writing isn't a freewheeling process. Let them know that writers study the techniques of others and use that knowledge to hone and refine their work.

Reserve time for students to study and practice the writing techniques below. Integrate these techniques into your workshop demonstrations by reflecting on your writing and by studying the writing of published and student authors.

- dialogue
- cause/effect
- compare/contrast
- chronological order
- stream of consciousness
- point of view
- stanzas
- bibliography
- onomatopoeia
- characterization

- setting
- mood
- flashback
- foreshadowing
- irony
- couplets
- titles
- repetition
- alliteration
- plot

What constitutes a good writing program is a question that all teachers must consider. In addition to writing techniques, a good writing program introduces children to a variety of literary forms by connecting children's reading to writing. Our responsibility is to give children a wide range of choices so they can select the form that will best express a writing topic.

In a self-contained classroom, teachers can integrate process writing throughout the curriculum, encouraging children to write fiction and nonfiction. In departmentalized middle schools, where teachers work apart, frequent communication can insure that students engage in a variety of writing that genuinely relates to their studies. Writing an article, essay, editorial, feature story, or report that grows out of independent research or a theme cycle study is as important as writing from personal experiences. Choice of topic within a genre should always be present.

Teacher demonstrations, which focus children on how published writers use literary forms, give students access to all kinds of print. As the year unfolds, I post a list of the literary structures and techniques that have been modeled and discussed. Students visit this list to refresh memories and make writing decisions. The list below illustrates the range of writing (and reading) that students should experience during their elementary school years:

- biography and autobiography
- mystery
- realistic fiction
- poetry: lyric, free verse, prose poem, the ballad, haiku, cinquain, limerick, concrete poems

- fantasy

- science fiction

- historical fiction

- scripts: radio, puppet, readers theater, skits, plays

- folk- and fairy tales

- picture books

- nonfiction

- essays: informative, critical, persuasive

- newspapers: editorials, human interest and feature stories, letters, news items, cartoons, horoscopes, local news, reviews, advertisements

- field guides

- speeches: informative, persuasive, campaign

- schedules: bus, train, school

- magazines

- journals: free writing, description, doodles, notes, unsent letters, guided imagery, lists, word portraits, maps

- diaries

- reports

- interviews

- photographic essays

- wordless picture books

In a writing workshop, the students carry many responsibilities, and the teacher is coach and guide, helping students climb those mountains. My kids write all the time and confer with each other as they revise for content and mechanics. My job is to set up situations where the students can help each other as I confer with individuals. Students are always setting content and editing goals and working to meet them.

I listen to their drafts during group share and take careful notes for student-teacher conferences. Sure, I spend time reading their work, but I don't mark the corrections; they do. My job is to guide them through revisions and editing during minilessons and conferences.

A good writing program establishes helpful partnerships among students and between teacher and students. You'll find you spend more time reflecting on your process as a

Two sixth graders write their drafts on chart paper to share with their class.

means to guiding students and on ways to help your students progress through their own efforts and understanding.

WRITING CONFERENCES

Whole Group Conferences. Whole group conferences are the place for teachers to model positive ways to respond to students' writing. I set aside the last fifteen to twenty minutes of workshop, two to three times a week, for group share. Those who wish to read a draft to the class place their names on the blackboard. It's clear to everyone that if the list is too long, some might have to wait.

To encourage positive responses from the class, I model possibilities before share sessions, offering students ways to begin their comments and celebrate successes. First reactions to a piece of writing should be a warm response to content. Tell the writer what the story meant to you, what mattered and touched you, or what you remembered most. To read a piece of writing and hear only comments about punctuation, omissions, or a particular word transmits the message that what the author said mattered little. The purpose of conferencing is to teach writers, to encourage them as they struggle to find voice and meaning.

All writers are vulnerable and easily wounded. A writer who dares to share craves and deserves positive response to content; it's the listener's job to explain the effects of content. Many of the kids I teach are so bent on cutdowns that I require they open responses with prompts such as "I liked the way you . . ."; "You touched my feelings because . . ."; "I noticed how well you created . . ." Modeling positive responses to

content, before the entire group, lets children know your expectations. When the children are ready to take over responding during group share, the author chooses two classmates. Setting such reasonable limits allows time for several to read their work.

After you've modeled a response, place it on a chart for students to review before they begin group share sessions. The suggestions below provide young writers with positive feedback:

- Tell how the writer made you feel.

- Point to exciting, sad, suspenseful, or humorous parts.

- Show how the writer connected you to a story or event.

- Point to effective use of dialogue.

- Tell how the writer used lots of details to make you see clear pictures.

- Ask the writer to reread a part you liked and explain why you liked it.

- Tell the writer what the story meant to you.

After you've modeled and charted many ways to respond, ask the author if she or he would like to request specific feedback from classmates. I often schedule a group share one day in advance and invite writers to think about the kind of help they need. Many students arrive with several thoughtful calls for advice. As the year progresses, more and more students arrive at group share with problems for peers to consider. But there are many who almost never prepare prior to our sessions.

There will be times when you'll sense the need to ask the group to recap key observations made during group share. I asked a fourth-grade class to tell one another what they learned after everyone had read and commented on first drafts. Students' comments had advanced from general and not too helpful remarks such as "I liked it; it was good," or "I noticed how fun it was," to insights important enough for all to see. The class offered these suggestions, based on two days of listening and commenting:

• Include lots of very, very specific details.

• Make your characters speak so you show how they are different people.

• You can use dialogue to move the action ahead.

• Humor makes some stories fun to listen to.

As you listen to group share, you'll come to know when to recap and when to move on.

Miniconferences should occur daily as you meander around the room. Question students, comment on what you observe, or respond to a plea for help. Keep these informal conferences short, allowing children to write and you to make many visits. I circulate around the room, pausing briefly at each desk, asking or answering a question; those working feverishly get a pat on the back as I scan their writing. Clipboard in hand, these informal conferences, which take no more than one to three minutes, allow me to note where students are with their writing. Within four to six weeks, students come to know that I'll make the rounds, and eventually they develop the patience to wait their turn.

Minivisits quickly inform me of kids who need longer chats. I stop at seventh grader Emmie's desk; she sits, chin cupped in her left hand, staring at the empty sheet of paper. It's

February, and Emmie, who struggles with writing, has only headed her paper for the last two days.

EMMIE: I can't write—got nothing to say anymore.
[Pause. I wait and say nothing.]
EMMIE: Sometimes I hate this paper. Everyone else writes and I'm sitting here.
ROBB: I know how you feel. That happens to me. Other writers, too. [Silence.]
EMMIE: My life's boring.
ROBB: Why not make a list of all the things that bore you?
EMMIE: Don't want to do that.
ROBB: How about reading your book or a magazine? Or looking out the window?
EMMIE: Don't want to. Just want to sit.

This conversation, like many, doesn't result in immediate turnabout. Inner voices chide me for "being easy" and "letting Emmie off the hook." But I recognize that I can't force Emmie, or any child, to write. She usually meets deadlines we've negotiated, so I move on. Those students who don't meet deadlines—and I have many of those—meet with me, one-on-one, during lunch and after school, to sort out issues and difficulties. The extra time involved here is usually a worthwhile investment. It's taken several years to build up anger and low self-esteem, and often a large amount of time passes before students begin to write. D.J. wrote his first piece two days before Thanksgiving break after twelve weeks of filling pages with "I have nothing to write," doodles, and drawings (figure 5).

I was ecstatic, elated, and wanted to sing and dance around the room. Fearful that too much praise might cause D.J. to retreat, I told him how his grandfather's bout with cancer touched me and made me think about my father, who died of cancer eleven years ago.

Free writing

One day when I was little I got bit bye a dog and I screamed. From that day on Ive been afraid of that dog but, I heard It got hit by a car the other day. I dont know If I should be sad or happy. Because I know how it feels to have someone taken away from you. It feels awful I had a cat when I was about five and It got hit, I cryed and cryed I cryed so much it felt like my eyes were swolen shut. So I guess I should feel sorry for the owner!

Tomorrow after noon I might go hunting with my dad. When we go hunting we go on my grandmothers lot. Speaking about my grand mother my grand father has canser, I hope there's a cure and he can get out of bed soon. My grand-father is building an air plane and I hope he get to fly it because before he got canser that was his dream and I think know his dream is to

get out of that bed and fly.

I think this is an improvement in my writing, because all I did in the others is draw or waste time writing the same thing over and over.

Fig. 5

Sure, I could have "insisted" D.J. write, and I would have received the one or two stilted sentences he had begrudgingly turned in to former teachers. My comment to students like D.J. is "I'm pleased that you can be honest about your feelings toward writing." The waiting, though, is agonizing. However, by offering support and time to vent frustrations, and through group share, which provides living examples of writing possibilities, locked doors can eventually open.

The following questions and statements will help you interact with students during mini-conferences:

- Tell me about your story.

- Retell the main parts of your story.

- Do you need help today?

- How do you feel about this piece?

- Would you like to read [a classmate's] story and talk to him/her?

- When will you need an editing conference?

- Do you need to work with a peer?

- Let me suggest you read _____. [I often offer a poem, story, or part of a book to a student who needs to learn more about a genre or technique.]

- Do you feel the genre's right for your topic?

- What do you want your piece to say?

- Have you read it aloud?

- Do you need to research the topic?

Wait for the writer to respond. Count to fifty and you'll be surprised how often the child jumps in with a suggestion. That's your goal—to model, model, model, so the kids absorb the process and begin to dialogue with their inner voice and solve problems independently.

The perfect prescription for demonstrating and building good conference techniques does not exist. Resist adopting one person's approach or point of view. Read the experiences of many teachers and writers (Donald Graves, Jane Hansen, Eudora Welty, Annie Dillard). But you'll learn the most from your own interactions with students and colleagues, and dialogues with yourself. With each new school year, you will affirm past techniques and discover new ones.

I schedule one-on-one writing conferences as soon as students have completed two first drafts. In addition to group share, individual conferences enable me to set a positive tone and model how to provide feedback to writers. It's best to establish a narrow focus for one-on-one writing conferences and select questions that are developmentally appropriate. You must study students' writing and confer with them to assess where they are and what the next steps should be. As much as possible, I try to prepare in advance for scheduled conferences, reviewing folders and notes to grasp strengths, establish a focus, and propose some reading. Below are suggested questions for scheduled conferences:

- Read me the best part. How can you build on it?

- Would you like to change anything? What?

- What parts do you think need revision?

- Do you have too many details? Too few?

- How do you feel about your lead? Do you want to write others?

- Does the lead make you want to read on?

- Do you have more than one story to tell here?

- Should this piece begin at another point?

- Where does the story take place? Is that clear to the audience?

- Are events too exaggerated? How can you change that?

- Is violence so exaggerated that it is not believable?

- Are there repetitions? Do you feel they're helpful?

- Have you read any books or poems about this subject or theme?

- Have you conferred with a peer? What did you learn from that conference?

- Does the title reflect the content?

- Is the title short and snappy?

- Are there confusing parts?

- Are parts in a logical order?

- Is dialogue needed?

- Is the dialogue realistic?

- What can be edited out of the piece?

- Does the ending grow out of the story?

- Does the ending drag on?

- Do sentences all begin the same way?

When teacher demonstrations and teacher-student conferences focus on strategies and questions that offer children ways to solve writing problems, conferencing among all class members quickly becomes an integral part of the workshop. In fact, students write and peer conference throughout workshop, exchanging stories about how to do things. Two fourth graders read each other's revised drafts, circling spelling errors. They return papers. Melly tells Jake, "This is a great mystery. I couldn't figure out till the end who stole the computer." In a loud voice, Melly announces, "I want to learn how to write mysteries like Jake's." And Jake offers to help Melly. The first question he asks is "How many mysteries have you read?" And I know that Melly is in good hands. Peer conferencing heightened Melly's interest in mystery, and Jake pointed her in the right direction.

Quite often I reserve a part of workshop time specifically for paired or group conferences. During those organized sessions, I give a specific focus that relates to a recent demonstration, such as "Discuss the lead. Does it draw you into the story? Write three alternate leads; share and evaluate them." Other times I print signs to announce the topic of a peer conference: introduction, conclusion, repetitious sentences, too many details, more showing and less telling, titles. There are times when I assign students to groups, but I always speak to them in advance to clarify the reasons.

The thrust of all conferring should be self-evaluation. Writers self-evaluate; that's why they revise or abandon a piece. And published writers know it's easier to think about a piece of writing once there is some distance, so ask students to revise a piece that's rested for at least two weeks. The first step in conferring with yourself is to read your writing aloud, several times.

Since a piece of writing has to communicate something, the first question a writer should ask is "What do I want this piece to say?" Read aloud again and think about the purpose. Then ask yourself if you achieved your purpose and see if you can explain why or why not.

For middle school students, I prepare a list of eight to ten questions for self-evaluation, questions culled from the list of individual conference questions on pages 123–124, or questions that arise during conferences. I check off different questions for each student, basing revision requirements on individual needs. The questions for self-conferencing should change throughout the year. Don't overwhelm them with too much to ponder and revise. Better to revise one thing well than give up in utter confusion and frustration by attempting multiple revisions.

Evaluating writing is tricky business, and a thoughtless comment or a low grade can obsessively replay itself, governing inner speech and the writing process. The words *needs improvement in writing,* deeply carved into my sixth-grade report card, still flash on the screen of my mind. Though my winning a community essay contest caused the teacher to erase the words, the depressed marks could be easily read. Negative phrases always replay more readily than positive feedback. Moreover, students can progress only by building on what they *can do*, not on what they can't do.

Evaluation in my classes considers the entire process, not just the end product. Under a deadline draft, students include all their drafts, revisions, brainstorming, and conference notes. Assessment notes discuss process and celebrate progress in organization, word choice, voice, structure, mechanics. Opening comments, always written on separate paper, point out strengths and growth. Rather

Sixth-grade students discuss their writing.

than make suggestions, I ask the writer one or two questions, such as "Could a man painted as so overwhelmingly evil have suddenly reformed at the end?" or "Have you read your poem out loud to listen to the words and picture the images?" Questions make the writer responsible, not the teacher. Effective writing assessment should guide the young author to continue to reflect on and revise a piece. If you must grade, emphasize the journey, not the arrival.

PUBLISHING STUDENTS' WRITING

"I'm an author, Mrs. Robb," second grader Jeff tells me as he leads me to the library bulletin board to show me his story. This sense of authorship develops when children, like professionals, publish writing for others to read. Katherine Paterson, in *Gates of Excellence,* says, "And finally, no matter how good the writing may be, a book is never complete until it is read. The writer does not pass through the gates of excellence alone, but in the company of readers."[3] Provide an abundance of publishing opportunities, for publication supplies the momentum to bring a work to deadline draft.

Publication can be as sophisticated as establishing a publishing house within a school with book binding and laminating machines. But many school systems do not have the financial or parent resources to initiate elaborate publishing procedures. You can display children's work on class and hall bulletin boards, in the principal's office, or in community libraries. Include their writing in a class magazine, newsletter, journal, or book. Submit writing to a local newspaper or magazines, such as *Stone Soup, Cricket,* and *Merlyn's Pen,* that publish children's work. Mail the letters children write and deliver their messages. Or ask students to write and laminate an original poem, attach it to a stick, and plant these around the school yard for all visitors and grades to read.

Include informal books in your classroom and school library; make books for other grades, day-care centers, nursing homes. Informal bookmaking can be as as simple as folding and stapling sheets of paper into the size and shape authors want. Ann Wheeler, librarian at Powhatan Schools, maintains that books by students have the widest circulation. "Even the eighth graders love to check out and read books by the primary children. They also love to reread their early works."

Publication can also mean reading a poem, story, readers theater script, or play to another grade. Open a school writers' café, an idea I adapted from college years when I attended poetry readings at New York City coffee houses and the Ninety-second Street Y. At Powhatan, the first writers' café paired sixth grade with second grade. Checkered tablecloths, donated by parents, covered wooden library tables. Students decorated each table with a Coke bottle capped with a candle. Fire regulations prevented us from lighting the colorful tapers, but they created the café atmosphere. Children gathered around tables, sipped cups of lemonade, and read, discussed, and celebrated their drafts.

Young authors' writing should become reading material for the real world of classmates, parents, other school members, and the surrounding community. Like adults, children write with sincerity and passion when choice, commitment, and genuine purposes drive the process. No significant writing will emerge from story starters and assigned topics.

The following list of authentic writing events has been compiled with the assistance of my students and the teachers I've mentored. These represent possibilities; your interactions with students, parents, and colleagues will generate other meaningful activities.

1. Student-made books: counting books, alphabet books, picture books, information books, chapter books, class journals, class books.

2. Calendars or coloring books with annotations or captions.

3. A field guide with pictures and text on topics such as birds, snakes, trees, wildflowers, mushrooms, fish, rocks.

4. An illustrated dictionary to explain new vocabulary, characters from myths and legends, sports such as fishing or tennis, or mathematical and scientific concepts. Primary children can draw and dictate the text.

5. Museum displays with written or taped texts: dioramas, wax museum, artifacts, paintings, sculpture, and so on.

6. Wall book with text and pictures: Cover the walls with chart paper and place the student-written text on the pages. Children illustrate the story, make a cover, a title, a dedication page.

7. Diaries: Students write entries in a diary that a fictitious character, historical figure, anthropologist, or scientist might have kept. Or students might wish to write their own stories, using the diary as their story structure.

8. Interviews: Students gather family and/or community histories, stories, opinions, and attitudes. Students can pretend they are story characters and answer interview questions as their character might respond.

9. Song lyrics: Protest songs, rap, ballads, work songs, chanteys, seasonal songs, street rhymes, or lyrics for a musical play.

10. Book advertisements.

11. Caption books: Write captions for wordless picture books. Make books from magazine pictures organized around a theme such as food, pets, weather, or people. Paste these in a booklet and print captions.

12. Scripts for radio plays, readers theater, one-act plays, and puppet plays.

13. Design and construct charts or graphs that organize information about characters, events, places, and scientific or historical data.

14. Make a map of all the settings in a story.

15. Create scroll or hand-rolled movies; write captions under each frame. Base these on books or original stories.

16. Letters: Write invitations, thank-yous, and requests for information to pen pals, other classes, and characters from books.

17. Compose the questions for a telephone interview with an author. Conduct the interview.

18. Develop a student-written monthly or bimonthly class newsletter to send to parents.

19. Correspond with another class in your school district or in another district.

20. A written conversation between two students.

References

1. Murray, Donald. *Write to Learn.* New York: Holt, Rinehart and Winston, 1987, pages 6–7.

2. Ibid. page 89.

3. Paterson, Katherine. *Gates of Excellence: On Reading and Writing Books for Children.* New York: Elsevier/Nelson, 1981, page 4.

AS I SEE IT

Rosemary Wells

These six doodads are made of plastic or metal. They are different colors and in general of no account. They are the stuff that collects in the bottom of the kitchen junk drawer. I travel with them all laid out on cotton in a fancy little box. The reason for this is the question everyone asks all authors again and again, which is, of course, "Where do you get your ideas?"

To groups of middle schoolers I reply, "Well, I'm glad you asked that question because here are my ideas, right in this box!" and everyone has a look and thinks I am crazy. "Now tell me what these doodads have in common," I ask them, and usually one very bright one will say, "Well, they're all bits of junk!" and that is the right answer.

"They have in common only their very ordinariness . . . just the way the minute details of our lives day-to-day are very ordinary, yet the small feelings, tones of voice, remembered expressions are what stories are made of. Did you ever think of that?"

Then I ask one of the kids to take the six bits of metal and plastic and put them in a cylinder with a glass end to it. "Now give it structure and light," I tell them. "Hold it up to your eye." The cylinder is, of course, a kaleidoscope. Each child turns the end piece until he or she gets a pleasing pattern, a rose window, entirely personal and completely different from their neighbors' on either side.

Each person's rose window is made of ordinary bits of life combined just so with structure and light. Each of our lives is different. Each of our stories is different. And yet those stories are common to all of us because we all come into the world with the same equipment. It's what we do with it that is interesting or not. The structure of the stories must have a familiar form. A beginning, middle, and end. This is the kaleidoscope body that lets us see each of our particular rose windows.

My work, a career as a professional writer (someone paid a fair living for making things up), requires talent. There is no question about this. But *talent* is a word used erroneously on artists alone. Marie Curie had great talent. Martina Navratilova has enormous talent. Talent is like the wind. All you have to do is put up your sail.

There are two kinds of writing: the kind I do, and the kind everyone must do. It is the kind everyone must do that teachers teach in the classroom. These are a few things I try to get across in a writers' workshop for middle schoolers.

1. Writing well is no different from having a phone conversation, but you must remember a phone conversation requires someone on the other end. Just so with writing. You are writing so that someone else will know what you think. You don't want to bore that person so they hang up the phone. You need to keep them interested. Make it short and to the point. Keep what you say colorful and original and intelligent.

2. Writing well means reading a lot. You can't hit a home run or serve an ace unless you do it all the time. The finest musicians in the world, the most famous, practice every day for a couple of hours. Reading shows you how other people use words to get their ideas across. It increases your vocabulary. I am not suggesting increasing your vocabulary to pass multiple choice tests. I mean the more words you know and use, the better your thinking is, the smarter you are as a person.

If you were to speak a small language (and there are such languages) where there is no word for blue, you could not think about the color blue. So in our language, if I do not know the meaning of words like *subtle, incisive, touchy, crass,* then I will not know what these things are in life and my thoughts and intelligence are diminished. Every word in our language has a meaning and a place all its own. Every word I do not know is a thought and an understanding that I cannot have.

3. Teachers of writing tell you to write about what you know. I like to turn this good advice on its head and say, know about what you write. At the moment I am doing research for a novel about the American Civil War. I have been to Virginia three times. I spend days reading original diaries from that time. This is not always fun because many of the accounts that have survived are poorly written. I have spoken to

historians, reenactors, and interpreters of that time, and each tells me something new and much that is repetitious. I will listen for an hour on how a flour mill operated and then, at the very end, the guide will throw in a gem of a detail and this is the thing I use. I find that three days of intensive research will appear only as a single sentence on a page. Yet that sentence will be something that walked right out of day-to-day life in 1861 and that everyone has forgotten existed.

I must know my material well enough to feel at home in Berryville, Virginia, on the afternoon of the third battle of Winchester. I must know the thoughts my heroine has and the notions she couldn't have had because this was a hundred and thirty years ago and there were ideas people just didn't have back then because they hadn't come to them yet.

Research is exactly like panning for gold. You get a hundred pounds of shale and rock for every nugget.

4. The other thing I like to bring into a classroom is a very old Etruscan coin that I bought in Rome. It is covered with verdigris and there is a creature of some sort engraved on one side. No two children ever guess the same creature when they handle the coin. I take it back and give them a new silver coin all shined up with a horse on it. I tell them, "Look what happens when you polish it up! It shines. Everyone can see what is pictured there. In the same way I take a first draft and polish it up again and again until what I want to say is plain. I love doing this. Three-quarters of a writer's time is spent revising. Nothing is ever good enough the first time."

"How many times do you rewrite?" they ask.

"As many times as it takes to get it perfect" is the answer.

5. Every writer works differently. Every book is different for me. One book may require intricate graphing out of the action of a plot. Another will come to me all complete in a minute and fall onto the page as if it were being dictated. Yet another book is slow and tedious and almost dies or goes into hibernation. Some come at me words first. Some require pictures to expand the text.

There is no process, nothing concrete, no secret to this that can be told. Still, I go on writing because that is where I live. Some people say writing a book is like giving birth. I disagree. When I was just in grammar school, there was a woman in our town who'd been a U.S. Olympic team figure skater (probably 1936).

Mary Mapes used to park her nine-year-old daughter with me on the edges of the frozen Shrewsbury River. Then she would take off in great loops and twirls, racing backward and suddenly forward, spinning and leaping, swift and graceful as an antelope, with only the sound of the skate blades crisply cutting the slick ice.

How I wanted to do that. How I struggled with frozen toes and awkward motions to imitate her. I never could. But when I write well, when I smile at my day's work after it comes through the printer, when I am able to make people laugh or cry, then it is like that skating. Writing well feels like being Mary Mapes at last, dancing so beautifully on the ice against the red winter sun.

SELECTED BOOKS WRITTEN
AND ILLUSTRATED BY ROSEMARY WELLS

Benjamin and Tulip. New York: Dial, 1973.
Fritz and the Mess Fairy. New York: Dial, 1991.
Hazel's Amazing Mother. New York: Dial, 1985.
A Lion for Lewis. New York: Dial, 1982.
The Little Lame Prince. New York: Dial, 1990.
Max's Chocolate Chicken. New York: Dial, 1989.
Max's Christmas. New York: Dial, 1986.
Max's Dragon Shirt. New York: Dial, 1991.
Morris's Disappearing Bag. New York: Dial, 1975.
Noisy Nora. New York: Dial, 1973.
Peabody. New York: Dial, 1983.
Shy Charles. New York: Dial, 1988.
Stanley and Rhoda. New York: Dial, 1978.
Timothy Goes to School. New York: Dial, 1981.
Voyage to the Bunny Planet. (Set of three in a box). New York: Dial, 1992.
    First Tomato.
    The Island Light.
    Moss Pillows.

SELECTED BOOKS WRITTEN
BY ROSEMARY WELLS

Forest of Dreams. Illustrated by Susan Jeffers. New York: Dial, 1988.
Leave Well Enough Alone. New York: Dial, 1977.
Lucy Comes to Stay. Illustrated by Mark Graham. New York: Dial, 1994.
The Man in the Woods. New York: Dial, 1981.
Night Sounds, Morning Colors. Illustrated by David McPhail. New York: Dial, 1994.
Through the Hidden Door. New York: Dial, 1987.
Waiting for the Evening Star. Illustrated by Susan Jeffers. New York: Dial, 1993.
When No One Was Looking. New York: Dial, 1979.

PART THREE

THEORY
INTO PRACTICE

LITERATURE DISCUSSION GROUPS: TALKING TO REFLECT AND INTERPRET

Talk is a shared language experience between two or more people, and as they communicate, as they story together, they write oral texts. These oral texts are guides that involve and connect our lives to others; in the process, we reveal parts of what we believe and feel, daily becoming more aware of who we are.

Collaborative talk can build literate learning communities where teachers and students inquire, explore, read, research, and write. For talk is an exchange of information, feelings, gossip, hypotheses, and questions. That's why talk is a key to connecting what we already know to new information and ideas.

Transactions between reader and text initiate an inner dialogue, the first interactions with texts; talk extends the transaction. Interactive talk about reading and research is central to all learning. It involves listening to alternate points of view, permits us to view the past and present from another's perspective, and offers opportunities to clarify information and raise additional questions.

In talk-focused classrooms where children read multiple texts, they can learn a great deal about the structure of texts and the information included. As part of an eighth-grade study of the Holocaust, groups read nonfiction, history textbooks, magazines, poetry, and novels. The conversation below demonstrates three students' frustration with textbook information.

CARL: This textbook only has one column about the Holocaust.

KIM: Mine is so impersonal. It just says "six million Jews died in concentration camps" and gives a bunch of facts about Hitler's rise to power.

HARRY: What was it like? How did they die? What did they think and feel? Weren't these Jews Germans? Mine doesn't answer any of these questions.

KIM: All this is, is facts and facts. I want to know the stories about the people back then.

By the end of the study, the class rated historical fiction and personal interviews as stimulating the best group discussions and answering many of their questions. "If we just read one or even two or three textbooks, we never would have learned about people and what happened to them," Harry told the class. They all agreed. This excerpt, however, illustrates more than Harry's comment: Kim and Carl evaluated the information in the textbooks; Harry raised questions that motivated the group to read on. And their discussions continued to raise questions that inspired them to search for answers by reading nonfiction and fiction and doing research. A variety of literary genres became their resources, enabling them to arrive at a broader view of the Holocaust.

Early in my teaching career I learned from students the power of group discussions. Whole group learning and discussions dominated my first two years of teaching. From my perspective, managing classes of twenty-five and thirty students appeared simpler if everyone read the same book, participated in the same discussions, or worked on writing and fine arts projects at the same time. A transformation began during my third teaching year.

Six courageous boys and girls changed the way I viewed grouping and learning. The catalyst was a study of fairy and folktales. One afternoon, following dismissal, I noticed an envelope on my desk addressed to "Mrs. Robb." The handwritten note inside requested a "private meeting to talk about an idea." All afternoon and evening, right up to bedtime, I felt like a kid, absolutely dying to know the topic of this meeting. None of my

hunches seemed plausible. The six students and I met during lunch, and their spokesperson confessed they were "bored" with everyone discussing the same story, the same questions. "Couldn't you do something about it?" Though I sincerely promised to think about their concerns and get back to them in a few days, I felt wounded and hurt. This was the only class in the school that used real books. What did they want? Once I shoved aside personal feelings and thought rationally about their request, I took a giant step forward in my concept of learners and learning.

That year I experimented with various small groupings and asked students to pose questions they wanted to discuss. Believe me, I did not reach nirvana then or now. Over the years groups have continued to meet to discuss free-choice library books, research, books relating to author, illustrator, and theme cycle; to share poetry; and to explore literary genres. Throughout the year I incorporate formally organized literature discussion groups and allow time for less formal impromptu discussions.

I have come to believe that there is no one right way to organize discussion groups. I prefer to offer students a wide range of experiences that emerge from our studies. If there's a book everyone's burning to read, we read and discuss it. Know your comfort level and begin there. If it's everyone reading the same book, fine! Once comfortable with the process, propose an author or theme cycle, with each group reading a different title. The merit of using multiple texts is that each student can read a book at his or her independent reading level. Moreover, you make better use of budget dollars when you purchase fifteen to thirty different titles instead of many copies of just one.

I continue to refine and play with the group discussion process, even today. Five issues, though, drive my philosophy of literature response groups:

Variety. Change the size of groups; use pairs or groups of three to six.

Diverse Membership. Group heterogeneously, rotating membership frequently. Keep records of groupings to insure that students work with all class members during the school year. Part of response group dynamics is learning to value diversity.

Teacher Modeling. The teacher, through minilessons, demonstrates questioning techniques and literature discussion strategies.

Choice. Students have many opportunities to pose questions, choose books, and select the strategy that focuses discussion.

Meaningful Reading and Talking. Students read the entire book, then reread and discuss, or they read large, meaningful sections to discuss. Talking about books is a reflective activity that drives readers back into the story to share passages that support hypotheses. Locating support and designing discussion questions provide a genuine reason to reread. Rereading becomes a natural part of book discussions and can improve recall and comprehension. Talk and rereading, like cooking with herbs and spices, reclaim hidden flavors within the story. And like gourmet cooking, this reflective process takes time.

Reading response groups also foster the social and individual aspects of learning. Students collaborate on two basic levels: They learn how to function as a positive social unit and as individuals conversing about books they've read. Competition can diminish when grading disappears, and the spirit of a common shared focus directs the groups. Group members working together can reap the following benefits:

Diverse Ideas. A diverse group membership guarantees divergent interpretations of literature. Children come to accept that they can explore what stories mean to them; it's okay to end up in different places than do their peers, and to hold different beliefs.

Shared Goals and Commitment. A group's common goal of reading, thinking, and talking about literature supplies positive direction. As the group works collaboratively, members become problem solvers, devising guidelines to share ideas and feelings successfully.

Changing Roles. A democratic spirit emerges, allowing equal opportunity for all members to talk about their ideas. Students themselves prevent one member from dominating conversations and encourage silent students to share. Members take turns as spokesperson for the group when asked to bring group ideas before the entire class.

Shared Risk-taking. Equality among members develops as they come to value and respect other ideas and beliefs. Once the group accepts the merits of diversity, a safe atmosphere can be created where students learn to challenge ideas, not people.

Responsibility. Students cooperate and compromise to establish guidelines for managing response groups, based on personal experiences and common goals. The guidelines reflect individual and group responsibilities.

Community. Working together in a spirit of cooperation gradually develops a productive learning community. Bonded by shared reading, by shared vulnerability through voicing different ideas, and by shared management of response group dynamics, children experience firsthand the steps that lead to building a cohesive community.

Teachers are key players in helping students organize successful response groups. Groups can discuss books organized by theme, topic, author, or genre, or talk about free-choice reading books. The teacher talks about several books to the entire class or to each group, offering the children choice within a selection. You can ask children to talk about books they love or to browse through the library and check out books that relate to a common topic.

Whether you use multiple texts or one book for all, your role as demonstrator, guide, and co-learner will assist in the establishment of a nurturing atmosphere for student collaboration. Share some of your expertise about the group discussion process. Help students dip into their give-and-take experiences with family, friends, and school. Together devise a first-draft list of response-group guidelines. Repeat this process throughout the year so that students base revisions on real experiences.

Remember, your students will make too much noise, will stray from their topic, will argue and not value classmates' opinions. Your job is to help them think about problems that arise and find positive solutions. It will take many weeks to establish a risk-free, congenial atmosphere in which group members have the right to make errors and learn, not retreat. The only way to learn is to experience and evaluate the process, discuss options, and then reach consensus on solutions.

Response-group discussions can last for one period or continue over several weeks. Time constraints and limitations stem from schedules, age of students, goals set by teacher and students, and the riches within the text. It's impossible ever to feel a book has been totally and thoroughly explored. But that's the joy of literature!

Set reasonable time limits for discussions. Work with your students to establish deadlines, helping them focus their energies on the topic. Circulate among groups as listener and observer. Keep a clipboard handy to jot down notes on students' interactions and quality of participation.

Join groups as a member. Your job as facilitator is to occasionally ask a telling question when conversation lulls. Don't take sides when students answer, for as soon as you utter, "That's right" or "Great answer," you inhibit further thinking. Instead, recognize and affirm thinking during whole class discussions with such phrases as: That's interesting; That's one way to look at it; You support that position well; It's clear you've thought carefully about your response; or I don't quite understand, could you clarify that point. Since I can't participate fully with every group, I occasionally tape a conversation to evaluate later with the children.

Model and encourage students to adopt follow-up questioning techniques that not only move discussions forward but also foster diverse thinking. Students can ask each other: What do you think about that response? What makes you say or think that? Why do you think you feel that way? Does anyone have other points of view? Are there any other questions? Reactions? Remind students that periods of silence are natural to discussions, for silence permits time to revise ideas and gather additional evidence from the text.

Reserve class time for groups to present their ideas to everyone. Ask for comments from the class. Set reasonable time limits so all groups have the chance to report.

For collaborative discussions about literature to educate students' hearts and minds, the students must be decision makers and actively contribute to the success of the process. Success arrives slowly. Groups struggle; student performance and interest level vary. But that's true of any community learning and working together. Most students enjoy discussions and, like Sallie (figure 1), come to understand how collaborative talk empowers learners to think deeply about reading and, in the process, develop an enthusiasm for thinking.

Not all students enjoy group exchanges and interactions. Over time, many change their negative feelings; however, you might find students who are always reluctant to participate in a group. There are usually good reasons for such negative feelings. An important teacher role is to help students recognize and understand negative attitudes. Seventh grader Dave, in an unsent journal letter, explores his fears (figure 2).

He wrote this letter at the end of February. Confronting his feelings, then conferring with me, eventually enabled Dave to participate more freely in group discussions. Some students, like Greta, who told me, "I don't want to talk about my ideas, I want to talk about my boyfriend or the weekend," might remain on the periphery of the group all year. Every class has its share of Gretas and Daves who challenge us daily. Whole class success stories are unrealistic goals. Struggles and a range of reactions are the norm.

Students new to small group book discussions often stray from the topic because sustaining a discussion is difficult. Arguments might erupt, since all students do not value diverse ideas. Here is a transcript of a fifth

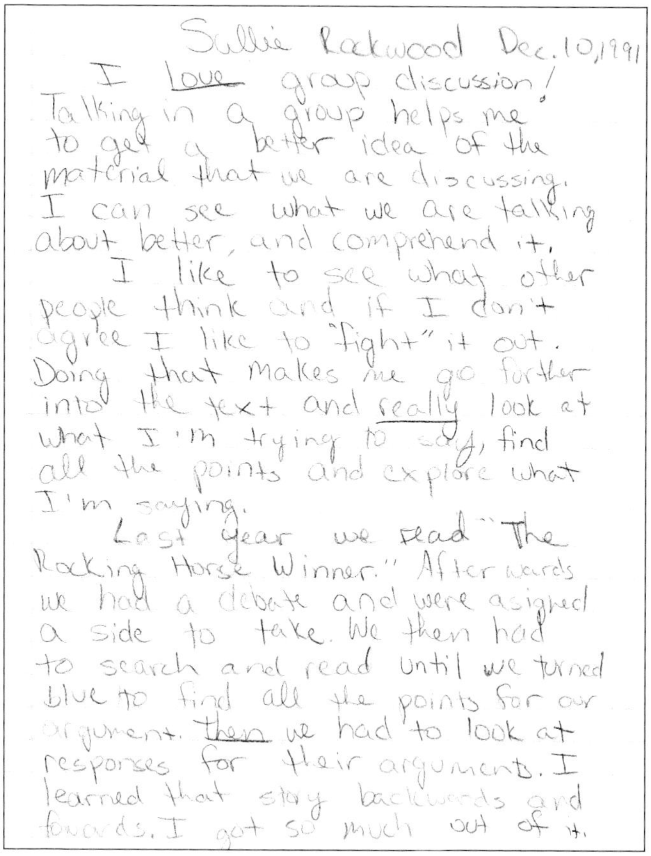
Sallie Rockwood Dec. 10, 1991

I love group discussion! Talking in a group helps me to get a better idea of the material that we are discussing. I can see what we are talking about better, and comprehend it.

I like to see what other people think and if I don't agree I like to "fight" it out. Doing that makes me go further into the text and really look at what I'm trying to say, find all the points and explore what I'm saying.

Last year we read "The Rocking Horse Winner." Afterwards we had a debate and were asighed a side to take. We then had to search and read until we turned blue to find all the points for our argument. then we had to look at responses for their arguments. I learned that story backwards and fowards. I got so much out of it.

Fig. 1 An eighth grader's assessment of group discussion.

grade's early experiences discussing three fairy tales by Hans Christian Andersen: "The Wild Swans," "The Little Match Girl," and "The Little Mermaid." The topic this group of three chose was to describe the tasks of the heroine in their particular story, then compare their heroine to others. Students 1 and 2 start the discussions and attempt to stick to the topic, while Student 3 tries to move the pair to a social agenda.

STUDENT 3: Are you playing soccer this weekend?

STUDENT 2: We're going to my uncle's.

STUDENT 3: I'll call you on Sunday.

STUDENT 1: [Interrupting] Hey, we're supposed to talk about these stories.

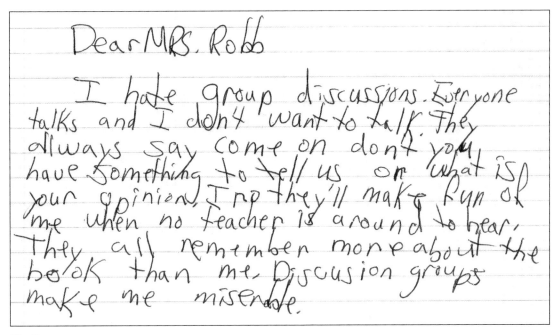

Dear MRS. Robb

I hate group discussions. Everyone talks and I don't want to talk. They always say come on don't you have something to tell us or what is your opinion. I no they'll make fun of me when no teacher is around to hear. They all remember more about the book than me. Discussion groups make me miserable.

Fig. 2

STUDENT 3: Whatever you say, Miss Goody-Goody.

STUDENT 2: In "The Wild Swans" Eliza tries to save her brothers. The evil stepmother turned them to swans. She's gotta weave jackets from these awful nettles found in graveyards, and she can't say a word until she's done. They think she's a witch, and she almost gets burned at the stake. One theme is you can't talk if you've got a task.

STUDENT 1: The little match girl can talk.

STUDENT 3: So, big deal.

STUDENT 2: They all worked hard to get someplace.

STUDENT 3: But the match girl dies and the others live.

STUDENT 1: But the match girl is happier dead. She goes to her grandmother, who loves her. Her life here was horrible. Look, I'll read this part.

STUDENT 3: This is getting boring [in a singsong voice].

STUDENT 2: Maybe the stories are all trying to say what happens if you work hard for something good.

STUDENT 3: Okay. Now that we've got it, let's talk about teams for recess.

STUDENT 2: I'm on Jack's team.

These students and I listened to the tape of their discussion. "We never thought you'd really listen to it," one said apologetically. Rather than embarrass them further and dwell on the negative aspects, I asked them to tell me what was working here and what goals they could set for their next discussion. All three agreed that even though they had strayed from the topic, they did gain some insights into the stories. The group agreed on three goals for their next meeting: 1) stick to the topic; 2) don't cut someone down if he or she is trying to follow directions; 3) help each person have a turn to talk about his or her story.

Students who have participated in literature response group discussions increase their ability to focus on the topic. Previous experiences with collaborative book talk heighten the importance of individual preparation. "It's not fair if you're not prepared," said one student. "Discussions get boring, and it's really embarrassing when everyone counts on your part."

A group of four seventh graders has completed *Of Nightingales That Weep,* by Katherine Paterson. Since second grade, these boys and girls have participated in literature response groups. The exchange illustrates student interactions, questioning techniques, and the assistance they offer one another in locating information and clarifying ideas. There's no formal raising of hands, but from experience, the group listens until a member finishes. Their discussion always returns to the story to prove points, and they remind each other that support is necessary. The topic the group selected was to point out the changes in Takiko by the end of the story. The selection below, transcribed from a tape recording, illustrates the power of joint discussions to lead students into deeper understandings of texts.

STUDENT 1: She learned a lot about what's important in life.

STUDENT 2: Yeah, she's kinda like a nightingale now, all gray and plain outside and beautiful inside.

STUDENT 3: You have to prove those ideas.

STUDENT 1: She thinks Hideo loves her—I mean for who Takiko is. But he doesn't even recognize her. I think that's when she knows outside beauty isn't everything.

STUDENT 4: That part is on the bottom of page 158. [Student 4 reads and others follow.]

STUDENT 2: If they didn't have manners they would've lost it. There's no way I could have gotten through that.

STUDENT 1: When she says farewell it's like her whole past life blows up in her face. [About two minutes of silence here.]

STUDENT 3: She still keeps her music. She practices her koto even with her swollen hands.

STUDENT 2: Yeah, but that's not a change.

STUDENT 1: She marries Goro. That's a bang of a change. She's hated him since her mother married him.

STUDENT 3: Give examples.

STUDENT 1: Well, on page 151, she thinks about Goro as a monster. She says he's so ugly he looks like a monkey.

STUDENT 2: Goro scars her face, and then nurses her from her fever. She invites him to spend the evening with her and says it saves on oil. But I think she's changing her feelings.

STUDENT 3: But she plans to leave him. That's in chapter 17. She's gonna become a nun. And when the empress tells her that "perhaps we are meant to learn that beauty can heal," it makes Takiko think.

STUDENT 1: I never thought they'd marry. Takiko learned that you have to love for more than looks. Goro's kind and gentle. It says: "His big hand rested gently on her hair."

STUDENT 2: You know what else changed? At the end the peasants, the ones who work hard, are important.

STUDENT 3: Not just the rich and royalty. What do you think? [Long pause]

STUDENT 4: I think that Takiko changed from being stuck on herself. At court she only worked on looking beautiful. I don't think she'll raise her daughter to be like she was.

Through their conversation, students move to valid interpretations. Notice the pauses and silences; the students understand that thinking takes time. Student 4 rarely spoke when group discussions began. Not only did Student 3's last question draw Student 4 into the discussion, but the group accepted the silent thinking time without immediately filling in with additional discussion.

As children read and talk about a variety of genres, many, like these third graders, begin to develop a set of evaluation standards. The brief exchange below was part of a discussion on Karen Wallace's *Think of an Eel*.

STUDENT 1: This book is different from other nonfictions I read.

STUDENT 2: I know. The pictures are so real. And the extra pictures with words.

STUDENT 1: Yeah. All the extra writing under the pictures gives more facts.

STUDENT 3: The pictures made me think that eels are beautiful. I always said "yuck" to eels.

STUDENT 1: The words are different from other nonfiction. They look like poems do.

The students' firsthand experiences with poetry helped Student 1 make a powerful connection, for Wallace's poetic text does depart from that of most nonfiction books.

Student selection of discussion topics or questions is crucial to building literature response groups. Begin with open-ended questions and statements, which are ways of talking about books that are not story specific. Open-ended strategies provide a common basis for group discussions as members confer about a different title or the same title. In my classroom there are stacks of cards that relate to story structure, personal response, and specific genres. I write one question on each four-by-six-inch index card, and each group receives its own card stack. Groups can choose to focus on one question or respond to several questions. Sometimes I limit choices by asking them to select from a particular set of questions. You'll want to establish standards of support for students, suggesting whether students need two, three, or four pieces of evidence to own a position.

The strategies below will stimulate discussions that can develop critical analysis, comprehension of story structure, and personal connections.

Problems Characters Faced. Describe the problem(s) a character faced. Can you identify events, conversations, or past experiences in the story that caused this problem? Describe and evaluate the solutions. If the character could not find a solution, try to explain why. Present your own solution.

Events and Dialogue. Talk about several events and conversations in the story and explain what you believe they taught you about that character. Or describe a character and find events and dialogue that support your conclusions.

Setting. Identify the various settings in a novel or story. Decide if the different settings affect a character's actions or personality.

From Beginning to Ending. Small groups discuss a character's personality at the beginning of the story (first three to four chapters) and at the end of a story. Identify the causes for change and growth within the character.

Form a Hypothesis. Write a statement that takes a position about a character, event, theme, or ecological or social problem. Find two to three supporting pieces of evidence. Statements that cannot be supported make invalid hypotheses.

Identify Mood. Find passages that create a particular mood, such as suspense, horror,

Two students explain their group's circular map for Millions of Cats, *by Wanda Gág.*

romance, anger, hatred, fear, or humor. Read the passage aloud and explain what the author did to create the mood. How does the creation of a mood affect your enjoyment of a book?

A Character's Decisions. Examine two or three decisions a character made. Evaluate these decisions by discussing how they affected the character and others in the story. Think about the decision you might make in a similar position and compare your decision to the character's.

What Did You Learn? Present the new information you learned from this book. What questions did the book raise but not answer? Identify and discuss any values and issues the book made you aware of.

Evaluate Photographs or Illustrations. What attracts you to the pictures? Or, if you dislike them, why? Discuss the information the pictures convey. Compare these pictures to those in other works by the author, other versions of the story, or other books on the same topic. Discuss the endpaper illustrations and how they affect you. What is the relationship between the text and the pictures?

Select a Quote. Each student selects a quotation from a book that speaks to him or her personally or relates to a theme. Copy the quote into a journal, noting the title, author, and page number. Students read and discuss their quotations with group members.

In addition to selecting from the above strategies, students give high ratings to the following questions, which you can place on index cards:

• Talk about the title and how it relates to the story.

• Choose some favorite illustrations and explain why you like them and how they help you understand the story.

• What made you like or dislike the book?

• Tell about some new information you learned.

• Do you want to read other books by this author? Why?

• Did the ending satisfy you? Tell why or why not.

• Would you reread the book? Give your reasons.

• Was there a character you really related to? What made the connection between you and that character?

• Was there a character you hated? What made you feel that way?

• What do you look for in a good reading book? How did this book measure up to your standards?

• Did the book offer you new experiences? Discuss these.

• What feelings did the book arouse in you? Can you explain what in the story did this?

• Are characters and events stereotyped? If so, how?

When children pose the specific questions they want to discuss about a particular text, they are more likely to invest in the discussion. After all, the questions we teachers create, or the authors of guides write, are from an adult's perspective and too often have little to do with a child's wonderings. Permitting children to write specific story questions requires that they have a detailed knowledge of the text and familiarity with higher-level questioning techniques.

Research demonstrates that students increase their questioning powers by imitating the models teachers present. Vaughan and Estes (*Reading and Reasoning Beyond the Primary Grades*) discuss this research and state, "The quality of questions asked by students is directly related to the quality of questions asked by teachers."[1] Teachers who ask interpretive, open-ended questions supply students with a model to imitate. However, for students to develop as authors of interpretive questions, I find it necessary to present minilessons that demonstrate the range of questions students can design. To simplify the process of modeling questioning techniques, I compiled a chart of verbs that follows Bloom's Taxonomy of Questions (figure 3). Easily accessible on my clipboard, I refer to the chart when I am questioning students and during minilessons.

Your demonstrations should include the necessity of returning to the text to design and test the quality of questions. Model how you would respond. Explain the difference between memory questions and questions that trigger diverse responses. Point out the verbs that signal Bloom's questioning categories.

Sixth graders studying the novels of Jean Craighead George wrote their discussion questions (figure 4), which some groups decided to separate into scientific and story issues. The separation highlighted the scientific issues, which students then researched and discussed.

Three periods of serious collaboration resulted in sets of questions for six novels. Groups discussed their questions and discovered the necessity to set a standard for neat writing. "If we can't read it [the question], we can't discuss it" was a comment I heard repeatedly. Some groups selected one person to write the questions legibly; others shared the writing.

Comfortable and familiar with the process of literature response groups, these sixth graders were able to direct their learning for the entire study. I invited them into the first round of reading by displaying and talking about these book titles: *Julie of the Wolves*, *The Cry of the Crow*, *My Side of the Mountain*, *The Talking Earth, Water Sky*, and *The Summer of the Falcon*. Students selected their first book and formed six groups with three to seven members each. We negotiated deadlines for completing the books, and students agreed that one week of reading daily in class and at home was adequate time for completing a novel. Groups spent the first two days of the second week freely talking about their book. Then each group designed questions they wanted to discuss and wrote project suggestions on a large sheet of construction paper. As students read different novels, they added ideas to the project list because they preferred to read and discuss many books before completing an extension activity.

After the first round of books, students directed the study. Each group presented to the class a two- to three-minute book talk that celebrated their creative spirits. Their repertoire included bag and stick puppets, an original poem or song about a book, a dramatization, a short monologue, interviews . . . all geared at enticing others to read their book. Students agreed that book talks should "give enough to make them pant for the book." Panting for books, panting to read, what better goal could I want!

Periodically, I asked the sixth graders to reflect on the process of designing their own questions and activities. Jill's comments (figure 5) point to the compromise that eventually emerged from disagreements. Expect arguments; expect disagreements. Allow time for students to work through issues that divide the group. The process increases the level of cooperation it takes to solve problems. Independence in learning takes practice. The observations made by Jill about her group's efforts to write questions and list activities clearly reflect the bumpy road that leads to compromise and success.

In addition to author studies, introduce students, through genre studies, to the various literary forms writers use. Genre discussions can lead students to a deeper understanding of a particular form and acquaint children with literature they might not select independently. Fifth grader Sam told me during a book conference, "I wasn't much into historical fiction, and when I read *The Sign of the Chrysanthemum*, by Katherine Paterson, I told myself this stuff's great!" Eighth grader Peden admitted he found biography "miserably boring" but fell in love with the genre after reading Jean

VERBS FOR QUESTIONING: Following Bloom's Taxonomy

<u>MEMORY</u>: asks student to recall factual information and data.

define	name	tell
repeat	recall	what
list	label	

<u>TRANSLATION</u>: asks student to transform information into another form such as paraphrase or draw.

summarize	explain	retell	create a mental image
discuss	identify	draw	
describe	locate	restate	

<u>INTERPRETATION</u>: asks student to use facts and information in order to discover relationships among these. Students draw inferences and conclusions.

why	relate
compare	determine
contrast	cause/effect

<u>APPLICATION</u>: asks students to solve problems faced in daily living. Students infer, combine ideas, connect ideas to other texts and situations. New learning occurs as previous knowledge supports new data.

apply	connect
dramatize	show
construct	design

<u>ANALYSIS</u>: asks students to analyze and evaluate thinking used to arrive at conclusions. Students evaluate the support offered and identify false stereotypes, propaganda and sweeping generalizations.

interpret	contrast	arrange
analyze	categorize	examine
compare	classify	survey

```
SYNTHESIS: asks students to problem solve and offer original ideas
to support solutions.  Students use data to infer, conclude and
support original thinking.


compose          design          construct
plan             infer           develop
hypothesize      conclude


EVALUATION: asks students to make value judgments based on a a set
of established standards.  Students can design standards and then
measure their value judgment against pre-set standards.
The difficult aspect is to weed out personal values which are often
veiwed as facts.


judge        rate         recommend
decide       critique     justify
evaluate     assess
```

Fig. 3 Above and at left.

Fritz's *Traitor: The Case of Benedict Arnold.* Peden told his partner, "I couldn't put it down. She [Fritz] made me think about all the wild and crazy things he [Arnold] did that made him dream of being a hero. The book was like a thriller, and you're with him to the bitter final chapter."

Repeating genre studies each year deepens children's insights into forms and how they work. At times the entire class reads within one genre, and at other times groups each study a different genre. I'm always distressed with schools that want to assign specific genres to each grade, careful not to repeat one in two consecutive years. While planning a cross-grade project with a third-grade teacher, I was informed that "they do tall tales in grade two, so I can't do them in grade three. We're not allowed to repeat a genre; we have to find something different." Granted, students should be introduced to a range of genres, but such limitations placed on teachers restrict student-teacher negotiations and restrain teachers' ability to be responsive to changing and evolving student interests.

Genre studies have the potential to enhance learning across the curriculum because students can engage in genre response group discussions in mathematics, social studies, science, health, physical education, art, and music. There are books to support all these subjects, enabling students to discuss issues and problems in departmentalized content area classes.

I initiate a new genre study by asking pairs or small groups to tell each other what they know or think they know about it. As they exchange ideas, students or I collect them on chart paper, and we read our books to confirm or change hunches. The charts that follow represent what a fifth-grade class knew before and after an investigation of science fiction.

The Cry of the Crow

Ron Geris
Immy Byrd
Meribeth Praml
Whizzie Demney

1) Why did "I've got you'u" stay in Nina's mind?
2) Why did Mandy name the bird Nina Terrance?
3) Why did Mandy take in Nina Terrance for a pet?
4) Why do the people think Nina speaks so well?
5) Why doesn't Mandy want Nina around people alot?
6) Why didn't Drummer want Mandy to kill Nina?

1) What is an eya?
2) Why do people dislike crows?
3) Why would crows have a warning call?
4) Do crows migrate?
5) Are crows intelligent? Why or why not.
6) Do you think Barbra understood Mandy having Nina?

Fig. 4 At left.

Fig. 5 Below.

My group argued alot. about which questions and projects we should include. Everyone had a different booktalk idea. I had to adap some of my ideas. Finally we compromised!!! I didnt like that at First. But when the other group did our projects that we desigined I Felt. proud.

Science Fiction: Before Reading

1. Takes place in future.

2. Couldn't happen.

3. Far-out gadgets.

4. Robots.

5. Other planets.

Science Fiction: After Reading

1. Set in future worlds.

2. Great advances, like space travel.

3. Time travel.

4. Spaceships and travel among galaxies.

5. People face problems like we do about friends and family, romance, dreams, and hopes.

6. Daily living changes.

7. Magic part of story.

8. Science is more advanced than now.

9. Alien worlds.

10. Explains what life will be like in the future.

After demonstrating how to turn statements into questions, have students design discussion questions from their chart(s), then select a book and read along with them.

The children led me into the challenging realms of fantasy, a genre that I had avoided. Fifth grader Ross, who dined on a steady diet of high fantasy, convinced his classmates to read and discuss that genre. Thanks to Ross, I entered the world of Susan Cooper, Ursula Le Guin, Lloyd Alexander, and Robin McKinley.

Literature discussions introduce children to many new topics, genres, authors, and illustrators. Every child can observe peers making connections with, inferring from, and analyzing texts. These repeated observations can assist children to risk voicing ideas and reflecting deeply about story. A long waiting list for titles students burn to read emerges from students' book conversations. I find that the children are the best vendors when it comes to "selling" books.

Collaborative discussions, where children learn to think about books worth reading and rereading, where they can exchange ideas and delight in the many ways to interpret a story, where they can passionately argue a point, where they find themselves subtly changed by their reading and conversations, where they make friends with many story structures—those groups and books are the ingredients that lure children into a reflective reading life. Such interactive talk can lead to valid interpretations of literature, interpretations that change as the children change.

I've included lists of student-written open-ended genre questions for teachers to use during minilessons, for students to critique and adapt, or as a beginning place for teachers new to the adventures of literature response groups. Middle school students assisted with the selection of their all-time favorite questions for each genre.

Biography

1. Why is this person important?

2. Did your opinion of this person change as you read the book? Point to these changes and discuss what caused them.

3. Discuss the problems this person had to overcome.

4. Evaluate some of the key decisions this person made, and try to explain how these decisions influenced his or her life.

5. How is your life similar to, or different from, this person's?

6. How did family, friends, and education influence this person?

7. Why do you think this person was able to realize personal hopes and dreams?

8. Has the book affected or changed your way of thinking? Explain how.

Realistic Fiction

1. What problems do the main character and other characters face? Evaluate how they solved their problems.

2. Describe the setting(s) and explain how setting influences the events and characters' actions and decisions.

3. How does the main character change from the beginning to the end of the story? Why do you think she or he changed?

4. Identify important decisions particular characters made. Why did they make each decision, and how did the decision affect their lives?

5. How do minor characters view the main character?

6. Realistic fiction deals with themes such as growing up, peer pressure, friendships, family relationships, survival, suicide, divorce, prejudice, gender issues, stereotyping, aging, death and dying, multicultural issues, sports, physical handicaps. Discuss the themes and issues in your book. Relate them to your experiences and other books you've read. Evaluate the way the author presented the themes.

7. What problems do you and the characters have in common? Compare the way you deal with those problems to the way the character dealt with similar problems.

Folk- and Fairy Tales

1. How does the story follow the traditional folktale pattern of "Once upon a time . . ." and ". . . happily ever after"?

2. Classify your folktale as cumulative, circular, realistic, wonder, beast, numbskull, giant, or quest. Support your choices with story details.

3. Does the tale revolve around magic numbers? If so, explain the role of these magic numbers in the story and how they affected the adventures and characters.

4. Why must heroic tasks or deeds be accomplished?

5. How are the characters changed by their adventures?

6. Describe the clash and struggle between good and evil. Who wins? Offer support for your opinion on the victory.

7. How do the adventures, the magic, and other characters change the life of the hero or heroine?

8. Discuss some of the difficult decisions characters make. What influences their decisions? How do their decisions change their lives?

9. What human characteristics do animals and toys have? How are their qualities similar to yours?

Fantasy

1. Describe the fantastic elements in the story.

2. How does the author help you, the reader, enter the fantasy world? Are there realistic elements? Discuss these elements and how they affect the story.

3. How do trips to other times or other worlds help the characters cope with the present?

4. Evaluate the way enchantment and magical powers determine the actions and decisions of many characters.

5. Does the story deal with values and themes such as death, friendship, love, wisdom?

Find details in the story that support a theme or themes.

6. Are there supernatural elements? Identify them and explain how they enhance the themes and events.

7. How is the main character changed by events and interactions with other characters?

High Fantasy

1. Describe the imaginary world or kingdom.

2. How do ancient powers affect the actions and beliefs of characters?

3. Why do good and evil clash? Does one side win? Explain why or why not.

4. Is the author commenting on good and evil, justice and injustice, courage and cowardice, wisdom and folly, and so on? Discuss the themes you see and compare the viewpoint of the book with your own personal views.

5. How do the quests and tasks change the characters and their society?

6. Can you connect the fantastic story elements to your own life and to society?

7. What do characters learn about themselves as a result of their experiences? Has their self-knowledge increased your own self-knowledge? How?

8. Discuss the symbols in your book and explain what you believe each represents.

9. Compare what the characters view as important in life at the beginning and at the end of the story.

Historical Fiction

1. How is the past similar to the present?

2. Compare what you knew about the historical period presented in the book with what you learned after completing it.

3. Compare and contrast family relationships and people's values in the novel with your family life and values.

4. Did the events create social, economic, and political change? Discuss these changes and compare them to those in our society.

5. Could the historical issues this book presents have been handled or solved differently? Use hindsight to explain how things might have been different.

6. Do you think the same situation(s) could occur today? Explain your position.

7. Do you feel that the historical events controlled the people and society or that the people were in control? Find support for your position from the story.

8. How are women and minorities portrayed? Are they stereotyped?

9. How do people cope with economic problems such as scarcity of food, housing, jobs?

10. What did you learn about a different culture and way of life?

11. How do you feel the events in this book might have affected present-day events?

Science Fiction

1. Point out the scientific advances in the society. How do these advances in technology affect characters' decisions and actions?

2. Compare the problems characters face in the story with problems people face today. How are they alike? Different?

3. Evaluate life in the future as described in your book. Would you like to live there? Are there advantages and disadvantages? Include setting in your discussion.

4. Does the author deal with such present-day issues as population, food supplies, ecology? Compare the author's views with your own.

5. Does the story offer hope for humankind or is it a warning? Explain your conclusion.

6. Why might you consider this future world alien?

7. How do people fit into this futuristic society? Are they subordinate to machines? Has democracy vanished? See if you can identify changes and offer reasons for these changes.

Mystery

1. How does the author build suspense and excitement?

2. Describe the nature of the mystery.

3. Why do the characters get involved in solving the mystery?

4. Can you point to the clues the author used to sidetrack you from solving the mystery?

5. At what point in the book were you able to solve the mystery? Why could you do this?

6. Did solving the mystery cause the characters to change? Discuss these changes and compare the characters at the beginning and the end of the story.

7. Does your book comment on issues such as ecology, handicaps, family relations? Or does the mystery grow out of a true historical event? Or is it one of the "formula" type of mysteries? Classify your book and explain the issues the story addressed.

8. How does danger affect the decisions and actions of the characters?

9. Why do you think the sleuths were good problem solvers? Could you apply their techniques to your own life? How?

Information Books

1. What is the book about?

2. Did the book make you question the topic in any way? What were these questions?

3. Use the questions the book posed for further research. Explain what you learned and share the additional books you read.

4. What new information did you learn from the book?

5. Does the author help you separate fact from opinion? Can you find examples of each?

6. What aids (illustrations, photographs, charts, graphs) did the author use? How did these help you? What did they teach you?

7. Did the author present information using anecdotes, series of facts, story? Evaluate the methods the author used. How did the author capture and hold your interest?

8. Reread the lead and ending. Were they effective? Did they draw you into the book?

Reference

1. Vaughan, Joseph L., and Thomas H. Estes. *Reading and Reasoning Beyond the Primary Grades*. Boston: Allyn and Bacon, 1986, page 180.

AS I SEE IT

M. E. Kerr

When I was a kid, I talked about Charles Dickens's novels with my dad. It was then, I think, that I began to realize the importance of a character's name. We'd both delight in remembering the names of characters like Mrs. Sparsit, Mr. Sleary, Josiah Bounderby, and Slackbridge—all from *Hard Times*. My dad would say that they could never have been called Mrs. Smith, or Tom Allen, or Joe Brown—those names just wouldn't sound right. You had to come up with the right name for your characters.

And I remember my father imitating Mr. Sleary when he'd suggest a break from doing homework. "People mutht be amuthed. They can't be alwayth a-learning, not yet they can't be alwayth a-working, they ain't made for it."

We'd talk about the "hard times" Dickens had experienced growing up, and how all of it was reflected in his novels, and I developed a social consciousness without even being aware of it, and an interest in the haves and the have-nots of the world.

In my teen years I discovered Thomas Wolfe, and my girlfriends and I read passages aloud to each other, swooning over his lyrical laments, wallowing in his melancholy, convinced, for some reason (teenage angst) that we were lost, lonely souls . . . and we talked about getting out of our small town, and we talked of great love: the dark and agonizing kind . . . and I developed romantic yearning in these discussions, and a conviction I was misunderstood and too sophisticated for my small hometown. . . . And later in junior college came Carson McCullers with her love of oddballs. My friends and I discussed all the "crazies" in our own home-towns. I wanted to be a writer, and for a time I wrote only about the misfits and the strange.

In college I met a Hungarian boy who had been smuggled out of Hungary by communists. He was a great reader, and we exchanged books. He would chide me for reading "gib-berish"—Scott Fitzgerald and Hemingway and Virginia Woolf—and he would bring me the novels of Kafka, Dostoyevski, Camus, and Howard Fast . . . and we would argue about "a worldly view" as opposed to "a selfish, introspective view."

I still have books I lent him where he made notes in the margin: "Sentimental rubbish!";

"Where is his concern for the workingman?"; and "Typical, capitalistic self-involvement!"

After college, in the fifties in New York, everyone was being "analyzed," and this greatly affected discussions of books . . . and we had Salinger in our "debates," and Capote, and Philip Roth, Mailer, and Cheever. . . . Introspection was back, with a Freudian slant. Our book discussions were filled with new words: Oedipus complex, paranoia, compulsion, superego, etc. We began to talk about ways an author developed a character through child-hood trauma, and what "complexes" resulted to explain his actions.

Now there is an ethnic awareness as we read Márquez, Tan, Rushdie, Gordimer, Morrison, Naipaul, Fuentes, and the like.

All of my writing has been informed by my discussion of books with friends. From the early days, when I first became aware of thinking up a "good name" for a character, to now, when I no longer limit myself to the WASPy group I grew up with, I've benefited from knowing readers who don't stop after they say they liked or didn't like a book. They quote, critique, argue, and *lend*, and I do the same.

SELECTED BOOKS BY M.E. KERR

Dinky Hocker Shoots Smack! New York: Harper & Row, 1972.
Fell. New York: Harper & Row, 1987.
Fell Back. New York: Harper & Row, 1989.
Fell Down. New York: HarperCollins, 1991.
Gentlehands. New York: Harper & Row, 1978.
Him She Loves? New York: Harper & Row, 1984.
If I Love You, Am I Trapped Forever? New York: Harper & Row, 1973.
I'll Love You When You're More Like Me. New York: Harper & Row, 1977.
I Stay Near You. New York: Harper & Row, 1985.
Is That You, Miss Blue? New York: Harper & Row, 1975.
Linger. New York: HarperCollins, 1993.
Little Little. New York: Harper & Row, 1981.
Love Is a Missing Person. New York: Harper & Row, 1975.
ME ME ME ME ME: Not a Novel. New York: Harper & Row, 1983.
Night Kites. New York: Harper & Row, 1986.
The Son of Someone Famous. New York: Harper & Row, 1974.
What I Really Think of You. New York: Harper & Row, 1982.

SELECTED BOOKS BY MARY JAMES
(A PEN NAME OF M.E. KERR)

Frankenlouse. New York: Scholastic, 1994.
Shoebag. New York: Scholastic, 1990.
Shuteyes. New York: Scholastic, 1993.

TOWARD
VALID
INTERPRETATIONS

Reflection is an evolutionary process that takes readers beyond first transactions between self and text to an exploration of meaning that can lead to valid interpretations. "Reflection on the literary experience," Rosenblatt writes, "becomes a reexperiencing, a reenacting, of the work-as-evoked, and an ordering and elaborating of our responses to it."[1] Reflection, then, is the process by which we rethink, sort, clarify, revise, reconsider, and confirm early responses to written and oral texts.

Interactive and reflective classroom experiences such as discussions, drama, readers theater, and journal writing can assist children in moving personal transactions to a more objective understanding of their relationship to the text. These experiences create situations where children come to understand how their values, experiences, and emotions are similar to, and different from, the author's. As readers move to validity, they should not devalue early personal responses. Interpretation is, according to Rosenblatt, "a process in time," affirming the evolutionary nature of the search for validity

and implying that there are many readings of a text. Such diversity, in responses to texts, can generate an excitement for teaching and learning. Jane, a fifth-grade teacher, felt bored and burned out. "Every year," she told me, "the same stories, the same workbook pages, the same answers." She began her transition with a whole class study of *Cracker Jackson,* by Betsy Byars. One day Jane bumped into me at school and literally dragged me into her classroom, proudly directing me to a bulletin board crowded with paragraphs written by students. "They're all different. And look here." Jane's index finger danced back and forth between two paragraphs. "One proves the book was hilarious, the other terribly sad. And you know what? They're both right!"

According to Jane, talk about the novel connected her students to Cracker, Alma, and Goat. She had observed that talk is a way to discover what we feel, believe, question, and don't understand. Second grader Tasha, sitting in the reader's chair, summed up the importance of talking about books: "I talk about a

156

story, then I know how I feel about it." Talk combined with exploratory journal entries can lead readers to valid interpretations. In your classroom, talking, writing, and reflecting should always precede any call for valid interpretations of texts.

Dramatizations, rich in talk and reflection, can foster valid interpretations of texts by allowing children to repeatedly experience the lives of characters. They enter the thoughts, emotions, and language of others. Atticus Finch, in Harper Lee's *To Kill a Mockingbird*, listens to his daughter, Scout, complain about Miss Caroline, her first-grade teacher. He offers this thoughtful advice: "First of all, if you can learn a simple trick, Scout, you'll get along a lot better with all kinds of folks. You never really understand a person until you consider things from his point of view."[2]

Pretending, which is what drama is all about, is in the child's imagination. Dramatic play naturally allows children to try on roles, test voice, gesture, and emotions, and explore relationships and situations on levels that deepen with each rehearsal. "Let's try it this way" or "See how the words sound with an angry voice" are comments that emerge from drama rehearsals.

The act of becoming a character seems to free children from their own self-conscious selves as they explore story beyond the realms of plot and into the uncharted terrain of the hearts and minds of others. The interactions that dramas require of pairs and small groups force members to consider elements of the story beyond their particular role. Discussions among the players arise naturally during rehearsals—discussions that lead them to deeper meanings within the story. Eighth graders, rehearsing a scene from James Agee's "Rufus," try to understand why young Rufus brags to strangers and boys from school about his father's sudden death in

a car accident. They rotate parts, by choice, each taking turns portraying Rufus. "It's easier being one of the mean kids or the strange man," Tim tells the group, "I can't get into Rufus's feelings."

"Why *does* he show off about his dad dying?" Kelly asks. "We'd better figure that out or they [the class] will know we don't know." The group sits on the floor; several thumb through the story, searching for a clue.

"I got an idea," says Jerry. "It says that his [Rufus's] dad was disappointed in him because the kids always teased him and Rufus did nothing. He was kinda like a wimp, not the kinda kid a dad would be proud of."

"I know, I know," Kelly says. "You see he never was really like he thought his dad wanted. And now he can never show his dad 'cause he's dead. That's it! That's why he says all that stuff to strangers and the kids."

"Yeah . . . it's sad and not Rufus's fault. He'll never have a chance to get his dad's approval." The group returns to rehearsing the scenes and supports Jerry, who plays Rufus, by encouraging Jerry to feel Rufus's loss.

Five second graders have decided to dramatize a nonfiction book by Karen Wallace, *Think of an Eel*. Three take turns reading the text, while the other two mime the eel's journey. "Next time we'll make things like eel eggs, the Sargasso Sea, and a tomb of weeds," David tells the group. Then he turns to Meg and says, "Suck in your cheeks, and stretch out your body so you look good and dead before you lay those eggs." The miming and discussions of the eel's life cycle guide the children into the eel's world and help them learn new information.

Impromptu discussions occur all through drama rehearsals. Frequently I stop a group and ask the members to share their probes with the class, demonstrating the process of discovering what makes a character tick.

A second grader tries out a lion mask made with a sixth grader for a dramatization of The Lazy Lion.

- exploration
- impromptu discussion
- rehearsal

- performance
- postperformance discussion
- continued use

After a presentation, the audience is always anxious to discuss what it saw, and quite often what the audience perceives is not exactly what the players intend. A powerful result of this tension between players and audience is a deeper understanding of the story. "One thing you guys didn't show," Diana says after the Rufus troupe performs, "is this kid's in shock. I mean, he can't deal with his dad being alive one day and dead the next. He's desperate for someone to say it's okay for your dad to have gone off and died." Often revelations like Diana's come from watching dramatizations by classmates that seem to deeply involve the audience in the players' words and actions.

Incorporating music, mime, movement, and art can enhance the dramatization of historic events, stories, and poems. They bring players and audience to greater self-awareness as both explore meaning through active involvement. Drama enhances children's search for meaning because actors travel back and forth among the following stages:

As students continue to take part in dramatizations, they can develop greater confidence in their ability to speak and role-play. Video- and audiotaping presentations permit children to see and hear themselves in order to self-evaluate and set reasonable goals for future dramatizations.

Readers theater, like dramatizations, is an interactive process that can lead to valid interpretations of a text. Modeled upon professional readers theater, the actors read their parts from scripts, using voice and gesture to project the emotions and state of mind of the characters. Readers theater places more demands on the imaginations of the performer and the audience, for both must create mental images of the characters, stage set, costumes, and props.

The interactive process leads to an interpretation of a readers theater script, with the performance the culmination of the groups' explorations.

Individual students' concepts about the text differ. The varied ideas about character and theme that emerge can enrich the search for an interpretation. Collaboration occurs as the actors exchange personal visions, using the script as a reference. During rehearsal actors revise and shape these visions. When students collectively write a readers theater script, this process heightens as they consider the text from two points of view: writer's and performer's.

Ready-made readers theater scripts are available and can serve as classroom models for children; they also simplify teachers' overburdened lives. However, readers theater scripts are simple to write, following these guidelines, which students learn through teacher demonstrations.

• Select a scene or chapter rich in dialogue.

• Establish narrators to summarize events leading up to the scene.

• Narrators set the stage for a scene, make transitions, and move the action along.

• The words characters speak in the text remain unchanged in the script.

• Set up dialogue like a playwright's script; begin with a character's name, followed by a colon. Then write the characters' lines.

• Place directions for tone of voice, facial expressions, gestures, or sound effects in parentheses.

Publish student-written scripts for other classes to perform. Catalog them in the school library.

When students record, in journals, the oral texts they compose during drama rehearsals and literature discussion groups, they construct a permanent place to reflect, test, and change ideas. Response journals become a thoughtful document providing students with the story of their thinking.

In my classes, students combine literature response with reflections on life in and out of school. Dialogue, buddy, and content area journals are separate. Children should choose or make their journal. Like Kate Bloomfield in Jean Little's *Hey World, Here I Am!*, I believe that "getting a journal is like buying shoes. You have to find one that fits. And you are the only person who can tell if it pinches."[3]

Two second-grade students read journal entries.

Journal entries should be viewed as first-draft writing that explores new and shaky territory. The purposes of journals are to discover thoughts, stories, and revelations, to construct new meanings, and to make connections. View each child's journal as an extension of the very core of that child's being. Therefore, the child who writes little or nothing sends just as powerful a message as the child who floods a journal with notes and writing.

So the students can readily locate material or return to and enlarge an entry, I ask them to head each entry with name, date, and a title. The title might be a topic, the name of a book, poem, story, article, or a personal experience.

Meet with the child whose journal is confusing due to illegible penmanship, abundant spelling errors, or unclear sentence structure. Ask the student to suggest ways to improve communication. The goal is to try, practice, and adopt strategies that make meaningful communication possible.

Grades are a reality for many teachers. Grades can be based upon the fulfillment of requirements negotiated between teacher and student. Since teachers use many kinds of journals throughout a school year, some might be graded and others not. The children should evaluate parts of each other's journals and their own journal. One way to improve children's journal entries is to allow them to read and reflect on a peer's work. Observing how others use journals opens diverse possibilities.

In order to gain insight into their reactions, connections, learning, thinking, and writing, it's crucial for teachers to read students' journals at least twice each month. Make comments positive. Equally important, however, is that children reread their journals to connect or revise entries, discover meaning, and, like real authors, unearth topics for writing and research.

Reserve time for children to read sections of their journals to the entire class. Doing this affirms the importance of the journal in the learning community. However, don't force a child to share.

Use minilessons to model, on chart paper, suggestions for organizing journals. Refrain from establishing a rigid pattern, such as picture on top half, writing on the bottom. Instead, let the discussion of the strategy guide your demonstrations, and then allow students to modify them as they translate your model into their own models.

Sixth grader Christy discusses with her group the opening chapters of James Vance Marshall's *Walkabout*. She organizes her journal notes by separating the incident from what it reveals (figure 1).

Interpretive statements such as "Mary—big sister to mother" illustrate the critical thinking that's taking place. Christy insisted that Mary and Peter should remain near the crash. Others disagreed, saying they would starve.

Undaunted by the disagreement, Christy added, "The logical thing to do is to stay near the plane." Christy was able to risk voicing and writing a different opinion without fear of recess reprisals, for her group valued diverse voices. "That's what I believe," she staunchly told her group, "and I supported it when I said that searchers would find the plane before two wandering children."

Brianna's entry (figure 2) reveals several aspects of the discussion-response-evaluate process. She has organized her evaluation of the parents in "The Veldt," by Ray Bradbury, into two columns. Brianna then responded, in a short essay, to a question the group posed and invited Susann to read and evaluate her paragraph. Susann's questions assist Brianna as she rethinks and revises a paragraph that begins with the inference that "greed" motivates Peter and Wendy. Editing each other's work for content can further the development of the reader as thinker, interpreter.

Choosing a meaningful quote, after completing a book, discussing with group members why the quote was so meaningful in terms of story and self, then writing about the quote, can forge connections. The process of selecting the quote invites the reader to skim and reexamine parts of the text. It's the return to the story that increases reflection and can spark new ideas and/or affirm original hunches. Tanette, a seventh grader, has selected this quote from *The River*, by Gary Paulsen: "I have, Brian thought, always been wet. Always. Even my soul is wet."[4]

Tanette's journal entry (figure 3) connects Brian's feelings about the rain, early in the book, to rafting down the river with the comatose Derek in the final section of the novel. Tanette mixes interpretation of the story with personal experiences when she observes the control some decisions have over our lives. Rosenblatt has described experiences such as

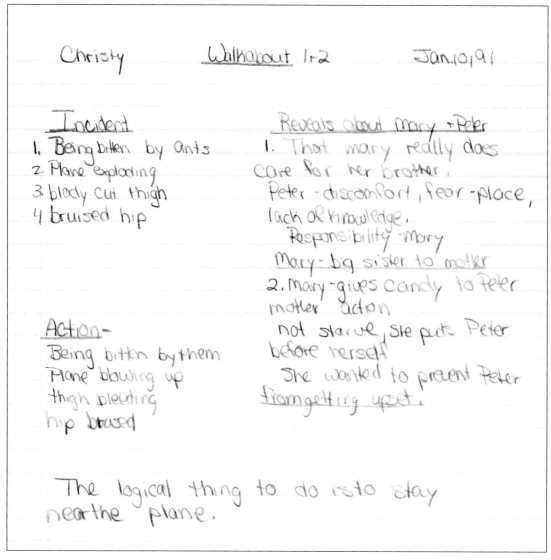

Christy   Walkabout 1-2   Jan.10,91

Incident
1. Being bitten by ants
2. Plane exploding
3. blody cut thigh
4. bruised hip

Action-
Being bitten by them
Plane blowing up
thigh bleeding
hip bruised

Reveals about Mary + Peter
1. That mary really does care for her brother.
Peter - discomfort, fear - place, lack of knowledge.
Responsibility - Mary
Mary - big sister to mother
2. mary - gives candy to Peter
mother action
not starve, she puts Peter before herself
She wanted to prevent Peter from getting upset.

The logical thing to do is to stay near the plane.

Fig. 1

Tanette's in terms of literature being a bridge to our lives. She writes, "Vicariously experiencing the life of a character in fiction or participating in another's emotion expressed in a poem may enable the reader to bring into consciousness similar elements in his own nature and emotional life."[5]

To vary the talk-then-respond pattern of literature discussion groups, I invite students to pair up for written conversations. Pairs dialogue on paper about questions they pose, each placing his or her name before a response. Susan and Whizzie, both eighth graders, have completed reading Irene Hunt's moving account of the depression, *No Promises in the Wind*. Susan begins the written conversation with an interpretive statement, and through the exchange that follows, the pair gather support from the story that validates Susan's opening statement.

"The Veldt"

Evaluwat Lyndia + George	Find reasons to explain why
as parents	Peter and Wendy murdered their
spoil	parents.
don't get to know children	No, rocket trip
depends on machinery	didn't know their parents
weren't fond	Didn't want nursery shut down
"stuck up"	No imaganation
mean	Spoiled to much
ruining lives	could't take a "no"
kids were independent	shut down house
parents depended on kids	Wanted to do what they pleased
nerdy	lacked trust
kids use imagenation	lacked love ♥ ♡
cared to much	don't know love
used money for love.	
old fashioned	

Short Essay

Why did Peter and Wendy murder their parents?

Peter and Wendy murdered their ∧parents because of greed!

why? Peter and Wendy thought that money bought more things than love. They depended on machenir y and the nursey so when their parents toke it away they felt that they couldn't do anything

How do you know? any more. Peter and Wendy had not yet began to underotand love.

Good lead! NEEDS more proof! Susann Carter

Revised

SUSAN: I think part of this story was about how parents feel when their children defy them.

WHIZZIE: Yeah, I know—but how did they defy them?

SUSAN: Josh left home because he thought his dad wanted him to. And Joey followed.

WHIZZIE: But their mom had mixed feelings. She loved them, but she knew they [the parents] couldn't feed them.

SUSAN: But she did say she thought it was best they go. At the end, when they're reunited, Josh's father cries and you know he's been upset and sad about the way he talked to Josh and pushed him out.

WHIZZIE: Yeah, and his dad wasn't the kinda person to cry.

Mapping data in journals is a way to visually organize information from the reading and talking of individuals, pairs, small groups, or the entire class. The process asks readers to select information, infer, conclude, analyze, make judgments, and understand relationships such as cause and effect, hypothesis and proof, compare and contrast. When mapping involves critical thinking and making choices or judgments, it becomes a graphic summary of students' interpretations of texts.

Teacher demonstrations of mapping techniques and student collaboration on map construction can illustrate the possibilities for organizing data. The making of maps should always be preceded by talk and discussion, and move from whole group efforts to small groups, and finally to pairs and individuals. As with the writing plans, students play with presented models and, through use, devise their own structure. I've selected some mapping strategies that can guide students toward interpretation of texts and data.

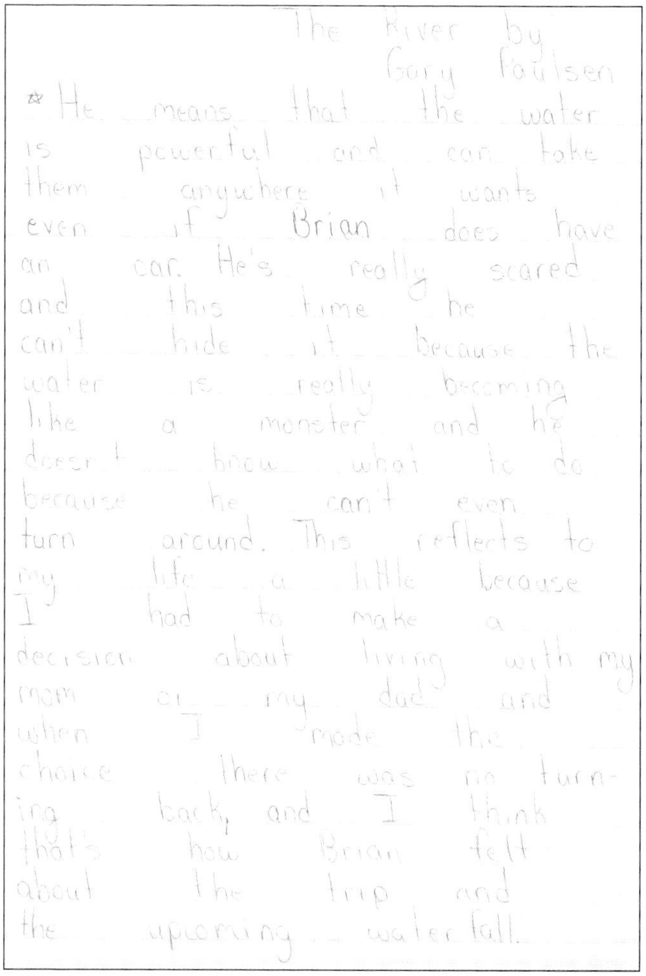

Fig. 3

Venn Diagrams. Traditionally a mathematical map, the Venn diagram graphically illustrates the concepts of set theory's union and intersection. The Venn diagram clearly visualizes similar features that fill the area where the two circles overlap and contrasting features that fill the separate sections. Children can use Venn diagrams to compare and contrast an author's use of setting within the same book or in two different books, variations of fairy and folktales, a character at the beginning and at the end of a story, or the methods different characters employ to solve problems. With nonfiction texts, students might construct a Venn diagram to compare and contrast historical periods, revolutions, wars, societies, governments, or men and women who shaped history. The possibilities for compare/contrast diagrams to organize scientific investigation graphically might include planets, insects, habitats, bodies of water, animal, fish, plants . . . the possibilities are endless.

Lorrie Aikens asked second graders to each plan and complete a Venn diagram as a culminating activity for the group's study of Steven Kellogg's *The Mystery of the Missing Red Mitten* and Jan Brett's *Annie and the Wild Animals* (figure 4).

She posted the diagrams on a wall and a bulletin board for students to read. The dis-

play became a popular gathering place during recess and free-choice reading period. "I got more thinking ideas from reading the others," several students told me. Lorrie had helped the children understand that by reading each other's maps they could learn more.

Since the thinking that goes into a compare/contrast Venn diagram for a theme cycle takes time, many teachers extend the collaboration with students over several weeks. Draw an oversized diagram on construction paper that covers a large portion of a classroom wall. Spend eight to ten minutes each day adding students' contributions. Always ask children to support ideas with facts and inferences from the texts. Enthusiasm for thinking builds as the children daily observe the growth of the Venn diagram.

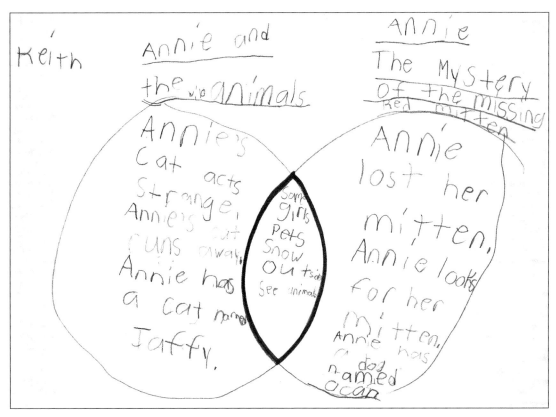

Fig. 4

Data Grids. Corporations, advertising and government agencies, libraries, and businesses all use data grids to present information in an organized fashion. Organizing information on a chart permits viewers to survey, monitor, and analyze data. Older students find the data chart an excellent way to periodically review large amounts of material, forcing them back to their notes, journals, books, and each other as they compile large amounts of information. After collecting information, students, via exhaustive discussions and questioning, can draw conclusions and make inferences, comparisons, and connections.

Data grids are evolutionary charts ideal for collecting and retrieving information throughout a theme cycle. Teacher and students jointly plan the title and headings of the grid; the children work cooperatively to fill in the grid with pictures and words. Primary teachers print the dictated words of children on the grid, but the children can draw and color illustrations on separate paper, placing these in the appropriate box. The headings, over each box of a grid, differ from theme to theme and topic to topic. Studies of authors and illustrators, different versions of fairy and folktales, transportation, the solar system, animals, pets, dinosaurs, family celebrations and holidays, and governments are only a few topics for data grids.

Cover a section of a classroom wall with an extra-large piece of paper. I use electrical tape, colored masking tape, or a thick colored marker pen to outline the ruled squares. Students plan the headings for the chart *after* they have completed some reading and research. This way the headings reflect areas of interest and students' emerging concept of the theme. Feel free to adjust these headings as you and students gain more knowledge. As students study and discuss in pairs, small groups, or independently, they record findings in journals and

decide which information will be published. Older students can write their research on the chart or tape on a separate piece of paper. I encourage teachers of emergent or beginning readers to write data on the chart and invite the children to draw illustrations on separate paper and tape these in the appropriate box. Below is a copy of a seventh-grade group's data grid for three survival books (figure 5).

Students scrutinized the data and drew the following conclusions, which they wrote in journals and shared with classmates:

1. The will to stay alive is unbelievable.

2. Kids can adapt to drastic changes.

3. When a kid is close to death, you realize how great living is.

4. Put to the test of making it changes you forever.

5. What school says is smart might not help if you have to survive in the middle of nowhere.

Cause/Effect Maps. The ability to comprehend cause-and-effect relationships has long been a measure of children's critical thinking ability in basal workbooks, informal reading inventories, and standardized tests. In those formats, children read a cause statement and select the logical effects from a prepared list. Thoroughly frustrated, Gloria Moranski, a second-grade teacher, brought a work sheet from a "whole language teacher guide" for *Nate the Great,* by Marjorie Sharmat. On the left-hand side were cause statements that second graders were to connect to effect statements on the right-hand side. "There are too many, and they can't figure it out. It even confuses me," she sighed. "What can I do?"

Together, we brainstormed ways to hand the thinking and writing over to the children. First they would work together, Gloria writing a cause statement on chart paper and second graders dictating effects, supporting their ideas with the story. Not surprising was the fact that the children shared more than the work sheet offered. Lively discussion and debate peppered the entire process. Kindergartners and first and second graders can draw an effect of a cause statement (figure 6) after rereading, discussing, and dramatizing the story. Jaime, a first grader, draws pictures to interpret her cause statement based on Rosemary Wells's *Hazel's Amazing Mother.*

Once students have demonstrated the ability to think in terms of cause and effect, they can assume responsibility for the entire process. Pairs collaborate, writing cause statements for a story or novel, and then list the effects. They exchange cause statements with others who have read the same book or story. The students own all of the reflective processes and also begin to understand that an effect of one cause can become the cause for other effects. After eighth grader Amy read

	Main Character's Problems	Main Character at End	Forces that Change	Themes

Hatchet	- pilot dies
	- Brian guides plane
	- plane crash
	- survive alone
	  Food, Shelter
	  Mosquitoes, Fire
	- adapt to woods
	- parents divorce
	- alone
		- food obsession
		- grows up fast
		- life more precious
		- accepts divorce
		- hears sounds of nature
		- can read nature to tell rain, etc.
			- hatchet
			- flint rock
			- will to live
			- primitive surroundings
				- man tested
				- boy to man
				- survival skills not part of our world
				- will to live
				- eats & does things never would do at home

The River	- Brian returns without supplies - Derek comes - raft - river - is map accurate? - food - no radio - mother worries - Derek's coma - Survive alone & make it with D. alive	- can't plan a survival trip - can't duplicate survival - chance - understands adult's worries - survival not a game	- Derek's coma - storm - will to keep both alive - need to adapt for both - responsible feelings for Derek	- responsiblity beyond self - survival isn't a game - love of nature
Walkabout	- plane crash - food, water - adapt to bush - hold onto memories of South Carolina - leave crash site - Bush Boy's illness - Mary's fears - communicating with Bush Boy	- Mary still close to life in South Car. - Peter adapts & forgets other life - both learn how to survive: water, food, fire - grow up quickly - Bush Boy's death makes them know extremes at young age	- Bush Boy - outback - will to return (Mary) - trusting Bush Boy - letting go of past values - adapt. need to - will to live	- grow up quickly - irony of Bush Boy dying - Mary & Peter live - ways to communicate without a common language - will to live - you do things you'd never do here.

Fig. 5

her list of the results (effects) of Jerry's decision to disturb the universe in Robert Cormier's *The Chocolate War* (figure 7) she looked up at me and her classmates and said, "Lots of these can be causes, like brother Leon hated him. [Pause] I could do this for lots on my list." Such insight can occur when students are in charge of their thinking.

Story Maps. The "agonists" map can assist middle school students' understanding of conflict and antagonistic forces in short stories and novels (figure 8). First I ask small groups of students to establish story-specific conflict categories, such as nature, parents, friends, adults, inner drives, thoughts, feelings, fears,

and goals. Then together, on chart paper, we complete the map and identify protagonist and problem, climax and outcome, and identify antagonistic forces and conflicts. Students record the map in their journals and work in groups to find at least one example from the text to support each category.

Group members share findings with each other and the entire class. "What I like best," Susan tells everyone as we talk about the process, "is I can add ideas to my map. You know, I used to feel so bad that I don't think of every angle. Now I see I'm not the only one. Making the categories is the part that really helps me. Sometimes it's the category that makes me think of another idea."

Fig. 6

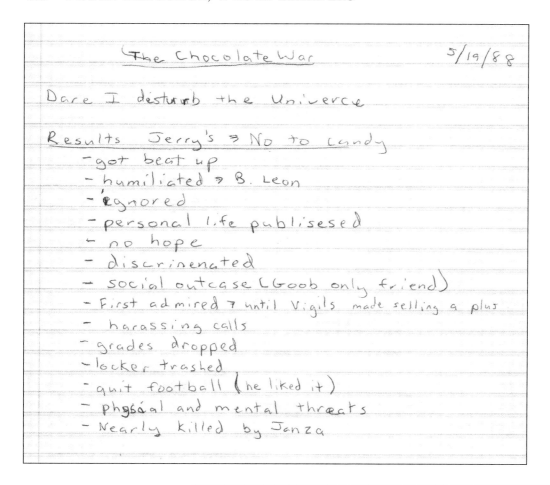

The Chocolate War   5/19/88

Dare I desturb the Univerce

Results Jerry's ⊃ No to candy
   -got beat up
   - humiliated ⊃ B. Leon
   - ignored
   - personal life publisesed
   - no hope
   - discrinenated
   - social outcase (Goob only friend)
   - First admired ⊃ until Vigils made selling a plus
   - harassing calls
   - grades dropped
   - locker trashed
   - quit football (he liked it)
   - physical and mental threats
   - Nearly killed by Janza

Fig. 7 An eighth grader's cause-and-effect list for Robert Cormier's The Chocolate War.

Fig. 8 At right.

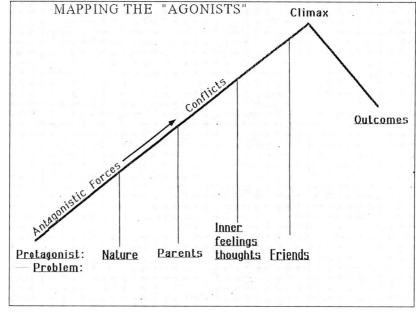

MAPPING THE "AGONISTS"

Climax

Conflicts

Antagonistic Forces

Outcomes

Protagonist: Nature   Parents   Inner feelings thoughts   Friends
  Problem:

Students eventually take ownership of the entire process, gaining insights into the conflicts, formulating and supporting interpretations.

Younger children can draw story maps in journals by dividing a page into four sections. In the boxes, children can identify and illustrate structural elements, such as setting, character, problem, or outcome; changes in the character; events they're connected to; or information from nonfiction books. Model the process many times and organize collaborative mapping experiences. Then turn the process over to the children, asking them to decide what to map and how much space they'll require. Resist preorganized materials, which limit creativity and problem solving and never enable you to see how children use an empty piece of paper.

Always reserve time for children to discuss their maps, for their explanations of choices often enable them to make amazing connections. Third grader Emily, explaining her *Mike Fink* map, points to her second picture and informs the class, "Mike Fink went from land to sea, and that's when he really became important and made the steamboats important. It wouldn't happen if he hadn't seen that river." As children think aloud, they can begin to reflect on, and interpret, texts.

Collaborative and individual maps can serve as outlines for translating thinking into critical paragraphs and essays. The central idea becomes the thesis sentence or introduction. Selected categories outline the points to prove; mustering additional support from the text enlarges and develops the ideas, making for a valid interpretation. Not all maps have to result in formal paragraphs or essays. There will be times when you'll offer students a choice in selecting an essay topic; other times, you might require they choose a topic that relates to a particular genre or theme.

My writing outlines, and those of middle school students, are messy; the structure differs with each topic. With maps, students review data, select and sort relevant from irrelevant information, and break the whole into related parts for the purposes of writing to support a position. Mapping achieves the purposes of creating a writing plan without locking authors into rigid forms.

And it's in the writing, whether collaborative or independent, that students think and discover meaning as they clarify and validate interpretations. Lloyd Alexander, in his essay "Travel Notes," clearly explains the elements of surprise and thinking that authors experience as they write to liberate ideas:

But we also need to understand that we know many things, more than we suppose. Our work lies in discovering what they are, in discovering what matters to us.[6]

The writing occurs only after students have truly lived their way into the text, engaging in many discussions, projects, and journal entries. At this juncture, the children work in twos and threes and review journal notes and responses, maps, folders, charts, and class and individual projects, searching for essay ideas. If students are tentative about finding issues for critical analysis, offer several suggestions so they have a choice.

Teacher modeling and think-alouds, student observation, and collaborative practice can open the doors of literary analysis. Over the years, I've compiled a file of students' paragraphs and essays. Groups read writing by students who no longer attend our school; they discuss content, organization, leads, and conclusions. Students move through seven stages:

1. Read journal entries, discussion notes, and collaborative charts.

2. Pairs or small groups share journal highlights and confer.

3. Pairs or small groups develop several theses or positions and test against the text.

4. Individuals decide on a position they'd like to pursue in a paragraph or essay.

5. Each student prepares a map or list of notes to support this position.

6. Compose a first draft; identify position in a lead sentence or brief introduction; write a conclusion.

7. Revise, draft, conference, and edit, following the process modeled in writing workshop.

Younger children are also able to formulate interpretations of stories, which teachers can record in a class book. Using the writing process, the teacher offers the children opportunities to rethink and revise interpretations. Nancy Hall's second graders composed what several children proudly named "a thinking book," based on Patricia MacLachlan's *Through Grandpa's Eyes*. The statements below, from their final draft, interpret why John turned the lights off after Grandpa, who is blind, left John's bedroom.

• He didn't want to make Grandpa feel bad.

• He loved his grandpa and didn't want to hurt him.

• John didn't want his grandpa to think about being blind.

• John didn't want him to think back to when he was three and could see.

Nancy Hall has begun to show her second graders how reading, reflecting, talking, and writing are guides to interpreting stories; through the process, she celebrates her students' critical thinking powers.

Once middle school students have observed, practiced, and used the seven-step procedure many times, they begin to adapt it to their own needs. The essays that follow reveal the interpretive thinking of middle school students, whose talk and journal notes assisted them in writing critical analyses of texts.

Eighth grader Alison uses her Venn diagram (figure 9) and journal notes to compare and contrast the personality of Josh and his dad from Irene Hunt's *No Promises in the Wind*.

She opens her essay with "I think Josh and his father have their differences and similarities even though they sometimes don't want to admit they have anything in common," and then proceeds to support her interpretation. The paragraph below is an outgrowth of the notes in Alison's Venn diagram.

Both Josh and his dad blamed everything that went wrong on their fathers. Josh blamed his problems on his dad, and in the past, Mr. Grandowski had also blamed everything on his father. Another major problem in their relationship was their inability to openly express feelings. I think if they had been able to do this, they would have been closer, and they could have discussed and solved some of their problems and differences. But instead, they kept everything bottled up inside.

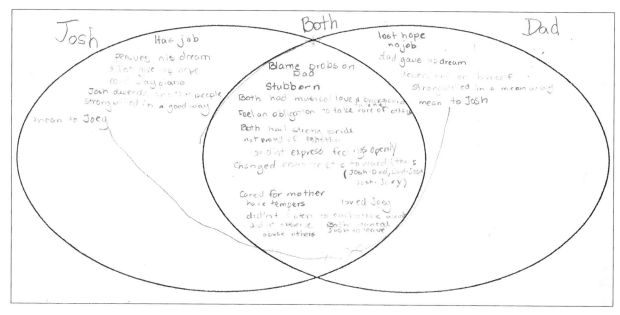

Fig. 9

Alison carefully offers inferences and facts from the novel to support her thinking. I reserved time for Alison and her classmates to confer with each other and move through the writing process stages. "I couldn't do this [write critical essays] without my journal notes," Alison wrote in one of her self-evaluations.

The fifth-grade essay that follows evolved from the independent rereading of discussion summaries and reflective entries for a study of the Trojan War based on Olivia Coolidge's retelling. Groups then conferred to identify possible theses for topics. Matthew, who struggled with the technical aspects of writing, was able to think on paper and prove his opinion of Agamemnon's leadership abilities (figure 10). Matthew's essay is an example of building on a student's strengths, in this case his thinking ability.

Readers' reflections on texts can lead to confirmation of their initial transactions. When Jean Craighead George visited my sixth-grade class on the heels of a survival theme cycle, several students had just completed essays on issues in *Julie of the Wolves*. Julie buries her beloved falcon, Tornait, and sings to the spirit of the murdered Amaroq, her wolf brother. The final words of the book are "Julie pointed her boots toward Kapugen." Sierra and Caroline asked Ms. George how she interpreted the final sentence. "Julie returns to Kapugen," came the immediate reply. "That's what the pointing of the boots means to Eskimos." But Sierra had argued, from the moment she completed the novel and in her essay, that the pointing of the boots was symbolic, meant only to give honor to the changed Kapugen. The girls' concluding paragraphs illustrate divergent yet equally valid interpretations of the same text.

SIERRA: Julie's main influence, to live in the wild, was seeing her father turn American. This made her more determined to keep the Eskimo ways alive. It also showed her what things were really important. In a way, the end of her journey was the beginning of her life.

CAROLINE: At the end of the book it says, "The totem of Amaroq was in her pocket. Her fingers ran across it, but she did not take it out." And then it says, "She slowly sang the song of Amaroq in her best English." I think both of these points mean that now it was time to return to her father.

Evidence could be mustered to support both points of view, and Ms. George's comments did not shake either student's position. Students whose conclusion affirmed the author's interpretation did not, as I feared, chide others. Trina's remark "I think we helped her [Jean Craighead George] see other points of view" illustrated the students' confidence in their reflective processes and the level of excitement that opposing conclusions generated.

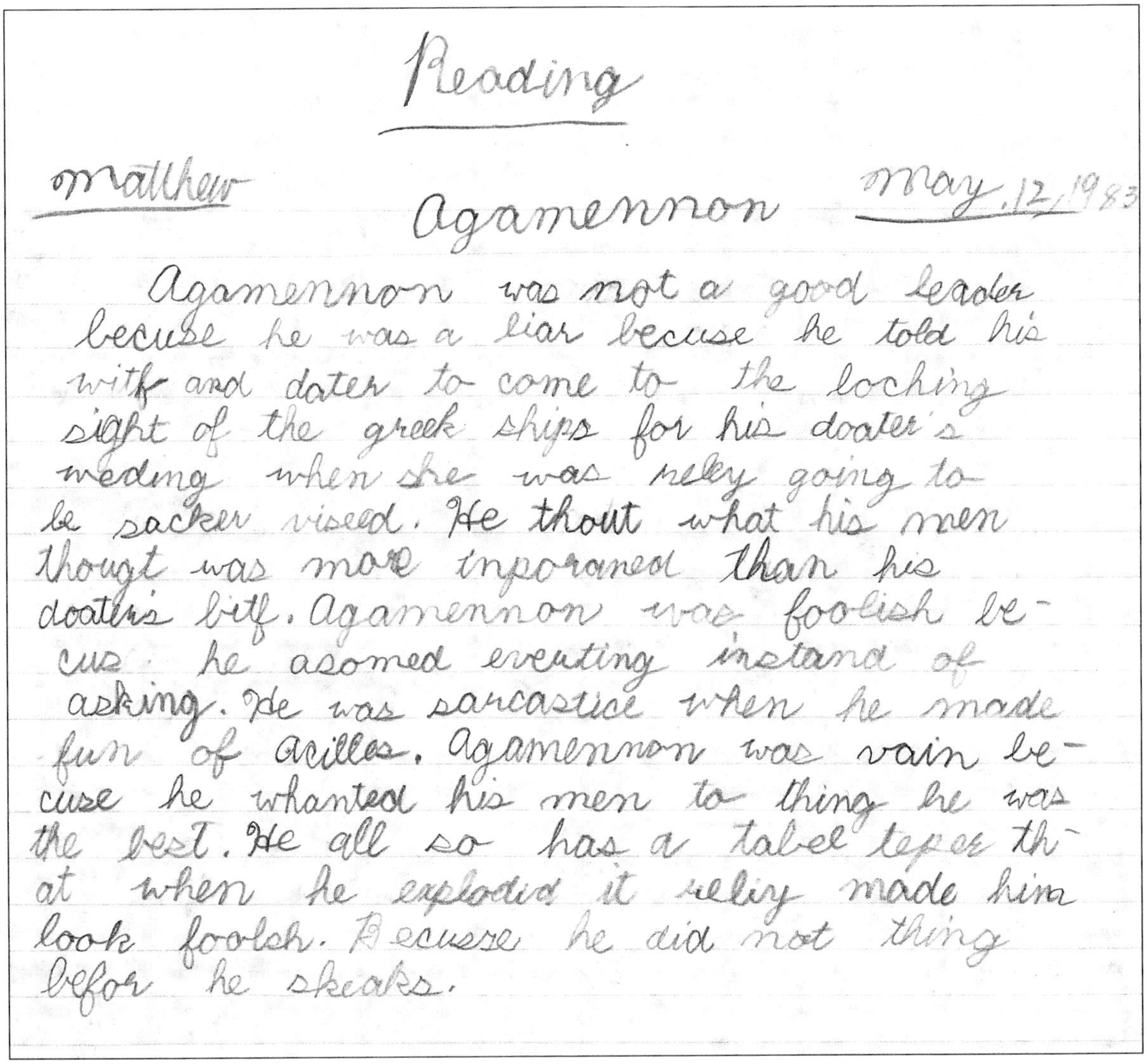

Reading

matthew   _Agamennon_   May 12, 1983

Agamennon was not a good leader becuse he was a liar becuse he told his witf and dater to come to the loching sight of the greek ships for his doater's meding when she was relly going to be sacker viseed. He thout what his men thougt was more inporaned than his doater's bitf. Agamennon was foolish becus he asomed eventing instand of asking. He was sarcastice when he made fun of Acilles. Agamennon was vain becuse he whanted his men to thing he was the best. He all so has a tabel teper that when he explodid it relly made him look foolsh. Becuse he did not thing befor he skeaks.

Fig. 10

Students' interpretations always jog my views of a story, and every year many introduce me to new ways of experiencing a text. One year Forrest, an eighth grader, chose for his final project to write an essay proving that Harper Lee's novel *To Kill a Mockingbird* contained many characters who themselves were mockingbirds. Like Tom Robinson, there were other innocent victims who had done nothing to earn the pain and suffering that came their way. Forrest, in his essay, extended the meaning of "mockingbird" beyond that of an innocent victim, to people who managed to turn their pain and silent suffering into an unwavering example of their beliefs. The last paragraph of Forrest's essay also bridges Atticus to mockingbirds on another level:

The final and most important mockingbird in the entire story was Atticus Finch. Atticus Finch was a small-town lawyer, nothing big, nothing small. Atticus never followed another's thoughts or instincts. He followed his own thoughts. This was well shown during the Robinson case, and during the times leading up to the case. The entire time before the case, he had received threats, vile names thrown at him, and other such absurdities. I say the word "absurdities" because it shows just how stupid all of the trial was. Atticus never let Tom down because he was never being influenced by the words and never dropped the case, no matter what odds were against him. This shows how much of a mockingbird Atticus Finch is, and will always be. And also, if you look close enough into Atticus Finch's name, you just might see a bird closely related to the mockingbird: the finch. Indeed, the mockingbird is gray, drab, and perhaps dismal; but, it is far from unbeautiful.

Literature response journals are the sole domain of the student—a place to explore, rethink, and revise literary and personal reflections. The dialogue journal, developed by Nancie Atwell (*In the Middle: Writing, Reading and Learning with Adolescents*), is correspondence about books between teacher and individual students. It allows the pair to think, question, and explore texts and, through their letters, learn about each other as reader, writer, and thinker.

The correspondence begins with a letter of invitation, written by the teacher to each student (see appendix). I like to begin dialoguing after the first eight weeks of school. During those opening weeks, I work to discover students' interests, reading habits, and attitudes and introduce them to reading response groups and journals. I view this as a warm-up period for me and students and a time when I can draw the children to reading.

Students read and write at school and can take their journals home. By Monday of each week, I expect students to place journals on a bookshelf labeled *For Mrs. Robb*. Journals arrive throughout the week, and this staggering allows me time to respond. Students retrieve their journals from a plastic crate.

Dialogue journal letters are personal. They're conversational and relaxed, so students and I feel free to write our feelings about a book and comment on each other's entries. My job is to relate to each child with empathy as I nurture growth and encourage a real reading life through free choice. The letters offer me opportunities to suggest books that students might enjoy. But I must always remember that the student is under no obligation to follow my suggestions, nor do I require a specific number of books to be read.

Four types of comments are always part of my letters:

Honor the content of the student's letter. Confirm good thinking and verify that you've read the letter with care by referring to specific ideas.

React to the book on a personal level; honestly relate your feelings about the story. I find that students prefer when I frankly state my opinions, disagree, and chat about my reading tastes. I want them to know that it's desirable and natural to have differences.

Stretch each student through your correspondence. Ask for clarification of a point or issue, ask a question about an omitted issue, ask for support. However, don't pelt students with questions or they'll feel as if they're being tested.

Suggest, ever so gently, other ways to respond to a book, possible titles the student might wish to read, or a literary technique to try in writing workshop.

This writing back and forth gives me the chance to model ways to think about books. Through letters, I connect genre, reading and writing minilessons, response group discussions, and paired and whole class discussions. In the back of their journals, students can jot down ways to talk about books based on teacher demonstrations and class discussions, accumulating their own reference guides for book chatting. With classes new to dialoguing, I compile a chart paper list entitled "Ways to Talk about Books." The list grows throughout the year and is a valued student resource.

Since grades are a reality, I devised a system that satisfies school policy but does not squelch students' growth. After the last entry has been completed, the students evaluate their own progress, studying the entire journal. The key here is reviewing the journal from beginning to end. Through conferences, students become more aware of their strengths and how to build on them. Together, we establish a grade, which I must give, but which I defer until the end of each marking period. Not only do grades get in the way of learning, students also become less sincere and honest in their responses, playing the game of "Let's find out what the teacher wants—and do it"—a game that does not foster risk taking and individual growth.

Students grow as thinkers, and they broaden their literary tastes and their knowledge of how books work. Cherie, a seventh grader, fell in love with James Giblin's books after reading *The Riddle of the Rosetta Stone: Key to Ancient Egypt*. An Egyptologist at heart, who devoured every book in the school library on that period, Cherie wrote, "I think I'll read all of James Giblin." And she did. After completing *The Truth about Unicorns*, Cherie made the type of connection that can result from reading within a genre:

I noticed that James Giblin uses a certain method of writing. First, his titles really attract me, like *The Truth about Santa Claus*. Every title makes me curious to read the book. Books always open with a story or a quote that makes the book exciting. Giblin puts lots of stories and conversations in his books that he got from research. I'm beginning to see how much research a writer needs to do.

My response begins:

Wow! What terrific connections you've made based on your reading. I've heard James Giblin speak about his process, and he talks about the very things you've observed.

Teachers can make dialoguing so risk-free that students begin to ask for help with their reading process through their letters. Sara, a sixth grader, wrote in her first letter on *The Sign of the Beaver*:

I don't understand what these words mean: blunderbuss, puncheon, oiled paper, and yourn.

At a conference, Sara and I returned to the story to attempt to determine the word meanings from rereading sections and from story clues. We referred to the dictionary to refine meanings of *blunderbuss* and *puncheon*. Sara then decided that while she read, she would highlight words she didn't understand and reread sections. And she discovered:

I can figure out so many words just from the story.

And I respond:

You are really improving at getting the meanings from story clues. I appreciate the way you set up the words by writing the page and paragraph. That helps me find each one. I also noticed that you are using some of these words in your discussions. That's really exciting!

Sara came to sixth grade from a basal reading program; reading real books had been a home activity or for a written book report. When Sara completed the first two parts of *Julie of the Wolves*, she wrote:

It's kind of hard to pridict whats going to happen next because I'm starting another

A sixth grader writes in her dialogue journal.

part of the book. I don't understand why the author didn't put part 2 before part 1 because how it is written it's like I'm reading the book from end to begining.

Yipes! I thought. How terrific that Sara noticed the literary technique of flashback. I took this "teachable" moment to explain the technique in my reply and suggested that Sara might wish to play with flashback in one of her own stories. Sara can start where she is and progress because dialoguing individualizes reading, writing, and thinking.

In her letters, Sara chatted about characters she liked and disliked. She praised Julie for "being an independent and tough female who loved animals and the ways of her people" and railed at Kapugen because "he hurt Julie so when he left the old ways and killed the wolves." She fell in love with Pam Conrad's books and read them all. Sara's January 13 entry marked a significant change in her view of herself as a reader: She changed her closing from "Sincerely" to "Your Reader."

Because of the time involved, dialoguing is demanding for teachers. Even using reading workshop time to read journals and respond to students, I frequently feel overwhelmed, especially when corresponding with two or three English classes. My first solution was to stagger dialogue journals and concentrate on one group each trimester. But another idea leaped to mind, an idea that turned more responsibility over to students: partner journals, where students correspond about books with peers or with an adult at home.

Although my intention for partner journals, whether with peers or with an adult, was to correspond about literature, personal entries crept into most of the journals. Some students marked an entry "Personal," and I never squelched their innovation.

This was a project that I initiated in January, after students had experienced dialogue and response journals. Chance determined a peer buddy, and partners changed once or twice during a twelve-week period. The kids developed the idea of "secret partners." Once names had been drawn, no student discovered who his or her partner was until letters of invitation had been written and delivered.

Choice is an important element of partner journals. Pairs select their own books to share, or choose from several books that I introduce through short book talks. Buddies design the journal cover, using construction paper for front and back and filling the inside with lined or unlined paper. Peer partners write letters and hand deliver them or place them in the class mailbox.

Managing time became one of the first issues we discussed. The class established a weekly due date, and students quickly learned that to meet the negotiated deadline, communication was crucial, especially if a pair had to share one book.

I offered no direction to partners in order to observe what they chose to include in letters. Each week we invested thirty to fifty minutes to exchange entries for this ungraded project. Students never read personal sections, only the book talk. The share sessions alternated between small group and whole class.

In their letters, students began to ask each other questions. The level of thinking in the exchanges between Abigail and Carla, who were reading *The Wonderful Story of Henry Sugar and Six More,* by Roald Dahl, matures as the pair corresponds. Carla, by example, leads Abigail into more thoughtful responses. Nowhere do the girls judge each other's letters.

Oct. 10, 1988

Dear Abigail,
I thought the story ["The Boy Who Talked to the Animals"] was strange. It was strange because the boy could communicate with the turtle. Also it was boring in the beginning but fun in the end. I think the turtle had taken the boy to a secret paradise to thank the boy for saving him. The turtle felt he had a friend he needed to keep! I thought it was unusual because a huge, enormous animal and a small boy would have a bond together.
　　　　　Carla

Oct. 12, 1988

Dear Carla,
I thought it was strange because he didn't like his parents enough to come back.
　　　　　Abigail

Oct. 17, 1988

Dear Abigail,
I thought the boy went with the turtle because he thought the man would probably catch it again and that he did not like it in the human world. I feel like that

every day, and I plan things to make them [parents] feel bad but I never do them.

Carla

The pair continue their correspondence, and Abigail ends a personal note about their history test with "Sorry I don't write much! I'll write more." Carla never addresses the issue of amount, but continues to write until she's had her say. By December Abigail's letters have more thoughtful content. "The Swan" has touched Carla, and really upset Abigail, who pours out intense feelings.

Dec. 12, 1988

Dear Carla,

I felt sympathy for Peter because he was trapped in a one way situation, I did not think that they [Ernie and Raymond] would go as far as to shoot him but they did! I think Ernie was a mean person & he got it from his father! I think he belonged in jail, shooting someone, gosh there is nothing worse. I thought that at the End he should have gone to jail! Or paid a fine also, his father should go with him because he gave him a gun without a license.

Abigail

Abigail, Carla, and I discussed their correspondence, which continued until winter holiday. Abigail said, "I felt better about what I was writing every time I read Carla's and listened to what others wrote. At first I didn't think my thoughts were good enough to put down."

A variation of peer partner journals is corresponding about literature with an adult at home. This project had two benefits. First, it opened lines of communication between chil-dren and adults. Second, it introduced parents to children's literature and allowed them a glimpse into their children's reading and thinking lives. The kids reveled in asking an adult to do work and in selecting the book to be shared. However, before journals went home with the students, we discussed these issues and set the following guidelines:

- Journal partners decorate their cover together.

- Students initiated a "getting ready to read" discussion and explained the purpose of this activity.

- Students were responsible for negotiating reading and writing times to successfully meet the weekly deadline.

- Reading could be completed separately; one partner could read aloud to the other or both could take turns reading aloud.

- The focus of the letters was content, not mechanics.

- Each week, there would be class time to share journals. Reading a journal was optional, and a student could read both entries or one entry.

Fortunately, no child has ever been without a home partner. Opening the choices to include any adult meant that a brother or sister, a baby-sitter, a grandparent, aunt or uncle, tutor, or close neighbor could accept the invitation. However, each year, should the need arise, I was fully prepared to be a partner.

When a third-grade class buddied with an adult at home, the children and adults asked for guidance. "My grandma doesn't know what to write" or "My baby-sitter isn't sure what she should say in her letter" were typical comments that prompted students and me to compile a list of ways to respond. We included these suggestions in a collaborative letter, which I typed and the students delivered (see appendix).

Parents and students wrote letters about books, stories, poems; personal comments about friendships, a bad day, and a low test grade also entered the correspondence. Some parents expressed concerns over their writing conventions. A third grader reported that her dad worried "because he can't spell very well. So I told him that was okay because in first drafts the content was the most important thing."

One eighth-grade parent rebelled at the thought of not having "perfect writing." His teary child brought me the journal, marred with circled words, instructions for rewriting sections, paragraphing, and so on. He summed up the errors in one sentence: "GRAMMAR, SPELLING, MISSING TITLE OR 'DEAR DAD'!" Devastated, the youngster refused to correspond with him. The father, a single parent, told me in one of many conferences that he was "trying to get this child educated for the real world." Reluctantly, he agreed to focus on the content. But his child would write only short, safe letters and refrained from taking risks during the project.

Sometimes the correspondence gained so much momentum that it turned into a written conversation. Third grader Joseph buddies with his dad, Barry, about *The Castle in the Attic*, by Elizabeth Winthrop. The pair really get into their discussion, and letters become an unsigned dialogue, driven by the force of ideas and pleasure in communicating them:

Sir Simon surely is a fascinating fellow with a very interesting story to explain his size. He also speaks in a very polite manner.

I find it a bit upsetting that William continues to lie so often.

I had thought of the end of chapter Number 5. Do you worry about the gray cat next door?

Barry

I think that the gray cat is going to try to eat Sir Simon. But Sir Simon might make the cat small so he could stick him. What do you think will happen to the cat?

Joseph

I am afraid that the cat may confront Sir Simon. I hope that neither gets hurt. I don't like violence.

[Barry]

But if you were in front of the Lion wood you kill him or wood you yell at him.

[Joseph]

I would do whatever was necessary to survive. However, Sir Simon can talk and the cat is a house pet.

[Barry]

But the cat eats mise and smal animals. Why shood he eat Sir Simon.

[Joseph]

I accept all your thoughts as fair, reasonable, and accurate assessments. However, I always hope for peaceful solutions to conflict because I am not a wild animal.

[Barry]

I agree that I want a peaceful solution.

[Joseph]

Stories connected home and school, and all the kids rated the extra time spent with an adult as the best part of partner journals. Luncheons that celebrated the writers became a desirable component because of the camaraderie of eating and chatting together; several pairs were bold enough to share entries.

Chatting and eating always concluded with a discussion of the partner journaling process. At one sixth-grade luncheon, most adults agreed that writing ideas on paper was difficult. "I began to view my son's writing differently," one mother said. "When I had trouble writing my ideas, I told myself, back off, and don't expect perfection from your kid." Another said, "Instead of fighting, we worked together. My daughter learned things about me that I might never have told her."

The majority of parents agreed that the most difficult task, at first, was to reserve unrushed time to complete the reading and letters. "I was angry with you [the teacher]," one told the group. "Because now I was getting homework again and losing my time. But now I'd say the time I spent with Reba was worth it."

In democratic learning communities, teachers honor, value, and encourage the diversity of children's visions and thinking. The task of teachers is to support and guide children as they construct meaning, absorb new information, and use story as a framework for reflection. Talk, drama, and writing can pave the way for illuminations and valid interpretations.

References

1. Rosenblatt, Louise M. *The Reader, the Text, the Poem*, page 134.

2. Lee, Harper. *To Kill a Mockingbird*. New York: Warner Books, 1982, page 34.

3. Little, Jean. *Hey World, Here I Am!* New York: Harper & Row, 1989, pages 73–74.

4. Paulsen, Gary. *The River*. New York: Dell, 1991, page 38.

5. Rosenblatt, Louise M. *Literature as Exploration*, page 201.

6. Alexander, Lloyd. "Travel Notes." *Innocence & Experience: Essays and Conversations on Children's Literature*, ed. Barbara Harrison. New York: Lothrop, Lee & Shepard, 1987, page 62.

AS I SEE IT

Jerry Pinkney with Gloria Jean Pinkney

Movement, mime, props, and research all contribute to the personal vision of stories I illustrate. Photographs of models, dressed in costumes, miming scenes, have always guided me into the secrets within stories, surprising me with meaning, connecting words and mental images, shaping the pictures in my mind.

My first models were my wife, Gloria Jean, myself, and our children, dressed in costumes; Polaroid photographs recorded story scenes. And these photos, combined with diligent research about a place, an era, are my treasure, treasure I sift through to develop my conception of a character. Today, with the assistance of Gloria Jean, I search for models who resemble, as closely as possible, the characters to be portrayed. To bring the models into the heart and soul of the story, we ask them to read and dramatize the text. Working with children has been a challenging experience. It's difficult to pose children in front of the camera, but if they feel a connection between the story, the character, and their drama, they enter the text more deeply and convincingly.

Polaroid photographs capture the models' body language and facial expressions. I paint from photographs that are rich in movement, for movement develops a stronger relationship between the story and the illustrations. As a result, paintings are more active and connected to the story's rhythms and motion.

For *Pretend You're a Cat*, we enlisted children from our granddaughter's day school, "Children's Space." I spent a day with the group, showing them the dummy book and encouraging them to respond freely to it. The children acted out the movements of the creatures in the text. At first, they responded only by imitating movements suggested in the dummy book. After repeated dramatizations, they began to interpret the poems in unique ways. The evolution of experiencing the poems was exciting to observe, and I learned how the constant interplay between Jean Marzollo's words and the children impacted on their interpretative process. When I returned to the day school to share the finished artwork, excitement ran high as the children saw themselves in the art.

In *Back Home*, written by Gloria Jean, Gloria found the perfect model for the main character, Ernestine. We then had to outfit her with clothing appropriate to the time period in the text. We rummaged through racks and cartons in secondhand clothing stores to uncover suitable outfits. The models Gloria Jean chose for Jack, Aunt Beula, and Uncle June were all from North Carolina. Their family stories provided information about the South and farm life that enriched my mental images of Gloria's childhood home and family.

Whether a story is about animals or people, research is crucial. My large reference file, which I constantly update, overflows with pictures and articles about animals, places, and people, and unusual items, such as photographs of different kinds of fire hydrants. Surrounding the tall black metal file cabinet are library shelves with over four hundred titles about American history, nature, animals, and other countries, and books about unusual topics, such as the history of ice-cream trucks or clocks. Each new book presents a research challenge, and I must use my resources as well as museums and libraries so I can *accurately* illustrate the text. Accuracy means that readers will gain a true vision of the story.

The first step to envisioning a creature is for me to pretend to be that particular animal. I think about the size and the sound it makes, how it moves (slowly or quickly), where it lives. I try to capture the essence of the creature, as well as its true-to-life characteristics. There are times when stories call for the animals to be anthropomorphic, and I pose, dressed as the animal, while Gloria photographs me. That's how the animal characters in the *Uncle Remus* tales evolved.

Each book presents challenges that I must solve in order to combine authenticity and creativity. To find the right model for the farmhouse in *Back Home,* we searched through books about barns and old houses until we came upon a section in North Carolina. Then Gloria spotted the picture of a house that matched her warm memories. Next we had to find pictures of fields and trees that resembled the family farm and conceive of the various stagings for Ernestine and her family.

Photographs based on *my conception* of the story are only one of the building blocks in my interpretive foundation. All of these elements—research, staging, discussing, reading, and rereading—blend together as I succumb to images and personal visions that I invent in my imagination and translate into paintings for stories.

SELECTED BOOKS ILLUSTRATED
BY JERRY PINKNEY

Aardema, Verna. *Rabbit Makes a Monkey of Lion: A Swahili Tale.* New York: Dial, 1989.
Carlstrom, Nancy White. *Wild Wild Sunflower Child Anna.* New York: Macmillan, 1987.
Dragonwagon, Crescent. *Half a Moon and One Whole Star.* New York: Macmillan, 1986.
———. *Home Place.* New York: Macmillan, 1990.
Eisler, Colin. *David's Songs: His Psalms and Their Story.* New York: Dial, 1992.
Flournoy, Valerie. *The Patchwork Quilt.* New York: Dial, 1985.
Hamilton, Virginia. *Drylongso.* San Diego: Harcourt Brace, 1992.

Hurwitz, Johanna. *New Shoes for Silvia*. New York: Morrow, 1993.

Lester, Julius. *Further Tales of Uncle Remus*. New York: Dial, 1990.

———. *More Tales of Uncle Remus*. New York: Dial, 1988.

———. *The Tales of Uncle Remus*. New York: Dial, 1987.

Levitin, Sonia. *The Man Who Kept His Heart in a Bucket*. New York: Dial, 1991.

Martel, Cruz. *Yagua Days*. New York: Dial, 1976.

Marzollo, Jean. *Pretend You're a Cat*. New York: Dial, 1990.

McKissack, Patricia. *Mirandy and Brother Wind*. New York: Knopf, 1988.

Moss, Thylias. *I Want to Be*. New York: Dial, 1993.

Pinkney, Gloria Jean. *Back Home*. New York: Dial, 1992.

———. *Sunday Outing*. New York: Dial, 1994.

San Souci, Robert. *The Talking Eggs*. New York: Dial, 1989.

Singer, Marilyn. *Turtle in July*. New York: Macmillan, 1989.

Taylor, Mildred. *Song of the Trees*. New York: Dial, 1975.

Willard, Nancy. *A Starlit Somersault Downhill*. Boston: Little, Brown, 1993.

Yellow Robe, Rosebud. *Tonweya and the Eagles and Other Lakota Indian Tales*. New York: Dial, 1979.

READING TO WRITE

All texts, written and oral, can inform writers. Young adult author Richard Peck frequently spends several early weekday mornings in a New York coffee shop, watching and listening to the conversations of students who congregate there before school. Their interactions, their dress, and the rhythms and content of their conversations tune Peck in to the ways young adults communicate, the language they use, and the topics they discuss. Peck incorporates his research on young adult oral texts in his novels.

Patricia MacLachlan, author of *Sarah, Plain and Tall,* in a speech at a children's literature workshop at Shenandoah College, confessed that when she decided to write books for children, she read over one hundred titles to discover what published authors did. When children read, listen, and observe their world, they can sharpen and heighten their imagination and grow as communicators.

Classrooms, then, should celebrate the joy of thinking about everyday happenings, everyday living, and encourage children to imagine these in unfamiliar and unaccustomed ways. In such learning communities, teachers and children will delight in the natural curiosity that taught us all so well before we entered school. Together they will inquire, listen, watch, and explore surroundings and interests, stockpiling meaningful experiences and sparking their imaginations.

For the imagination to thrive, for children to understand how reading, listening, and observing can inform their writing, five conditions must be present in classrooms:

Opportunity. Make available a rich supply of books for children to read and reread. Reserve time to listen, watch, create mental images, and practice using language to translate inner visions. For students to link their reading to writing and to gain insight into a genre's structure, encourage them to immerse themselves in texts by many authors. Your demonstrations and students' discussions should focus on the diverse ways authors treat a genre and the literary techniques they include.

Second graders read together during choice time.

Involvement. Offer choice, combined with time—time to explore and browse through many titles, time to settle into a book and read at a comfortable pace, and time to fantasize and play with a story. Build in sustained silent reading periods long enough to get into a book.

Discussion. Engage in playful composing by talking about stories, experiences, problems, and observations so readers can hear their own thoughts and emotions and observe how others react to them.

Clarification. Present minilessons to clarify writing technique and genre structures and encourage students to experiment with literary techniques in their writing. Works by published authors and students form the backbone of these minilessons.

Collaborative Writing. Generate questions about story structures and process through collaborative writing. Students can scrutinize messy first drafts, noting that revision necessitates crossing out words and phrases or rewriting sections. They can listen to each other's suggestions on how to write a lead, phrase a sentence, shape a poem, or solve a character's problem. The mysteries of drafting and revising can be solved through class collaborations.

Hang collaborative writing around the room to celebrate class efforts and to provide resources for students to review and study. Or copy the collaborative piece onto a ditto and run copies off for students to keep in their writing folders.

Tune students in to the sounds and rhythms of language through listening and reading, helping students to, like Beowulf, *see* where others merely look. In addition to reading and discussing literature, children will practice transforming their eyes into a camera, noting details and reflecting on what they might mean. School, home, and community surroundings, as well as family photographs, can all become seeing experiences. Listening experiences should encompass the dialogue of others along with exploring the sounds in our world. These experiences are what I call writing warm-ups because they sharpen our senses and intensify perception. They can focus children's attention to lunch remains on a desk or floor, a particular area at school, a small section of a paved walkway, a tree, insects, a rotting log, the kitchen sink—the possibilities are endless. Students work silently, noting in great detail what they have seen and heard.

The teacher's task is to demonstrate how these warm-ups connect to the children's reading and writing. Through minilessons, teachers show how authors' heightened and well-developed ability to see and hear affects their writing.

When teachers incorporate portions of books and poems in reading-writing demonstrations, they must also bring to light for the children how the text reveals the writer's use of specific details to paint character, set a

A sixth grader works intensely on her story during a reading-writing workshop.

scene, and achieve authenticity of dialogue and language. In such classrooms, reading truly informs writing as children practice specific techniques in writing exercises or create innovations on authors' texts.

The writing of collaborative innovations on patterned and predictable books can extend young children's knowledge of the rhythms, repetitions, and rhymes in these books and act as springboards for creative writing. Once children, through repeated readings, understand the pattern of such books as Eric Carle's *The Very Busy Spider* and *The Very Hungry Caterpillar,* Shigeo Watanabe's *What a Good Lunch!,* Ezra Jack Keats's *Over in the Meadow,* and Bill Martin, Jr.'s, *Brown Bear, Brown Bear, What Do You See?,* you can introduce writing innovations.

Second-grade teacher Dick Koblitz, who teaches at the Dorris School in Colinsville,

Illinois, says, "Collaborative innovations on texts mean I can model the writing process. The first drafts I record are messy, and we often pull out a word like *small* on the side of the chart paper and brainstorm synonyms or rhyming words. As I write their texts I point out commas, capital letters, periods, direct quotations. Even though every child doesn't contribute at first, every child has the opportunity to observe." Many teachers prefer to print the class text on final draft paper, asking the children to illustrate each page. "This way," as Dick Koblitz says, "the text is accessible to all, since there exists a great variation in the penmanship of young children." Class innovations on texts are natural ways to explore story structures and increase children's vocabulary. Dick's second graders combine their knowledge of dinosaurs in a collaborative innovation on *The Very Busy Spider* entitled *The Very Busy Bee*.

The Very Busy Bee
by Grade 2

Page 1: Early one morning a bee flew out of its hive.

Page 2: It went to a flower patch and began to collect sweet nectar.

Page 3: Along came a tyrannosaurus rex and said, "Do you want to come and hunt with me?"

Page 4: The bee didn't answer, he was very busy collecting sweet nectar.

The text continues until the bee falls asleep because of his very busy day. Children incorporated recently completed research on dinosaurs in their text. The class matched the dinosaurs' invitations with what each ancient reptile could logically do. So the pterodactyl invites the bee to fly, the triceratops to fight, the dimetrodon to ride, and so on.

Cumulative and circular folktales lend themselves to innovations, but the texts are more complex than many of the simpler patterned and predictable stories. Children can write innovations of such cumulative stories as Paul Galdone's *The Gingerbread Boy* and *There Was an Old Woman*, retold by Steven Kellogg. They can study such takeoffs of traditional fairy tales as James Marshall's *Goldilocks and the Three Bears* and *The Three Little Pigs*; Ed Young's *Lon Po Po: A Red Riding Hood Story from China*; Al-Ling Louie's *Yeh-Shen: A Cinderella Story from China*; and John Steptoe's *Mufaro's Beautiful Daughters*. Then students can write their own variations.

Introduce the wonderful variety of informational books, including alphabet, counting, life-cycle, and how-to. Also introduce photographic essays and informational picture books to children. Then work together to create collaborative and individual books. Integrate research; let students vote on the topic they'd like to investigate; connect the book project to a theme cycle. Don't rush. Collaborative innovations can take several weeks to complete as children discuss, research, reflect, and create. Here are four points to think about as you embark on collaborative innovations:

1. Help students decide what elements in the pattern they wish to change.

2. Complete one or two pages of the innovation each day, reserving time to make group decisions.

3. Books that require research take more time to plan, write, and illustrate.

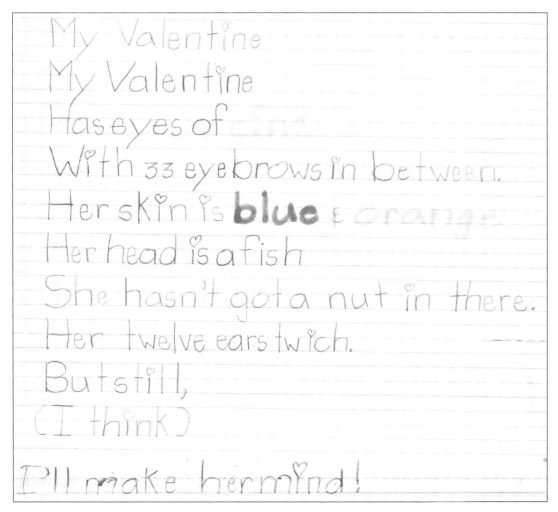

My Valentine
My Valentine
Has eyes of
With 33 eyebrows in between.
Her skin is **blue** & orange
Her head is a fish
She hasn't got a nut in there.
Her twelve ears twitch.
But still,
(I think)

I'll make her mind!

Fig. 1 A second grader's innovation on Myra Cohn Livingston's "My Valentine."

4. As the book unfolds, hang pages around the room for all to read. This provides the momentum to continue and complete the project, plus opportunities for children to reread their texts.

Once children understand story patterns and structures, many experiment with the patterns they've studied and write original texts. Susan Flynn's second graders adore Myra Cohn Livingston's poem "My Valentine" (from *Celebrations*). Nina composes an innovation (figure 1) that allows her to get deep inside the language of the original, as she composes a poem that uses exaggeration to poke fun at the super-sentimental quality of many valentine poems. Patterning poems can also call children's attention to the shape of poems.

William Joyce's *George Shrinks* has become *the* book to read among my second-grade workshop students. The kids adore the hilarious illustrations, and they read the story with ease. Carrie writes an original book, patterned after Joyce's, called *Ann Shrack!* (figure 2).

Fig. 2

Fig. 3

Once upon a time there lived a little girl named Katie. Katie had everything she had ever wanted. Also a golden ball.

Like Joyce, Carrie includes parents who give orders, illustrations with text, and illustrations without text. "I know how to write a shrink book," Carrie tells her class during group share.

Circular stories, like the classic *Millions of Cats*, by Wanda Gág, begin and end in the same place. In order to understand the circular story structure, Carol Chapman's second graders first work as a whole class, then collaborate. Small groups map four to six important events from stories such as Steven Kellogg's *The Mysterious Tadpole* and Pat Hutchins's *Rosie's Walk*. During writing workshop, several children decide to write original circular stories, and, like a forest fire, writing circular stories spreads throughout the class. "I'm making a plan," announced Katherine, and she drew a story map before writing. Katherine felt such pride in her map that it became the cover for her circular fairy tale (figure 3).

Some second graders imitated Katherine's plan; others plunged into writing and then illustrated their story. Authors sat in a wide circle and read their stories. During a class writing process share, Katherine explained her reasons for making the circle story map before writing:

> What was I going to write? I thought a long time and felt better when I made the map. It took me a long time and was more work. But I think my story was better and easier to write from the map.

Sharing process enables authors to learn from each other as they strive to make reading-writing connections. Ongoing writing process shares can make students keenly aware of how they write, and many note thoughts in their journals. Eighth grader Megan plays with rhyme and at the top of her journal reflects on writing with and without rhyme. On the page she draws, plays with rhyme, and writes two lyrical poems (figure 4).

Megan has begun studying Myra Cohn Livingston's *Poem-Making* and has also been reading lyric poetry.

In addition to teacher demonstrations, student writing process shares, and rereading, I've noticed that students often attempt to make sense out of text structures by recopying. Seventh grader Stacie told me during a mini-conference, "I copied this [poem] because I like it and to figure out how the author does it." These seventh graders, immersed in poetry for the first time, spent two weeks reading aloud to each other and silently to themselves, and copying poetry into their literature response journals.

Literature response journals, therefore, can also provide a place for students to reflect on, and figure out, literary genres, as well as respond to stories, map, free-write, copy poems and lines from books, draw, and record warm-ups, personal descriptions, and written conversations with classmates. A full and rich journal, like humus, is the planting soil for writing seeds. And these seeds, sparked by a child's reflection on the treasure within the journal, can become the basis for composing books, narratives, poems, essays, letters, diaries, editorials, articles, speeches, illustrations, paintings, or sculpture.

Lucy Calkins and Shelly Harwayne, in *Living Between the Lines*, present research on students keeping notebooks like authors. The personal and literature response journal, like an author's notebook, stores the creative wealth of the imagination, waiting to be released into an art form. I encourage my students to keep writing notes and early drafts in their journals so they can review their entire process, and other reflections, before deciding to revise a draft or begin a new piece.

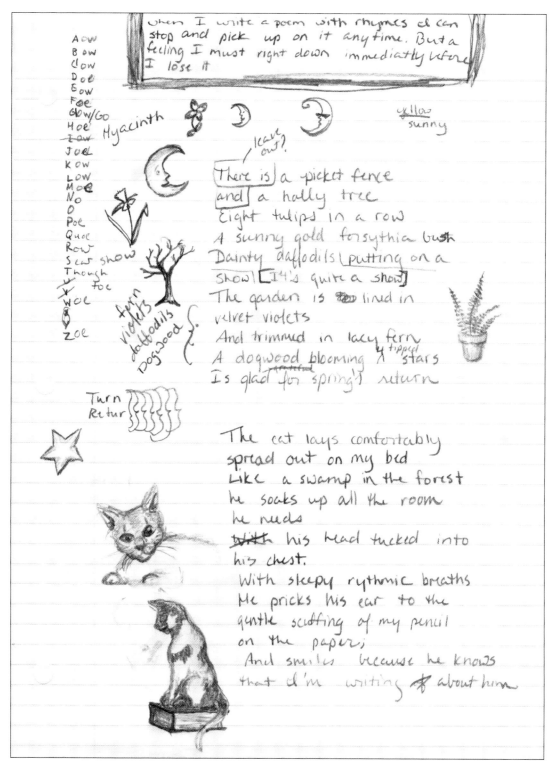

A ow
B ow
C ow
D oe
E ow
F oe
G ow/Go
H oe
I ow
J oe
K ow
L ow
M oe
No
O
Poe
Quoe
Row
Sew show
Though
t foe
W oe
Zoe

when I write a poem with rhymes el can stop and pick up on it any time. But a feeling I must right down immediatly before I lose it

Hyacinth

yellow sunny

leave out?

There is a picket fence
and a holly tree
Eight tulips in a row
A sunny gold forsythia bush
Dainty daffodils putting on a
show It's quite a show
The garden is too lined in
velvet violets
And trimmed in lacy fern
A dogwood blooming tipped stars
Is glad for spring's return

turn violets daffodils Dogwood

Turn
Retur

The cat lays comfortably
spread out on my bed
Like a swamp in the forest
he soaks up all the room
he needs
With his head tucked into
his chest.
With sleepy rythmic breaths
He pricks his ear to the
gentle scuffing of my pencil
on the paper;
And smiles because he knows
that el'm writing about him

Fig. 4

Small Poems

Jennifer   March 18, 1991

spider webs - different sizes, shapes

donuts - glaze, chocalate, cinnoman

meadow - flowing, apartment buildings

trees - large, woodly, trunk, branches, leaves

bush - dense, low-growing branches, shrub

awakening - rousing from sleep, a sudden

meadow - piece of land - where grass and flowers grow

ocean - whole body of salt water, a great expanse

penny - bronze, small, circle, coin

dimple - hollow hole or dent in cheek or chin

button - small knob holding *to fasten* parts of a garment together

stupid
dreamy about
gaze around
wander idly

moon - heavenly body, resolves about the earth, crescnt

peace - end war, agreement, freedom, quiet, stillness, *ad sense of noise*

blue - color, low in spirits; sad, clear sky, sea

red - color,

orange - color,

cheese - curb of milk, pressed into food

sunrise -

swollows -

elephtants -

beetles - four wings, insects

The End

light - not heavy, easy

darkness - dark, absence of light

time -

air -

book - sheets of paper bound or strung together.

shadows - image, a ghost, shade,

clouds - visible mars or tiny bits of water or

ice hanging in the air, black to white,

gloom?, anxiety, ill-temper.

Fig. 5

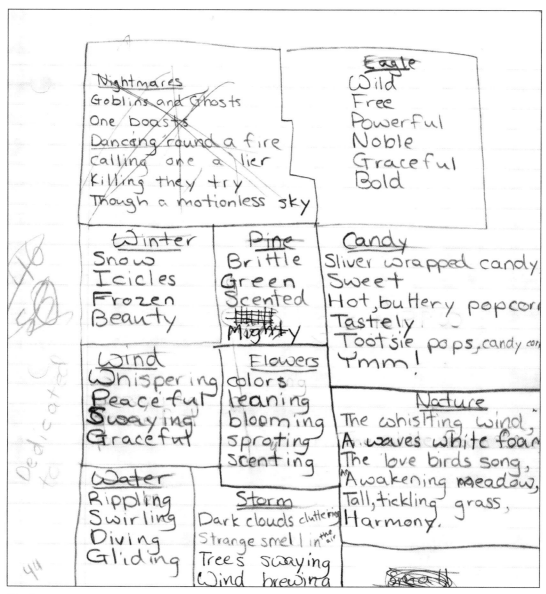

Nightmares
Goblins and Ghosts
One boasts
Dancing round a fire
Calling one a lier
Killing they try
Though a motionless sky

Eagle
Wild
Free
Powerful
Noble
Graceful
Bold

Winter
Snow
Icicles
Frozen
Beauty

Pine
Brittle
Green
Scented
Mighty

Candy
Sliver wrapped candy
Sweet
Hot, buttery popcorn
Tastely
Tootsie pops, candy corn
Ymm!

Wind
Whispering
Peaceful
Swaying
Graceful

Flowers
colors
leaning
blooming
sprouting
scenting

Nature
The whistling wind,
A waves white foam
The love birds song,
Awakening meadow,
Tall, tickling grass,
Harmony.

Water
Rippling
Swirling
Diving
Gliding

Storm
Dark clouds cluttering
Strange smell in the air
Trees swaying
Wind brewing

Dedicated to

Fig. 6

Several sixth graders develop a passion for Valerie Worth's collections of small poems. Some members of the group read aloud, into a tape recorder; others read silently. Jennifer decides to write her own book of small poems because, she tells me, "I want to see if I can write so much with so few words." Already she has understood Valerie Worth's remarkable economy of language, and she notes some favorite phrases in her journal.

Jennifer's journal entries illustrate the complexity of her writing and thinking process. First she brainstormed ideas for poems, and I've included part of her detailed list (figure 5).

On the following journal page are drafts of small poems (figure 6). "I'm just playing

Jenn   March 1991

Prairie Falcon

short quick wing beats
bold, daring hunter
small rodents, squirrels

Bald Eagle   Black & White Warbler

                                    black & white stripes
white mask   crown
dark brown   weesy, weesy, weesy
strong, large   hunts for insects
keen eye sight   at night

Mourning Dove

long, pointed tail
gray
coo-ah, coo, coo

Common Grackle

black
bright yellow eyes
long wedge-shaped tail
iridesent green to bronze

Fig. 7

around to see what I want to do," Jennifer tells me during a miniconference.

Then suddenly Jennifer turns from writing small poems to reading guidebooks on birds. "We're watching and identifying birds in science," she explains as I pause at her table. "I think I might use birds for my small poems." Figure 7 illustrates some of the notes from research and bird-watching that enter Jennifer's journal.

Several weeks later, she turns in *Bird Poems*, a collection of five small poems, and like Worth's poems, each one of Jennifer's poems has an accompanying illustration, as in "Praire Falcon" (figure 8).

The point is that Jennifer invested large chunks of time reading and researching, talking and sharing, reflecting on journal notes about Worth's poetry and her own ideas for small poems. She explored, revised, abandoned, and rethought before she completed her book. "I'll use the other notes sometime, when I'm ready," she informed her group during a writing process share. And

then added, "Maybe." The choice will always rest with Jennifer because she is the author making decisions about investing time and creative energy in her writing.

Structure and technique are not the only functions of stories in reading-writing-research classrooms. Books can reclaim stories buried deep inside memory—stories, characters, topics, themes that might find their way into our own writing. I learned about stories reclaiming memory seeds twelve years ago. During a group share, eighth grader Jordan prefaced the reading of her story with, "Well, guys, Cinderella is alive and well in this class, and she's got a lot in common with this one." Jordan brandished a copy of the Cinderella fairy tale before she began. The story, based on Jordan's experiences, was a humorous yet pointed tale about doing all the drudge work at her parents' parties. Jordan gave me the idea of reading picture books and poems during workshop with the specific hope of resurrecting students' past experiences. Memory seeds are

Fig. 8

barred and buried experiences, stories that all of us carry. They wait, silently, ready to germinate and spring through the closed doors of our minds when stories reach and reclaim them.

I read aloud or students read alone, in pairs or small groups, and the workshop concludes with ten to fifteen minutes of free, unprompted responses to the book or poem. An eighth-grade class and I explore poems written in the voice of apostrophe. I read several from *Poem-Making,* and we discuss the poet's voice, which speaks to things that cannot answer. Students dig in to anthologies to unearth examples of this poetic voice. Some choose to play with this new voice and immediately compose poems; others elect to pursue different writing routes.

Brianna, having heard me read Alvin Tresselt's *The Gift of the Tree,* returned later in the year to the voice of apostrophe. Her journal page (figure 9) included a response to Tresselt's poem and the note at the side to "talk to the earth."

Brianna drafted a poem that grew out of Tresselt's book and another that grew out of her daily living. Like many students, Brianna did not immediately incorporate a reading-writing demonstration into her own work. But the notes and responses in her journal, which she periodically reads, hold what Brianna calls "possibilities." She explains to the class during a process share, "I don't always try a new technique right away. I need time. These poems I might work on later—now I'm just collecting lots of possibilities."

In the midst of a fairy and folktale study with sixth- and eighth-grade students, I phoned Amy Ehrlich. She and I were to speak at a program and address the use of fairy tales to reclaim barred memories. Amy told me about *Lucy's Winter Tale,* which grew out of her childhood fears of being kidnapped. She mailed me the manuscript of her contemporary fairy tale to read to students. Lucy, abducted from her home, views this abduction as a grand adventure with Ivan the juggler, Henry, his dancing bear, and Martina, Ivan's sweetheart. Only Lucy's father and brothers see the kidnapping as an evil act. To my surprise, the story resurrected fears in sixth grader Soren, who freely reacted to the read-aloud in his journal (figure 10).

And his poem, which Soren composed several days later (figure 11), transforms the fearful emotions reclaimed by Lucy's tale into hopeful suggestions.

"When I reread my reactions," Soren said, "I wanted to say there was a way to fight those thoughts." Story and reflection provided the seeds for his lyrical poem.

Three eighth-grade boys read Ashley Bryan's *Turtle Knows Your Name.* For one week the three enter workshop class rhythmically chanting "Upsillimana Temperlerado." Their infectious entrance made the story a hot class item, and the book rapidly circulated among twenty-two boys and girls. The three boys discussed the unimportance of name, wealth, and station. They agreed that getting to know a person from the inside was the key to understanding and fair play. Steve wrote the dialogue eight days after the boys read and discussed Bryan's tale (figure 12).

The brief conversation reveals the tension between Steve's desire to be perceived as mature by his friends and his mom's continued use of a diminutive form of his name.

The same Bryan tale prompted Zach's entry (figure 13).

The Gift of the Tree
The tree gave home to different animals - even
its enemies.
As the tree rots into the earth, its like it
will be born again

Brainstorm   Earth troubles - by: Brianna Monroe
talk to the Earth   Earth, Earth, why do you put up with us?
                      We pollute your seas and oceans,
                      killing all your ocean life.
                      We deforest your land all over
                      to make new cities and raise our beef.
                      We pollute your air with toxins,
                      to get where we want faster.
                      - All this to make life better -
                      but to make your's worse

Why, table, do you stand in my path,
so I have to go another route?
Why, clock, do your hands move slower,
when I'm sitting in history class?
Why, t.V., do you stop working,
when I'm watching my favorite show
Why, telephone, do you ring for my parents,
when I'm waiting for an important call?
Why, chair, do you move away,
when I'm just about to sit down? ⟶

Fig. 9

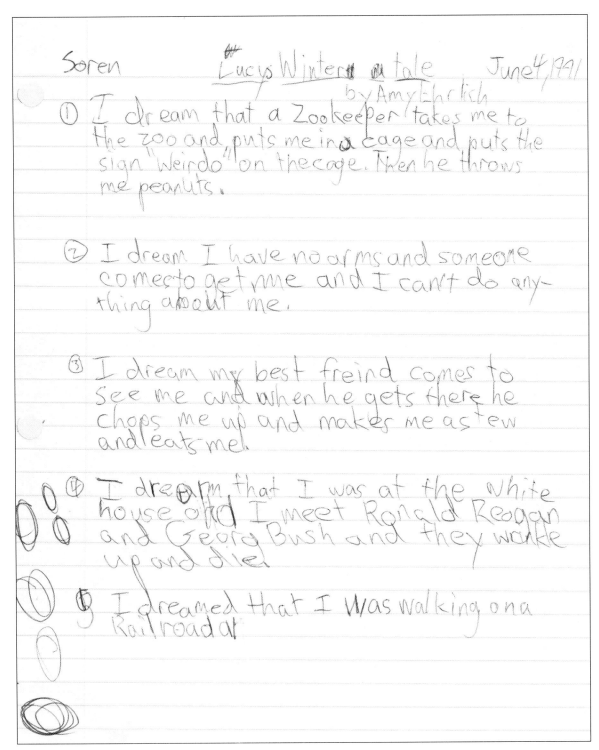

Fig. 10

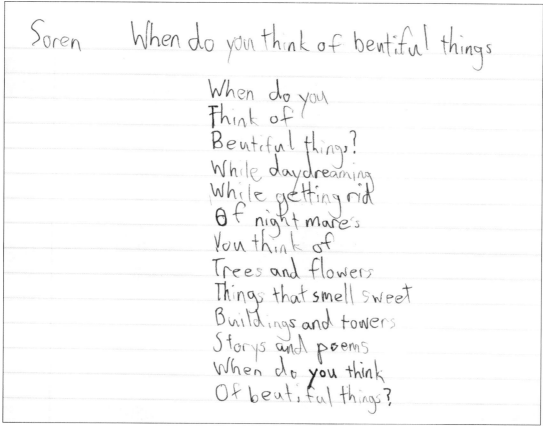

Fig. 11

The top half of Zach's notes summarizes his group's discussion, but in the bottom half he shapes some of his thoughts into a poem. Three days later, Zach writes this one sentence in his journal:

His name in Greek means "of great strength," but look at him. He's puny and weak.

In a conference, Zach tells me that's the way he feels about one of his classmates, and that he's putting all his feelings into a poem. Two weeks later, after a group share of journal entries, Zach wrote a poem (figure 14) and volunteered to read it to the class.

Zach prefaced the reading of his poem with this comment: "I've stood being called 'fat,' 'tubbo,' and 'roly poly,' and I hope this poem makes you [his classmates] stop." Privately I asked Zach why he made those comments. "I've been teased in this school in sports and on the bus and in the locker room forever. After the story and our discussion, I decided it was time to have my say and see if *they* [classmates] meant what they said." *Turtle Knows Your Name*, group discussions, written responses, and journal reflections all assisted Zach in writing a poem about deeply rooted feelings.

Often a student's connections and associations interested me and their peers more

NICKNAME

Steve   May 24, 1991

"Hello."

"Hey Steve, what are you doing"?

"OH, not much. How about you."

"Well, I'm just watching t.v."

The conversation began just like any normal one would. The same old "Hello" and the same old "what are you doing" formality. Little did I know, my conversation would soon be interrupted in the worst possible way.

"So Kenny, what are you going to do this weekend"?

"I don't — CLICK

"Stevieeee, get off the phone and finish your homework"!

I think to myself. I hate when she does that! I hate it!

"Okay Mom". I answer politely. "Litsen Kenny, I'll call you back in a little while."

"Okay Stevie, you call me back." Mocks Kenny in the most exaggerated voice I've ever heard. I hear a snicker while he hangs up and I can only think to myself.

Why can't she call me, Steve?

Fig. 12

May 16, 1991

Turtle Knows your name

A type of prejudice. A name is a label. Names are not meant to hurt anyone. You can always change your name. Your name does'nt determine your personality → its What you do.

Happiness, humor   [Lip-service]

Take sides because of relationship - countries/people

Prejudice

why do we have names?
I do.
you do.
LABEL ME.
Give me a name.
why?
A name is a name,
they are never the same,
sometimes..............

Fig. 13 Above.

Fig. 14 At left.

I've had my name for many years,
theres nothing different about it.

But when those people have nothing better to do,
they come and poke fun at it.

They are the infamous name-changers,
everyone's name is in danger.

They laugh and laugh and laugh and laugh
until thier satisfaction.

Frankly, I cant stand them. They must be
stopped. Do something before they get you.

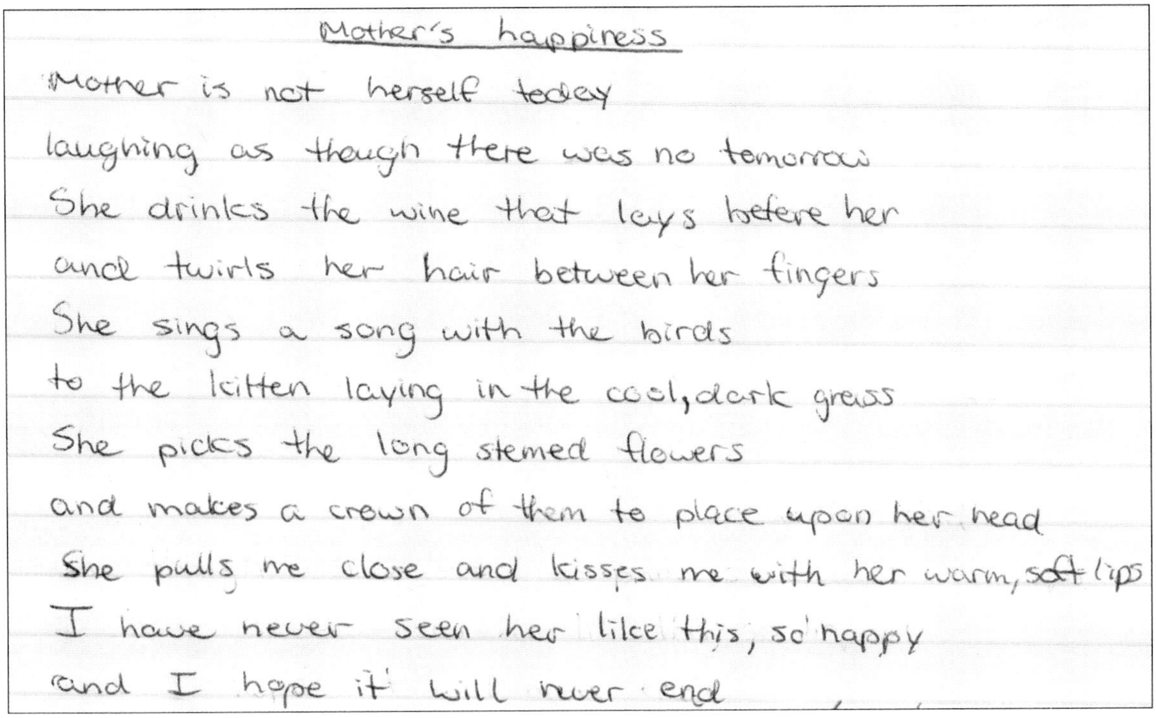

Mother's happiness

Mother is not herself today
laughing as though there was no tomorrow
She drinks the wine that lays before her
and twirls her hair between her fingers
She sings a song with the birds
to the kitten laying in the cool, dark grass
She picks the long stemed flowers
and makes a crown of them to place upon her head
She pulls me close and kisses me with her warm, soft lips
I have never seen her like this, so happy
and I hope it will never end

Fig. 15

than they interested the student. After sixth grader Brianna read her response to the Grimms' "Jorinda and Joringal," several classmates suggested that Brianna pursue the idea. But Brianna wasn't interested. More than a year later, I read Gail Haley's *Birdsong.* Brianna, now a seventh grader, brought me her poem "Mother's Happiness," breathless with excitement. "You know how everyone wanted me to write about Mr. Smith and his bird and I never did. Today, when you read *Birdsong,* I heard my mother singing." And Brianna read the poem to me (figure 15).

Connections stories make can surprise us, like Brianna, and catch us unawares, long after we think we've forgotten initial responses. I tell stories like Brianna's to classes to encourage them to save their journals and continue to use them as writing seeds.

Every student did not have a powerful and transforming experience with each tale. Deep, personal connections did not always result in a story or poem. Ilse's summary of *Why the Tides Ebb and Flow,* by Joan Bowden, ends with this statement: "This story reminded me of nothing." I repeatedly received that sentence from students and include it as a reminder of the range and diversity of student reactions.

Reading picture books and poetry aloud during reading-writing workshop occurs every day in my classroom. Selection is crucial, and I look for books that transmit values, that arouse tears and laughter, that make us gasp for the beauty they transmit and the emotions and thoughts they stir. I read such books as the following to first and second graders, as well as to middle school students: Sam Swope's *The Araboolies of Liberty Street,* Alberto

Blanco's *The Desert Mermaid*, Eve Bunting's *Terrible Things: An Allegory of the Holocaust*, Shonto Begay's *Maii and Cousin Horned Toad*, and Roberto Innocenti's *Rose Blanche*. The choice to respond to the stories and create original work is theirs. But the seeds have been planted.

Stories can reclaim memories, but words help us shape memories into stories. In *Gates of Excellence*, Katherine Paterson writes: "I believe that words, too, are necessities—and to give the children of the world the words they need is, in a real sense, to give them life and growth and refreshment."[1] Words are a writer's bricks, for what more does a writer have than words with which to transmit personal vision and universal meaning?

Students and I collect words and compile our collections on chart paper for all to see. A student with legible penmanship volunteers to record the chart on a ditto master. I store word lists in a box, and it's not unusual for classes to dip into each other's lists; many tape the word lists into their journals. Here are some ways to compile word lists:

Poems and Stories. After reading poems and stories that relate to a theme or topic, ask groups of students to select words for the list.

Free Association. Place a topic or theme on chart paper and let students spontaneously free-associate words to each other's responses.

Interviews. Students interview parents, peers, other teachers, relatives, and others to gather words from them.

Word Graffiti Board. Create a graffiti word board so all members of the school community can write words relating to a theme or topic.

The list below is an outgrowth of listening to and reading poems, brainstorming, and interviews:

Autumn Word List

equinox	spectral	somber
crisp	blaze	linger
bloodcurdling	dismal	sorcerer
murky	woebegone	beckons
wizard	sated	gnarled
fragile	demonic	menacing
dusky	cackles	rustle
phantom	eerie	mystify
sparkle	desolate	doomed
penetrate	shriek	fields
inferno	hollow	hay
whistles	tumble	merciless
revenge	crimson	bloody
bleak	leaf burning	solitary
mingle	shuffle	

Creating collaborative lists with your class models the process of collecting words. I post the lists in a prominent space and encourage students to enlarge them as new ideas spring to mind. This is what I hope they will do in their journals, especially as they develop the habit of rereading pages.

I urge students to jot down in journals intriguing words they find as they read poems, stories, and books. Certainly, this is a form of research—research into language. Danny, a sixth grader who decided to write and illustrate Halloween poems, began to collect words at the end of September. To enlarge his list, Danny frequently read it to classmates, asking for their input and jotting down the words they offered.

On a foggy, gray day, I read Carl Sandburg's "Fog" to sixth graders. That bleak December morning, Crystal uses workshop to create a list of "fog" words and notes, with specific details, what

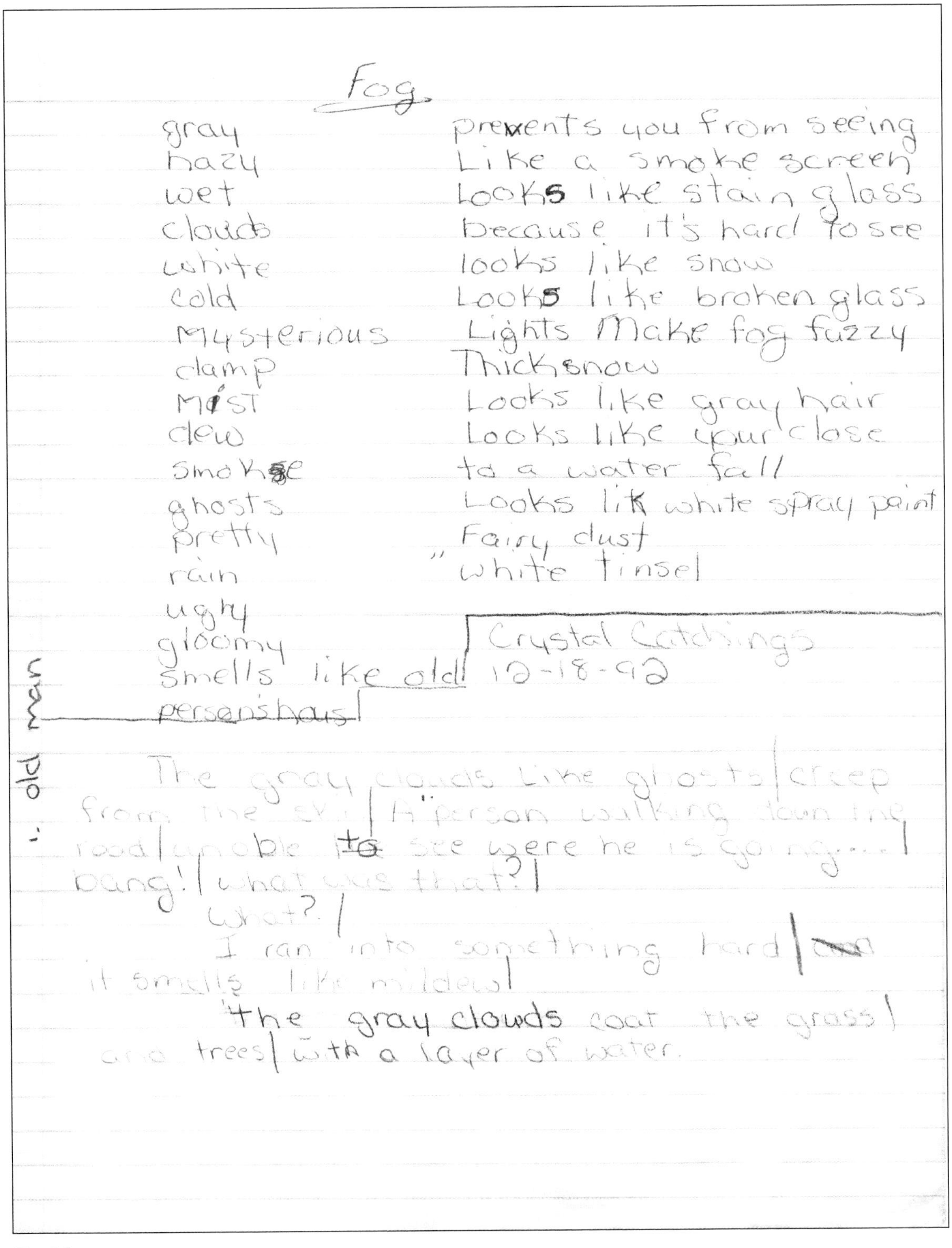

Fog

gray	prewents you from seeing
hazy	Like a smoke screen
wet	Looks like stain glass
clouds	because it's hard to see
white	looks like snow
cold	Looks like brohen glass
Mysterious	Lights Make fog fuzzy
damp	Thick snow
MiST	Looks like gray hair
dew	Looks like your close
smokse	to a water fall
ghosts	Looks lik white spray paint
pretty	„Fairy dust
rain	„white tinsel
ugly	
gloomy	Crystal Catchings
smells like old	12-18-92
persenshaus	

... old man

The gray clouds Like ghosts/creep from the sky./ A person walking down the road/unable to see were he is going.... / bang!/what was that?/
What?/
I ran into something hard/ and it smells like mildew/
the gray clouds coat the grass/ and trees/ with a layer of water.

Fig. 16

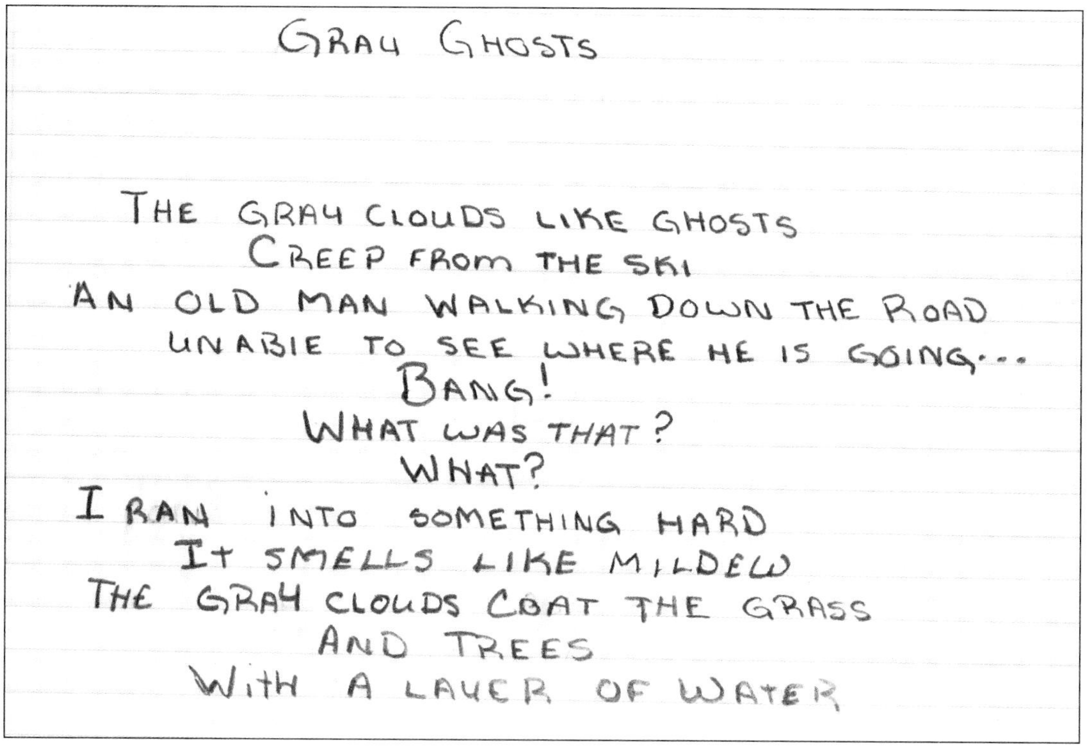

GRAY GHOSTS

THE GRAY CLOUDS LIKE GHOSTS
CREEP FROM THE SKI
AN OLD MAN WALKING DOWN THE ROAD
UNABLE TO SEE WHERE HE IS GOING...
BANG!
WHAT WAS THAT?
WHAT?
I RAN INTO SOMETHING HARD
IT SMELLS LIKE MILDEW
THE GRAY CLOUDS COAT THE GRASS
AND TREES
WITH A LAYER OF WATER

Fig. 17

fog looks like. Two days later, she writes and lines a poem on the same journal page (figure 16).

Crystal then revised her poem (figure 17).

The entries reveal how Crystal integrated into a poem the following elements: her own vision of fog, Sandburg's poem, a search for words, and specific details describing fog. Making lists of words is also a revision technique; young authors turn to word lists for fresher and more accurate ways to transmit inner visions to paper. Sixth graders Jimmie and Bob collaborate to create a list of alternate words for *scary,* which they feel they've overused. A group of students writing dialogue asks if we could help them make a list of ways to say *said.* Many students copy this list into journals so, as Trina put it, "I can use it whenever I get stuck."

As a teacher, I am always demonstrating reading-writing connections. My goal is to inspire students to reflect on the potential every book, poem, story, and article carries. And I know that the richer a learner's reading life, the greater the chance of enlarging knowledge and experiences and nurturing the imagination. My hope for all learners is that reading will fortify their endless struggle to communicate through writing, knowing full well that ultimately, as Donald Murray wrote, "Inspiration comes from the chair and that part of the anatomy that belongs there."[2]

References

1. Paterson, Katherine. *Gates of Excellence,* page 6.

2. Murray, Donald. *Write to Learn,* page 228.

AS I SEE IT

Robert Cormier

I have never kept a journal—or have I?

Bear with me.

As a reporter/editor/columnist for almost thirty years, I recorded the daily events of the cities in which I lived and worked. I wrote a twice-a-week human-interest column for ten years. In almost one thousand of these columns, I put down on paper my observations of small-city life and sought to inflict shocks of recognition on my readers by writing about what I had seen and heard and *felt* in my daily rounds. The columns were most often ignited by my emotional response to events, just as my novels and short stories have been sparked by emotions that send me to the typewriter.

As a journalist, I was, in a sense, invisible; present at the scene of fires and accidents, political meetings, elections, and places where acts of violence had occurred; present, yes, but not accounted for; present but not part of the event. This gave me a great advantage: the opportunity to observe, to scrutinize, to ponder, to view objectively the events before me, and, paradoxically, to also absorb the emotions rising from what had happened.

Baseball legend Yogi Berra amused many people who poked fun at his famous sayings ("It was like déjà vu all over again"). He also made people smile when he said: "You can observe a lot by watching." Frankly, many people don't actually observe while watching. They look without really seeing. They pass through events untouched and unaffected.

As a reporter, I had to train myself to do all that so that I would be able to put down on paper later what I had seen and heard and felt.

This is the kind of daily journal I kept for almost three decades.

When I left newspaper work to devote myself full-time to writing novels (I was working on what became *After the First Death*), I began to keep a record of the daily events of my life. Before going to bed late at night or early in the morning, I filled out one side of those three-by-five filing cards.

I did not regard the cards as a journal. I didn't ponder the meaning of events or philosophize about them. I *did* record whether a novel I read or a movie I saw was good or bad. I commented on the weather, recorded how many birds and what kinds visited the feeder that I could see from my typewriter. Who I met downtown or at the library. Who called or dropped in to visit. What kind of mail arrived. Mundane, everyday stuff that would bore the life out of anyone reading the cards.

Why did I do this? I wasn't sure then, and I'm not sure now. But I have some thoughts on the matter. I think I wrote on the cards because I had a need to keep reporting on the daily events of my life. Writing novels draws on the imagination, on memories and remembered emotions, but not on my current experiences. I was compelled, apparently, to go on doing what I had done most of my life.

This brings me, in a roundabout way, to how I feel about keeping a journal.

I think journals are important for a number of reasons, most of which have nothing to do with content. Discipline: the act of writing on a daily basis. Observing: really seeing what's going on during the hours of your days and evenings. Absorbing: opening your pores to the emotional content of your daily landscapes and events.

That's the kind of journal I kept—both consciously and unconsciously—all these years. Perhaps it has made me the writer I have tried to be, perhaps not. But perhaps there is a clue here somewhere for those who wonder about such things.

SELECTED BOOKS BY ROBERT CORMIER

After the First Death. New York: Avon, 1979.

Beyond the Chocolate War. New York: Knopf, 1985.

The Bumblebee Flies Away. New York: Dell, 1991.

The Chocolate War. New York: Pantheon, 1974.

Eight + One. New York: Dell, 1991.

Fade. New York: Delacorte, 1988.

I Am the Cheese. New York: Pantheon, 1977.

I Have Words to Spend: Reflections of a Small Town Editor. New York: Delacorte, 1994.

A Little Raw on Monday Mornings. New York: Dell, 1992.

Now and at the Hour. New York: Dell, 1991.

Other Bells for Us to Ring. Illustrated by Deborah Kogan Ray. New York: Delacorte, 1990.

Tunes for Bears to Dance To. New York: Delacorte, 1992.

We All Fall Down. New York: Delacorte, 1991.

INQUIRY AND CONTENT AREA JOURNALS

"I have to read every book there is on spiders," fifth grader Nina announces as the class and I return from a spider hunt. "I saw three different webs in that old barn. One looked like a funnel and I wonder what spider made it." Nina shows me the drawing she's made of the funnel web. "Can I go to the library now?" she pleads. I nod and Nina races ahead of the group. Twenty minutes later she returns to class with an armful of books about spiders.

Nina's passion to know more about spiders also sends her to the science teacher, to the insect zoo in the Smithsonian Institution, to the yard behind her house. Drawings, notes, and questions fill her journal as Nina researches her subject. On one page she writes, "Lots of my friends believe spiders are disgusting. But they help us by eating insects inside the house and in gardens." Nina heads a page Unusual Things and notes information she's learned such as "most spiders have tiny claws at the end of their feet. I didn't know that before."

Nina's methods of learning are worth noting. Beginning with a topic she's itching to study, Nina reads, questions, observes, finds additional resources, and thinks about what she's learning. In her journal, Nina stores drawings, questions, answers, and data. My job is to support her interests by providing books and articles, by talking to Nina about her research and notes, by creating situations where she can talk about experiences with classmates, by negotiating ways she can share knowledge with an audience, and by encouraging Nina to observe, question, read, write, and think.

If writing is, as Donald Murray points out, "the most disciplined form of thinking,"[1] then writing to learn should be integrated into content area subjects. In this way, children can collect and sift through information with the purpose of solving problems and making connections to self, community, and world.

Nina used the knowledge she gained about spiders eating bugs to try to convince classmates that they should not destroy them. Nina went beyond learning data for the sake of memorizing facts. She used knowledge to benefit people and spiders, to change misconceptions and actions, to think.

The use of journals across the curriculum can facilitate writing to learn as students collect and analyze information. Collecting data can come from reading, observing, talking, and listening. But the need to collect data arises from inquiries within the child. In this context, journals become sanctuaries, safe places to wonder and to discover what you do and don't know. Studies and investigations move beyond reliance on one textbook to reading poetry, nonfiction, historical fiction, magazines, and charts and to interviewing people, viewing a film, and listening to

students' observations. And the purpose of these investigations is to stimulate reflection and critical thinking.

The curiosity of the young makes them keen observers of their environment, and before they come to school, they have repeatedly engaged in inquiry learning. Questions drive inquiry learning, and in order to find answers to the mysteries that surround them, children observe, experiment, predict, classify, and draw conclusions. In every subject, then, the children should have opportunities to pose the questions they investigate.

On a bright and sunny autumn day, I paused at the door of a second-grade class studying the sun. An open textbook covered each desk, and the teacher was compiling a list of facts

Three eighth graders study the behavior of a milk snake.

about the sun on the board. The children repeated the list with the teacher, put their books away, and copied the board information into a journal. No questions. No discussion. Now, this classroom had a wall of oversized windows and that sun was shining right into the room, begging to be observed and wondered about. The teacher never suggested this, and sad to say, no child asked permission to look at or think about the "real sun." A primary task of teachers is to unleash all the questions within children, so we can discover what they want to know and supply the materials required to help them on their journey.

Children's questions, then, form the core of inquiry learning; collaborative charts and journal and inquiry notebooks are places to pose questions for content area studies. Carol Chapman's second graders and I study natural phenomena and disasters. In their notebooks, students constantly pose questions. This questioning process begins before our research and continues as we study. The more children learn, the more questions they seem to have. Jennifer asks page after page of questions.

Every book she browses through, every discussion, stimulates more things she wants to know. The journal page below is an example of some things Jennifer wants to know about tornadoes and storms (figure 1). Jennifer opens her questions with "I want to know . . ." Her urgent tone sets a strong purpose for her research.

Fourth-grade teacher Ellen Benjamin and I discuss a theme cycle on the human body. Even though the topic is a required part of Ellen's curriculum, the children can have choices, provided we tap into their interests.

A spin-off of writing questions in a journal is to create an "inquiry notebook." We have the class aide make these four-by-six-inch booklets for the children. Even though the study will begin at the end of January, Ellen and I introduce the inquiry notebooks on January 4. We ask the children to keep them on their desks for the rest of the month. Whenever a question about the human body, or any other topic, pops into their minds, they record it in their notebook. We place no restrictions on their questioning in order to learn more about the kinds of questions they have. The excerpts

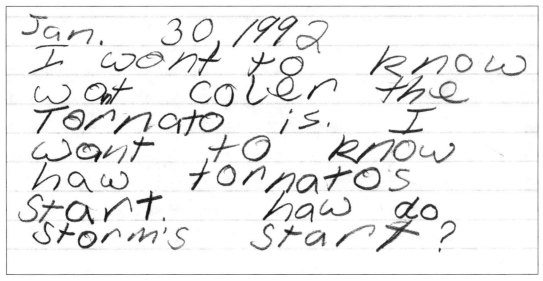

Fig. 1

from their notebooks (figure 2) illustrate the excellent questions that were on the children's minds. Reviewing students' questions in advance permitted Ellen and me to order additional materials that supported the children's inquiries.

Ginny, our aide, typed students' questions and filled three pages; the children researched and discussed them (see appendix).

The combination of inquiry, talk, research, and writing led some fourth-grade boys and girls beyond the facts to deeper understandings. The high point of their discussions occurred when William and Bobby discovered books with differing information on dreams. William, basing his argument on his reading, insisted that some dreams last as long as an hour; Bobby countered by reading a portion from his book that stated that most dreams occur within a minute. I asked, "What might you conclude from this difference in information?" Silence. Fidgeting. I waited.

Fig. 2 Excerpts from inquiry notebooks for study of the human body.

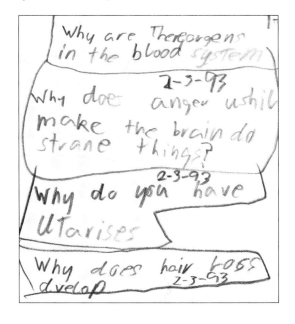

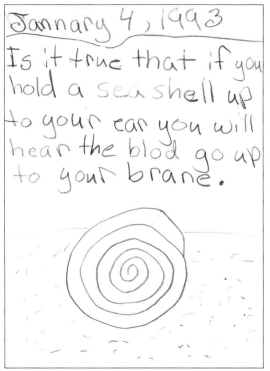

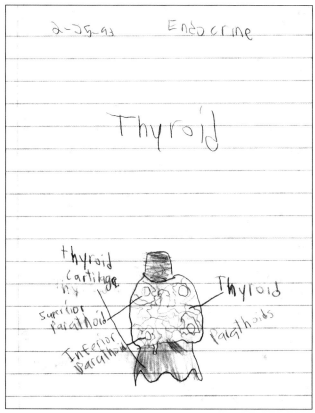

2-25-93   Endocrine

Thyroid

thyroid
cartilage
Superior
parathyroid
Inferior
parathyroid
Thyroid
Parathyroids

The Thyroid is found in your neck. It is behind your adams apple. Thyroids are part of the endocrine. The most important part of the endocr system are the hormons. Hormons help you grow. If you didn't have any hormons you would stay the size you were when you were born. If you had to few hormons, you would be a midget. If you had to many hormons, you would be a giant. That's why hormons are important.

Fig. 3

Finally, Peter tentatively raised his hand. Words formed slowly, hesitantly, as he spoke. "Well, maybe neither book is right—maybe—maybe it's just their [the authors'] theories [pause], and theories need proof." Ellen Benjamin and I, in unison, shouted, "Yes!" Huge grins erupted across our faces. Mere facts about the human body no longer dominated this theme cycle. Through research and collaboration, we observed children testing hypotheses and making connections.

Sometimes students' questions reveal the level of connections they can make between their own lives and new information. Arthur Kearns introduced a sixth-grade study of the Renaissance by asking students to first discuss in groups what they would like to know about this period, then pose questions in journals.

Laurie Houck begins her question list with "What in the heck is the Renaissance?" and then poses questions such as: "Was it a time of peace or war? Were there any problems with the environment? Were there taxes? Why? Was religion important to them?" Though Laurie had little knowledge of this period when she framed these questions, she has taken some familiar contemporary issues and wondered how people dealt with them at that time.

To encourage students to go beyond the collection of data and think, the double-entry journal graphically organizes notebook pages. Students set up their journals so that the left-hand page is for notes, pictures, lists, maps, and so on. The right-hand side is for reflection, summaries, hypotheses, explanations, critiques, opinions, feelings, and conclusions. Fourth graders used double-entry journals to focus on a specific part of a system in the human body that interested them. Kenny's illustrations of the endocrine system (figure 3) reveal the care he invested in his drawing. His "think" paragraph on the right-hand side integrates information and conclusions about why hormones are important.

Double-entry journals benefit inquiry learning in all subjects. In social studies, students can illustrate a physical feature of the earth and explain how that feature determines the way people live. A drawing of terraced mountains or irrigation ditches could be accompanied with thoughts about why people devised that particular method of farming. Or drawings of the physical features and notes on the climate of ancient Mesopotamia can spark written discussions of why that area is called the cradle of civilization.

The purpose of any double entry is to encourage children to move beyond recording information and lead them to think systematically about data. Reading their entries to groups often raises questions of validity and returns children to the research mode. My response to incorrect information or invalid conclusions is always a question that will, I hope, motivate the child to investigate further.

Writing to learn in mathematics means that students take the time to reflect on their process, to explain in words the meaning of a concept or how they arrived at an answer. Journals in mathematics class offer time for such reflections, which can let the kids and teacher know what is and isn't understood.

I'm fortunate enough to work with Harry Holloway, an adventurous, probing, and unorthodox middle school mathematics teacher. His students write in mathematics journals from the day they enter class. Harry himself keeps a journal that documents his discoveries and searches for ways to demonstrate problem solving, computation, patterns, and effective uses of the journal in his class. His journal also comments on articles and books he reads for personal and professional growth. In January, Harry writes,

> Experiences lead to learning?!
>
> However, *reflection* and *critical reflection* is important. Experience alone does not teach. However, reflection on experience does teach.

Harry is careful to present minilessons that model specific journal responses. In addition to voicing his processes to students, Harry encourages them to exchange their processes with each other.

Seventh-grade students begin the year by defining old concepts. Below are two examples of definitions of multiplying and dividing based on students' prior experiences. The first student explains division and multiplication, but, judging by her words, she does not clearly understand decimals. The second student takes the concepts beyond mathematics and uses story examples.

Student 1

Dividing:
> You have a number and you want to find out how many times it fits into another number.

Multiplying:
> It is a shortcut of addition because you are increasing a certain number by a certain number of times. If you multiply two numbers and it gets smaller you use decimals.
>
> To make bigger numbers in division you use decimals.

Student 2

Dividing:

Dividing is the way to split something into smaller parts. Dividing a word used in English into parts. Multiplying is a way to add something. To do addition over and over. More people in the class is multiplying the class. To have babies is to multiply.

Third-grade teacher Carolyn Morgoglione asks her students to write what they think they know about a math topic to determine the range of prior knowledge among students. Children regularly write about their investigations and work during and after completing a unit of study. In addition to a computation test on adding and subtracting decimals, Mrs. Morgoglione wanted to know whether the class understood the concept of tenths and hundredths. Weeks had been spent manipulating Cuisenaire rods. Journal entries responding to the question "What are tenths?" brought a range of explanations. Success on the test did not necessarily correspond with a deep understanding of the concept of tenths, for the test measured computation, while the journal writing clearly revealed those children who had grasped the concept and those who required additional support:

- Tenths they are very easy. 0.04.

- Tenthes are like one orange rode [rind]. it is also like ten centimeters.

- Tenths are a part of someing. Like one tenth of a hundred becaus there are ten thenths in a hundred so a thenth is part of a hundred.

- if you give someone a Tenth your giveing them more than if your giving Then a hundred.

- tenths are decimals meaning one 1 tenth 2 tenths and on. Say I had a candy bar and broke it into ten pieces and I took 2 pieces or 2 tenths.

Below are some writing to learn math strategies to use with students. Before asking students to use a strategy, model the strategy and the thinking process in minilessons. Record these on chart paper and display them for students to review.

Reading a Mathematics Textbook. Adapt the K-W-L strategy described previously to introduce a chapter or section of your text. Have students preview the pages, reading boldface headings, words, sample solutions, charts, and graphs, then write what they already know about this topic. Next, students list the new information they expect to learn from the section. Students set individual goals for their

Eighth grader records possible solutions to a math problem.

studies and read their textbook, becoming familiar with technical writing. After completing the study, students can record what they have learned.

Brainstorming. Brainstorm lists of what you know and understand and what confuses you.

Questions. Record questions about a particular type of problem or a set of procedures or methods.

Predictions. Write estimates or predict a method or outcome using given information. Compare predictions with actual solutions.

Summaries. Summarize findings—what you learned or the particular process you used to arrive at a solution.

Definitions. In your own words, explain the meaning of terms. Definitions can be refined throughout the unit and the school year. Provide time for students to review their early definitions and compare them to later explanations.

Personal Responses. Write about feelings and attitudes toward specific topics. These personal reactions help teachers identify students' needs.

Directions. Write how-to explanations of the process used to compute whole and rational numbers. Students who have difficulty writing explanations usually are having difficulty with the topic.

Notes. Students write what they observe in a minilesson, a small group project, or a section of the text. Notes in the child's own words are a form of remembering, storing, clarifying, and studying.

Descriptions and Explanations. Write a detailed description of your plan for solving a problem or of the procedures you actually used. Ask students to study a series of solutions to see if they can discover and write about a pattern.

Graphs and Charts. Organize surveys and data collected, in math and other subjects, into graphs and charts. Introduce students to different charts and graphs such as circle, bar, and line. Practice selecting the graph that will best summarize specific data.

Words and Phrases. In journals, have students compile an ongoing list of words and phrases that signal addition, subtraction, multiplication, and division. The teacher might wish to place these words on a chart or a bulletin board. Use these words to write original story problems and as clues to decide how to solve a problem. For addition: *total, how many, how far, sum, combined, more, how much.* For subtraction: *remain, profit, reduced, difference, diminished, exceed, change (money).* For multiplication: *of, percent, volume, area, times, each, product, square or cubic units.* For division: *equal parts, shares, quotient, average, pieces, partition.* Some words, like *reduced* and *average,* may require more than one step or operation.

Draw Pictures. Ask students to picture and illustrate the information in a problem and fill in numerical data. Then write possible solutions, using the pictures and data to discover a pattern or as clues that lead to a logical solution.

Solutions. List all the ways to solve a problem or to compute whole or rational numbers. Explain which way works best for you.

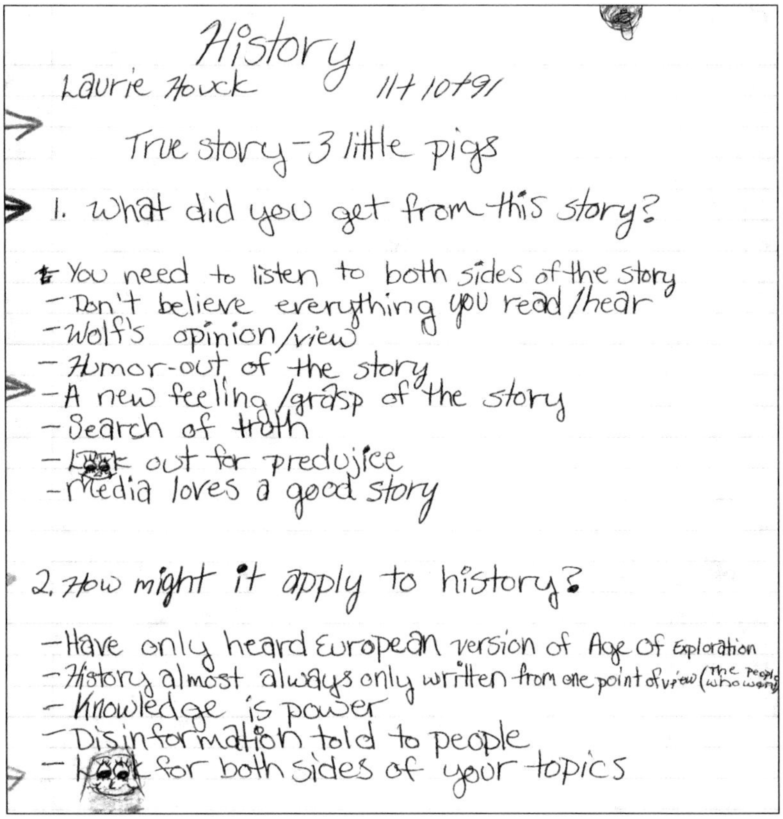

History

Laurie Houck   11+10+91

   True story - 3 little pigs

1. what did you get from this story?

- You need to listen to both sides of the story
  - Don't believe everything you read/hear
  - Wolf's opinion/view
  - Humor - out of the story
  - A new feeling/grasp of the story
  - Search of truth
  - Look out for predujice
  - Media loves a good story

2. How might it apply to history?

  - Have only heard European version of Age of Exploration
  - History almost always only written from one point of view (The people who won)
  - Knowledge is power
  - Disinformation told to people
  - Look for both sides of your topics

Fig. 4 At left.

Fig. 5 Below. Eighth grader summarizes and reflects on her research
for a debate on the American
Revolution.

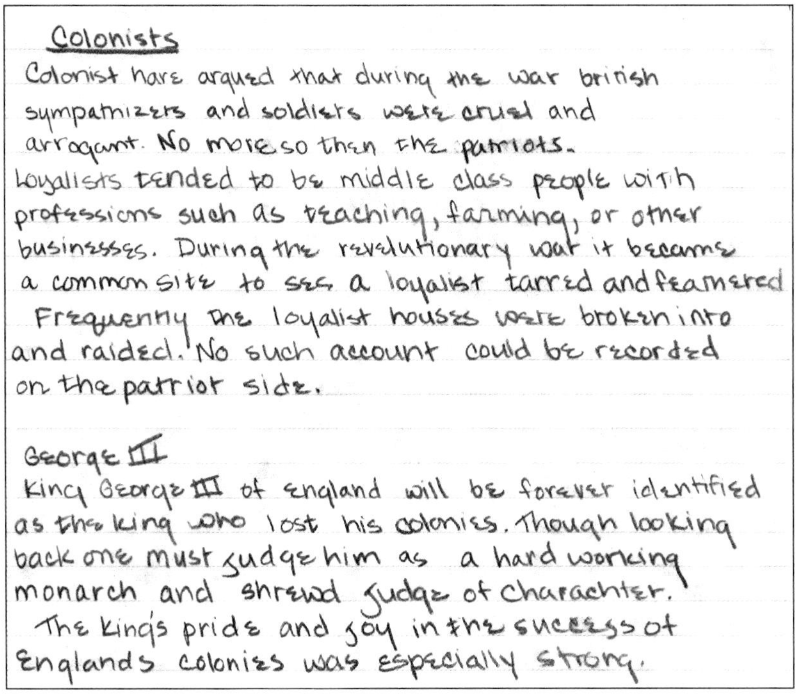

Colonists

Colonist have argued that during the war british
sympatizers and soldiers were cruel and
arrogant. No more so then the patriots.
Loyalists tended to be middle class people with
professions such as teaching, farming, or other
businesses. During the revolutionary war it became
a common site to see a loyalist tarred and feamered
   Frequently the loyalist houses were broken into
and raided. No such account could be recorded
on the patriot side.

George III

King George III of England will be forever identified
as the king who lost his colonies. Though looking
back one must judge him as a hard working
monarch and shrewd judge of character.
   The king's pride and joy in the success of
Englands colonies was especially strong.

Writing Original Problems. Groups, pairs, or individuals write story problems to exchange and solve. Place one story problem on an index card and build a deck of problem cards for individuals or groups to use.

Learning logs in social studies can become reflective documents that open the possibility for children to understand what history is and why we study the past. Determined to offer his sixth-grade class opportunities to study the Age of Exploration from several cultural perspectives, Arthur Kearns read Jon Scieszka's *The True Story of the Three Little Pigs*. Arthur began with this read-aloud and posed two open-ended questions for discussion and writing: 1) What did you get from this story? 2) How might it apply to history? Laurie's journal entry (figure 4) summarizes her group's ability to connect the themes in Scieszka's story to their study of history. Arthur has used literature to set the tone for a study that would include researching 1492 from many perspectives.

I designed a humanities class for eighth graders titled "Peaceful Resolutions to Conflict." Billy Peebles, headmaster of Powhatan, team taught that class with me. The class followed students' interests, drew on current events, and relied heavily on literature and primary sources. Students studied conflicts among peers, within families and in surrounding communities, and among nations. What the students did, Mr. Peebles and I did; we read, researched, kept journals, and participated in discussions, and learned. Journals documented twelve intensive weeks of study; because we combined history and English, the class met for twelve periods each week.

To prepare for a debate on whether the colonists had the right to break away from England, students raided the school library and community libraries and stacked the room with books. For three weeks teams read, discussed, took pages of notes, and planned their strategy—recording all of their thoughts in journals. Notes often reflected opinions and critiques rather than parroting information. Heath began his summary of a book with:

> To tell you the truth, this book taught me very little about the American Revolution that I didn't already know.

And Emily collected evidence against the colonists in her journal (figure 5), selecting information that equated the cruelty attributed to loyalists with that of the patriots. Thinking with the facts, which is what students began to do, occurred because the class members immersed themselves in reading and research until they had absorbed the stories of that period.

Preparing for debate forced students to look at opposing sides of the American Revolution and select data that supported their position. They also learned that history was interpretation of information when, after the debate, Justin admitted, "We purposely left out information to make our argument stronger; I guess that's what some historians do."

In journals, students explored feelings about their reading and research. Julie read an article on the Japanese relocation camps of World War II. She began her journal entry:

> The article that I read both astonished and confused me. I was astonished at the fact that Americans, while condemning the Nazis, treated Japanese-Americans in much the same way. This is what confused me. How could we shed tears for the Jews suffering in death camps, yet still watch dry-eyed as the same injustices occurred right under our noses?

> the story makes me depressed, sad
> seems unjust, but for some reason I feel
> it was right that we did it (I don't know why)
> I feel sorry for the people of Hiroshima and Nagasaki
> I wish the war could have ended another way or
> not even started at all
> Japanese did bomb Pearl Harber and sometimes I
> feel that the U.S. dropped the A-bomb out
> of revenge - If that was the reason It really
> doesn't seem that we should have done it, We
> ended the war but by killing huge numbers
> of people, We destroyed two large cities completely
> and killed off almost everyone living in it

Fig. 6 Eighth grader responds to a reading of Hiroshima No Pika, *by Toshi Maruki.*

Julie's confusion represents critical analysis of the illogical reactions of many Americans who attempted to rationalize the internment of the Japanese-Americans during the war.

Nuclear war was an issue that students pleaded to research and study. In science they had learned about nuclear winter and the aftereffects of war. We viewed several films on the bombing of Hiroshima and Nagasaki. I read aloud *Hiroshima No Pika*, by Toshi Maruki, and Steve wondered in his journal response (figure 6) if there is a link between Pearl Harbor and the United States dropping the bomb on Hiroshima and Nagasaki. His research disproved his theory, but without the opportunity to inquire, Steve might have incorrectly perceived the bombing. The class, knowledgeable about nuclear weapons and their destructive capabilities, read *Wolf of Shadows*, by Whitley Strieber, and decided to research wolves to determine why Strieber selected the wolf to survive and help the mother and daughter.

Here is what Heath wrote in his journal following a discussion on *Wolf of Shadows*. The entry, entitled "Reactions—Wolf and Nuclear Winter Discussion," begins, "This was one of my most favorite discussions of all this year." The group discussed and listed the facts that the story gave about nuclear winter and wolves and the facts their research revealed. Heath's conclusion demonstrates the kind of thinking that reading multiple texts, research, discussions, and journal records can develop:

> I can safely assume that the author knows more about wolves than he does about nuclear winter. However, he made an effort to show the effects of nuclear war, and I think this counts for something. Who knows, there is a chance he could be right. After all, we've never had a full-scale nuclear war before.

Many students in this humanities class felt compelled to take action for the cause of peace by writing letters to their representatives in state and federal legislatures. Julia's letter (figure 7) displays her knowledge of the status of nuclear weapons, her comprehension of "trust and fear," and her positive school experiences with the democratic process.

Her cogent letter demonstrates the thinking that students are capable of once we move them beyond facts and a single point of view, to researching multiple resources and diverse points of view.

In my school days and in far too many schools today, the word *research* receives a verbal rating of "Yuk" or "Ugh" because it triggers two thoughts: writing a boring report and looking up information in the encyclopedia. We diligently teach children not to plagiarize, so they rearrange sentences and change conjunctions to satisfy this charge. Now, with photocopying machines, students copy pages and don't even spend time reading in the library. But no real learning takes place under this system.

The purpose of research is to learn more about a subject, to clarify our present knowledge, or to learn about something totally new. The goal of all research, for me, is to acquire new stories and make them my own, so I can think and talk and write using these stories. I want nothing less for the students I teach.

Story gathering comes from reading, talking, observing, questioning, and writing. All these activities are part of a research-driven curriculum, whether it's researching variations of folktale motifs or learning about suspension bridges.

I believe school is the place to learn research. Unfortunately, reports assigned for homework do not expose children to the complexities of the process. Good research takes time to complete and time to learn. As children research, the teacher conducts whole class and small group minilessons. Record all minilessons on chart paper and hang them, like a book, on a wall for reference. Observing students will offer many topics for additional demonstrations. When a student discovers a technique that works, ask the student to model it for the class. Here are some strategies you'll want to model again and again: using the library, keeping track of sources, summarizing information, focusing information, and determining the purpose of, and how to set up, a bibliography.

If you work closely with your students as they progress through the research process, you'll be better equipped to guide them through rough spots. When the noise levels in the fourth-grade room prevented Ellen Benjamin, me, and several children from working, we called a meeting to discuss the problem. The class agreed that a quiet room would help them concentrate and remember what they read. Together, we negotiated a terrific solution that satisfied their need to read and talk: silent reading for twenty minutes, followed by a ten-minute exchange of information.

Take the time to spotlight the supportive and democratic behaviors you observe so the

Powhatan School
Rt. 2A, Box 177A
Boyce, Va. 22620
June 1, 1989

Mr. H. George White III
Administrative Assistant
1404 Longworth House Office Building
Washington, D.C. 20515

Dear Mr. White:

I am in the 8th Grade at Powhatan School in Boyce, Va.. In our school we have many conflicts. When we do, we are taught to sit down and resolve our problems in a peaceful, democratic way. I see no reason why this cannot be the course of action in our difficulties with other countries. I am aware that the government often uses this method. However, I am also aware that smaller nations, both hostile and peaceful, fear our country as a dominant power capable of destroying them; trust does not begin with fear. I was very happy when the middle-ranged nuclear weapons were disarmed, but we still have a long way to go. I do not suggest that we simply throw these dangerous arms into the ocean, for that would only worsen the state of our already battered environment. I just think that if we could establish an unbreakable trust with other nations instead of building up our country's threat, we and other countries could begin to make concessions until the danger of nuclear war is no longer so frighteningly imminent. Not only do these nuclear weapons invoke fear upon foreign peoples, but our own countrymen as well. Americans live with the constant knowledge that all we love could be destroyed with the push of a button. I know that the trust and the hope that I have may seem a naïve concept to some, but I also know that without these things, I would not love being alive as much as I do.

Very Truly Yours,
Julia E. Aitcheson

Fig. 7

children can build on them. Participate with the kids, and you'll find plenty to celebrate, such as the day four kids in Ellen Benjamin's class figured out a way to share the same book.

Think about the research process in terms of four recursive stages: deciding, collecting, sharing, and selecting. Store every note, drawing, summary, and reaction in a journal. Know that by the end of the first session, students will be at different points within the collecting stage. Here again, deadline dates can help bring closure; your chief task is to figure out how to support the students who lag behind.

Deciding. Book browsing, brainstorming, and group discussion can help children discover topics to investigate.

Collecting. Prior to collecting, help kids discover what they already know and what they would like to learn. The K-W-L strategy can provide a framework for writing questions about "What do I want to learn?"

Reserve several class periods for reading books, magazines, and charts. Ask students to record the titles and authors of books, magazine names, and pages read. The purpose of this is to know your resources, so you can easily return to them to clarify information or accurately note statistics. During the last fifteen minutes of research time, ask students to write, from memory, everything they recall from reading. If recall is minimal after many reading periods, that is a sign that students have not connected to the new information. Boost students' progress with your assistance and/or peer support.

Sharing. Ask students to reread their journals and consider how they would like to share their research. After students offer suggestions, add some of yours. Offer choices from a wide

Eighth graders study and write about fish and their environment.

range of projects, such as a speech, play, dramatic monologue, interview, article, book, editorial, puzzle, narrative, poem, chart, or essay.

Selecting. Help students understand that they must consider their project in relation to their audience, for genre and audience will impact on decisions about what information to include. I ask children to work in small groups, rereading journals, circling information they think they'll need, and discussing plans with peers. What usually occurs is that students raise additional questions and identify data that requires clarification, returning them to reading and collecting. Questions become categories on a writing plan, map, or index cards; students collect information from journals that answers their questions.

To help younger students organize information under question headings, I use large envelopes. On the outside of each envelope, students write the topic category. Working on one question at a time, they record notes on paper or index cards, placing them in the

Three third graders research bears.

appropriate envelope. Pairs read the contents of their envelopes to each other, to make sure the notes support the question.

At this point, students begin drafting and follow the writing process as they work to bring their project to a deadline draft.

Even kindergartners can research and document their learning. Nancy Chambers brings her kindergarten girls and boys into the school library, and she conducts research with her students in two ways. One is to let the children browse freely through the library and find books to study. The other is to gather their interests through questioning and give the list to Anne Wheeler, the librarian, who then places piles of books on a special reserve bookshelf for the children to explore. Research consists of studying the photographs and illustrations of books and magazines. The chil-

dren arrive in the library with large sheets of paper to "write" what they've learned. Most of them draw pictures and dictate thoughts to Nancy and her aide. Grayson drew and wrote about space and spaceships (figure 8).

Another child, studying dragons, wrote "The Dragon" and drew five different dragons. All the children share their research with classmates. In Nancy's class, kids pursue interests and discover, as one child put it, "all the things in the world to learn."

Research can lead students to reading-writing connections. Sixth graders decided to study animals as an outgrowth of reading books by Jean Craighead George. For several weeks, students read books and magazines such as *Zoobook*, *National Geographic*, *Smithsonian*, *Cricket*, and *Ranger Rick* to collect information, but in the process, they discovered different types of leads. Groups

Third graders record their research and place note cards in category envelopes.

printed their reading-writing connections on chart paper and shared these observations with the entire class:

1. Ask a question.

2. Create interest with a far-out statement.

3. Identify the animal.

4. Give an unusual, interesting fact.

5. Explain what the reader can look forward to.

6. Use a short, short story.

7. Compare to another animal or humans.

8. Create mystery with a story or statistic.

Here are a few of their leads, which, the children agreed, resulted from reflecting on "how published writers did it."

Zebras

Wow! Did you know that a zebra can see in all directions at one time! Also an adult zebra eats about twenty pounds of grass per day! Zebras have been clocked at speeds of up to sixty MPH. And there's lots, lots more!

Soren

Turtles

Did you know turtles (on the average) travel only about seven miles in their lives! One turtle had been tracked with a tracking device. He traveled eight miles in one-and-a-half years. He was held up at a hedge for six months because he couldn't crawl under.

Emma

Do Bats Really Deserve Their Bad Name?

Did you know there are over 1,200 kinds of bats. The little brown bats are only one of these interesting creatures. Bats' wings are so thin you can almost see threw them. They are only two layers of skin, but, stronger than rubber gloves.

Reveley

The Monkeys in Africa

Suppose that one day you might be walking through the jungles of Africa or maybe Asia. The leaves are bright green and there are plants and flowers all around you. Sunlight glitters down on your head as you look about. You hear a rustle and a crunching of leaves behind you as though someone were following. You turn around only to see a large mandrill monkey following you!

Chris

A research project can generate further research. Fourth graders, after completing their research on the human body, decided they had to "research ways authors write up information." Their possible project list included alphabet books, question-answer books, picture books, and calendars. Students designed and revised plans that identified and sequenced content, like William's calendar plan (figure 9).

Annie's alphabet book, *The Human Body: A-Z*, resulted from three months of research and information recorded in her journal. An excerpt represents the amount of learning that took place, Annie's pride in authorship, and the fact that knowledge learned can be assessed in ways other than testing (figure 10).

Teachers always ask me how many journals are necessary for each student. There is no pat answer. For some projects, like buddy and dialogue journals, students can make separate notebooks. In self-contained classrooms, every child might have one journal to explore literature and record personal experiences, then divide another notebook into sections for

Fig. 8

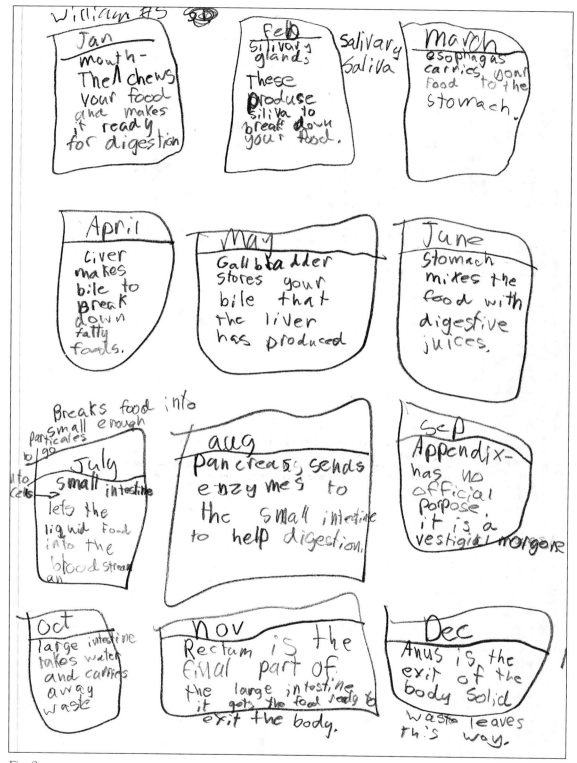

William #5

Jan
mouth—
The chews
your food
and makes
it ready
for digestion

Feb
silivary
glands
These
produse
siliva to
break down
your food.

salivary
saliva

March
esophagas
carries down
food to the
stomach.

April
Liver
makes
bile to
break
down
fatty
foods.

May
Gallbladder
stores your
bile that
the liver
has produced

June
Stomach
mixes the
food with
digestive
juices.

Breaks food into
small enough
particales
to go
into
cells

July
small intestine
lets the
liquid food
into the
bloodstream
an

aug
pancreas sends
enzymes to
the small intestine
to help digestion.

Sep
Appendix—
has no
official
porpose.
it is a
vestigial morgon

Oct
large intestine
takes water
and carries
away
waste

Nov
Rectum is the
final part of
the large intestine
it gets the food ready to
exit the body.

Dec
Anus is the
exit of the
body solid
waste leaves
this way.

Fig. 9

Fig. 10 At left, below,
and opposite page.

subjects or theme cycles. Many middle school teachers working in departmentalized schedules prefer students to have a separate journal for each subject. Explore and discuss the problem with your students, then experiment. That's how you'll get most of your ideas.

The key issue, however, is that you help students recognize journals are safe places to collect, explore, and reflect upon information and ideas, to analyze data, and to solve problems. The journal, then, becomes a record of each child's thinking and learning—a storehouse of language, information, and feelings that can lead young authors to discover knowledge about their world and answers to the question "Who am I?" Most important, in journals, learners *use* language to discover what they know and what they must find out. In the process, children can grow as readers, writers, thinkers, researchers, and observers.

Reference

1. Murray, Donald. *Write to Learn,* pages 3–4.

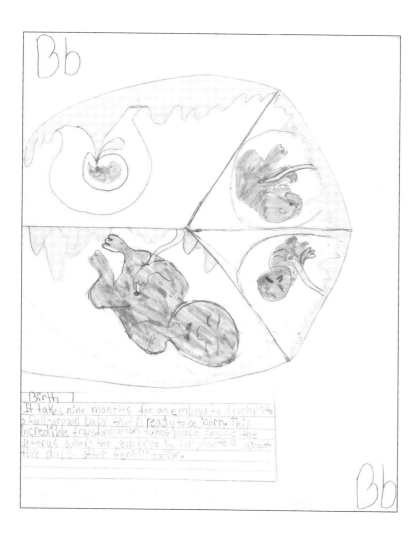

AS I SEE IT

Seymour Simon

The world doesn't always make sense.

Think about it. Does it make sense that the white light that comes from the sun is really all the colors of a rainbow mixed together? That the carrots, lettuce, and bread you eat turn into you? That the people on the other side of the earth are standing upside down yet don't fall off into space? That we're closer to the sun during winter than we are during summer? That bees do a dance to tell other bees where food is located? That a heavy object and a light object fall at the same speed? Does it make sense that some of the atoms that make up your body are the same atoms that made up a dinosaur's body one hundred million years ago?

What does it mean to "make sense" anyway? It means that something is obvious to our senses. But what's obvious to our senses may not be true. Look around you. The ground looks flat (more or less), the oceans look flat, the world looks flat. Does it make sense that the earth is round?

In a book of mine on optical illusions, nothing makes sense, because your senses are always being fooled. One line looks longer than another even though both are the same length. A drawing looks like a duck to some people and a rabbit to others. Another drawing seems to be either an old woman or a young lady, depending upon how you're looking at it. An image of wavy lines looks as if the lines are in constant motion even though they are really not moving at all. Illusions show us that what we think is clear and correct may not be correct at all. Richard Feynman, a Nobel Prize–winning scientist, put it this way: "Science is a long history of learning how not to fool ourselves."

There are at least two other things about science that have always attracted me and that I've tried to put into my books. One is that scientists are always playing around, and the other is that science is fun. You see, play for a scientist means trying something just to see what happens. Only they may call it an experiment. Some scientists play with telescopes, looking here and there in the night sky, perhaps discovering a comet or a new star or something strange about the surface of Mars. Other scientists play with microscopes, perhaps discovering little creatures swimming around in a drop of water or little cells in a piece of skin. Still other scientists play with equations or with thought experiments. Einstein, for example, imagined how one person traveling in a spaceship almost as fast as the speed of light would not get old as fast as another person remaining on earth. It's all part of the theory of relativity.

I guess the fact that science is fun is what attracted me when I was a child, attracted me when I became a science teacher and an author of science books, and still attracts me today. One of the first books I wrote was about how to make and fly paper airplanes. Not science? Oh, but it was all about experimenting, hypothesizing, examining ideas, and coming to conclusions. Just what scientists do. And the book was really a result of teaching that very same thing to my eighth-grade science classes.

Even when I turned to fiction, in the *Einstein Anderson, Science Sleuth* series, what I tried to do was show how much fun science could be. The fact that when some solids and liquids are mixed together they behave in strange ways was the idea behind "The Fastest Ketchup in the Cafeteria." Newton's second law of motion as applied to baseball became "The Batty Invention." And the sun's rising in the east and setting in the west helped Einstein solve the mystery in "The Incredible Shrinking Machine."

One of the basic laws of the universe when I was a teacher seemed to be "If anything can go wrong, it will go wrong." To which I suppose I have a correlative theorem: "Things don't go wrong all the time, so don't depend upon it." That especially applies to experiments and science investigations that were carried out in my class.

Sometimes things that I or the children expected to happen did happen. A magnet attracted an iron nail but not a copper penny. Seeds kept in a refrigerator germinated slowly, if at all. But often things didn't come out the way the children (and their teacher) expected. Mold didn't grown on a moist piece of bread but grew quite nicely, thank you, on the blotter around the bread. Fertilized plants quickly gave up and keeled over, while unfertilized plants grew like Jack's beanstalk. But these "wrong" results were often more fun and more instructive than those that came out just the way I expected they would.

My students and I thought about what happened and tried to figure out why it happened. We came up with a hypothesis about what might be the reason and then tested the hypothesis. The importance of carefully observing, checking, keeping records, questioning, rethinking, and coming to a new conclusion became obvious. And all this time we were having fun trying to figure out why the world is the way it is (and sometimes isn't). I'm still doing much the same thing when I write books nowadays—having fun and playing around with a world that doesn't make sense.

SELECTED BOOKS BY SEYMOUR SIMON

Autumn Across America. New York: Hyperion, 1993.
Big Cats. New York: HarperCollins, 1991.
Deserts. New York: Morrow, 1990.

The Dinosaur Is the Biggest Animal That Ever Lived, and Other Wrong Ideas You Thought Were True. Illustrated by Giulio Maestro. New York: Harper & Row, 1984.

Einstein Anderson, Science Sleuth. Illustrated by Fred Winkowski. New York: Penguin, 1986.

Galaxies. New York: Morrow, 1988.

Hidden Worlds: Pictures of the Invisible. New York: Morrow, 1983.

How to Be an Ocean Scientist in Your Own Home. Illustrated by David A. Carter. New York: Lippincott, 1988.

How to Be a Space Scientist in Your Own Home. Illustrated by Bill Morrison. New York: Lippincott, 1982.

Icebergs and Glaciers. New York: Morrow, 1987.

Jupiter. New York: Morrow, 1985.

Little Giants. Illustrated by Pamela Carroll. New York: Morrow, 1983.

Look to the Night Sky: An Introduction to Star Watching. New York: Penguin, 1979.

Mars. New York: Morrow, 1987.

Mountains. New York: Morrow, 1994.

New Questions and Answers about Dinosaurs. Illustrated by Jennifer Dewey. New York: Morrow, 1990.

Oceans. New York: Morrow, 1990.

The Optical Illusion Book. Illustrated by Constance Ftera. New York: Morrow, 1984.

Our Solar System. New York: Morrow, 1992.

The Paper Airplane Book. Illustrated by Byron Barton. New York: Viking, 1971.

Pets in a Jar: Collecting and Caring for Small Animals. New York: Penguin, 1979.

Professor I.Q. Explores the Brain. Illustrated by Dennis Kendrick. Honesdale, PA: Boyds Mills Press, 1993.

Professor I.Q. Explores the Senses. Illustrated by Dennis Kendrick. Honesdale, PA: Boyds Mills Press, 1993.

Saturn. New York: Morrow, 1985.

Seymour Simon's Science Dictionary. New York: HarperCollins, 1994.

Shadow Magic. Illustrated by Stella Ormai. New York: Lothrop, Lee & Shepard, 1985.

Snakes. New York: HarperCollins, 1992.

Soap Bubble Magic. Illustrated by Stella Ormai. New York: Lothrop, Lee & Shepard, 1985.

Space Words: A Dictionary. Illustrated by Randy Chewning. New York: HarperCollins, 1991.

Stars. New York: Morrow, 1986.

Storms. New York: Morrow, 1989.

The Sun. New York: Morrow, 1986.

Uranus. New York: Morrow, 1987.

Volcanoes. New York: Morrow, 1988.

Weather. New York: Morrow, 1993.

Whales. New York: HarperCollins, 1989.

Wolves. New York: HarperCollins, 1993.

SPELLING AND WORD STUDY

Controversy surrounds the teaching of spelling and word study. At meetings, I am most often attacked by parents who insist whole language teachers ignore spelling. At one meeting, when I boldly stated that all of us employ spelling inventions, four parents jumped out of their seats in unison, angry fists waving in my direction. They feared that my work with the teachers would ruin their children's spelling ability forever! Like these parents, many administrators and teachers hold fast to such spelling beliefs as: Spelling is a separate subject; earning high grades on memorized, weekly spelling tests is an indication of spelling power; filling in workbook pages teaches spelling; children should be made to spell correctly, and if that means marking them down for misspelled words, so be it. Schools all over the country invest long hours preparing star spellers for national contests. Winners receive grand prizes and national publicity. Underlying these attitudes toward spelling is the certainty that good spelling is a mark of intelligence. Once we equate intelligence and spelling, these spelling myths become logical conclusions.

Many teachers perpetuate spelling myths by asking children to memorize lists of words and complete fill-in-the-blank workbooks and dittos. They celebrate those perfect spelling grades by displaying them on bulletin boards. Yet teachers daily observe that many children who score 100 percent on weekly tests spell poorly on written work. They wring their hands and begin yet another search for the "perfect" program—the program that will make kids spell right! However, programs don't make kids spell correctly.

Relieved to be able to ditch their basal spelling program, many teachers turn to literature rather than workbooks to design word study units. I've observed children plowing through wonderful stories to find words with long or short vowels, consonant digraphs. "They've had two days of fun with the story," said one teacher, "and now we use it for phonics and word study." And indeed, her class was searching diligently through the pages of Maurice Sendak's *Where the Wild Things Are*, compiling lists of words with long and short *a*'s and *i*'s. "But they love searching for words," their teacher rationalized, thoroughly frustrated. "How else can I teach phonics? I don't have a workbook. What else can I use?" And my response is always "Use the children's collaborative writing and their innovations on patterned texts, poems, and songs for language study." For it's through their written language that children learn about spelling and writing conventions, becoming more efficient communicators.

Classrooms immersed in print, signs; classrooms filled with books; classrooms where children read and are read to are places where children can observe and connect their growing knowledge of print and how language works. Models abound with which they can test hypotheses about how words and print conventions operate. "Maurice Sendak uses capital letters," first grader Tommy notes as he thumbs through *Chicken Soup with Rice.* Reading *Henry and Mudge in the Green Time,* by Cynthia Rylant, to a small group of second graders, Monisha looked up and told them "*Gingersnaps* is a compound word." Two emissaries from the group questioned me about the accuracy of Monisha's observation. What they didn't know was that Monisha had given me a minilesson topic and for three weeks we accumulated compound words on a huge wall chart. Children brought words from home, such as *bathtub* and *carport*; they pointed to words on classroom charts and signs such as *doorway* and *shortcake*. Language study can be a vital, authentic activity when teachers respond to questions and observations children make about literature and their own and classmates' writing.

Words, the tools of thought and communication, shape writing and speech; the study of language and how language functions is a worthwhile and important task for all children. Spelling is only one aspect of language. During their elementary school years children should also study etymology, the history of language, variations in language registers, and written conventions.

To plan an effective child-centered language program requires a knowledge of spelling development. Edmund Henderson's extensive research at the University of Virginia and Shane Templeton's at the University of Nevada, Reno, identified five developmental spelling stages that all of us pass through. Letter-sound relationships, word patterns, and meaning all contribute to understanding ways our language works and how to spell correctly. Therefore, a spelling program should include all three elements of word study at developmentally appropriate times.

Stage I: Preliterate. (Ages 1–7) This stage includes prephonemic and early phonemic spellers—children who might know their alphabet but are unable to match letters and sounds and early phonemic spellers who have begun to associate sounds with letters.

Prephonemic spellers have ideas of what written language should look like. Though they usually know their alphabet, they cannot match letters and sounds. Their writing inventions consist of random strings of alphabet letters, numerals, and squiggly marks with no relationship between the words intended and the written marks produced. Through constant exposure to stories, print, and opportunities to write and experiment with language, these children move into the early phonemic stage.

With early phonemic spellers, there is a clearer link between written letters and some speech sounds. Children at this stage repeat a word or word part, diligently listening to sounds until they can relate sound to letter. Only one or two phonemes, or sounds, spell each word, and so an entire word will first be spelled with only its initial consonant. As children rehearse and experiment with matching letters and sounds, the final consonant sound heard joins the initial consonant, and two consonants represent an entire word. At this stage, children are unable to engage in phonemic segmentation or the ability to break a word down into its phonemes. They cannot match sounds in spoken words with letters.

Prephonemic and early phonemic spellers are prereaders unable to accurately point to memorized print; they lack a stable concept of *word*, and don't recognize the difference between words and the spaces that separate them.

Stage II: Letter Name. (Ages 5–9) Children spell according to the alphabetic principle, which means matching the sounds in a word to the letter name sounds. As they slowly and deliberately repeat the sounds of a word, they substitute the closest letter-name sound for vowel consonant digraphs such as *ch*, *sh*, *th*, *wh*, and *qu* and consonant blends or clusters. *Bus* might be spelled *bs*; *chip*, *jip*; *night*, *nit*. Their spelling inventions honor the short and long vowels, but letter-name spellers classify vowels according to the way they hear them. *Bed* might be spelled *bad*; *love*, *luv*; *rake*, *rak*. Not only do these children have a stable concept of word, able to point correctly to words as they read poems and patterned books from memory, but they've accumulated a core of sight words that they can accurately spell. Late letter-name spellers demonstrate they are making the transition to Stage III (Within-Word Pattern) when they begin to spell short vowel words and many common long vowel words correctly. These children also begin to include in their spelling the preconsonantal nasal sounds such as the *m* in *thump*. Basically phonetic spellers, these children benefit from activities that lead them to study medial vowel patterns in words.

Stage III: Within-Word Pattern. (Ages 6–12) These children's spellings reflect control over many consonant blends and short vowels. Difficulty with complex long vowel patterns continues, but a knowledge of syllables, each with a vowel sound, develops. Errors still occur with many long vowel patterns—children write *beaf* for *beef*, *swet* for *sweat*, *saler* for *sailor*. Confusion often exists with spelling consonant digraphs such as *ch/sh*, *th*, *wh*, and consonant blends such as *dr/tr/cr* and *c/k/ck*. Confusions often appear with the spelling of prefixes and unstressed final syllables.

Stage IV: Syllable Juncture. (Ages 8–10) During this developmental stage, children work to understand the conditions that guide spelling at the point that syllables join together. Invented spelling errors occur at syllable junctures and schwa positions, affecting the spelling of open and closed syllables, consonant doubling conventions, prefix assimilation, such as *ad* meaning *to* or *toward*, and homophones.

Stage V: Derivational Principles. (Ages 10–100) Word patterns have been memorized, and these children transfer this knowledge to spell other words. At this stage, spellers combine their knowledge of the alphabetic principle, word patterns, word meanings, silent letters, vowel alternation and reduction, and Latin and Greek derivations. Children and adults in this stage, when faced with a difficult or unfamiliar word, may revert to spelling inventions that employ phonetic principles.

The knowledge researchers have accumulated about the alphabetic, pattern, and meaning conventions of spelling in the English language has implications for the study of spelling—implications that suggest

```
BEGINNERS' FEATURES LIST

1.    late
2.    wind
3.    shed
4.    jumped
5.    geese
6.    yell
7.    chirped
8.    once
9.    learned
10.   shove
11.   trained
12.   year
13.   shock
14.   stained
15.   chick
16.   drive

ADVANCED FEATURES LIST -

1.    setter
2.    shove
3.    grocery
4.    button
5.    prison
6.    nature
7.    peeked
8.    special
9.    preacher
10.   slowed
11.   sail
12.   feature
13.   batter
14.   sailor
```

Fig. 1 Features lists from Understanding Reading Problems, *by Gillet and Temple.*

we link the *order* of word study with a child's development. To assess students' spelling needs you must be able to identify the developmental stage of each child.

There are several ways to study a child's spelling errors in order to assess spelling development. The key to all helpful assessment lies in studying children's word inventions, for their inventions offer insights into the rules and concepts they are using. You can study your students' word inventions by analyzing their writing, or by administering and analyzing a features list or qualitative spelling inventory.

Children's Writing. Careful review of children's writing informs teachers about their spelling knowledge and language conventions. Use the features list guidelines described below for assessing a child's developmental spelling stage through writing samples. However, young children tend to search for correct spellings by asking peers and by using available print. That is why writing samples should not be the only assessment tool you use.

Spelling Features List. These are words specifically selected to evaluate certain word features apparent in children's spelling inventions. Gillet and Temple offer two lists: a beginners' list for children in grades kindergarten to two, and an advanced list for grades three and up (figure 1).

You might need to use the beginners' list with older students who are weak spellers and the advanced list with younger students who are strong spellers. Before administering the word features test make sure you explain to the children that you don't expect them to know how to spell all or even many of the dictated words. Encourage students to write the word the way they think it is spelled. Read each word clearly as you dictate it, and use each in a sentence that clearly illustrates the word's meaning.

Scoring a Features List

Using the guidelines below, the teacher studies each word to determine whether the spelling is prephonemic, early phonemic, letter-name, transitional, or correct.

1. **Prephonemic Speller.** No letters in the word relate to any sound in the word. Example: *pt* for *book*. Score 1 point.

2. **Early Phonemic Speller.** Fewer than half the letters in a word relate to sounds in the word. The child uses the letter-name strategy to match sounds and letters. Example: *hs* for *house*. Score 2 points.

3. **Letter-Name Speller.** Letters represent half or more than half of the sounds in the word. A similarity exists between the sound of the letter and the name of the letter selected to represent that sound because children sound out a word, letter by letter. Example: *luv* for *love*. Score 3 points.

4. **Transitional Speller.** Children in the stages Henderson identifies as Within-Word Pattern and Syllable Juncture are transitional spellers. More than half the sounds in a word are spelled correctly. Spellings have moved beyond letter-sound relationships; and digraphs, consonants, and short vowels are spelled correctly. Attempts at using the final silent *e* appear. Example: *lernd* for *learned, plase* for *place*. Score 4 points.

5. **Correct Speller.** The entire word is spelled correctly. Any error, no matter how slight, scores the word as transitional spelling. Score 5 points.

The sample spelling features analyses are for a second and a sixth grader (figures 2 and 3).

Using the above definitions, put each word into a category. Assign points according to the scoring guidelines. The category where the majority of spellings fall is an indication of a child's stage of spelling development.

Qualitative spelling inventories have been developed from graded or basal spelling series. They can assist teachers in identifying students' developmental stage of spelling and designing a word study program. You can use the qualitative inventory from the McGuffey Reading Center of the University of Virginia, which follows the spelling features that children must master at each developmental stage (see appendix).

Remember that you, the teacher, are the best judge of a student's development and needs. Every student error will not necessarily neatly fit a particular stage. Discussions with students will help you develop a feeling for how students think about words and spelling inventions. Careful review of students' writing folders can offer additional insights into spelling performance. The judgments you make about a child's spelling development, therefore, are subjective and qualitative. With a firm grasp of the developmental stages and the three principles that govern spelling—phonetic, pattern, and meaning—you will be able to assess students' needs.

Below are some guidelines for you to follow when administering a qualitative spelling inventory.

1. Ask children to put name and date on the paper.

2. Dictate word lists I and II to first graders.

3. Dictate three word lists to grades two to seven: one list below grade level, one list at grade level, and one list above grade level.

4. Have children begin a new test on a different sheet of paper.

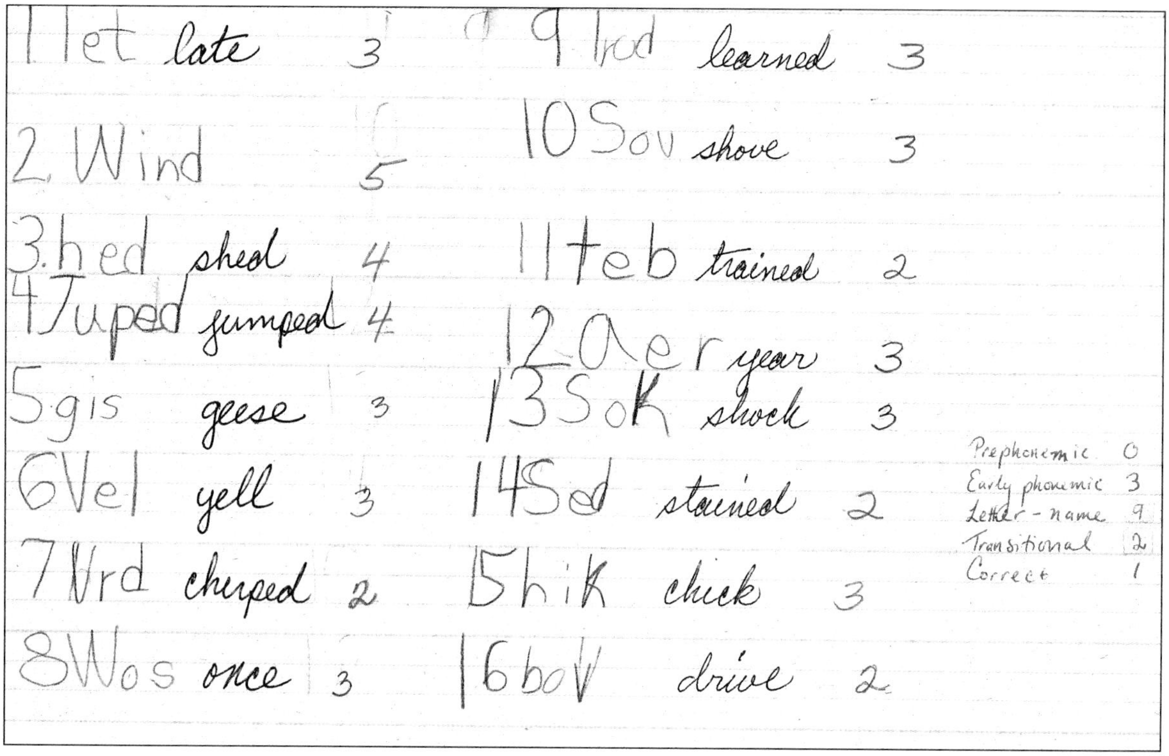

1 et	late	3	9 lrd	learned	3
2. Wind		5	10 Sov	shove	3
3. h ed	shed	4	11 teb	trained	2
4 Juped	jumped	4	12 Aer	year	3
5 gis	geese	3	13 Sok	shock	3
6 Vel	yell	3	14 Sd	stained	2
7 Vrd	chirped	2	15 hiK	chick	3
8 Wos	once	3	16 boV	drive	2

Prephonemic 0
Early phonemic 3
Letter-name 9
Transitional 2
Correct 1

Fig. 2

5. Pronounce each word clearly and use it in a sentence that demonstrates the meaning of the word.

6. In your introduction, include remarks such as those that follow: "Today I am going to administer a spelling inventory to you so that we can work together on spelling and word knowledge. This inventory will not be graded; it will only be used for us to set helpful learning goals together. Try to spell each word correctly. If you can't spell a word correctly, I want you to make the very best guess that you can."

7. Administer only one test per day. Score each test. Beside each error the child makes, rewrite the word correctly. Rewriting the word helps you reflect upon and analyze students' inventions.

8. Continue administering lower to higher spelling lists until you have acquired for each child:
   - One score below 50 percent
   - One score between 50 percent and 70 percent
   - One score above 70 percent (if possible)

9. Now carefully review each error and try to categorize the students' pattern of errors; place each student in a developmental stage.

As you plan your program, keep in mind several key conclusions about how children learn language based on the research of Henderson, Graves, Read, and Chomsky. The suggestions that follow should influence the kinds of language study you offer students.

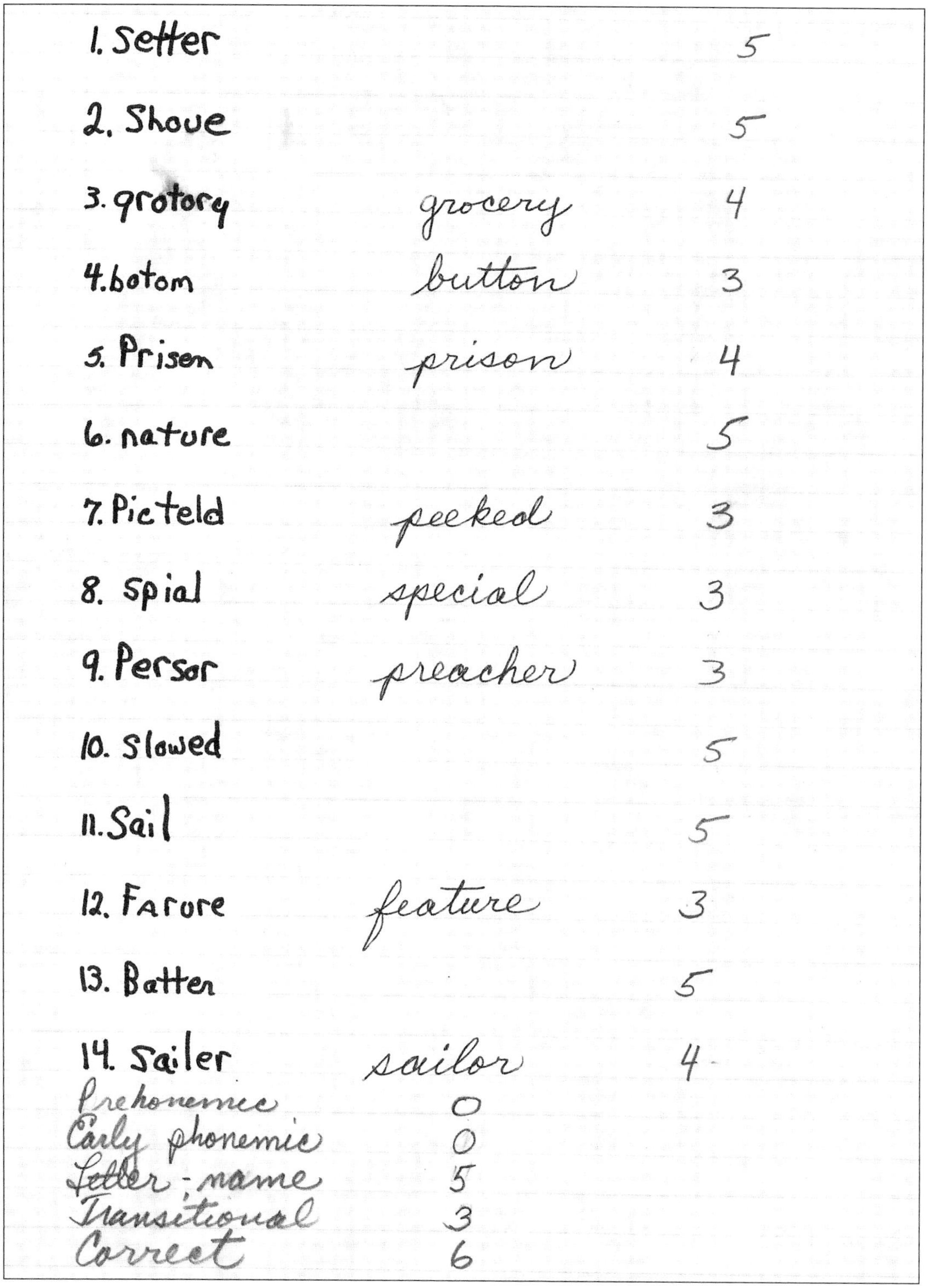

1. Setter   5

2. Shove   5

3. qrotory   grocery   4

4. botom   button   3

5. Prison   prison   4

6. nature   5

7. Picteld   peeked   3

8. spial   special   3

9. Persor   preacher   3

10. slowed   5

11. Sail   5

12. Farore   feature   3

13. Batter   5

14. sailer   sailor   4

Prehonemic   0

Early phonemic   0

Letter-name   5

Transitional   3

Correct   6

Fig. 3

- Word study should begin *after* children have developed a stable concept of the written word. Children with a stable concept of word can accurately match print and speech by pointing to each word in a text; they also know the difference between words and spaces and can identify the beginning and end of a word.

- Study of our language includes three principles of spelling in this developmental sequence: alphabetic, word patterns, and word meanings.

- Spelling inventions are temporary. Children and adults use such inventions to match sounds with letters. All spellers, whether child or adult, usually turn to the phonetic principles of our language to attempt to spell an unfamiliar word. That is why a phonics-driven program will often limit children's understanding of how our language works.

- We learn to spell only those words whose meaning we comprehend.

- Experiential learning offers children opportunities to observe and think about how our language works. Rules or generalizations result from active learning experiences.

- Children's writing enables you to observe whether or not they apply their spelling knowledge.

- At each developmental stage of spelling, children must memorize sample words from their studies, in correct form, once they've demonstrated a clear understanding of the specific spelling features. In this context, memorization can support their study of higher-order principles.

Spelling, then, is individualized; the words children study should come from their writing, theme cycles, word banks, spelling lists, and texts. If your district mandates that you cover a basal text, then use the text to support each child's spelling development by selecting words that broaden a student's knowledge of sounds, patterns, and meanings.

A child-centered spelling program can be organized around whole group, small group, and independent experiences. The data you collected by analyzing children's writing and their word features inventories can provide you with a variety of ways to group children; these groups will change as your students progress.

Through minilessons and during reading-writing conferences, you can demonstrate how the alphabetic, word patterns, and word meanings principles affect spelling; explain and model word-sorting activities; and share researchers' observations, so children can understand how successful learners think about language as they use language.

For the small percentage of natural spellers in your class, those children with incredible spelling facility, design a program that acquaints them with word derivations, word meanings, and the political and social aspects of language. Help these students move beyond the information they've internalized.

Diverse resources can define a middle school language study program. I collect basal spelling texts that span several grade levels. These become one resource for the study of word patterns and meanings. Make available to students folders in a file cabinet that contain all kinds of word lists for different grade levels—lists organized by rules, frequency of use in writing, spelling demons, and so on. The children become word collectors, copying words from edited writing or new vocabulary from theme cycles into spelling word

Sixth graders work in pairs administering individualized spelling tests.

logs. Support their word searches to insure they make choices that are developmentally appropriate. Students can easily make their own spelling logs by folding in half, lengthwise, a nine-by-twelve-inch piece of construction paper. Staple several sheets of folded, lined composition paper inside the construction paper cover. Middle school students fill two to three logs each year.

On classroom shelves are several different editions of dictionaries, thesauri, and books to explore word histories and etymologies. Stock your room with books such as Wilfred Funk's *Word Origins and Their Romantic Stories,* Charles Funk's *Thereby Hangs a Tale: Stories of Curious Word Origins,* and *Eight Ate: A Feast of Homonym Riddles,* by Marvin Terban. My students enjoy taking turns telling word stories they've read about to their class and younger grades.

Assessing children's word knowledge and progress should move beyond weekly whole class spelling tests to a program that includes individual word lists, group word lists, and words everyone in a class should study and memorize. Children can work in pairs and select ten to twenty words from their spelling logs or group list, then administer individualized spelling tests to each other. Students and teacher also agree on words that everyone should memorize; testing comes after careful discussion and study of these words.

During reading-writing workshop, you can set aside specific days for word study and reserve time for partner and whole class tests. Or you can suggest that children use part of choice time for partner spelling quizzes. Help children set word study goals and then establish deadlines for memorization once

Two second-grade students discuss their key words.

individuals can explain and demonstrate how a concept works.

You can start young children on word collections with word banks, which consist of an individual student's sight words, printed on cards by the teacher and stored in a cylindrical container such as a coffee can or oatmeal carton. Teachers gather words that children recognize and read from stories they dictate, as well as from signs, labels, and trade books. Word banks can become a spelling resource in writing workshop.

Key words, a concept developed by Sylvia Ashton-Warner while working with Maori children, can broaden sight and writing words. Children sit in a circle and tell words they would like to read; the teacher records these on cards. Store cards on a metal ring or in a canister. Pairs or small groups read and talk about their words.

Many primary teachers establish classroom word banks, collecting words in cans according to specific features, such as short, long, and *r*-controlled vowel spellings, consonant digraphs, final *k* spellings, homophones, compound words, and so on. These can enrich sorting experiences, and you'll often observe the children adding words to the cans.

Word collections are a rich resource for word sorting, which is an experience-based word study strategy that calls children's attention to the likenesses and differences among words. Sorting allows children to solve language problems actively as they analyze word sounds, patterns, and meanings. Such experiences foster the ability to generalize common features and transfer knowledge to unfamiliar words with similar patterns.

Children can sort words independently or in small groups. By monitoring individuals, you can observe a child's process and listen to explanations. When groups work collaboratively on a sorting problem, they can enlarge each other's word knowledge and vocabulary by sharing what they know. No matter how you group your students, always have them pronounce each word as they categorize it.

Open Sorts. Divergent thinking results from open sorting because the child sets the criteria for categorizing a set of words. As you observe the open sorts of small groups of younger children, ask each child to explain the reasoning behind the sort; older students can write their explanations. In either case, you can gain insights into students' reasoning and knowledge of word features.

Closed Sorts. You, the teacher, define the nature of the sorting activity, asking the children to search for words that illustrate certain features. The children's writing and open sorting can furnish you with specific principles that require further study. Once you select the criteria for the sorting activity, carefully model the process, then ask the children to organize their words. Through closed sorts you offer students practice based on observed needs.

Shared Features Sort. To assess a child's ability to use what she or he knows and to analyze what isn't known, create situations that require students to transfer their knowledge to new situations. For example, Greta has in her word bank these sight words:

hand   sand   and

If Greta can use the shared feature of *and* to recognize and categorize unknown words such as *land* and *band*, then she has demonstrated the ability to move from a known set of features to unknown words with similar features. You can supply the unknown words on cards and/or ask the child to add similar words.

A Sample Open Sort. I ask eighth graders to select ten to twelve words from their spelling logs to categorize, for I want to see how much of their word features knowledge they can transfer to a random selection. Gail's list, which follows, informs me that she has internalized our study of Latin and Greek roots and can identify words from the French language.

beginning *f* sound spellings
pharmacist, forage, felon
Latin root *spect*; it means "to watch"
spectator, spectacle, inspector
Greek root *tele*
telegraph, telecommunications, telethon
endings of words *ent* and *ant*
defendant, adolescent, independent
long *a* spellings
x-ray, sleigh, saint
words from French
felon, saint, revenue

She also applies her knowledge of vowel and end-of-word patterns and letter-sound associations. Through this sort, Gail has demonstrated her knowledge of the three

Age 1-7	Age 5-9	Age 6-12	Age 8-18	Age 10-100
Stage 1	Stage 2	Stage 3	Stage 4	Stage 5
Preliterate	Letter Name	Within Word Pattern	Syllable Juncture	Derivational Constancies
Scribbles	Most sight words spelled correctly	Most sight words spelled correctly	Sight words may or may not be transferred to spelling performance	Sight words may or may not transfer
Identifies pictures				
Draws	Invented spelling by letter name	Invented spellings honor short vowels and long vowel markers	Invented-spelling errors occur at juncture and schwa positions	Invented spellings "most frequently misspelled"
Imitates writing				
Learns letters				
	Episode 1 (Concept of Word)	Episode 2 (Silent Reading)	Episode 3 (Abstract Thought)	
Readiness	Beginning Reading	Early Reading	Toward Maturity in Reading	
Talks	Steady acquisition of sight vocabulary	Semantic support sufficient	Functional vocabulary mastered	Classical vocabulary expands rapidly
Listens to stories				
Requests stories	Support for reading necessary	Silent reading established	Common plot complexities mastered	Metalinguistic reasoning applied to form and content
Identifies symbols				
Recites to print	Oral reading	Prosodic oral reading	Basic discipline mastered	
	Word-by-word reading: prosodic form delayed	Rapid word acquisition		
	Basic story form used functionally	Predictions accurate for simple stories and expository material		

Fig. 4 From Teaching Spelling, *by Edmund Henderson.*

spelling principles: sound, pattern, and meaning.

A Sample Closed Sort. A large group of third graders consistently spell the short *e* sound phonetically. Their sole reliance on sound-letter relationships will continue to reinforce misspellings unless they gain insight into the different short *e* patterns. And so the sort I model for short *e* spellings might look like this:

E PATTERN	EA PATTERN	OTHER
shed	lead	said
fed	health	friend
bed	read	
men	bread	

My goal is to draw children's attention to the patterns within words. You can increase the complexity of closed sorting by asking children to sort words into three and four patterns. For example, sort words under these three headings—*box, slow, coat*—to illustrate ways to spell short or long *o* sounds; or under these four ways to spell *a* sounds—*flat, rake, trail, way*; or even move to five ways to spell a sound, such as *bug, rough, burn, blue, fruit.*

You'll find a comprehensive list of words organized by sound, pattern, and meaning in the appendix of Edmund Henderson's *Teaching Spelling*. Lists such as Henderson's are extremely useful to teachers implementing a spelling and word study program based on the developmental stages we all pass through.

Spelling patterns, however, do not affect mature readers the way they affect beginning readers. Henderson's chart (figure 4) is an overview of the relationship between the developmental spelling stages and reading. The research that this chart summarizes dispels the myth that all excellent readers should be terrific spellers. The only measure of competent readers' acquisition of spelling knowledge should be in the application: their daily writing.

As you consider and rethink the role of spelling in your classroom, reflect on ways you can integrate spelling into authentic language experiences. Writing for an audience offers an authentic way to test and revise new knowledge and furnishes real reasons for functional spelling, legible handwriting, and comprehensible grammar and usage. Reading offers models of how authors use these conventions to communicate with others. All

Sorting words in a sixth-grade reading-writing workshop.

spelling knowledge your children gain will make sense only in the context of using the knowledge and reflecting on ways others use the same knowledge. That's why your whole language curriculum should focus on meaningful reading, writing, and research. This way you can link children to ways people use language in the real world.

Since research demonstrates that children can learn to spell and retain only words they understand, acquisition of new vocabulary should play a starring role in a language curriculum. There's no doubt that vocabulary development concerns teachers, parents, and administrators from preschool through graduate school, no matter what subject they teach. And this concern stems from the knowledge that children and adults can't think about concepts and theories for which they have no words. Words are the meaningful labels that enable us to think about topics, theories, ideas, and concepts.

The principles of *introduce, pronounce, define,* and *memorize* drive many vocabulary programs. Words memorized in isolation are less likely to be retained than words in meaningful phrases. Variations of this method include "word of the day," where students "enlarge" their vocabularies by memorizing a new word each day and weekly receiving lists of words to define and memorize. One high school English teacher handed seniors a list of one hundred vocabulary words on Friday. Students defined and memorized the words for a quiz on the following Friday; no class discussions about the words ensued. The weekly quiz, however, consisted of four words the teacher selected from the hundred. One senior told me that most students never defined the words or studied. "It's like playing Russian roulette with the vocabulary sheet," the student told me. "We take chances; you win some, and you lose others."

Perhaps students retain memorized definitions long enough to pass quizzes. However, words memorized swiftly depart. To understand a new word, the child has to have prior experiences, knowledge, and stories to bring to the new label. Only then can the child link the word to a stored body of knowledge. Uncovering story connections to new words is the first step toward comprehension of a new vocabulary.

My students supply me with words for vocabulary demonstrations. They collect words from their independent reading and enter the words in journals. Another method asks students before beginning a theme cycle to compile lists of unfamiliar words after browsing through books, magazines, and charts, or previewing a textbook. For minilessons, I select those words that most students identified. Our reading and group discussions can broaden their knowledge of new vocabulary not analyzed. Below is the list of words one of my seventh-grade classes compiled after browsing through many books about medieval Japan:

Kabuki	Bushido	child emperor
hara-kiri	tea ceremony	kimono
samurai	bonsai	kowtow
shogun	Heike and Genge	calligraphy
koto	samisen	
Shinto	Bunraku	

I immediately knew which words stumped students. Had I culled the words, they might have had little to do with student needs. Your students will be more willing to invest time learning new vocabulary if they identify unfamiliar words.

Begin your minilesson by explaining that you too at times meet words you don't understand. I introduce two to three words each week following these steps:

For Upper Elementary Students

1. Trade stories and experiences related to the word with students. Ask questions to facilitate storying about a word. For the word *commotion* I ask, "Have you ever been in a situation surrounded by loud noise and lots of activity?" After trading stories, record the word and its other forms.

2. Ask students to write in journals the new word and the story that connects them to it. On a chart, I record the word and some of the shared stories that relate to the word.

3. Write these three column headings on the chart paper: Category, Like, Examples. Under *category,* students classify the word; under *like,* they search for words and phrases that describe a word's features; under *examples,* they suggest situations where the word might be used.

4. Evaluate the information in the categories and make changes if necessary.

5. On the chart, write several sentences that you and students create to model the way the words work.

6. Use the word frequently during discussions.

7. Invite students to check the dictionary entries for the word.

Work collaboratively with students to produce several charts. Students can record the collaborative models in their journals. Display the charts in the classroom, for they provide students with examples of the process and usage.

Here is a chart compiled by a group of sixth graders identified as reluctant readers:

HUDDLE, HUDDLED, HUDDLING

Stories:
1. What football players do to make a game plan.
2. You do it to keep warm. Like stick together.
3. You get together when you're scared.
4. Tell secrets and gossip in little groups.

Category	Like	Examples
you do it	bodies in a bunch	football game
action	heads together	to keep warm
a verb	people stand close	basketball game
	a bunch of people	when you're scared
	jump	at a party or dance

Sentences:
1. The team *huddled* in order to change their strategy.
2. We *huddled* by the fire to keep warm.
3. Three girls told secrets in a *huddle*.
4. James was *huddling* in the corner of the garage.

Dictionary Check:
Results, presented to the class, of James's and Keri's dictionary study of *huddle*.
1. It's also a noun.
2. Using it to mean "to gossip" or "tell secrets" is slang.
3. It can also mean to push into something.
   Example: The teacher huddled the students onto the bus.

Jaime Grahson
4-20-

rove   roving. You get Spring Fever.

Story- In math I always day dream

Category	Whats it like?	Examples
verb	happy feeling	staring
	makes you feel good	cats
	you have happy thoughts	dogs
	staring at something	writing one place
		board
		walks in a park
		nowy mind
		bumping into something

My mind always roves in Math class.

In the Spring my mind roves.
I always think of going to the Mall and going on a vacation.

Fig. 5

Fig. 6 A second grader uses a drawing to explain the concept of a tornado.

For Lower Elementary Students

1. Repeat Step 1 from the list for Upper Elementary Students.

2. In journals, students draw or write the story that connects them to the new word. The teacher writes several connecting stories on the chart.

3. Ask groups of students to discuss various situations where they might use the word. Collect students' ideas on chart paper. Print two sections on the chart: Situations and Other Ways of Saying.

4. Organize small groups to find words with similar meanings; record these on the chart. Introduce the term *synonym* after you've collected and talked about students' suggestions.

5. On the chart, model the way the word works in several sentences; students contribute sentences.

6. Have students write original sentences in journals.

7. Display chart and use the word frequently.

This is the chart a group of third graders constructed for the word *astonishment*: They were reading *Ramona Quimby, Age 8,* by Beverly Cleary.

ASTONISHMENT, ASTONISH, ASTONISHED, ASTONISHING

Stories:
1. Miss Whaley's patience from Beverly Cleary's *Ramona Quimby, Age 8.*
2. When I got a present I wished for.
3. The day my mom let my dog sit at the dinner table.
4. I thought everyone forgot my birthday, and then I had a huge surprise party at the roller rink.

Situations:
1. That Danny would kick the back of Ramona's desk.
2. Kids throwing paper balls in class.
3. When you get something unexpected.
4. When my brother tried to kill me.
5. When my brother had pneumonia and we thought it was a cold.
6. When my little brother bit me.
7. When someone does something that doesn't go with that person. Like not doing your work when you always do it.

Other Ways of Saying *Astonished:*

shocked	excited	amazed
remarkable	surprised	real
jumpy	unexpected	startling

Students' Sentences:

1. Jill felt *astonished* when she saw a hippo in her yard.
2. My friend was *astonished* when she saw an alligator eating at the table.
3. Erica was *astonished* when she had a surprise party.

Collaborate as a class until the process is clear. Then small groups record work on charts to present to the entire class; each group stories and researches a different word. Move from groups to pairs to individuals, always encouraging students to support each other. Once students understand the process, they can work on individual words. By April, Jaime, a seventh grader, is able to connect *rove* to her prior knowledge, conferring with peers when needed (figure 5).

Learning vocabulary this way is a joint venture, and dictionary work becomes a friendly experience. "Using the dictionary at the end didn't make my stomach hurt," Kayla told me. "I used to just copy the definitions; now I understand, so I can use my own words." Dictionary use gains authenticity and can become a thoughtful, problem-solving activity that takes time.

Painting and drawing new words can also link new to prior knowledge, as long as the children talk about their pictures to small groups or the entire class. This stimulates questions and stories from classmates. Some children even organize their drawings into word books, adding written explanations.

Conversation, thought, and rehearsing with drawings precede final drafts. "It's hard to draw a word so others know what it means," second grader John said to his group. Greg's drawing is his visual conception of a tornado (figure 6). Greg has labeled the drawing *Powerful*. Fascinated with airplanes, Greg manages to weave one into his picture, which leads the group to wonder if a plane could safely fly near the funnel cloud. "We can try to look that up," says Gabe, and the group is off on another investigation.

Words are thinking, reading, and writing tools. The words we own determine our ability to think, comprehend, and communicate. The very best way to enlarge children's vocabulary is by reading aloud the books and poems you treasure. This daily modeling will hopefully transmit your passion for story and love of language and entice the children you learn with into the reading life. Words are the tools of reader, writer, thinker, and dreamer. And we all want our students to read, write, think, and dream.

AS I SEE IT

Karla Kuskin

Sing and song.
Ping and pong.
Some words just belong together.

French and France.
Shirt and pants.
Glide and glance.
Shoe and leather.
Some words simply dance together.

KARLA KUSKIN FROM SOAP SOUP

The more words one has, the more one begins to understand.

KENNETH BRANAGH

It is hard to imagine tools more useful than words. Without them, talkers, philosophers, actors, writers would simply be out of business. When I think back to my early childhood, to that time of first putting names on things, putting words together, making sentences, I remember my fascination with the sounds of words, the tuneful humor in strings of syllables, the rhythms of scanning lines and rhymes and the wonderful secret each new word held like a nut meat in a shell: its meaning.

I was just learning to read when my mother got me a copy of "The Night Before Christmas" at a local Woolworth's. This was the pre-paperback era (shortly after the paleolithic) and I remember the look and feel of the thin hardcover book with its black-and-white illustrations. In particular I remember these lines:

As dry leaves before a wild hurricane fly
and then with an obstacle mount to the sky
the coursers they came
and he whistled and shouted
and called them by name.

That verse riveted itself into my head because, although I could make my way through the lines phonetically, I did not know what a hurricane was, or an obstacle, or what coursers were. The sounds of those rich words were so promising that I had to remember them in order to find out what they meant.

"When *I* use a word," Humpty Dumpty said, "it means just what I choose it to mean—neither more nor less." That is all right for an egg or maybe a very young child. My son Nick's first word was mainly sound: "Gung." The clang of a round bell, it was always pronounced with vigor and served both as greeting and exclamation. My daughter, Julia, used to call her breakfast cereal "shredded weak," and when she pronounced *toast* or *tights* the final *t*'s at the ends of those words were rendered with such precision they sounded like tiny explosions. I remember, as a child, my early troubles trying to get my tongue around the words *spaghetti* and *yellow* and settling for "pisghetti" and "lallo." Tongue twisters make hay of the humor in complicated word sounds. Song lyrics, limericks, poetry make music, sense, or nonsense out of the sound and swing of words.

Does you husband misbehave?
Grunt and grumble?
Rant and rave?
Shoot the brute some
Burma Shave.
ADVERTISEMENT ON ROADSIDE SIGNS

There were a lot of words around when I was growing up. Television had not yet wrapped the world in wall-to-wall images, and language was still vital for getting a point across. My father was a natural writer who wrote the way he spoke. He was also a versifier. I picked that trait up very early. Before I could write, my mother would copy my words down, encouraging my efforts. Both my parents were avid readers who loved to read to each other and to their only child. So early on I came under the spell of a well-loved voice drawing me into the world of a poem or story. Words beckoned.

When I was about eight we were introduced to a school word game that went something like this: First, a teacher would write a rather silly story filled with description. But instead of adjectives she, Miss Sailor, put in blanks. Next, we all took turns supplying the adjectives (the more outlandish the better) needed to fill the blanks. And finally the completed story was read aloud to much hilarity. Sometimes we also contributed nouns, and I think there was a variation in which we wrote the story ourselves, each supplying a line or two and filling our blanks in later.

I have another memory from around the same age, of a bunch of us memorizing all the lyrics to Gilbert and Sullivan's "When you're lying awake with a dismal headache and repose is tabooed by anxiety . . . " Then for a week or two we competed to see who could recite it fastest. Taking advantage of this youthful talent, our smart teachers helped us pick favorite speeches or poems to learn by heart rather than insisting we fill our heads with words that did not interest us.

As an adult still trying to find the right words, I sometimes have the chance to give young classes writing assignments. I begin by asking for the description of a thing, anything: a sneaker, a favorite stuffed animal, the picture over your bed that you hardly see anymore. Look very carefully at the subject you are going to describe and find those details that make it special. Do not say something is nice or pretty; rather, let the details show us that. Help us see what you see. Try to paint a picture with words.

Maybe E. M. Forster comes closest to describing the power of words with his: "How can I tell what I think till I see what I say?"

SELECTED BOOKS WRITTEN
AND ILLUSTRATED BY KARLA KUSKIN

Any Me I Want to Be: Poems. New York: Harper & Row, 1972.
City Dog. New York: Clarion, 1994.
The Dallas Titans Get Ready for Bed. New York: Harper & Row, 1986.
Dogs and Dragons, Trees and Dreams: A Collection of Poems. New York: Harper & Row, 1980.
Near the Window Tree: Poems and Notes. New York: Harper & Row, 1975.
Roar and More. New York: Harper & Brothers, 1956.
Soap Soup and Other Verses. New York: HarperCollins, 1992.
Something Sleeping in the Hall. New York: Harper & Row, 1985.
Which Horse Is William? New York: Greenwillow, 1992.

SELECTED BOOKS WRITTEN
BY KARLA KUSKIN

City Noise. Illustrated by Renee Flower. New York: HarperCollins, 1994.
A Great Miracle Happened There. Illustrated by Robert Andrew Parker. New York: HarperCollins, 1993.
Jerusalem, Shining Still. Illustrated by David Frampton. New York: Harper & Row, 1987.
Patchwork Island. Illustrated by Petra Mathers. New York: HarperCollins, 1994.
Paul. Illustrated by Milton Avery. New York: HarperCollins, 1994.
The Philharmonic Gets Dressed. Illustrated by Marc Simont. New York: Harper & Row, 1982.

AUTHENTIC
ASSESSMENT

I sat across from Principal Mary Ann Biggs talking about two sixth graders, previously tracked in the low-ability class, who had admitted me into their reading and writing lives. We both crowed over their poems, which hung on Mary Ann's office walls—poems offered as gifts to a school principal deeply involved in the learning of four hundred children at Johnson Williams Middle School.

Mary Ann leaned across her desk, "Laura," she said, "I've got to tell you a story that I've not told anyone. Last summer, I attended meetings with all the fifth-grade teachers, to preview the incoming sixth-grade class. By the end of the day, lists of negative social and academic behaviors filled my briefcase." I nodded, for the experience certainly was part of my own past. "You know what I did with those papers?" Mary Ann asked, her blue eyes daring me to guess. But she barely paused, eager to continue. "I gathered them up and tossed them in the school recycling bin." The blue eyes hardened. "I want every kid entering sixth grade to have a new beginning, a fair chance."

Mary Ann's genuine love for children prevent-

ed the passing on of all these negatives to the sixth-grade team. She knew an endless list of what kids do wrong would set incoming students up for failure. And she was right on target.

A more positive approach to informing new teachers about incoming students is to invite children to reflect on their growth and interests in a letter. Sixth-grade teacher Cindy Hughes, together with her colleagues, decided that in addition to writing samples to send on to seventh grade, students would review and reflect on their writing folders and journals, then write letters to next year's teachers, noting strengths and progress, likes and dislikes. Dana's letter (figure 1) reveals the nature of learning experiences in her sixth-grade classroom. She points out that reading is enjoyable when she gets to read her own book.

Letters like Dana's confirm a strong whole language belief that assessment, the collection of each learner's work and stories, must reveal what children like and can do, for progress can proceed only from strengths, not weaknesses. Evaluation, which emerges from assessment, is the student's, teacher's, and parent's interpretation of data and stories.

252

A good deal of authentic assessment is an informal, ongoing daily process: teacher observations and notes, peer and teacher-student conferences, and on-the-spot teacher-student interviews. Authentic assessment is also holistic, considering all the stories that contribute to a child's growth: stories about school, home, and community. Assessment, to be holistic and authentic, must not only embrace the whole child but also concentrate on self-evaluation, for self-evaluation is a pathway to self-awareness.

The child who acquires self-awareness by thinking about herself or himself as a learner and a friend, and as a family, team, group, and community member, can come to appreciate and understand the complexities of learning in social contexts. Evaluation and assessment that consider the whole child and the whole teacher concentrate on how our stories affect our learning.

Assessment then becomes the way for you and your students to comprehend process. Therefore, it's crucial to separate authentic assessment from school district evaluation requirements, which can be product- and test-oriented. The question you must resolve is how to reconcile the system with personal beliefs about evaluation.

You can meet district requirements along with assessing children's process; you might even be able to adapt your philosophy to specific regulations. Required to give final exams for many years at Powhatan, I changed the concept of English exams, which are no longer a mystery game of "What will she ask? How will she trick us?" Such games divide students into two camps: One group compulsively studies everything, stockpiling anger, anxiety, fear, and physical discomfort; the others elect the flippant pose and avoid studying.

Students now collaborate and design the essay questions for English exams and tests.

They receive the test two weeks in advance, for my goal is to have them think about and discuss the literature and form interpretations. They arrive with pages of notes and spend two hours writing with pleasure in a more reasonable situation.

Authentic assessment actively involves you as much as your students, for as you assist them in comprehending their process, you can also come to know yourself better as teacher-learner. Your self-evaluative process can become deeper and more meaningful by keeping a journal on classroom practices and events. Like your students, you'll want to reread and reflect on these entries; they can furnish you with valuable information and insights about yourself.

My journal has supported decisions I might not have made if I had relied solely on memory and daily emotional reactions. Here's part of an entry that altered my thinking on content time:

> Kids all seemed to enjoy the survival theme. One complaint, though, that came through was not enough time. Most felt rushed and didn't like doing stuff at home that would have been more fun with groups at school.

Rereading this entry caused me to rethink the theme cycle; I had to either reserve more time or work out more reasonable goals.

My journal is also a place to pour out the anger, frustration, and weariness I sometimes feel due to my assessment goals:

> Sometimes I am weary with recording observations. This week especially. I need to focus on a few kids a day; I'm trying to do too much, and it makes me want to scream by dismissal time. Why am I doing this?

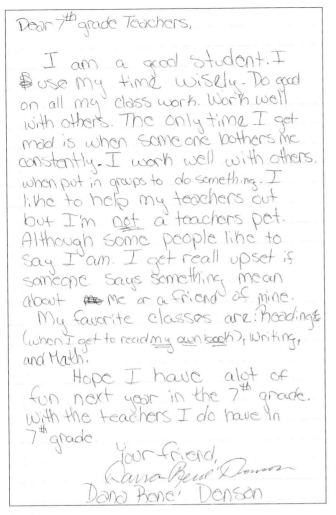

Dear 7th grade Teachers,

I am a good student. I use my time wisely. Do good on all my class work. Work well with others. The only time I get mad is when some one bothers me constantly. I work well with others. when put in groups to do something. I like to help my teachers out but I'm not a teachers pet. Although some people like to say I am. I get reall upset if someone says something mean about me or a friend of mine.

My favorite classes are: Reading (when I get to read my own book), Writing, and Math.

Hope I have alot of fun next year in the 7th grade. with the teachers I do have in 7th grade.

Your friend,
Dana Rene' Denson
Dana Rene' Denson

Fig. 1

I vividly recall why I wrote this in my journal. The week was gray, with chilly rain and drizzle. I was recovering from a cold, dragging myself to school, and hating every nugget of extra work I'd created. Anecdotal records were high on the list. Thirty restless sixth graders. The lugubrious days affected them as well. Grumping, I continued to observe and write on my clipboard; no chiding voices could stop me. That was October. In December, the child study group at Johnson Williams Middle School met to discuss Dillon because of his poor grades, behavior, and attitude. The group invited me to offer opinions, since Dillon spent two hours a day with me in reading-writing workshop. Of course, I patted myself on the back for the copious notes I had compiled about Dillon—notes based on classroom behavior and work, group interactions, listening, reading and writing conferences, and two interviews—all neatly tucked in Dillon's folder and my computer. Here are three of the anecdotes I reported, transcribed from the shorthand spellings I use:

- Writes the same story over and over in w.w. [writing workshop] 4 lines.

- Dillon has trouble reading the 4 lines. Tiny letter, misspellings, no punctuation.

- Yawns continuously after reading or writing independently for 10–15 minutes.

- Goes to bathroom several times a period.

- During interview told me he's failing a subject. "I know the answers—I just can't write it all. The textbook don't make sense," Dillon tells me. "My dad says I don't read the words that's there."

The conclusion of the child study group could have been that Dillon was careless, lazy, didn't try hard enough, could do better if he wanted to, didn't study or complete homework. Some of his teachers held those opinions. Though several members felt that Dillon had pulled the wool over my eyes, the detailed anecdotes opened *their* eyes and the door for further probing.

Dillon now receives one-on-one help three days a week. During a session he told me, "They're [teachers] always telling me to work harder. So I work harder and nothing happens. And they say, 'Work harder, Dillon, you're not trying' when I'm busting my butt. And nothing's happening." Stories about Dillon painted a powerful ongoing picture of his reading, writing, and social life. They supplied the evidence to refute generalizations such as "careless, lazy, and doesn't try" and to draw a different set of conclusions.

Equally as important as the sharing of these stories with colleagues and administrators is reviewing notes during student-teacher conferences, to gain insights into the child's way of seeing things. Teachers who use anecdotal records find them quite helpful during parent conferences, provided they can share stories they've previously discussed with students. I caution teachers about relating anecdotes they've not discussed with students to parents. That practice can leave you open to parent comments such as "That's the way *you* see it," or "How do I know it happened that way?" And even worse, "What did my child say?"

One of the enduring rewards of kid watching and anecdotal stories is that your knowledge of how children learn continually expands. I always have more questions than answers, but that's as it should be. I bring these questions to support group meetings, to a colleague on lunch or bus duty, or to an evening phone conversation. Questions provoke thinking and are an indication that you continue to grow.

The anecdotal note-writing suggestions that follow can help you initiate a powerful method of assessment.

- Let your class know what anecdotal records are and why you take them, so students don't make incorrect assumptions.

- At times, decide on a focus for your observations, such as group participation, peer conferences, or organized choice time. Note your particular focus on your record sheet.

- Describe the event with specific details.

- Report impartially; don't personalize, draw conclusions, find solutions, or judge.

- Concentrate on strengths observed and note first what a child is doing right.

- Develop a shorthand system you can read back, so you can write quickly. Transcribe these notes sooner rather than later to maintain accuracy.

- Date each note.

Finding the format for anecdotal record keeping that works best for you can relieve tension and anxiety. I've tested many note-taking methods: indexed notebooks, Post-its, or large self-sticking mailing labels on a clipboard. None worked. Finally I designed a form for a clipboard, with a child's name at the bottom for easy access (figure 2).

In addition to a record column, I included a column for comments by students, parents, and colleagues, and, near the bottom, an evaluation box for suggestions, observed patterns, and follow-ups. The form can easily be adapted for observing small groups. Change the heading Date to Names. Write the date at the bottom of the form in the space provided for individual student names. Space your list of group members' names, establish a focus, and take notes (see appendix).

Try this method, ask colleagues for suggestions, but determine the method that suits *your* teaching style. Anecdotal records support our quest for what children know and can do. They can assist us in finding ways to take a child from where the child is to where the child is able to go. Following are some suggestions for using your anecdotal notes. Don't limit yourself to this list.

Date	Teacher's Observations	Comments by student, parents, other teacher
week of Jan. 11	_Choices_ – SSR – reads 10 min. then talks to Jack asks to go to library to check out dif. books. Returns in 10 min. choice over.	Phy Ed + Art Teacher – top performance here.
	Discussion Group – active participation listens to others – asks them to prove with example from story – relates to other books discussed – Soto's "Growing Up" to "Through the Tunnel." Writes brief discussion summary in journal.	
	Choice Write – into horror stories works then time. Mini-conf. – made plan – figured out way to build suspense – reads me one section – details-rich – "scary" sounds, sights – Sits in corner on floor – say "enjoys writing his kind of stories."	Conf. on homework + Sci. report – "waited too long to start report" hates homework – rather be outside after all day at school. Say thinks needs help managing time.
	Homework – unprepared 2 × this wk. Stays in recess to complete reading log – 1 entry for 6 days says "doesn't like to read at home or in SSR that much – likes short books-stories.	No Science 1st draft report – spotty notes – Suggestion: try to set up some extra help sessions to get him started. Phone Conf. with mom – says he's done all his work at school. – Schedule conf. to talk together.

Evaluation Notes

Build on art talent – illustrate – puppets – drama sets
Administer IRI to get deeper view on reading.
Paired reading – discuss reading buddy in primary grade

Name_____   Grade 6

Fig. 2 Anecdotal notes for a student.

Be vigilant for new ways of thinking about and interpreting data. You'll find these as you collaborate with children, faculty, parents.

- Study a range of observations, looking for patterns in students' writing, reading, interactions, and projects. Look for content patterns, spelling and punctuation patterns, organization patterns, completion patterns, and so on.

- Focus on positives and frame recommendations so they build on what children can do.

- Reflect carefully on students' comments and connect their perspective to your observations.

- Meet with colleagues who teach the child and compare their observations with yours; include the parents' point of view.

- Evaluate, with students, their goals and recommendations to insure they are reasonable. Compare student goals to the goals you've set.

- Make inferences about a child's reading and writing strategies based on your study of a *series* of anecdotes and conferences.

- Discuss notes with students and, when appropriate, share with parents.

- Use anecdotes to adjust classroom practices and theme cycle expectations.

- Review anecdotes to raise questions about a child's progress, the class's progress, and your progress. Discuss these with others; react to them in your journal.

I have learned to develop an outer protective skin as I share anecdotes with students because their responses are not always what I want to hear. But that's the only way to determine their perspective and how they view themselves in relation to school events.

Portfolios can furnish additional insight into children's views of themselves in and out of school. Jane Hansen makes this point in "The Manchester Portfolio Project," broadening our concept of portfolio to include artifacts from home, school, and community.

Portfolios have been around in the real world much longer than in schools. Artists, copywriters, and authors all use portfolios to demonstrate versatility by including samples of their work that represent the depth and range of their talents.

Unfortunately, many schools limit the scope of portfolios. "Our portfolios are reading-writing portfolios. No other kinds of work go into them." I had to conceal the wave of sadness that surged through me as I listened to this presenter at a national conference. "The only artwork they can put in has to relate to writing or reading." A reading-writing portfolio reflects only a partial view of a child's literacy development.

Choice is crucial to the success of holistic portfolios, and choice begins with deciding what to use as a portfolio. Like book talking, I portfolio talk, bringing in an array of folders and binders that efficiently store papers. Then I ask students to bring in a portfolio that will hold a variety of papers and objects such as school papers, letters, photos, souvenirs, buttons, and magazine pictures. Portfolios range from extra-thick three-ring binders to accordion envelopes. If it works, let kids use it. I keep a portfolio along with students. Doing it myself forced me to become aware of the need to set aside enough time to reflect on, discuss, add to, and change the contents.

Students select the items for portfolios independently and during conferences with peers and me. The content range is limitless. After students decorate portfolios, groups discuss what to include to represent themselves as readers, writers, researchers, friends, artists, doodlers, cartoonists, and people with feelings, tastes, beliefs, and attitudes. Recording everyone's ideas on a large chart creates a resource that reminds students about what they can include. Here are some items you might find on a chart of What Can I Put in My Portfolio?:

- selections from a journal (can be photocopied)

- cartoons, drawings, doodles

- a reading log selection

- papers illustrating revision

- writing from first to deadline draft

- content area work

- a favorite poster

- peer conference notes

- self-evaluations and goals

- personal letters

- photos

- magazine or newspaper clippings

- interest inventory

- a reading/writing survey

- advertisements

- buttons

- travel brochures

- letters from other people

- lists

- song lyrics

- a poem or story quote

- a running record

- an audiotape of a student reading aloud

- a T-shirt

Just as professional artists and writers update portfolios, so should students, for then they are truly anchored in the real world. Updating usually occurs after reviewing, rereading, or discussing the contents: a logical step in the self-evaluative process as we include papers that better represent who we are as people and learners. I file weeded-out classroom artifacts; personal items return home.

Many teachers are overwhelmed by the organization and time they and their students must invest to build and reflect on portfolios and make them available to parents, colleagues, and administrators. An overly enthusiastic beginning, "doing it all," can result in abandoning the concept or sporadically stuffing items into the portfolio, which transforms it into a work folder.

Begin slowly and enlist the aid of students by periodically asking them to evaluate how things are working. Your support group will be a valuable source of advice, and if there's a teacher in your building experienced with portfolios, buddy up with that person immediately! If you can convince other team members to be adventurous with you, then you'll be surrounded by a nucleus of support and comforting voices. Communicate with parents. Have students write letters home, explaining portfolios and inviting parents to come in and review the contents. Keep current through professional journals and books; share articles and experiences with colleagues and students.

Support and guide students with demonstrations and think-alouds, modeling the process to select representative pieces of work, interpret contents, discover strengths, self-evaluate, and set reasonable goals. Here are some possible minilessons; keeping your own portfolio and reviewing those of students will supply you with additional portfolio minilesson topics.

- Think aloud the process you use to select an item.

- Set criteria with students for the selection of representative school work. The criteria will change throughout the year.

- Model possible things to talk about when sharing your portfolio with a group or partner, such as why you like or dislike a piece, or what the piece illustrates about you as a learner.

- Encourage children to ask each other questions about selections and goals.

- On a chart, write ways to respond and ways to self-evaluate. After you've modeled, join a group and become part of the process.

Responding to portfolio selections as students choose them initiates a reflective process. Below are a selection of comments made by sixth graders in a reading-writing workshop for individual portfolio items:

- This shows I am writing better stories. My dialogue is better than it was. I do great with descriptions.

- This picture of Michael Jackson is because I want to be a rich singer like him.

- I can use complete sentences in my stories.

- This is my grandfather. He is sick and will die. He lives in California.

- I can read and write a good response. I learn how to read a nice size book. I improve in reading.

- I can understand the words.

The second graders in Carol Chapman's class select portfolios and explain their choices. Carol teaches them how to respond by offering reaction openings such as: I like this; I dislike this; This shows how I am doing better; I think I've improved because . . . Students can choose to build on one of Carol's suggestions or write their own. Carol works one-on-one with students' first selections, recording their responses after she assists them with the self-evaluative process. By January, Kathryn explains why she's doing better and expresses a goal that she will continue to work on (figure 3).

Once students become comfortable with self-evaluation, they are ready to share portfolios with partners. Students can choose partners or you can establish a rotating system. Partners exchange portfolios and read selections and students' comments. The pair discuss each other's progress, raise questions, and offer positive suggestions. The purpose of trading portfolios is to extend support and the celebration of progress to peers. By talking about each other's work, students learn

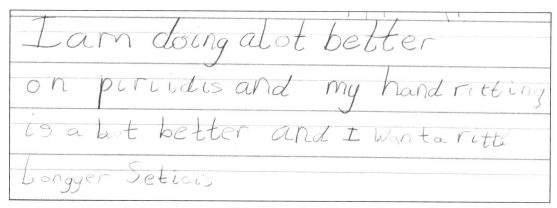

Fig. 3

alternate modes of responding and have opportunities to offer productive strategies and gain insights into the lives of peers outside of school.

Below are some practical portfolio management tips you might find helpful:

• Find a storage place that's accessible to the children: a countertop, bookshelf, table, or plastic crate.

• Students store daily work in their journals, writing folders, or file folders.

• Set aside a period of time every three to six weeks for students to select work, review their portfolios, and respond. Knowing they have their work folders will help students understand that the portfolio contains a limited number of items.

• Reserve time for students to read portfolios twice each marking period; share contents with a partner or group. Students self-evaluate on separate papers stapled to each item.

• Schedule teacher-student portfolio conferences toward the end of each marking period.

Think aloud the inferences you make by reviewing and reflecting on portfolio artifacts. Then write a positive note pointing to strengths, self-evaluations, and goals and praising progress.

• Permit students to read and reflect on portfolios during choice times and recesses.

• Use the portfolio during parent-teacher-student conferences. Show parents how you interpret data. Record parents' reactions and suggestions.

• Students update portfolios at the end of a marking period by returning some items to the work folder. I empty the contents of work folders at the end of each marking period and place them in a special filing cabinet. Students always have access to these papers, which they can take home at the end of the year.

Some teachers send portfolios home for parents' education and input; that works well when students have come to value a portfolio—the valuing insures the return. The high-risk students I teach don't always return portfolios; through conferences or home visits, students share portfolios with parents and me. They remain at school until students gain the self-esteem and responsibility needed to shuttle them back and forth.

Portfolios become meaningful and useful to students only when you set aside time to review and talk about stories the artifacts tell. Each fall, I must discover, through brainstorming and conversations, what words like *evaluate, assess, grade, test* mean to new classes. Their brainstorming supplies information about notions and beliefs they've collected from experiences at school and home; and these beliefs guide my introductory mini-lessons on self-evaluation and assessing progress.

For self-evaluation to affect children's learning, it should encompass students' behavior and academic experiences. Asking students to alter disruptive behaviors by confronting and reflecting on their actions takes more time than the traditional method of teacher-in-charge. Most of the teachers I've mentored are willing to use self-evaluation in academic areas, but show reluctance with behavioral issues. I've observed well-intentioned teachers demand respect by ordering students to speak in a pleasing tone of voice or to mold a face into a bland expression. The teacher-control method of discipline reaps instant rewards, but quite often student honesty departs, resentment increases, and unacceptable behaviors go underground. One fifth grader told me, "I tell her [the teacher] what she wants to hear. I'm not taking any chances." Control removes risk-taking and the opportunity for a lasting change. In a democratic classroom, learners come to accept social responsibilities by assessing their behaviors, setting appropriate guidelines for different classroom experiences, and exploring reasons to change.

Sixth grader Lenny's classroom behavior often disrupted workshop classes. Frustrations and anger ignited rapidly, and Lenny reacted by shouting abuses, storming out of the room, or punching a classmate. Cindy Hughes and I taught Lenny's class together, and Cindy agreed to try self-evaluation and conferences to reform disruptive behaviors. Each time Lenny lost control, Cindy or I would listen to his side, his feelings. We'd ask questions, attempting to help Lenny see alternatives to his choices: delay action, reflect, call for a peer conference, ask a teacher to intervene, or use journal writing. We hoped that discussion and written self-evaluations would eventually draw Lenny to strategies that would alter his behavior. Conferences disclosed that from Lenny's perspective, the problems belonged to everyone else. "Everyone picks on me" was his refrain.

Reports of disruptive behaviors plagued Lenny, especially in the cafeteria, where he engaged in food and verbal fights several times a week. The day that Lenny wrote, after an altercation, "I guess I got a problem" was a red-letter day, for Lenny had taken ownership of his behavior. Several times during workshop, Lenny voluntarily removed himself from class, steaming and fuming as he departed. Progress. He vented his anger out of the room, instead of acting out in front of peers. The cafeteria was a different story. "I can't stay out of trouble with all the noise and kids," he confessed. Yet Lenny found his own solution. He asked the principal if he could purchase lunch and then eat it in Cindy's classroom.

Lenny had begun to understand how his behavior affected him. In a conference with me he blurted, "The kids hate me after I yell and fight. I'm just dumb." Conferences also revealed that Lenny disrupted workshop when he didn't understand minilessons, when he noticed students writing dialogue and he didn't know where to begin. The trust and communication that developed through this process supplied Cindy and me with crucial information about Lenny. By the end of the year, Lenny's outbursts had markedly decreased. Change required time and a large investment of energy by Lenny and his teachers.

When a large group of middle school students is noisy or uncooperative, I immediately hand out paper and ask them to explain their behavior. In such cases, I find it better to discuss after writing. Discussions on the heels of the disruption often escalate into unproductive arguments. Writing can change students' focus and helps me gain insights into their actions.

The sixth grade arrived out of control: noisy, running around the room, throwing paper wads. Five out of twenty-nine students retrieved writing folders and checked the journal box. Several flicks of the light informed the class that they had stepped over the limits; each student received a blank piece of paper, and, as always, I received a range of reactions:

• Today we came in loud and I sat down and J. yelled at me to move and I told her no because I was in here first.

• We need more responsibility in our groups.

• I was very good coming in but I was late.

• I think the class came in loud cause they were excited about Miss Child's birthday last period. Nobody was listening. Some are even talking right now!

Two fourth graders review their portfolios.

Sometimes there are logical reasons for their behavior, like Miss Child's birthday party. During the discussion that followed, many suggested that they should have told me about the party and their high energy.

Our discussions always focus on choices, since students make the choices and must own their behaviors. Recognizing that you're aiming for gradual change through reflection will help you cope with repeated disruptions. Two third graders who talked all through music class offer sound and realistic advice:

I promis thet I will Lisin For all times well not for al time!! But for a lot of times.

I promis that I will lisen sometimes beacuse I might forgite about this note.

These third graders teach an important lesson: Count progress in terms of improvement, not in terms of impossible-to-reach standards.

The democratic process of a class conference, where everyone has the option to voice opinions and feelings about class behaviors that prevent learning, combined with elements of writing workshop's group share, can help students understand how others perceive disruptive behaviors. Both students and teachers can bring issues before the class.

Some second graders had begun to complain about the noise in Carol Chapman's classroom, especially during math peer-tutoring sessions. I urged Carol to first have the children write about math class and express positives and negatives. We structured the sessions like a writing workshop group share. A child sat in the math author's chair, read, and responded to questions from classmates;

whole class discussions followed. Carol taped sessions so we could both listen carefully and talk about what occurred.

Three share sessions later, the children had confronted and dealt with two key issues: noise levels and selection of peer tutors. The transcription below offers a glimpse into two conversations that led to change:

J.K.: It's [math] hard for me. Sometimes I just don't get my brain going, and it's just hard for me.

T.: What times does it make it not work?

J.K.: When somebody next to me is talking and whispering. It bothers me.

A.: If someone bothers you, can't you get it out of your brain and not hear it? Can't you say "Be quiet"?

J.K.: Not when people keep saying your name.

M.: Can you work with someone else?

J.K.: If I'm comfortable with them. I want to choose my tutor.

C.: [Reads paper] I don't understand it [subtracting], but it got easier when we used the number boards and chips. It got faster for me. We have been doing it for three weeks. It is getting easier every day.

J.K.: Does anyone get in your way?

C.: Yeah. [Pause] When people talk and come up and say, "Carol, Carol, can you help me?"

M.: People talk about exciting things and it makes your brain go "Oh." Like when they talk about an exciting movie, I go, "What movie is that?" and forget about math.

P.: You lose the math out of your head and take the fun stuff in your head.

A.: The noise makes me not concentrate. I get stuff wrong.

Mrs. C.: Do you want me to make the math class a quieter place?

"Yes, yes, yes," echoes throughout the room.

Two changes resulted: the establishment of quiet math work times and children's input in selecting peer tutors. As Justin said, "I'm afraid to work with just anyone—they might embarrass me when I don't know. I don't like being embarrassed."

Student-teacher, class, and peer conferences and written self-evaluations support students as they learn to read and write and experience democratic responsibilities. The process can be painful for some, like eighth grader Renee, who wrote:

> Some people reject your ideas and can easily cut you down. Then you leave class with a broken heart.

But she's quick to point out:

> The good part is that it tests your ability to cooperate. It challenges you and teaches you how to expand your cooperation. It helped me really understand how we all see things differently.

The last sentence reflects one of the major contributions of self-evaluation: self-awareness and a keener understanding of an issue. Many middle school students were initially negative about class conferences, consistently making comments like "boring," "stupid," "dumb," "nothing's going to happen anyway." Experiencing the process changed many students' attitudes. Understanding, not fixing, is the first goal of self-evaluation. Problems still arise, but now students have strategies that spotlight other points of view.

In conjunction with reflecting on behavior, I reserve times for students to self-evaluate progress in reading and writing. Their reflections furnish me with insights into each child's process, how individuals view their work, and the effectiveness of minilessons.

Before self-evaluation, students and I set specific criteria for the evaluation process.

For older students, criteria can be as general as inviting students to reflect on the strategies applied and the connections made. They can also be specific to the event, such as reviewing final drafts for content; editing for spelling, punctuation, or paragraphing; reviewing individual contributions to the group; or identifying and assessing the range of reading in a book log.

Younger students can assess their writing for title, name, and date; they can reflect on whether their narratives have a beginning, middle, and end; they can consider their use of sustained silent reading (SSR) time; or they can review what they learned from research and discussions. Whatever the set of criteria established, they should reflect *your classroom experiences*. Demonstrate how to weave criteria into a paragraph with specific examples. Always encourage students to draw inferences that move beyond the criteria in order to collect a broader range of reflections (see appendix).

Every three to four weeks, and at the end of a grading period, middle school workshop students review and reflect on one of these: writing folders, reading logs, response journals, revisions, final drafts. Content area teachers can do the same. The point is to develop the habit of rereading and reflecting on your work. Periodic reflections become the topic of peer and student-teacher conferences, enabling students to assess their work and set goals. Kisha reviewed her reading log for a six-week period (figure 4).

Armed with Kisha's reason for her empty reading log, I suggested at a conference that she might consider reading aloud to her ill aunt. "She might enjoy that," I added. Two weeks later, all smiles, Kisha hands me a log with entries. "My aunt loves when I read. She

> This six week I am suspused to read everynight but this six week I haven't been doing as well. I try to read from 20 to 40 mins a night. I guess it is because I have been so busy like I don't get home until 4:00 and then I have to go up to my Aunts house and do my homework and I stay up there until my cousin comes up there and then go back home. Because I go up there to watch my Aunt because she is very sick.
>
> For the next six weeks and days to come I will try to read everynight and complete the Reading sheet.

Fig. 4

wants me to continue now, even though she's better."

A zero or after-school detention, both traditional punishments, would have only manufactured resentment and anger toward reading. Self-evaluation clues can explain why students make choices and open the possibility of alternate choices.

Ben, tall, gangly, and extremely angry because he repeated a grade, wants to be a seventh, not a sixth grader, and has done little writing. A friendship with Garrett has resulted in a writing partnership. It's December, and Ben writes token pieces; the partnership changes Ben's feelings about writing, and both boys put all their energy into a baseball story. Ben's self-evaluations, to this point, have paid lip service to the process: "I wrote a lot for me," or "I didn't feel like writing much," or "I don't have anything to write about" were the

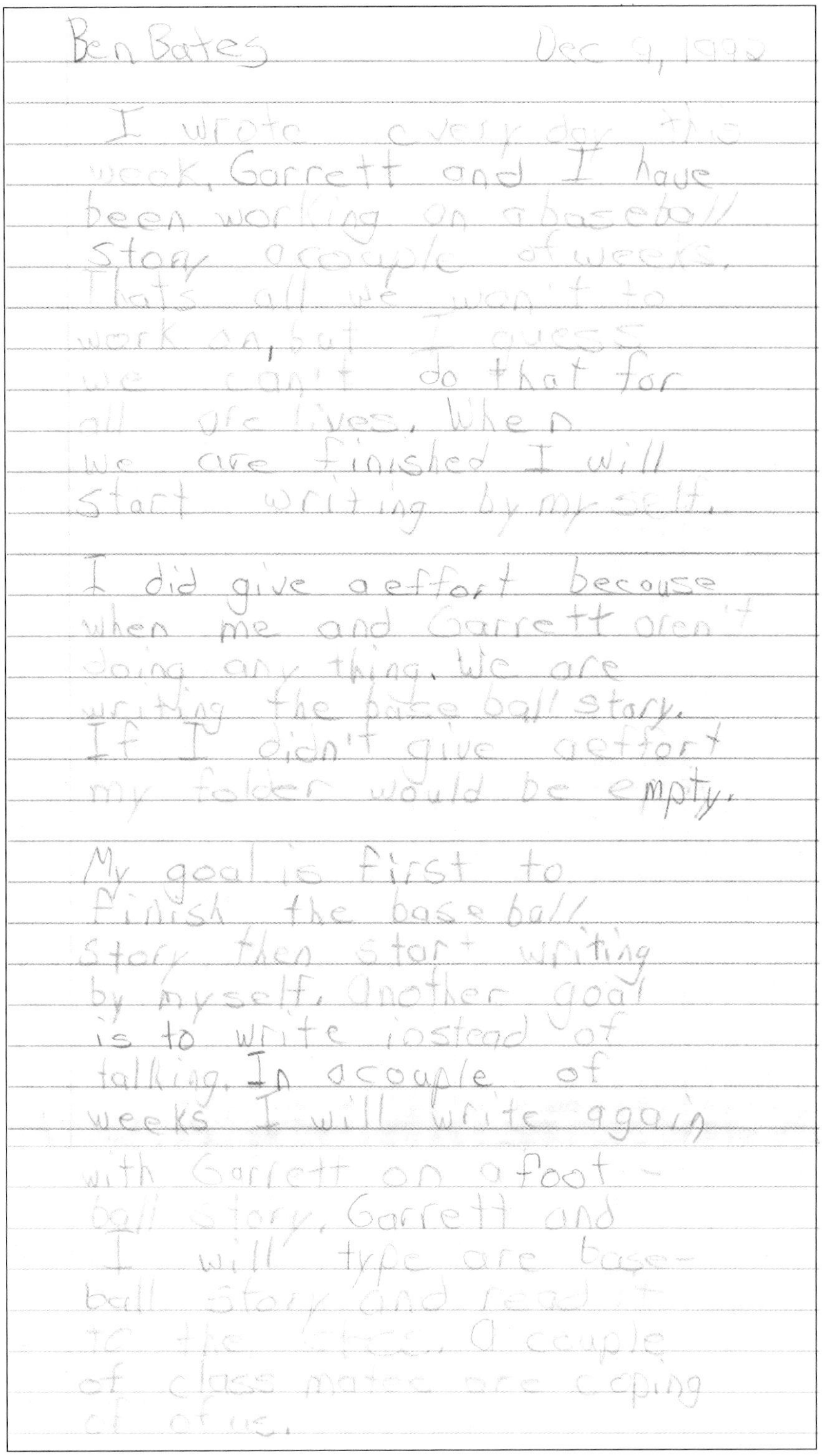

Ben Bates   Dec 9, 1992

I wrote every day this week. Garrett and I have been working on a baseball story a couple of weeks. Thats all we won't to work on, but I guess we can't do that for all ore lives. When we are finished I will start writing by myself.

I did give a effort becouse when me and Garrett oren't doing any thing. We are writing the base ball story. If I didn't give a effort my folder would be empty.

My goal is first to finish the baseball story then start writing by myself. Another goal is to write instead of talking. In a couple of weeks I will write again with Garrett on a foot-ball story. Garrett and I will type are base-ball story and read to the class. A couple of class mates are coping of or us.

Fig. 5

types of statements he turned in. The partnership changed Ben's feelings about writing, giving him the confidence to set some goals, and pour out a one-and-a-half-page self-evaluation (figure 5).

Ben went on to write a wonderful football story. Like a pendulum, he swings between writing and goofing off. The periods of writing are longer and more frequent. That's all the progress I can expect. And it's coming from within Ben, rather than being imposed by me. Students confront their folders and work habits more openly and honestly than I might; such candor can effect positive changes because the students set the goals.

John reviews three weeks of reading work (figure 6) and admits that he did not respond in his journal. His goal relates directly to the issue he confronted.

Stacey expresses feelings of great accomplishment and pleasure in understanding what she's read (figure 7). A slow reader, she is trying to increase her rate by reading! Notice how Stacey's words reflect her ownership of progress.

High and low points govern my teaching life. Low points occur when I get an evaluation like Carl's:

I didn't do anything this week because this week I decided to be lazy every day.

An honest appraisal. Sometimes notes like this demand I look for other reasons, and in Carl's case, his bravado was a cover for a real difficulty in expressing ideas on paper. Barriers can crumble as the children let us in to their lives through self-evaluation.

Once each marking period, I try to respond, in writing, to a student's self-evaluation. I consider the time invested worthwhile. Certainly, with limited time, you must decide how often you can manage a return letter. But children treasure these replies; they read them alone, to friends, and parents, and many turn up in portfolios (figure 8).

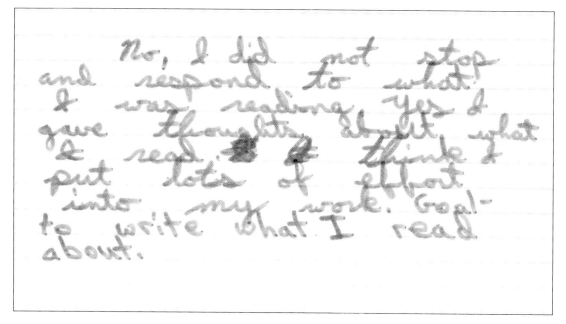

Fig. 6 After reviewing his work, this student's self-evaluation clearly states his goal.

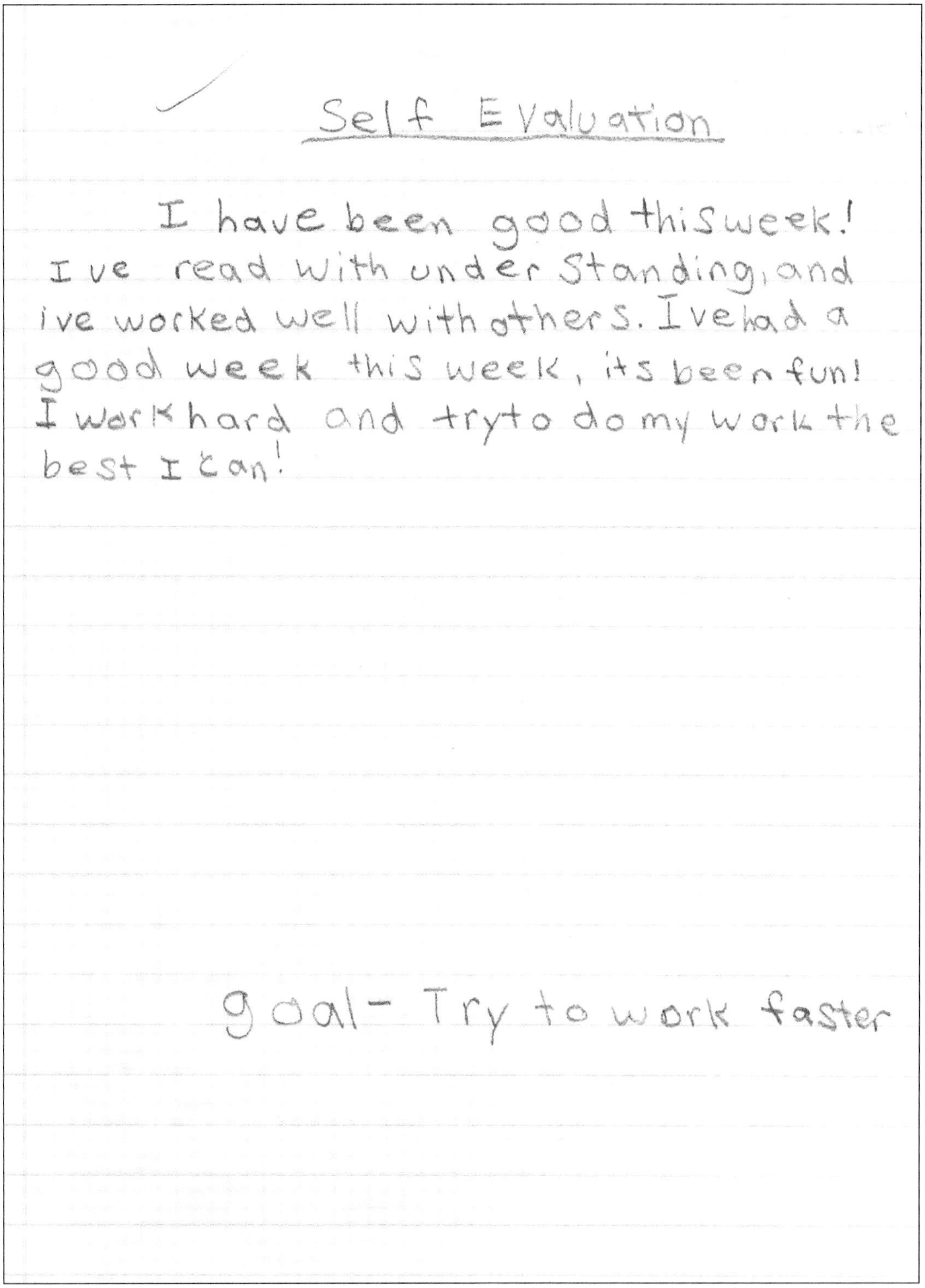

Self Evaluation

I have been good this week!
I've read with under standing, and
ive worked well with others. I've had a
good week this week, it's been fun!
I work hard and try to do my work the
best I can!

goal - Try to work faster

Fig. 7

Carol   APril. 7, 1992

I like my book becuse of the picshers thay exsplain the wrods beter than I can. my book has a cover, title and my name. I lit like my book very much.

.Gols. I nead to improv my riting

April 10, 1992

Dear Carol,

I, too, really admire your pictures. The illustration of the seismometer and inside of the earth have so much fine details. They help me understand what the machine and inside of the earth are like. I also learned about tsunami. Your explanations are filled with details. I enjoyed reading News About Earthquakes.

                                    Mrs. Robb

Fig. 8 A student's self-evaluation of her book and her teacher's reply.

Teacher demonstrations that model how to write self-evaluations, how to review specific, negotiated goals, and how to share evaluations in small groups can all guide children through the process. Before second graders evaluated their word books, the children reread the chart of word-book guidelines that they established and used these as the basis for self-evaluation. Below are some possibilities for student self-evaluation. Many items on this list are students' suggestions.

- Writing folders.

- Reading logs.

- What I've learned compared to what I thought I knew.

- Response journals.

- Retellings of stories: early retellings with retellings after reading and discussing.

- Content of group discussions.

- Content area journals.

- Portfolios.

- Themed studies.

- Resources such as real books, textbooks, films, interviews. Which worked best and why?

- Journaling techniques.

- Minilessons: to explain what they understood and what confused them.

- Research methods.

- Collaborative efforts.

- Projects.

- Tapes of reading recorded at different times.

Anecdotal stories, portfolios, students' self-evaluations, reading, writing, class conferences, and spelling inventories will supply you with insights into each child's learning. Such data can help you identify students who require additional evaluation.

To assess children's reading requires a knowledge of children's patterns of error as they read aloud. Kenneth and Yetta Goodman have identified and analyzed children's reading errors, or miscues. Their extensive research indicates that all readers make errors, and all readers do not detect many of their errors. Moreover, not all miscues impede comprehension.

The data accumulated from a miscue analysis offers information about miscue patterns and insights into children's reading process. Miscue analysis, according to Ken Goodman, is useless unless the teacher has "some sense of the theoretical context and the view of language and reading that's involved."[1] Yetta Goodman, in *The Whole Language Catalog*, points out that a knowledge of miscue analysis increases teachers' understanding of the reading process and aids them with helping children solve reading problems. Miscue analysis is not necessary for those children who read fluently, comprehend, and are self-monitoring. The goal of the Goodmans in using a miscue inventory is to assist the teacher in understanding and valuing what students can do well, proceeding to build on strengths, making readers aware of their process, and understanding that even the best readers make errors. To learn more about miscue analysis and how to use it in your classroom, study *Reading Miscue Inventory,* coauthored by Yetta Goodman.

Marie Clay outlines a system of documenting students' oral reading errors in *The Early Detection of Reading Difficulties.* Based on one-on-one observation of students, the taking of running records is a reading assessment tool that allows you to closely observe the strategies readers employ to comprehend print. The running record supplies teachers with information about students' reading behaviors. The method takes no more than fifteen minutes and provides the teacher with ongoing information about young children's reading behaviors and strategies.

Clay points out that taking running records develops teachers' powers of observation. The more running records completed, the more ear and eye become attuned to the reading process. Running records include a reading of three different passages: easy, instructional, and difficult. Each passage should contain one hundred to two hundred words. At very early reading levels, the text will drop below one hundred words, and teachers at this level might use caption books, teacher-made books, or very early readers. To use and analyze running records, I recommend a careful reading of two books by Marie Clay: *The Early Detection of Reading Difficulties* and *Reading: The Patterning of Complex Behavior.*

Establishing a baseline running record for each child within the first six to eight weeks of school separates kids developing appropriately from those who need additional monitoring and guidance. Collecting as much reading behavior data as possible early in the year helps you cue in on a smaller group of children. Repeat running records more frequently for students who exhibit difficulties.

Marie Clay recommends that teachers check off each correct word and mark error patterns. I mark only miscues to save time and more accurately record a child's error pattern. After establishing a baseline record of an easy, instructional, and difficult passage, I begin repeating running records with an instructional passage. This saves time and will help me determine, as I review the pattern of several running records, what kind of intervention to try—whether to use a more difficult or easier selection, seek additional guidance, or introduce a new strategy. Refer to Marie Clay's system of marking errors or adopt the system proposed by the informal reading inventory (IRI) you prefer.

Informal reading inventories assess sight word recognition, oral and silent reading, and the child's comprehension when listening to reading (called listening capacity). To evaluate all four areas of reading, an IRI, whether commercial or teacher-made, should contain three sets of different passages at each grade level. Sight-word recognition lists should range from

A student-teacher writing conference.

A parent-student-teacher conference.

at least preprimer or primer to grade six; reading passages should range from primer to preferably eighth or ninth grade. A variety of questions from factual to inferred and a scoring guide accompany each selection. Commercial IRIs are inexpensive and save teachers valuable time.

I've included a listing of commercial IRI resources for you to investigate:

Bader, Lois A. *Bader Reading and Language Inventory*. New York: Macmillan, 1983.

Ekwall, Eldon E. *Ekwall Reading and Language Inventory*, 2nd ed. Boston: Allyn and Bacon, 1985.

Johns, Jerry L. *Basic Reading Inventory*, 5th ed. Dubuque, IA: Kendall/Hunt, 1991.

Woods, Mary Lynn, and Alden Moe. *Analytical Reading Inventory*, 4th ed. Columbus, OH: Charles E. Merrill, 1989.

For additional information on administering and interpreting commercial IRIs and on creating your own inventory, refer to these resources:

Barr, Rebecca, Marilyn Sadow, and Camille Blachowicz. *Reading Diagnosis for Teachers: An Instructional Approach*. New York: Longman, 1990.

Gillet, Jean Wallace, and Charles Temple. *Understanding Reading Problems: Assessment and Instruction*, 3rd ed. Boston: Little, Brown, 1991.

Jongsma, Eugene A., and Kathleen S. Jongsma. "Test Review: Commercial Informal Reading Inventories." *Reading Teacher* 34, No. 6, March 1981, pages 697–705.

Many teachers design checklists to organize evaluation data. Collaboration with other teachers enhances the process of designing checklists by fostering an exchange of ideas and a close examination of items. Useful checklists (see appendix) change and should be updated to mirror classroom experiences. When I pointed this out to one administrator, the concern was more for the practicality of updating, rather than for the accuracy of reporting. The supervisor wanted to print the checklist report card in triplicate, and the expense of yearly changes would not be cost-effective. My fear of checklists is that administrators and teachers will embrace ready-made forms and shove the program and children into the form simply because it's easier.

Twice a year, Cindy Hughes and I ask middle school students to fill in checklists and write comments. During teacher-student conferences, we compare and contrast our checklists with those of students. The lists inspire questions and open a meaningful dialogue between teacher and student. Used this way, checklists become reflective and foster independence in learning. And twice a year is manageable!

As you review and rethink your student evaluation practices, consider which elements of authentic assessment you wish to incorporate. Don't do it all. Select one change, work out all the kinks with students, then introduce another change. Each innovation will support the new addition, and in time, you will form a firm and rewarding foundation.

Communicating with parents closes the circle of authentic assessment. Parents crave feedback about their children's school life. Moreover, information about a child, from the parents' perspective, can be extremely valuable in assessing and assisting that child. Parents bring us literacy stories from home that can reaffirm and enhance school observations. Parent conferences build a base of support at home for you and the child.

Many schools schedule on their calendar formal parent-conference days. Portfolios, self-evaluations, anecdotal stories, book logs, journals, writing folders—any work a student has completed—can be the subject of a conference. First I conference alone with the parents, giving them time and space to talk about their child and raise questions. Be a good listener and honor the parents' concerns and feelings. Invite the child to join part of the conference and encourage the child to share the contents of a portfolio, reading log, and writing folder. Let the child answer some parent questions. Close with a discussion of goals and the type of support home can supply. Don't confine parent conferences to fixed dates—invite parents in as often as necessary.

Newsletters, school bulletins, literary magazines, surveys, parent workshops, and seminars are ways students and teachers can communicate classroom experiences to parents. Teachers who maintain excellent communication with parents develop staunch supporters who come to understand and embrace changes in education and how these changes can benefit their child.

Reference

1. Goodman, Kenneth, Lois Bird Bridges, and Yetta Goodman, eds. *The Whole Language Catalog*. New York: American School Publishers, Macmillan/McGraw-Hill, 1991, page 100.

AS I SEE IT

Jean Van Leeuwen

When my son David was in first grade, he was slow in learning to read. Obviously bright and a child of intense interests (he had recently passed from his Dinosaur Period into his Indian Period), he loved being read to. But he did not seem to be making the leap to reading on his own. Along around the middle of the year, we as parents were made aware that this was a problem. David was placed in the lowest reading group, which though known by a code name clearly delivered the message that he was one of the slow ones. He was switched from a sight-reading text of the Sally, Dick, and Jane variety to a phonics book, called *A Pig Can Jig*. He was taken out of the classroom for extra help. None of these measures seemed to work. At the age of six, this child felt himself to be a failure.

As a last-ditch effort to get him on the right track, it was recommended that our son attend summer school. Looking back, fifteen years later, I am amazed that we went along with this recommendation. And we didn't even ask questions. Like: Where is it written that every child has to learn to read at precisely the same time? Wouldn't my son do better if he were surrounded by books about dinosaurs or Indians rather than those dull textbooks? And isn't it far worse to damage a child's self-esteem than to accept his being a little behind the "norm"? I feel guilty to this day that I never brought up any of these points. But David was our first child, and we lived in a community known for its educational excellence. So we went along with the experts.

Summer school did not work any miracles. Eventually, without joy, David was able to master *A Pig Can Jig*. And then something quite wonderful happened. In the early fall of second grade, David's teacher read a book out loud to the class. It was called *Charlie and the Chocolate Factory*, by Roald Dahl. The day she started the book, David came home from school in a state of high excitement. He insisted that we go straight to the library and take out that book so he could find out what happened next. We did, and amazingly, he could read it! A whole long chapter book filled with hard words! David was proud, and I was impressed. And greatly relieved. He never looked back after that, but went on to become an excellent and enthusiastic reader.

What is the moral of this story? To my mind, it is clear that every child develops at his or her own rate. I wish that in first grade my son had been given the gifts of time and a feeling of self-worth. More than that, I can't help wondering what might have happened if, a little earlier, a perceptive teacher had placed the right book in his hand, one where he couldn't wait to find out what happened next.

SELECTED BOOKS BY JEAN VAN LEEUWEN

Amanda Pig and Her Big Brother Oliver. Illustrated by Ann Schweninger. New York: Dial, 1982.

Amanda Pig on Her Own. Illustrated by Ann Schweninger. New York: Dial, 1991.

Benjy and the Power of Zingies. Illustrated by Margot Apple. New York: Dial, 1982.

Benjy in Business. Illustrated by Margot Apple. New York: Dial, 1983.

Benjy, the Football Hero. Illustrated by Gail Owens. New York: Dial, 1985.

Dear Mom, You're Ruining My Life. New York: Dial, 1989.

Emma Bean. Illustrated by Juan Wijngaard. New York: Dial, 1993.

Going West. Illustrated by Thomas B. Allen. New York: Dial, 1992.

The Great Christmas Kidnapping Caper. Illustrated by Steven Kellogg. New York: Dial, 1975.

The Great Rescue Operation. Illustrated by Margot Apple. New York: Dial, 1982.

The Great Summer Camp Catastrophe. Illustrated by Diane de Groat. New York: Dial, 1992.

More Tales of Amanda Pig. Illustrated by Arnold Lobel. New York: Dial, 1981.

More Tales of Oliver Pig. Illustrated by Arnold Lobel. New York: Dial, 1981.

Oliver, Amanda, and Grandmother Pig. Illustrated by Ann Schweninger. New York: Dial, 1987.

Oliver and Amanda's Christmas. Illustrated by Ann Schweninger. New York: Dial, 1989.

Oliver and Amanda's Halloween. Illustrated by Ann Schweninger. New York: Dial, 1992.

Oliver Pig at School. Illustrated by Ann Schweninger. New York: Dial, 1990.

Tales of Amanda Pig. Illustrated by Ann Schweninger. New York: Dial, 1983.

Tales of Oliver Pig. Illustrated by Arnold Lobel. New York: Dial, 1979.

Two Girls in Sister Dresses. Illustrated by Linda Benson. New York: Dial, 1994.

PART FOUR

SCHEDULING AND PLANNING

PLANNING A READING-WRITING WORKSHOP

In my early years of teaching, I separated "creative" writing from reading and responding to reading. But one stubborn fifth grader forced me to evaluate this separation. She was into writing poetry. Yet during class, I often observed her reading fairy tales instead of writing. At a conference, I asked her about reading in writing class. "I have to read," she told me. "That's how I'm learning how to write a fairy tale."

Combining reading and writing workshop not only made good sense, it caused me to lobby for longer blocks of workshop time. The guidelines for reading and writing that Atwell (*In the Middle*) and Hansen (*When Writers Read*) write about infuse the combined workshop where children choose to read, write, or do both. The following chart illustrates the close relationship between reading and writing:

Writing	Reading
Prior Knowledge: Preparation	
Get-Ready-to-Write	Get-Ready-to-Read
Discussion and Dialogue	
Consider Audience	Set Purposes for Reading
Discovery	
First Draft	First Reading
Finding Meaning	
Revise, Conference;	Reread, Reflect;
Revise, Conference;	Refine, Rethink;
Edit	Reflect
Connecting	
Final or Deadline Draft	New Knowledge; Interpretation

Managing a reading and writing workshop posed challenges that have lessened over the years. I have developed some personal guidelines to cope with the varied experiences that cause everyone to be at different stages of writing and research. Chaos defined those initial forays; a core of students produced minimal amounts of writing, and there were those who never developed the passion for reading I envisioned. The assumption was that choice and freedom to read and write motivated everyone. Well, they didn't! However, an intense belief in the concept kept me afloat and prevented my tossing the workshop overboard.

Now, during the first week of school, I spend time discussing the organization and goals of the workshop. By the end of the first month, students and I have begun to set individual, reachable goals. Records of these goals are in conference folders. Students have

choices, and many do read during choice time if they're into a good book. This is the way natural readers behave.

Compartmentalizing students' lives into short time periods, dominated by performance-objective goals, can turn students away from a book or piece of writing. Teachers who read and write soon know that ten to fifteen minutes here and there just isn't enough. Moreover, scheduling experiences in short bites of time teaches children not to focus and get involved with their work. "Just when I'm into a book," one youngster told me, "I've got to put it away. I hate that." Similar comments surface about writing.

Readers and writers should not turn their concentration on and off like water faucets. I asked a teacher I was mentoring when students could listen to a book on tape; she said their middle school schedule allowed for

Reading and discussing a free-choice book during a reading conference.

only two five-minute reading periods. Students rarely read during their forty-minute class. They had so much to cover that there just wasn't any time.

Integrating content and language arts in a reading-writing workshop creates an environment in which children are deeply involved in their work. Self-contained and departmentalized classrooms can incorporate shared reading, literature response groups, minilessons, read-alouds, research, spelling, and word study through theme cycles. But always allow time for free-choice reading and/or writing. I learn most about students as readers and writers from free-choice experiences. And during choice time I read, write, and confer with students. "While I'm reading and writing," I tell my students, "you need to conference with peers or note questions for later." Then I circulate around the classroom, making myself available.

The grade you teach, your students, and mandated curriculum requirements will all affect the way you structure a reading-writing workshop. Workshop requires flexibility from both students and teachers. As an artist mixes and changes colors and uses a variety of brushes to realize a vision, the reading-writing workshop is a palette of colors and textures whose spirit lies in teacher-student negotiations and interactions. An effective workshop environment, one that fosters reading and writing, has the energy, the renewal, and the constancy needed for success. Change, discovery, and surprise are what I treasure most about the workshop. That happens only when children and teachers use language in meaningful contexts to acquire new insights and new information.

I always begin and end a workshop with a whole class meeting. At opening meeting, we discuss the schedule and choice aspects of the class, we address specific student requests, and we set a time for whole group share of reading or writing. At the beginning of the school year, these opening group sessions dwell on establishing procedures for leaving the room, for discussion groups, for turning in work, and for choice times.

Closing meeting grew more out of my need for order than students' needs, though I believe it benefits them as well. Before closing meeting, many of my middle school students left class unclear about short- and long-term assignments; there were always unreturned folders and journals scattered on the floor and tables. During the closing five to ten minutes, I not only review assignments and remind students to store their work, I also praise the good things that happened that day. Class ends on a positive note and reminds students of the learning and cooperation that took place. I view this as evaluation that fosters community bonds and recognizes the daily progress that students don't always see because it often arrives in minute increments.

The sample schedules below (figures 1 and 2) are for self-contained classrooms and departmentalized middle grades. Scheduling language arts and reading back-to-back in the middle grades provides a one-and-a-half-hour block four to five times a week. Self-contained classrooms have greater time flexibility and often meet in two- to three-hour blocks. Adapt these schedules to suit your needs, shortening or lengthening suggested time frames. Limit the choices you offer primary children; gradually add choices once routines have been established.

You'll find that the choices you and your students make and those you jointly negotiate will change as a theme cycle matures. An event such as literature discussion groups might be the teacher's choice at one point and shift to the students' choice at different points during the study. In either case, students can

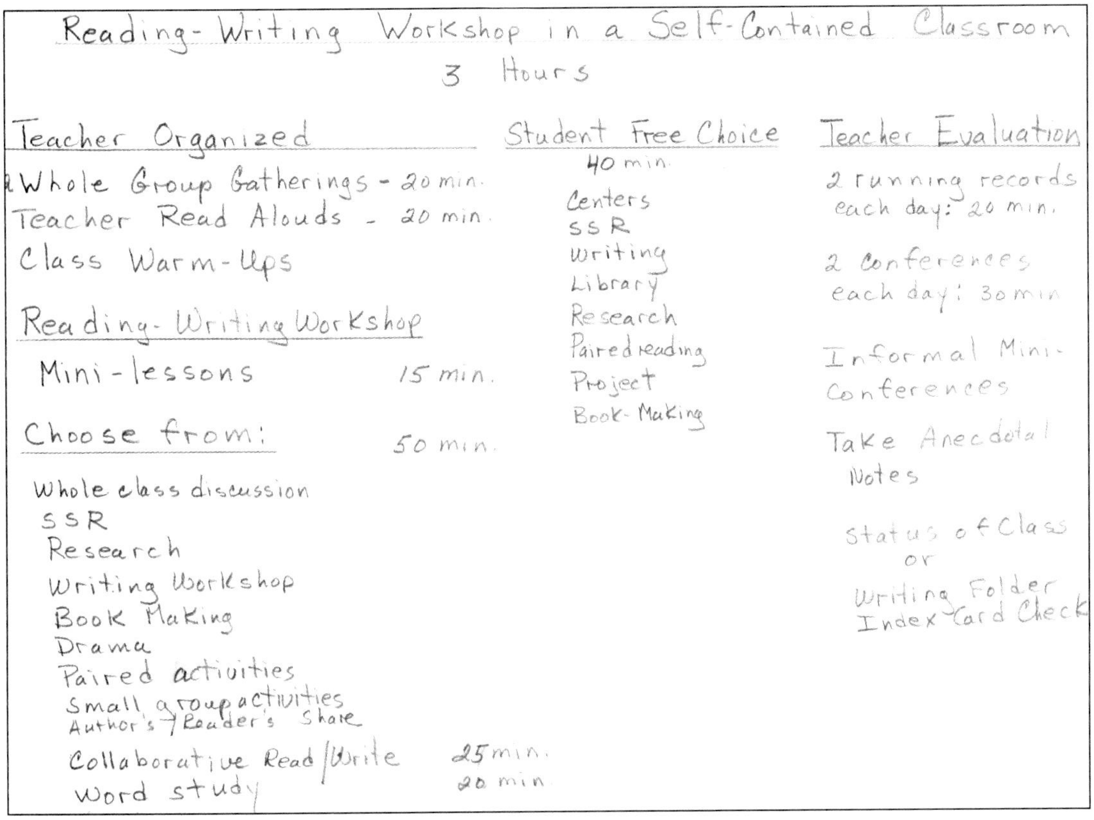

Reading-Writing Workshop in a Self-Contained Classroom
3 Hours

Teacher Organized

Whole Group Gatherings - 20 min.
Teacher Read Alouds - 20 min.
Class Warm-Ups

Reading-Writing Workshop

Mini-lessons   15 min.

Choose from: 50 min.

Whole class discussion
SSR
Research
Writing Workshop
Book Making
Drama
Paired activities
Small group activities
Author's / Reader's Share
Collaborative Read/Write   25 min.
Word study   20 min.

Student Free Choice
40 min.
Centers
SSR
Writing
Library
Research
Paired reading
Project
Book-Making

Teacher Evaluation

2 running records
each day: 20 min.

2 Conferences
each day: 30 min

Informal Mini-
Conferences

Take Anecdotal
Notes

Status of Class
or
Writing Folder
Index Card Check

Figs. 1 and 2 Sample reading-writing workshop schedules for self-contained and departmentalized middle-grade classrooms.

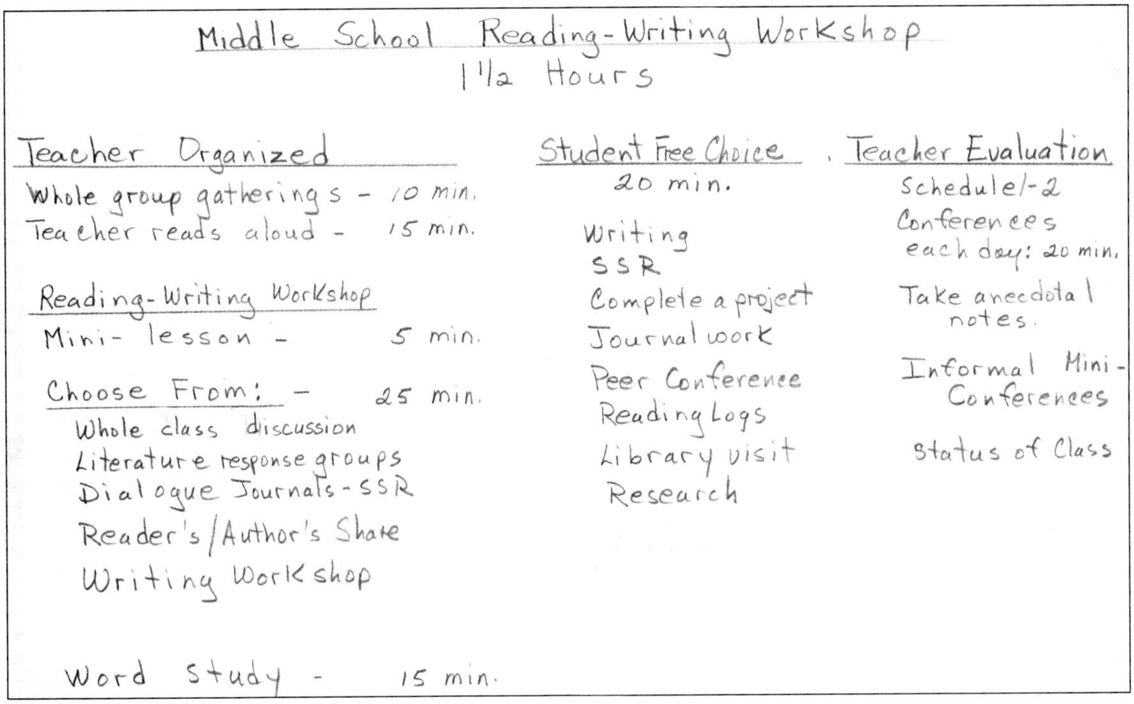

Middle School Reading-Writing Workshop
1½ Hours

Teacher Organized

Whole group gatherings - 10 min.
Teacher reads aloud - 15 min.

Reading-Writing Workshop

Mini-lesson -   5 min.

Choose From: -   25 min.
  Whole class discussion
  Literature response groups
  Dialogue Journals-SSR
  Reader's/Author's Share
  Writing Workshop

Word study -   15 min.

Student Free Choice
20 min.

Writing
SSR
Complete a project
Journal work
Peer Conference
Reading Logs
Library visit
Research

Teacher Evaluation

Schedule 1-2
Conferences
each day: 20 min.

Take anecdotal
notes.

Informal Mini-
Conferences

Status of Class

still have the right to select the book and/or topic to discuss within the framework of discussion groups. Whenever possible, offer students choices within the events you have selected.

Whole language teachers organize workshop experiences around a variety of flexible groupings. Flexible grouping refers not only to composition, but also to formation of groups that change throughout the year. Group memberships should represent a diversity of gender, ethnicity, and socioeconomic backgrounds so students can value and learn from divergent ideas. Sometimes you will determine the group's membership; other times chance or book choices will group students. There will also be educational experiences where students can group themselves.

Purposes for grouping can center around students' common interests, developmental needs, or in-class or cross-grade projects. Grouping decisions alter with content and the purposes of experiences and should include whole class, small group, pairs, and individual learning events.

Accept that your first attempts with grouping will present problems and difficulties, and discouragement won't replace your adventurous, inquiring spirit. I've organized a suggested list of diverse group events and summarized some of the benefits of each. Many events and corresponding benefits overlap. When and how to include them are choices you and students will make as you plan and experience theme cycles.

Experiences that include the whole class build community bonds as students engage in democratic planning and revision, work to solve social issues and behavior problems, and come to value diversity within the classroom. It's an opportunity for a community to share knowledge and vital information, to celebrate and affirm group and individual progress, and

to establish community goals and guidelines. Whole group events can be directed by the teacher and/or students; they provide moments to listen to and observe each other's process. As a kid watcher, you'll learn more about whole group interactions. You'll also be able to assess students' prior knowledge.

Some Whole Class Events

- gatherings
- activating prior knowledge

- discussions
- planning theme cycles

- negotiating rules
- minilessons

- author's and reader's chair
- making decisions

- self-evaluation
- presenting student projects

- read-alouds
- shared book experiences

- problem solving
- questions

- think-alouds
- book talks

- demonstrations
- speeches

Small groups and pairs can work at a faster pace, since fewer students are involved in collaboration and cooperation. Talk-focused partners and small groups work together, share responsibilities, compromise, and support each other in order to build a safe learning atmosphere where members can take risks. Students experience the role of teacher as they take turns working closely with peers to solve reading, writing, research, and mathematical problems. The joint ventures of pairs and groups sharpen their ability to make decisions and share expertise.

If your students have little or no experience with cooperative group work, I recommend you begin with partners. As pairs build and sharpen their social and interactive skills, they have opportunities to be successful and can learn to transfer their experiences to small groups.

Some Small Group and Paired Events

- activating prior knowledge
- peer tutoring
- discussions
- paired reading
- writing
- paired questioning
- negotiating rules
- storytelling
- minilessons
- research
- reading and writing conferences
- book talks
- collaborative evaluations
- self-evaluation
- problem solving
- setting goals
- questions
- making decisions
- dramatizations

All the benefits derived from small group and whole class events can support students' independent learning. Time to work alone permits children to pursue their interests, make choices, and become reflective, self-directed, self-monitoring learners. Such learning events occur within the context of a community that values diversity and supports each individual's set of goals.

Some Individual Events

- SSR
- writing
- research
- choice activities
- goal setting
- self-evaluation
- problem solving

As you and students plan and reflect on the framework of the reading-writing workshop, you should form two key relationships: one with your school librarian, the other with colleagues in a support and study group. Your librarian's book knowledge can furnish you with titles to support a theme cycle and a research project, as well as supplementary reading for individual students. Participation in a support group will keep you in touch with your process as you and colleagues collaborate about professional and children's books, learning as students learn, by using language.

Forming a partnership with your school librarian can help you assemble all the resources for a reading-writing workshop. A great challenge for schools is to construct bridges that forge relationships between school librarians and the learning community. Children and teachers can reap the benefits of their librarian's knowledge of, and love for, books and reading. Who can ever replace the feeling of responding to the beckoning finger of the librarian who secretly whispers previews of the delights that lie between the covers of a

Sixth graders trade bookmark notes and discuss their novels.

book saved especially for you? And what of the return visit that guarantees some time to exchange stories and search the shelves together for another book? "I always ask Mrs. Wheeler [Powhatan's librarian] to help me find a book. She knows every book and what I like to read." Year after year, children echo those words. Children who become aware of a beloved librarian's rich and loving story knowledge form a relationship that nourishes their reading lives.

The whole language librarian can influence the reading lives of all school members. The library, redefined, becomes the bustling hub of reading and research. Increasing the number of volumes in school libraries, acquiring books to support theme cycles, creating space for students' research, scheduling open times for students to use the library daily, keeping teachers, administrators, and parents abreast of new acquisitions, supporting family reading programs and classroom teachers, organizing and running book fairs are some of the duties that school librarians shoulder. No longer can the library be a room a class enters once each week, at a designated time, to check out books. I've overheard many a teacher tell groups of students, "You can't use the library now, it's not your turn." I've visited schools where kindergartners can't use the library because the school's policy is "only kids who can read can check out books."

In an inquiry-driven curriculum, where questions inspire learning, an open and accessible library provides children with the tools for research: books, magazines, newspapers. Restricting the availability of these tools to one period, one day per week, is unnatural and forces teachers to depend on textbook instruction. This sends a negative message to children about why people read and study. Teachers and librarians must meet frequently to negotiate ways the library can best serve and support classroom studies. Together, they can build into schedules open research times for various grades as well as guidelines for two or three students to collect materials as the need arises.

Collecting books for a study and bringing them into the classroom benefits children only when they are the collectors. I know many teachers—and I have been guilty of this myself—who work around the limited-library-use system and constantly carry library books into the classroom. And so we graduate students from high school who have rarely *used* a library's catalog, browsed through shelves, checked out materials, or referred to the *Reader's Guide to Periodical Literature*. Oh yes, they've filled in work sheets with drawings of library shelves, encyclopedias, card catalogs, and almanacs, when the real shelves are just around the corner. Library illiteracy results, and many students enter college suffering from library phobia, due to little or no active library experience.

Rethinking and redefining the librarian's role also means redefining relationships between teachers and librarians. Librarians can recommend books for theme cycles and free-choice reading. What frustrates a librarian is not compiling a list of recommended books for a teacher; it's being asked to assemble a list in one hour. Give your librarian as much notice as possible, and if there aren't enough books to support research, you can order materials or switch gears. Communication can result in assistance from your librarian that spawns the success of a project. Push school administrators for meeting time with the librarian in order to design a more flexible library policy. Invite librarians to curriculum-planning sessions so new acquisitions are consonant with your needs.

Rewards include an increase in book knowledge, a greater familiarity with your school's library collection, plus backing from the librarian for your programs. As with all learning, practice and use lead to comfort and pleasure. And that includes libraries and librarians. Many of us recall our childhood reading with warmth and delight: not only our ten-year-old selves riveted to a book, but also the library floor we sat on, the dusty book smells of wooden shelves, and the waxed tiles piled with books to browse through before check-out decisions. The reality of today's world is that the school library is the only one children can visit regularly. I've surveyed hundreds of elementary school children and discovered with sadness that very few belong to, or regularly visit, public libraries. School libraries, packed with books and kids and teachers, are vital for reading, research, and study.

Whole language philosophy has dramatically changed schedules and redefined the roles of learner and learning, yet most schools are not meeting the needs for teachers to support each other. If your school doesn't reserve common planning time for groups of teachers, then joining or forming a teacher support and study group is the best way for you to grow as a teacher-learner. Teacher support groups, whether within a school or part of a community network, provide time for faculties to learn and read together, to share problems, and to celebrate successes. I view support as a partner of change, professional growth, and innovation.

Groups that I participate in schedule bimonthly meetings at times convenient for teachers with and without family obligations. Using a survey sent to teachers, we organize one-hour sessions that alternate between evening, early morning, and after-school meetings. Flexible scheduling brings increased attendance. The open-ended time of evening meetings frees many to linger beyond the hour. At some schools, the principal and supervisors send teachers administrative notices in a premeeting memo and discuss only crucial issues after the support groups meet. At Johnson Williams Middle School, teaching teams at each grade level have forty-five minutes of common planning time during each day, permitting a support group to meet during the school day. A common lunch period for each grade at Cooley Elementary permits daily twenty-minute group meetings.

Attending a support group should not be required. I always issue an invitation that frees teachers to join at any point during the year and does not insist upon constant attendance. The first support group I organized grew out of a graduate class with thirty teachers from two area school districts. After the third meeting, we all agreed that getting together to read and discuss professional and children's literature was what we needed. I issued an invitation to thirty teachers, and three attended the first meeting. I was one of the three. The evening concluded with our brainstorming ideas to increase attendance. We decided that in two weeks we would each try to bring a teacher with us. Two more arrived at the second meeting, and we read poems and picture books, asked questions, and traded classroom experiences. The group, totally heterogeneous, at that point consisted of a high school English teacher, a high school business teacher, a kindergarten teacher, and a middle school English and science teacher. By May, twelve teachers regularly attended, including primary teachers and even a physical education teacher!

We learned, that year of reading and talking, lessons that a graduate class or test could never impart. Books and personal stories shared with the group affected our emotional lives. Our studies forced us to reexamine recommended expectations for students that just didn't work in class or in our group. What a revelation to discover that it took us longer to respond in a discussion or journal than the time we offered our students. Instead of falling into the complaining teacher cycle of faulting the kids and administration, our own experiences guided us as we tested the ice in classrooms.

Like homing pigeons, we returned to sessions again and again. Many of us entered dog-tired, muttering that this had to be the last meeting. And we left reluctantly, revitalized, chatting around cars and on porches, extending departure times. But most important, we were there for each other, at meetings, at our schools, and on the telephone.

One evening, Sadie, struggling with tenth-grade business students who daily expressed lack of interest in reading the text and learning the process for getting a job, brought her problem before the group. Our brainstorming resulted in suggesting that Sadie have her class research all the things a job seeker must know to obtain a position, and organize research into a guidebook. Sadie and all of us had just completed Eliot Wigginton's *Sometimes a Shining Moment: The Foxfire Experience*, and her students, armed with tape recorders and notebooks, interviewed men and women in the community. They had a real reason for reading and learning how to write a letter and clear suggestions for "the book." The project continued most of the year. "They had a reason to research and write and use the school computer lab," Sadie told us as she proudly passed out copies of the completed booklet.

Our support group met at my house one cold, dark wintry evening. Nancy, a kindergarten teacher, had to make three trips from her car to the house to bring in all her materials. Nancy and her children were studying the human body. That day, Nancy brought a steer heart and lungs to school, and the children completed a big book documenting their investigations. The bloody organs now lay on an oversize dark green plastic garbage bag atop my living room rug. Twelve teachers gathered round, feeling, poking, sticking fingers up an artery and into a chamber of the heart. Lots of talk and questions. Nancy set up a microscope with slides she and the children made, and we took turns looking at heart and lung tissue. The oversize book rested proudly on Nancy's lap as we read the children's story together. Nancy's contagious enthusiasm enveloped us, and the group wished we could be in her class.

The next year, our numbers grew so large that we divided into two groups. We read aloud to each other, choosing books that related to a theme; sometimes we'd have an open-choice share. That year we developed a method of keeping track of all the children's books shared. The form, on four-by-six-inch pieces of paper, fits into an index card filing box.

| TITLE |
| AUTHOR |
| PERSONAL CONNECTIONS |
| THEMES |
| CLASSROOM CONNECTIONS |

There was no way we could remember, each month, the twenty or more books and poems. Some teachers preferred recording notes on an index card. Choice was always an ingredient of our sessions, so we could remember to give similar options to our students.

We also experienced firsthand the difficulty of taking notes only from discussions. It was common to hear "Hold it, I need to finish this," words frequently heard in middle school and high school classes. These were words received by teachers with frustration and impatience until we lived through the note-taking process ourselves.

Support groups not only extend your knowledge of children's and professional literature, they simulate ways students learn. Step into students' shoes to gain insights into teaching by actively reading, writing, listening, talking, and trying on the various roles flexible grouping creates. But most important, over time, a reading and sharing fellowship emerges among members; tears and laughter mingle as teachers exchange stories of pain, suffering, frustration, and joy. The suggestions that follow can help you and colleagues construct an invaluable support network:

- Begin with an invitation, making choice a component from the start.

- Create a risk-free, relaxed atmosphere by recognizing that everyone can't attend every meeting or be prepared for each session. Set a flexible meeting schedule so teachers with young children can attend some sessions.

- The group decides what to read: different or same children's book; professional article or book. The facilitator and/or members can talk about book selections for members to choose from.

- Include your librarian—librarians are an invaluable resource for whole language teachers.

- Initiate discussion by having the person sharing express thoughts and feelings about the book.

- The group leader's role is to generate discussion. Keep the talk focused on the book with an open-ended question about character, theme, or setting; by asking others what they think about the book; or with a personal comment.

- Ask the person sharing if the book, poem, or article raised any questions within his or her mind.

- Accept silences as a natural part of thinking and discussing. Most silent periods are shorter than our perception of them. Time a silence and say nothing until at least one minute has passed.

- The leader's crucial role is to keep talk squarely on the text or issue before the group, for talk can easily move from the book to personal gossip.

- Encourage a diversity of interpretations and reactions.

- All sharing should be voluntary. Give those reluctant to share time to risk participating.

- The leader must be a good listener in order to keep the discussion going. Don't support one viewpoint over another.

- Reserve time periodically to discuss the group's process and how what's happening at meetings connects to classroom practices and expectations.

- Once comfortable with whole group discussions, try flexible groupings of pairs and smaller groups who discuss the same book, poem, or article.

- Use support meetings to learn more about children's books, especially multicultural books.

- Learn to check multicultural books for bias, such as portraying minorities as "the problem"; accepting poverty as inevitable; or relying on a white person or male to resolve problems.

- Reserve time for members to share and discuss teaching stories. Suggest that members keep journals about daily teaching experiences and support meetings.

- Encourage other members to act as the group leader and make this a rotating position.

Support groups actively involve you in learning by using language. In the first chapter, I noted that all learning is in the doing, the experiencing. Study groups engage you in the doing so you can come to know more about your process and colleagues' process. Such groups nurture members' gifts, focus members more on the mission of process, and foster professional growth by sharing classroom stories, journal articles, and professional books. The bonus is that you can transfer the knowledge you gain into your own classroom.

AS I SEE IT

Pam Conrad

I have always loved metaphors and symbols, and when I think of reading and writing, it occurs to me that if my brain were a country estate, with different parts of the estate corresponding to different parts of my brain, I imagine the furnace in my main building would be the part of my brain to control my involuntary muscles and organs; and the kitchen—full of aromas and herbs drying in fragrant clusters—would correspond to the place that controls all my carnal appetites; and perhaps the stables, with steaming, stomping dark horses, their eyes wild and ablaze, would be the place of my fears. So I ask myself, what part of my brain would be the part that reads and writes? And I know immediately. I knew that first, actually. The parts about the furnace, kitchen, and stables I had to think about awhile.

All books, all notebooks and diaries, all poetry and prose, all muses, would make up the garden of my brain. At first I had imagined this as a lovely roof garden in a sumptuous Manhattan apartment that overlooked the Statue of Liberty, but I soon realized such a garden would not be big or varied enough for all I had in mind.

I knew it had to be a very big garden with different views and a tremendous variety of flowers, shrubs, and trees. For poetry, there would be a topiary garden to meander through, with perfectly carved images, where everything would be precisely mathematical and symmetrical. But this wouldn't be the only place for poetry. There would also be the compost heap out behind the kitchen where avocado pits are tossed with leftover bean sprouts and orange rinds. (Some of my poetry is like this.)

So you ask, how was this magnificent rich garden planted? When was it planned, and how did it grow? I go to my bookshelves and pull down a copy of one of the first books I owned. It is *The House At Pooh Corner,* by A. A. Milne. Inside it is inscribed, *12 '51, To Pamela, To Help Make Your Heart Beautiful. From Mommy & Daddy.* This is in my father's handwriting. I was four and he was twenty-four. And still today, hovering over this garden mingled with birdsong and frogs, is the remembrance of my father's voice reading *Moby Dick* to my mother in bed, when they were young. This is how my garden began.

It is clear to me that my garden was originally planned by someone else. And as anyone who has ever had a garden knows, the greatest blessing is to have had it well planned years before you noticed it and began working on it yourself. My garden layout was more than adequate. I heard poetry recited out loud, things like "The Man on the Flying Trapeze" and "The Face on the Barroom Floor." And I was read to. My parents were not well educated, and I think maybe if they had been, I would have read other things, but besides Milne and a few other books, I had hundreds of Golden Books, inexpensive books that were part of a day's shopping, and although today I know they were perhaps not great literature or great art, I have been known to stand transfixed and stunned in Macy's furniture department, staring at a rough-hewn chair made from branches. *The Three Bears* vibrate through me. And oh, how I studied that Golden Book *Cinderella*! I tied a ribbon around my throat, and drew all my dancing girls with poofs like saddle bags on each side of their hooped skirts.

And then there were my own early attempts at writing—the stories in black notebooks that rambled on and on and went nowhere, their only glory being the number of pages they could consume; and also there were my poems—single ungainly attempts at something I blindly aimed at, shining there, in a row, like a child's garden of boisterous sunflowers. Ah, rhythm! Ah, meter! Ah, bumblebee yodeling round my plump seeds! My parents stood by and applauded.

I realize that my serious writing did not happen for me until I had begun to structure and plan the gardens of my own children. I read to them. We carried books wherever we went—to church, to the doctors, to picnics, and to stores. I read to them in their beds, even while they soaked in the bath. I remember reading aloud from Dickens's *Christmas Carol* along with winter breakfast one year. I even paid them to read, a dollar a book. I wrote notes, little poems, and tucked them in their lunch boxes. I sat under the dropping linden trees in their gardens and turned pages and wondered where the big trees had come from. I had certainly not planted them, but my children had come with parts of their gardens already formed and flourishing, as I suspect is the case in most children's gardens.

My daughters are grown women today, but I can still get my oldest daughter's attention by looking at her from across a room and saying quietly but with some urgency, "Pit, pat. Pit, pat. Pit, pat." We look in each other's eyes and feel the quivery thrill of a little elf running from tree to tree in our adjoining gardens, chased by his shoes.

But it was while my girls were young that I suddenly began to write again. I used them in stories. I opened the gate to my garden and even invited them in. They were boisterous and ornery. They toppled some of my more delicate plantings and had to be scolded. Sometimes they were expelled. I remember before closing the door to my writing room saying, "Now don't call me for anything."

"Nothing?"

"Absolutely nothing!"

"What if there's a fire?"

"If there's a fire call me. But nothing else!"

"What if a policeman comes to the door?"

"If there's a fire, or if a policeman comes to the door, call me! But nothing else! Good-bye!"

In those years we tromped back and forth through each other's gardens. I walked with care in theirs. I always brought a gift—a seed, a seedling, an interesting nut—and I would observe, like a squirrel in a dogwood tree. I watched to see what they were doing in their gardens.

Admittedly there have been dry periods in my own garden. I have walked through periods in my life where it seems that instead of spending time in the garden, I was in the stable, preoccupied with fears. Other times my garden has been barren and wintry. I have sat on a cement bench in a winter garden and felt the chill, like death all around me, and I have thought myself barren as well. Storms have ripped through my garden, tearing down trellises and taking away good soil. Snow has piled on top of precious shrubs, and then turned to ice, and like a pile of bricks, the ice has broken and split my shrubs. Tidewaters have risen, encrusting everything with salt, and neighboring dogs have barked and disturbed my peace. Sometimes I have abandoned my garden. Books have lain unread, journals and notebooks unopened, untouched.

But always there has been a spring. Croci whispering to be seen, dogwood blossoms like baby fists, waiting. And I would see a movie that would remind me of a book, and I would return to that book. Someone would invite me somewhere, and I would hear someone tremble their way through a poem, and on the way home—alone—I would scribble words on the back of my grocery list.

And while there must be quiet, solitary summers in my garden, I cannot bear to be alone in it for long. I have always enjoyed a little company. When my youngest daughter was twelve we had a birthday party in our house, and I discovered that all of her friends had just read my book *Holding Me Here*, and I was fascinated to see them wander through my house, realizing, "Here's the door Ted broke down." "And here's the desk Robin hid under." And my daughter, enjoying being a tour guide through her mother's garden, leaped up into the doorway and climbed to the top, just like Heather in *Staying Nine*, the book I had written for her when she was turning ten, and it had made me sad.

Then there was the time I had my writer's group to my house. I belong to a most extraordinary group of Long Island authors. I feel guilty mentioning their names, as though I'm name-dropping, but I knew I was rubbing shoulders with serious celebrities when my sophisticated teenage daughter nearly squealed, "The author of *Lyle Crocodile* is coming here! Tonight? Lyle! Oh, my God!"

Normally we meet and "network," as the magazines call it. Whoever's house it's at will pick a topic. We've talked about writer's block, getting ideas, best computers, loyalty to a publisher, contracts, and more. But this one time it was at my house, and I suggested we have a reading. While we were all children's book authors, and somewhat familiar with each other's work, a few were also poets, adult authors, and journalists of sorts. It would not be a critiquing, but rather an entertainment. We would offer each other gifts from our gardens. I was surprised at the reluctance and shyness. And I realized that behind our well-known "names," we all ran for the stables when it came time to open the doors to our own gardens. What I remember most from that night is watching one of our members—someone we had known to be a playwright as well as many other things, someone who probably uses his stables to store his paints and canvases—as he sang his way through a musical he had written about baseball. We laughed and marveled, relieved to spend time in someone else's lush and wondrous garden.

I guess it has always been easiest and least threatening to bring someone I love into my garden. This past summer my youngest daughter, my last child, was getting ready to go off to college, and I was watching her leave (from my stable window, as you may already have guessed). I got it into my head that I should *read* to her, that I needed her in my garden.

So this one particular summer evening we had plans to sleep overnight on our twenty-two-foot sailboat. Our boat is moored in the most beautiful place in the world—a little cove on the south shore of Shelter Island, which is out east, nestled in the fishtail of Long Island. We were going sailing the next day with a friend who would meet us in the morning. We had washed up and were ready to settle down for the night. I had brought along *The Bluest Eye,* by Toni Morrison.

We put our sleeping bags out in the cockpit and by eight-thirty or nine, when the light was fading, I began reading to Sarah. I read for a while, torn between the need to read and also the need to admire our peaceful surroundings. When I told Sarah I felt like I was missing the sunset, she offered to read, and then we began taking turns, until we were in the dark, reading with a flashlight, in the light rain and in our moldy old sleeping bags. At one point the rain did seem to threaten to do more than drizzle, and we moved the sleeping bags inside to keep them dry, but we continued to sit out in the cockpit anyway, reading. Sarah laughed in amusement at some of what we were reading and was silent and thoughtful for other parts. At one point there was a very graphic description of sex. I asked her if she was okay with reading this together, aloud. She shrugged and said, "Sure, *I* didn't write it." I laughed, and she went on.

When the rain eased up, we brought the sleeping bags back out and finally turned off the flashlight. We sleepily watched the stars come out and felt the boat rock gently beneath us. I thought that someday she'd be with her own children in a setting much like this one, and she'd remember this night and say to them, "My mother would have loved this." It was one of those timeless moments when the universe presents an instant that doesn't feel locked anywhere, and through this instant, we would always be able to conjure each other up.

So I can see now that my garden would have to have a sloping hill down to a bay, or at the very least, a cove. There would be a dock there and a sailboat. And because this is all metaphor and symbols, I can make it whatever I like, so there will be window boxes on the windows of my sleek little sailboat, like those I once saw on boats in the canals in Amsterdam, and there will be nasturtiums and impatiens growing there, and on your way to the boat, your fingers will brush the Shirley poppies beside the path.

I sit back and sigh, satisfied. But I know the greatest part of my garden is the fallow field beyond the herb garden. I haven't decided what to grow there next. Once it was Nebraska corn. Another time I set it with tombstones and pebbles. It waits for me. And now in my solitude, I walk though its richness.

Later today, when I get in my car and drive to the supermarket, my mind and my brain will be on other things, many other things, but my feet will be caked with mud.

SELECTED BOOKS BY PAM CONRAD

Holding Me Here. New York: Harper & Row, 1986.

I Don't Live Here! Illustrated by Diane de Groat. New York: Dutton, 1984.

The Lost Sailor. Illustrated by Richard Egielski. New York: HarperCollins, 1992.

Molly and the Strawberry Day. Illustrated by Mary Szilagyi. New York: HarperCollins, 1994.

My Daniel. New York: Harper & Row, 1989.

Pedro's Journal: A Voyage with Christopher Columbus. Honesdale, PA: Boyds Mills Press, 1991.

Prairie Songs. Illustrated by Darryl S. Zudeck. New York: Harper & Row, 1985.

Prairie Visions: The Life and Times of Soloman Butcher. New York: HarperCollins, 1991.

The Pumpkin Moon. New York: Harcourt Brace, 1994.

Seven Silly Circles. Illustrated by Mike Wimmer. New York: Harper & Row, 1987.

Staying Nine. Illustrated by Mike Wimmer. New York: Harper & Row, 1988.

Stonewords: A Ghost Story. New York: Harper & Row, 1990.

Taking the Ferry Home. New York: Harper & Row, 1990.

The Tub Grandfather. Illustrated by Richard Egielski. New York: HarperCollins, 1993.

The Tub People. Illustrated by Richard Egielski. New York: Harper & Row, 1989.

What I Did for Roman. New York: Harper & Row, 1987.

THEME CYCLES

In her first year of participating in a reading-writing workshop, Nancy Heisey, a sixth-grade teacher, said, "I've grown more these first months than in the last several years. I read with my students, I write with them, I listen to them and watch them. We're still in our theme cycle of World War II. It balloons instead of fizzling to an end. And the kids bring in books and ideas for field trips, visitors, and investigations that we all want to do." Nancy is experiencing the vitality and creative energy of a theme cycle.

A theme cycle, however, is not a themed unit, and it's essential to understand the differences between unit and cycle. There are an abundance of literature-centered whole language themed units available to teachers filled with thick, reproducible packets of activities more akin to basal workbooks than teachers like to admit. Moreover, the adult authors of themed units have completed all the thinking, questioning, and problem solving, not the children. Students' choices in a themed unit involve, at best, selecting an activity or a project. The unit remains unchanged during the weeks of study and is carefully filed away for future years.

Many connections in themed units are false, as the authors attempt to integrate the topic into all subjects. If no authentic math activities emerge, then children draw patriot hats to count or decorate the room with Pilgrim shoes in order to fulfill art requirements. In classrooms driven by themed units, teachers, bulletin boards, books, centers, and activities are predictable year after year. One teacher complained to me, "But I've finally arrived at the point where I have enough units to use through the year. And you want me to change?" The answer is yes—by considering classroom studies in terms of a theme cycle, which respects the range of children's development and makes the planning a joint venture.

The concept of theme cycles forms the core of a democratic classroom and demands as much of the teacher as of the student. Teachers don't have to know everything about a subject in order to teach it. Once the concept of "teaching it" transforms to "doing it," then a shift in the classroom power structure occurs: a shift from dispenser-of-knowledge to co-learner. Theme cycles change daily and are

An artist and her self-portrait—a student-choice project for a Renaissance theme cycle.

flexible enough to consider varied interests, new knowledge, experiences, and resources. The theme originates as an incomplete thought, matures, and takes on a life of its own.

Teachers get shaky when I tell them this. "How can we do new things every year? It's impossible." First, the teacher doesn't do all the work; the teacher acts as coach, resource person, adviser, and listener. Second, choice and negotiation balance the curriculum between district requirements and students' interests.

I might begin the school year by telling students that we're required to study space, Africa, the human body, and biography. Then I tell the class how other groups evaluated these themes, and ask them to choose which they want to study first. Though I have a history of experiences with the themes, each year I gather the children's questions and work to discover individual interests. Every year new books, resources, and fresh ways to investigate a theme arise because the children lead the way. And each year the children are different; so am I. Redoing the theme this way offers choice and values the children's interests and passions.

Teaching is easier because I'm more familiar with the resources and more comfortable in the facilitator and co-learner roles. Annually, I reexperience the theme through the children's vision and my research. That's the creative and exhilarating aspect of theme cycles: Growth and innovation are available to all community members.

Find out children's questions and interests with the inquiry notebook and student-made interest interviews. I always answer interview questions and participate in the share session. After all, isn't it equally important for them to know me and hear some of my stories?

Themes that develop from honest questions might not always please adults. Without honest inquiry, we'll always be playing the game of learning rather than engaging in real study. I've adopted the habit of spending the first days of school listening to students' stories to discover more about them. Kid watching also tunes me in to students' informal talk and conversations, yielding ideas that often form the core of our studies. The fear and depression over the possibility of a nuclear holocaust expressed by a group of eighth graders became a theme cycle called Peaceful Resolutions to Conflict. Another year, two sixth graders presented speeches on the use of animals for research in cosmetics and medicine. Their presentations blossomed into a theme cycle that polarized students into two camps: one for, the other against using animals for research. The point is that through a topic students burned to study, they were able to improve their reading, writing, speaking, thinking, and research abilities.

I like to think of a theme cycle as a gardener views annual flowers. Each year new ones must be planted, the earth recultivated, and the seedlings watered, weeded, and nourished so they'll thrive and mature. You'll even modify the planning process as you experience it.

The steps for coordinating a theme cycle that follow have worked for me. They are not an inflexible set of linear guidelines, and I can guarantee that as I continue to teach, I'll abandon or alter some and discover new and better strategies.

- Identify the theme with your students or offer them a choice from a set of required themes. Themes might center around an author or illustrator study, a literary genre, a topic, or required curriculum content.

- With your students, brainstorm all ideas the theme generates. On chart paper, organize suggestions in a list, web, flow chart, or map. Select the best method of organization for you.

- Have students help you categorize information to see which content area connections emerge.

- Collect from students areas they would like to investigate.

- Students, teacher, and librarian gather trade books, magazines, charts, maps, audiocassettes, newspapers, posters, and materials for research throughout the study. Consider the resources that parents, other classes, and the community can provide.

- With the children, list authentic reading, writing, and speaking activities on a chart or bulletin board. Allow time to add to this list throughout the cycle.

- Add goals that your school requests you and the children meet.

- Negotiate with the children the kinds and number of projects and investigations to be completed.

- Set aside large blocks of time so students can read and discuss and gain new knowledge. Learning and thinking take time.

- Schedule whole group and small group meetings to discuss specific needs, to revise goals, to remind children of deadlines, and to praise progress.

- Document the themed study as it unfolds.

- Students and teacher assess the theme cycle from their perspective and from negotiated guidelines and reflect on which experiences were most beneficial.

Students and I learned that unless we kept track of plans for a theme cycle, many experiences were shuffled to the side or simply forgotten. The theme cycle planning framework that

I find most helpful is the category chart. Some teachers publish the emerging plans on a chart or bulletin board and refer to them during morning gathering at any point in the study. Publishing also permits all community members to continually add to and modify their plan.

These models work for me; you need to adapt them to your needs. Students who don't have a knowledge of authentic reading and writing experiences will need suggestions from you.

Category Method of Planning

Eighth-Grade Theme Study: Peer Pressure, Brainstorming Ideas

teen magazine stories	real-life stories
newspaper stories	literature
advertisements	films, videos
drug and alcohol abuse	autobiography, biography
guests: teen rehab centers	visit a community rehab center

Books and Resources

books: students choose	visitors
films, videos	parents
magazines, newspapers	librarian

Authentic Experiences and Flexible Grouping. Students and I mark activities using this key: WG: whole group; SG: small group; P: pairs; I: independent. An asterisk (*) next to an item designates my input.

inquiry journal (I)

interviewing peers (I)

presentations (SG, P, I)

*conducting a community survey (P, I)

watching a film (WG)

reading response journal (I)

*interviewing adults (P, I)

buddy journal (P)

designing a survey (WG)

discussions (WG, SG, P)

readers theater (SG)

how-tos of an effective interview (SG, WG)

inviting guests (P, I)

phone calls, thank-you notes (I)

writing a magazine story (I)

checking out library books and other resources (WG)

book talk titles (I) plus Mrs. R.

writing an editorial (P, I)

reading literature (P, I)

interviewing guests (SG, P, I)

Evaluation	Notes
jointly set assessment criteria	readers theater the best
self-assessment and evaluation	make time for conferences
completed projects	more time to interview others
record keeping	record keeping easy to forget
group participation and group interactions	rotating class secretary works

This list is a framework that changes according to students' interests and available resources. My role is to assist students with the organization of their time, establishing reasonable deadline dates and setting aside quiet times for reading, research, and writing. In the Notes section, I record comments students make and my own reactions. The "make time for conferences" was a reminder to me to organize my time so every child received one-on-one assistance. I review these notes frequently, as they force me to reflect on student perspectives and highlight the smooth and bumpy aspects of each cycle.

I have identified, with the assistance of students, signs that advertise a theme cycle is working for the entire classroom community:

- Allows members to *read*, *write*, *think*, and *speak* in meaningful and authentic ways.

- Provides for the growth and development of all members, whether at-risk or gifted.

- Integrates the fine-art and content areas only when integration makes sense.

- Provides a wide range of experiences that meet the interests, developmental needs, and learning styles of all students.

- Reserves time to research and explore the theme.

- Promotes critical thinking as students solve academic, planning, and social problems.

- Uses minilessons, modeled by teacher and students, to improve the learning process.

- Encourages continual self-evaluation and goal setting.

- Provides ongoing opportunities to share new knowledge, research, books, music, and so on.

- Allows for flexible and changing groups.

- Promotes reflection, providing time to think, discuss, share, and review work in order to make personal connections and connections with other books and subjects.

- Creates a community of active learners.

It's helpful to know up front that a theme cycle doesn't run smoothly and perfectly with every student on task and super-productive, even when the learning arises from individual interests. Noise levels will become intolerable, children will waste time, disagreements and arguments will occur, students will adamantly refuse to compromise or share, many will use choice and freedom to plan time as an opportunity to waste time. Dealing with these issues is a crucial aspect of the learning process, especially the problem-solving model, which requires collaboration and cooperation. Children don't learn how to make less noise, how to set goals, how to organize time, how to concentrate unless they make mistakes and have a chance to analyze and revise them. Children don't arrive at school automatically knowing how to work in pairs and groups, how to compromise, research, manage time, meet deadlines, or make beneficial choices. It's the getting there that contains the learning, and your job is to provide ways for children to figure out how to interact in your classroom community so that each member can use language to learn.

A SECOND GRADE HELPS PLAN A THEME CYCLE

The story that follows recounts the evolution of a second grade's partnership with their teachers, Carol Chapman and myself, in planning a theme cycle on natural phenomena and natural disasters. Their story represents a coming together of many of the concepts discussed throughout this book.

"The hardest thing to learn is to step back, because you feel like you're not teaching." These were Carol's words in the midst of a second-grade theme cycle. I had approached her, during the final days of autumn, with a proposition: to work with the second grade on abstract science themes and let the children lead the way. Carol; Anne Wheeler, the school librarian; and I would offer suggestions, be resources for the children, and support them and each other. I also wanted to observe how much story would provide a framework or scaffolding for the children's understanding of concepts they had not directly experienced or observed.

Carol, extremely flexible and comfortable with her reading-writing workshop, had never fully placed on her children the responsibility for learning and developing a theme. Most of the planning, problem solving, and activities offered students had been completed by Carol. Though a bit skeptical, she agreed to let the children lead the way.

We obtained permission from the head of the school and from Carol's immediate supervisor. The only request both administrators made was that we keep the parents informed and involved. An easy charge, for that would definitely be the children's responsibility. Our only plan was to present two general themes to the class of eighteen children: natural phenomena and natural disasters. Documentation would occur in the journals Carol and I kept. The eight boys and ten girls in Carol's class lived in a small town or in the surrounding rural area. Several children were reading below grade level; others read and wrote fluently. Students' topic choices determined the membership of four heterogeneous groups.

Carol and I quickly discovered that the children had little prior knowledge about natural disasters and phenomena. Other than earthquakes, hurricanes, dinosaurs, and Venus's-flytraps, we did not compile a rich and varied list. But these children, sitting in groups of four and five, understood note taking. Without prompting, before brainstorming ideas, many went to the stack of scratch paper and brought a pile back to their groups. Their notes ranged from pictures to the first letter of a word, such as *V* for *volcano* and *H* for *hurricane*.

At this juncture, Carol and I had a choice: We could add to the chart or ask the children how they could learn more. "Go to the library," several said. "Ask Mr. Legge, the science teacher," was another suggestion. "You could tell us," Mary said. We began with the library, because that placed responsibility for expanding knowledge on the children. We invited the children to browse. However, every child took a book and began to read. Quickly we convened the group and demonstrated the art of browsing. Carol and I modeled and fielded questions. The class spent two leisurely library sessions browsing, surrounded by books, changing partners, exchanging discoveries. Carol and I browsed with the children, expanding our knowledge base. There were subjects I knew only a smattering about: comets, oceans, electricity, and quicksand.

The kids expressed surprise at first when I told them I needed to browse to learn. "You're supposed to know everything," they said, rather shocked. Catherine insisted on taking notes while reading. When I suggested she might want to wait until she had browsed through several books, she looked up and said, "This is serious browsing." Catherine had become so intrigued with a book on shooting stars, she wanted notes "so I can think more later."

Cara avoided browsing by spending the two periods looking at bulletin boards. Carol intervened and offered to browse with her. She happily browsed with her teacher, but she did not move into browsing with a peer or by herself. We accepted this behavior and said nothing.

Each browsing session ended with the children writing what they remembered in journals. Catherine's browsing resulted in a yearning to learn more about many topics she had not previously thought about (figure 1).

Back in the classroom, our list of possible topics to investigate filled two large charts. After reading the lists, Gregory shouted, "I just want to study the whole world!"

"Now you've done it," Carol said to me. "How are they going to decide? We can't possibly have them do everything." My insides felt as tentative as half-formed Jell-O, but I replied confidently, "They'll work it out."

Groups met and gradually eliminated topics from the lists. To help them narrow choices, I circled those topics our library could support with books and other resources. I also asked the four groups to try to agree on two to three topics to research. Two days later, we had a list of six topics. Every child wrote first and second choices on paper. Carol and I organized study groups around these topics: volcanoes and fire, tornadoes and storms, earthquakes and fire, and space and storms.

To activate prior knowledge, I offered the class a choice between composing a group mural or brainstorming, discussing, and charting. All groups voted to draw a mural. Carol and I asked them to make a plan and think about what each member would draw on a five-foot strip of brown paper. Ensuing arguments and personal sniping worried Carol and me. We repeated minilessons and modeled how we planned, imagined, took notes, respected each other's suggestions, and made room for ideas we each generated. The class commented on our process, and we compiled a list of their observations:

- You don't argue.

- You let the other finish.

- You accept each other's ideas.

- You didn't act as if you thought you had to agree.

- You compromised sometimes.

Back at the drawing board, groups solved decision-making problems. Three groups decided that each member would offer a plan of what she or he wanted to draw and present it to the group. One group brainstormed a list of all the possible things they could include in a mural and then divided the tasks. Desks and chairs piled against the wall, crayons and

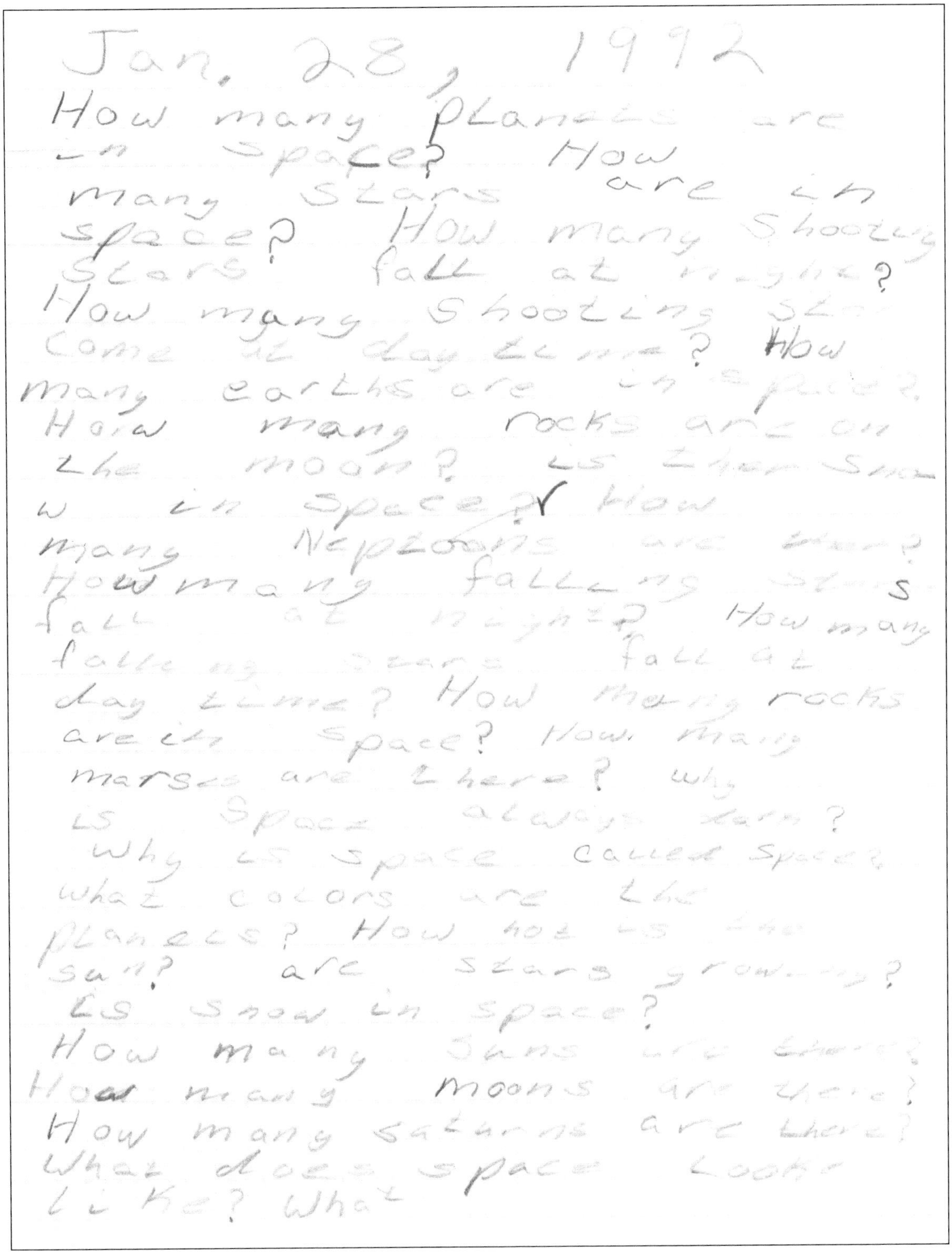

Jan. 28, 1992
How many planets are in space? How many stars are in space? How many shooting stars fall at night? How many shooting stars come at day time? How many earths are in space? How many rocks are on the moon? Is there snow in space? How many Neptoons are there? How many falling stars fall at night? How many falling stars fall at day time? How many rocks are in space? How many marses are there? Why is space always dark? Why is space called space? What colors are the planets? How hot is the sun? Are stars growing? Is snow in space? How many suns are there? How many moons are there? How many saturns are there? What does space look like? What

Fig. 1

markers and children transformed the plain brown paper into action-packed, detailed murals. We didn't have to offer a deadline for completing this project; everyone worked, groups paused only to study each other's progress and ask questions. Class artists solved illustration problems. The comments below show that the children viewed the murals as hard work, but fun!

• You might think it's just coloring. We think and work hard to draw.

• What I think is that work is imagining things and trying to tell them. This is work.

Carol and I hung completed murals on the walls and ceiling; groups rehearsed class presentations. Every group explained its mural in terms of stories; the illustrations were like wordless picture books, stories of what happened to people, buildings, animals, and nature during and after an earthquake, volcanic eruption, storm, fire, or tornado. The space group had four earths, and Catherine explained when questioned by peers, "We don't know what's out there; we've never been." Telling the stories of the murals became serious business, and most children wrote their lines in journals as detailed as Nicole's (figure 2).

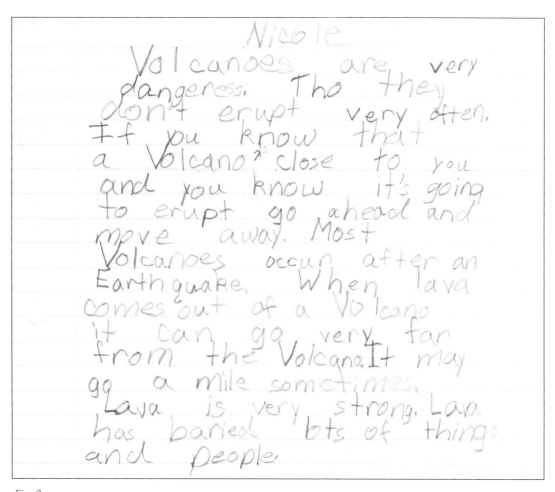

Fig. 2

~~and~~ christin e

I am mars
Mars has a polar ice cap on top fels
Mars is in between
Earth and Jupiter.
Pluto is the coldest
planet it is farthest
from the sun.
mercury is the closest
to the sun so it
is the hottest
the moon is very
bamppy Earth has
blue and green.
the green is land
the blue is water.
Jupiter has a red spot
the red spot is the
place wher storms ha
ppen. Space is the
darkest place. It is
darker than your room
and katherine

Fig. 3

Groups exhibited great pride in telling the stories about the mural. The discussion period that followed each presentation raised further questions, which Carol and I recorded on chart paper and displayed on a bulletin board. Here are some questions the class raised that were different from group members' questions:

• Are there different colored lavas?

• What color is a tornado?

• How powerful are tornadoes?

• Is there snow in space?

• Is there more than one earth?

• Where do most earthquakes happen?

• Can you predict when an earthquake will happen?

• Are meteors like rocks?

Reading dominated the next few weeks. However, the children quickly identified two problems: Where could we put books so groups didn't have to rummage constantly through boxes? What about books that more than one group needed? How simple it would have been for Carol and me to solve this problem for the class. We resisted and asked the children to discuss and offer possible solutions. Thirty minutes later, each group was making a topic sign and taping it to a section of a bookshelf. The sign on one bookshelf read Share Books; everyone pitched in and placed books on appropriate shelves. Children read independently, to a partner, or to a small group. They discussed pictures and text and read and discussed the questions each had

raised after browsing and before reading. We reserved the last ten to fifteen minutes for writing and drawing all they recalled in journals (figure 3).

Problems arose daily, and the kids brought the big ones to Carol and me; we brought these before the class. A large quantity of the books on the reserved classroom shelves were too difficult for the class to read. "We want more than just the pictures; we want the words," said Mark, a spokesperson for the class. So Carol and I began to make reading appointments with children. But this didn't work; many grumbled about waiting for a reader. This time, the children's solution was far superior to the teachers': invite an older class to come read to us. And they did. Letters of invitation went out to the fourth and seventh grades, and we spent several glorious periods together.

Both classes evaluated the buddy-reading sessions; older students felt they had learned much new information by reading to the second grade. "I didn't think the books would be compkated," wrote fourth grader Annie. "I learned about Saturn and want to go there on a space ship."

Parents had carloads of questions about our work and wondered why work folders did not arrive home on Fridays. One month into the cycle, the children dictated a letter to me. I typed the letter; each child signed and decorated it and asked a parent or adult at home to respond (figure 4). Children read and clipped their letters to a clothesline strung across the room.

Children also wrote to parents about their research and projects in their journals, and many parents responded. In fact, parents' enthusiasm increased throughout the project, and charts, additional books, and suggestions for guest speakers arrived daily.

January 30, 1992

Dear Parents,

Below is a collaborative letter from your children updating
you on their studies. Please read the letter, look at the
illustration, write back and return to school so we can
display them. Many, Many thanks!

                    Carol Chapman and Laura Robb

Dear Parents,

    We're studying rocks. There is water in rocks.

    We're studying sun. There's fire in it and when it
erupts it goes into rainbows.

    We're studying stars and all that we can learn about
space.

    We read books.

    We draw pictures about browsing.

    We made lists of questions for each group to find in
books.

    We write in our journals.

    We have lots of fun. You get to do stuff you don't
usually get to do, but Mrs. Robb is a little bit crazy.

    Catherine S. and Nicole brought in tornado experiments.

Amy, Kate and Nicole brought in a volcano experiment.

    We read a lot of books. We learn a lot of things.

                              Love, *MF H.*

Fig. 4 A collaborative letter to parents from a second-grade class and one parent's reply.

Dear Mary Frances,

All of you seem to be having a wonderful time studying and learning about many interesting things. Your illustration of a volcano reminds me of the country in which I was born, Japan. In Japan, erupting volcanoes and earthquakes happen very often. As you probably already know, Japan is a country of islands, which were formed from volcanoes.

You and your class keep up the great work!

Love,
Dad

During writing workshop, several children, consumed with their research, included what they learned in stories (figure 5).

Others drew pictures about their new knowledge on the blackboard and told stories about drawings. Stories entered conversations; the transcription of the volcano group's exchange is a mixture of story and fact:

M.: Did you know that a volcano looks like any mountain?

B.: Then how can you tell it's a volcano?

M.: Smoke comes out the top. My dad said that when he was in Hawaii, he could see the smoke.

F.: Lava is magma. Pressure melts the rock under the ground.

N.: Yeah, kinda like having lots of ovens and fires under the earth.

F.: There's a story about this god, Vulcan, who makes fires under the earth.

N.: Well there's no god doing it. It's from pressure. That's what the book says. [Points to book and reads.]

The moment I offered the children the option of creating a play based on research, they refused to discuss other options. Using books, journal notes, and illustrations, groups planned and rehearsed plays.

Parents sent in cartons of fabric scraps, old blankets, yarn, sheets—anything that might be transformed into a prop or a costume. Carol and I watched, totally enthralled by the children's process. For two weeks, they planned and rehearsed scripts in the classroom, changing their minds, adding or removing scenes. Groups selected a scribe to record script notes for everyone. Jennifer's notes document one of the tornado group's rehearsals (figure 6).

Once they had planned their scripts, we moved to the learning resource room, an empty classroom reserved for special projects.

Groups designed sets, made costumes, and had several dress rehearsals. An old plaid blanket, hung from the ceiling, was a funnel cloud; a child in a box, covered with a faded red blanket sprinkled with flames of red yarn, became a volcano ready to erupt. The earthquake group set up a helicopter and told their story through the eyes of two pilots, while other members mimed the narrative. The space group wrote a script called "Journey Through Space" for a narrator and created, with material and cardboard, planet costumes. At one rehearsal, Pluto was absent, and I was drafted for the part. "Ball up more, you're too big," ordered Jennifer, who kept telling me that Pluto was the smallest planet.

Journal entries varied; some children relied more on pictures to demonstrate learning, and others wrote far more than they drew. The children did what they were able to do. Carol and I grew to understand their learning styles and ability to use words to express meanings by not providing a rigid structure or set of standards or guidelines.

At this point, Carol became a bit shaky, for the cycle had encroached on more time than we had originally reserved. "We don't have any way to measure learning other than the kids' journals, our notes, and some tapes." Carol was searching for a product that would demonstrate the learning we knew was occurring and rationalize the extra time. We agreed to present this closing activity to the class: Each child would make a word book with a minimum of five new words learned during the study. Within the framework of the word book, we offered choices. Children could use words from their group or create a book based on words learned from interacting with other groups. Three decided to work on a different topic "because we'll have to read and talk more to others and we'll learn more."

Fig. 5 At right. A story in a writing workshop incorporates study on the planets.

Fig. 6 Below. A second-grade space group's stage directions for their play.

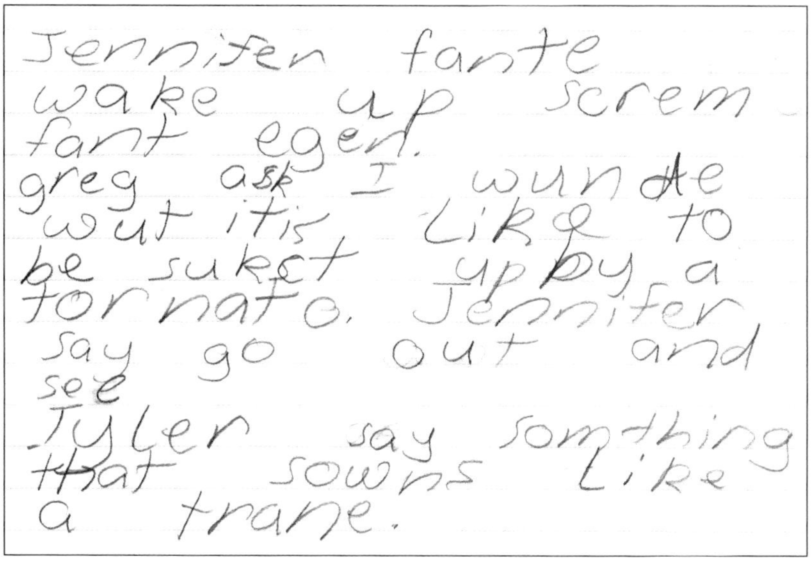

Jenniter fante
wake up screm
fant egen.
greg ask I wunde
wut itis Like to
be suket up by a
fornato. Jennifer
say go out and
see
Tyler say somthing
that sowns Like
a trane.

Earthquakes are powerful they can nock down bildings and they make craks in the erth. meny peple get kild or get hurt vary badly.

Fig. 7 Second-grade project for a theme cycle on natural phenomena.

Together, the class and I set guidelines for word books. Since the book would be for readers who knew nothing about the topic, they decided to include the word, a detailed illustration, and an explanation and/or story about the word. A title and the author's name would appear on the cover. Three weeks of intensive work went into these word books (figure 7). First drafts, more research, decisions on which words to include all took time.

The task of making decisions about what to include, organizing their books, then illustrating and explaining, was, as John put it, "a lot of hard work for second grade."

Self-evaluation was ongoing throughout the cycle for students and for Carol and me. We wanted to help each child set reasonable goals, meet them, and feel a sense of pride and accomplishment. Through conferences, written evaluations, and oral and written responses from me, the emphasis was on individual growth and not on competition. Though we never discussed formal grades, the children graded the cycle with words and letter grades. As always, they were honest.

- I wud becuas i like to dray the picher that we did it wus fun and I wun to go in a nuver groop so I can do this a gen and I lernd a lot becuas uv the books.

- I fill that i shod giv this werk an A+. This werk is fun my faverit thing that wev dun so far is the [word] book.

- We need more joling in groops. D.

- I do not like it becuse it is boning. I had to mak desins [decisions] to wrk. I giv it a B.

- Fun!, it is hrd, we did posr [posters] it was fun, it was to nocy, we did a play, I did lrnalot.

Problems arose, but they arise every day for adults. Why would children's lives be different? The children dealt with these and solved them. Some days were more productive than others, but all learners experience these swings in levels of productivity. Why would it be different for children at school?

Theme cycles can foster a commitment to the purposes of learning in a democratic community where curiosity is welcome and prized. Through joint and individual efforts, children can become socially responsible, self-directed learners and citizens who are capable of making choices that benefit themselves and others. Teachers contribute to each child's education by gently guiding them and creating an environment where children can learn new things on their own.

The list of theme cycle planning resources that follows can furnish you with resources, stories of other teachers' experiences, and alternate methods of organizing and planning a cycle.

Periodicals

BookLinks is a bimonthly magazine published by Booklist Publications, an imprint of the American Library Association. It is designed for classroom teachers. Articles written by teachers and librarians focus on themes, literary genres, authors, and illustrators and are rich with teaching ideas and extensive annotated bibliographies.

Booklist, published twice monthly by the American Library Association, contains reviews of children's books and audiovisual media. The starred section highlights books reviewers consider outstanding. Each issue includes an interview with a prominent author of books for children or adults.

The Horn Book Magazine is published six times a year by The Horn Book, Inc. Devoted to children's literature, the magazine is a cornucopia of timely reviews and articles by authors, illustrators, and children's book editors. "Books in the Classroom," written by teachers, offers ways to incorporate children's books across the curriculum.

Language Arts, published monthly from September through April by the National Association of Teachers of English, organizes articles by classroom teachers and college researchers around a current teaching and learning theme. Regular features include a biography of a children's author or illustrator, and articles on assessment, the computer, and themed annotated bibliographies.

The New Advocate is published four times a year by Christopher-Gordon Publishers. Contains articles penned by teachers, authors, teacher trainers, and illustrators; the focus is using children's literature and issues surrounding children's books. An annotated bibliography of new books concludes each issue.

The Reading Teacher, published monthly from September through May by the International Reading Association, includes "Children's Choices" and "Teachers' Choices," annual annotated book lists. Pieces by classroom teachers and college researchers include author and illustrator interviews and articles about teaching. In each issue is a themed annotated bibliography of children's books.

School Library Journal, published monthly from September through May, reviews most new children's books. It includes feature articles on children's literature and reviews written by teachers, librarians, and renowned children's literature critics.

The WEB: Wonderfully Exciting Books is published four times a year by the Reading Center, Ohio State University, Columbus, Ohio. It includes reviews of books by teachers and librarians and children's responses. Each issue contains a "web" of ideas centered around a book, genre, or theme.

Some Additional Bibliographies

Barstow, Barbara, and Judith Riggle. *First Readers: An Annotated Bibliography of Books for Children Beginning to Read.* New York: Bowker, 1989.

Cain, Melissa, Hughes Moir, and Leslie Prosak-Beres, eds. *Collected Perspective: Choosing and Using Books for the Classroom.* Boston: Christopher-Gordon, 1990.

Donavin, Denise Perry, ed. *American Library Association Best of the Best for Children.* New York: Random House, 1992.

Flowers, Ann A., ed. *The Horn Book Guide to Children's and Young Adult Books.* Boston: The Horn Book, Inc.

Freeman, Judy. *Books Kids Will Sit Still For.* New York: Bowker, 1990.

Gillespie, John T. *Best Books for Children, Preschool Through Grade 6.* New York: Bowker, 1990.

Gillespie, John T. *The Elementary School Paperback Collection.* Chicago: American Library Association, 1985.

Graves, Bonnie B., Michael B. Graves, and Randall J. Ryder. *Easy Reading: Book Series and Periodicals for Less Able Readers*, 2nd ed. Newark, DE: International Reading Association, 1989.

Hearne, Betsy, Zena Sutherland, and Roger Sutton. *The Best in Children's Books: 1985–90*. Chicago: University of Chicago Press, 1991.

Hearne, Betsy. *Choosing Books for Children: A Commonsense Guide*. Revised, expanded, and updated edition. New York: Delacorte, 1990.

Horning, Kathleen T., and Ginny Moore Kruse, with Merri V. Lindgren and Katherine Odahowski. *Multicultural Literature for Children and Young Adults,* 3rd ed. Madison, WI: Cooperative Children's Book Center, University of Wisconsin, Madison, 1991.

Kobrin, Beverly. *Eyeopeners! How to Choose and Use Children's Books about Real People, Places and Things*. New York: Penguin, 1988.

Lima, Carolyn W., and John A. Lima. *A to Zoo: Subject Access to Children's Picture Books,* 3rd ed. New York: Bowker, 1989.

Lynn, Ruth Nadelman. *Fantasy Literature for Children and Young Adults: An Annotated Bibliography*, 3rd ed. New York: Bowker, 1989.

Paperback Books for Children: A Selected List Through Age Thirteen. New York: Bank Street College, Child Study Children's Book Committee, 1988.

Subject Guide to Children's Books in Print. New York: Bowker, updated annually.

Books

Arbuthnot, May Hill, and Zena Sutherland. *Children and Books*. New York: HarperCollins, 1991.

Cohn, Amy, compiler. *From Sea to Shining Sea: A Treasury of American Folklore and Folksongs*. New York: Scholastic, 1993.

Cullinan, Bernice, and Janet Hickman, eds. *Children's Literature in the Classroom: Weaving Charlotte's Web*. Needham Heights, MA: Christopher-Gordon Publishing, 1989.

Cullinan, Bernice, ed. *Invitation to Read: More Children's Literature in the Reading Program*. Newark, DE: The International Reading Association, 1992.

Cullinan, Bernice. *Literature and the Child*. San Diego: Harcourt Brace, 1989.

Hepler, Susan, Janet Hickman, and Charlotte Huck. *Children's Literature in the Elementary Classroom*, 5th ed. San Diego: Harcourt Brace, 1992.

Lynch-Brown, Carol, and Carl Tomlinson. *Essentials of Children's Literature*. Boston: Allyn and Bacon, 1993.

AS I SEE IT

Susan Jeffers

As I sit at my drawing board, writing about how I choose a story to illustrate, I realize the task is similar to that of a teacher selecting a book to read aloud or books to include in a long-term project. Whether artist or teacher, we must live with our choices a long time, and satisfaction arrives from working with stories that speak to the heart.

First, a story has to attract me with a heart-pounding excitement. Day and night, the text beckons me to sketch and paint scenes. Like a deep-sea explorer, astonished by the world beneath the ocean, I am fascinated by the images a story evokes within my mind.

Stories have many purposes: to uplift, educate, or simply entertain. Not a small thing for a writer to effect. A story can have a personal theme, such as visual imagination, as in *Benjamin's Barn*; unconditional love, as in *The Snow Queen*; or how Black Beauty teaches us, through a horse's voice, what it means to be human. *Brother Eagle, Sister Sky* speaks of the magic of nature that we are all entitled to. All of these stories have a personal resonance for me.

I have learned by wonderful and painful experience to follow my heart in choosing stories to illustrate. Some books turn flat after several weeks, forcing me to abandon them. And even when I do love a story, there is no guarantee that I will paint with passion. But I know that without that juice, that compulsion to stay with the story, I am heading for disaster.

When I suggested *Hiawatha* to my publishers, they were quite dismayed with my choice. Their argument was that too many people had been forced to memorize the poem and therefore hated it. But I recollected my parents' voices, reading *Hiawatha* to me; fireflies danced outside the evening bedroom window as I drifted into sleep with Longfellow's words and images. I loved the poem for its beauty and the way it had been presented to me.

Many people have shied away from *Hansel and Gretel* because father and stepmother desert the children to save themselves. Horrible thought. But for me the story was about the love between sister and brother and their resourcefulness. My sister, Judy, and I shared a room when we were small. We would tell each other endless stories about magic animals and princesses before falling asleep. Judy and I assumed the personalities of Hansel and Gretel, caring for each other, replaying and resolving many scenes using our creative wits and always gloriously defeating the evil witch. No roles for our parents, for we were in charge of our destiny.

Brother Eagle, Sister Sky is a summation of much of what my parents held dear and passed on to Judy and me. They spent a great amount of time conveying reverence and respect for the natural world. My mother was the inspiration for the character in *Stopping by Woods*. For her, the trees were as full of life as her family and neighbors. During an ice storm, Judy and I would watch our mother standing in our yard, transfixed by the beauty surrounding her.

It has never worked for me to have "a good idea." And a true disaster is trying to figure out "what the market wants." Because these questions come from outside the heart. My criteria for illustrating a story is: Do I love it passionately, regardless of what anyone else thinks? And is the book worth all the trees that will be felled to make the paper?

The process sounds as if it might be simple, but I have had a great amount of difficulty separating myself from others' opinions and worrying about whether my perceptions are important enough. What has evolved over the years is the knowledge that it doesn't matter if it's important to the world. What matters is that it's meaningful to me, that it speaks to me. I think we all have something valuable to say that is just ours. It may be as a parent, a teacher, an artist, or a friend. What I have to overcome is comparing and judging my contribution long enough to make it! The good news is that along with acquiring years, I am also acquiring more ability to wend my way through the harmonious and strident voices within myself and pick out the true ones. The voices that, like a compass, point me to stories that speak to my heart and ignite my imagination, calling me to talk with paintings.

SELECTED BOOKS ILLUSTRATED BY SUSAN JEFFERS

Andersen, Hans Christian. *The Snow Queen*. Retold by Amy Ehrlich. New York: Dial, 1982.

———. *Thumbelina*. Retold by Amy Ehrlich. New York: Dial, 1979.

———. *The Wild Swans*. Retold by Amy Ehrlich. New York: Dial, 1981.

Brother Eagle, Sister Sky: A Message from Chief Seattle. New York: Dial, 1991.

Field, Eugene. *Wynken, Blynken, and Nod*. New York: Dutton, 1982.

Frost, Robert. *Stopping by Woods on a Snowy Evening*. New York: Dutton, 1978.

Grimm, the Brothers. *Hansel and Gretel*. New York: Dial, 1980.

If Wishes Were Horses: And Other Mother Goose Rhymes. New York: Dutton, 1979.

Jeffers, Susan, reteller. *Wild Robin*. New York: Dutton, 1976.

Lindbergh, Reeve. *Benjamin's Barn*. New York: Dial, 1990.

———. *Midnight Farm*. New York: Dial, 1987.

Longfellow, Henry Wadsworth. *Hiawatha*. New York: Dial, 1983.

Mohr, Joseph. *Silent Night*. New York: Dutton, 1984.

Perrault, Charles. *Cinderella*. Retold by Amy Ehrlich. New York: Dial, 1985.

Sewell, Anna. *Black Beauty*. Retold by Robin McKinley. New York: Random House, 1986.

Wells, Rosemary. *Forest of Dreams*. New York: Dial, 1988.

———. *Waiting for the Evening Star*. New York: Dial, 1993.

REFLECTIONS ON
JOURNEYS

Most of my childhood and teenage years were spent in a tiny three-room apartment in the Bronx. My journey into stories began in those three rooms on the seventh floor of a white brick building. School wasn't much fun for me. A restless child, I was always in trouble for talking too much and not being able to sit still. I remember filling in pages of workbooks and practicing making circles and ovals to improve poor penmanship. My fantasy life blossomed in kindergarten and continued to entertain me during school. Home was exciting; home was stories—stories my father told of Poland and Russia. I knew every inch of the farmhouse and planting fields, and the fear in my father's heart when the cossacks stormed their house and barn. Sunday mornings were the best. My brother and I snuggled close to my father in the enormous double bed and listened to stories until Mother fussed at us because breakfast was getting cold.

Grandmother lived across the street on the fourth floor of a red brick apartment building. On Sunday afternoons, Grandma's sisters or friends visited and told stories about the old country. I'd journey across the street, curl up next to the sofa by Grandma's bunioned feet. And listen. The grown-ups sipped dark brown tea from glasses with metal spoons. Thick lemon slices floated near the rim. To sweeten the hot brew, each balanced a sugar cube on the tip of her tongue. I never quite learned the knack of holding on to that sugar cube. The square cube would linger momentarily on my tongue and then fall into the hot glass, dissolving.

Those family stories are a tapestry of voices from the past that, like connecting rods, link me to people and places as if I had lived their lives. Like songs, they replay in my memory or when I tell them to my children and students. Life hasn't changed much since those early years. I'm still listening to, reading, and telling stories composed by children, teachers, family, and friends.

Becoming a whole language teacher is like writing a story that begins, flourishes, and never ends. Each teaching day begins with promises of the unexpected pleasures of stories that can actively shape our philosophy and teaching practices.

You can't have stories without readers, without listeners. Teachers, to gather stories, must listen and read. Stories sharpen and hone that gift that makes us human: *imagination*. When stories allow us to fully exercise our imagination, we know deep inside that something good, something right, has happened to us. And we are connected beyond the confines of our own spirits and bodies to the lives and imaginations of the children we teach, to our colleagues, to our community, to the world. To what we seemed incapable of knowing. Connections are what stories and poetry and drama thrive on. Connections are what whole language teaching and learning are all about.

Exercising the imagination, like exercising the muscles of our bodies, is hard work. Continuous work. Joyful work. Teachers are creative builders who daily shape the architecture of their classrooms with story. Years ago at a poetry conference, a kindergarten teacher, after three days of reading and listening and dramatizing poetry, confessed to the group: "I don't read poetry to my kids. But I'm going to try come September." In January, she wrote me a long letter that began with an account of the inner battle she fought to convince herself to read poetry to her students. "I still didn't believe they'd get anything out of this; left alone, I had returned to my doubts," she wrote. "But I secretly vowed I would try. And so I forced myself to begin." The letter concluded with a powerful connection:

I have no choice. The kids beg, no I'd say they demand, I read poems to them every day, all day. They show me their pleasure by chiming in, requesting repeats, laughing, and repeating lines. The best thing, though, is what's happened to me. The other day, Jonathan, asking me to help him plant his bean seed, called me Mrs. Poetry Lady. And when I asked him why he gave me that name, he said, "You love poems and you read lots."

To bring poetry to the kids, I have become a reader of poetry. I have become a reader of books. And that's made all the difference in my teaching and my life outside of school. I see the poetry in my children, Laura—and in me.

The poet Samuel Taylor Coleridge, in his efforts to explain poetry and poetic genius, also defined the essence of whole language teaching. I frequently reread portions of Coleridge's *Biographia Literaria*, not because I aspire to be a poet, but because his words elevate whole language teaching to an art that incorporates good sense, fancy, and imagination:

Finally, good sense is the body of poetic genius, fancy its drapery, motion its life, and imagination the soul that is everywhere and in each; and forms all into one graceful and intelligent whole.

The concept of teaching as an evolving work of art is within the reach of every professional who continues to learn and connect. As we learn by doing, we come to understand why and how our students, in order to learn, must have similar experiences. And we can better duplicate these experiences for them once we obtain a clearer image of our own process.

But it takes guts and a stout heart to traverse an unknown path only to leap into the next unknown. In our classrooms we assume the masks of writer-researcher, forming and testing hypotheses about our students, ourselves, and our classroom practices, and always with the poet's sense of surprise in discovering what we think, feel, and don't know. Daily we step across a threshold into a room that will certainly bring crises and joys, successes and failures, depression and revelation. More questions than answers. Where the unpredictable reigns. And so we live our lives on the high wire, continuously testing the mettle of our safety net. This takes courage. Remember: The same courage is required of our students and administrators and parents.

Each year my eighth graders read Steven Kellogg's *The Island of the Skog* as they construct democratic and totalitarian decision-making models. Discussions always involve an analysis of the fears of mice and skog. "We only fear what we don't know," says Bobby. "It takes lots of courage to face the unknown."

When whole language teachers daily face the unknown, they muster a combination of spunk and faith. Spunk to face the unknown—to sense the closeness of that safety net and return to the high wire. Faith that our students can learn to read, write, and think *if we allow them*, faith in students' desire to learn, and faith in our commitment to continue to listen to the stories of individual students, parents, and colleagues.

The joy and challenge is not knowing beforehand what will transpire, what the outcomes will be. The joy is in the surprises and discoveries that await us as we travel untrodden ways, constantly revising who we are and where we're going.

APPENDIX

HOME-SCHOOL CONNECTIONS

Take-home Stories
A family read aloud Festival

●Your child brings home a library book with folder to read and share at home with any family member.

●Reread the book often. Family member writes title and author and records comments by child about the book.

●Student returns book and folder when ready to exchange for another.

FAMILY MEMBER'S

Date	TITLE	COMMENTS	Initials

Take-home-stories form.

April 16, 1988

Dear Parents,

Kindergarten Puddle Week has been an interesting one considering that not only did we search for a puddle, but we had to construct one! Finding last Friday's puddle missing on Monday necessitated creative use of some collected rain water. We had to refill our puddle to carry out our puddle plans. We discovered it to be 1 and 1/2 inches in depth and 11 feet in circumference. We discussed some interesting concepts in the process, including different labels for measurement: inches, feet, centimeters, and our own made-up measurement. We came to the conclusion that as long as we all agree on it, we could call the measured area anything we wanted. Another concept discussed was that of evaporation and absorption. The class decided evaporation was simple -- just like rain, only it goes up instead of down. We read Jemimima Puddle-Duck again and decided why she was called a "puddle" duck. Puddle Week was concluded with the making of individual edible puddle cakes, the base of which was bran muffin mix, with a choice of bran fibers (for sticks), chocolate chips (for mud clumps), and nuts and raisin (in clumps for rocks).

Initiation of "student teachers" from the class started on Monday. Each child will pick an activity and be responsible for explaining the steps necessary for completion. It primarily involves sequencing skills, for example, four steps making various animal homes such as a woodpecker nest or a honeybee hive.

Many thanks to Sam's mother for teaching us how to make edible birds' nests.

Next week we will be geologists and collect and discuss how different rocks are used. We will observe our own pet rocks and describe them so other children can pick them out. We will be making rock sculpture and discussing different meanings of the word "rock" such as, "What is rock and roll", and "What does 'Rock-a-Bye Baby'" mean? Please have your child look for a rock to bring to school to share in these projects.

Sincerely,

Nancy Chambers

Nancy Chambers

A weekly kindergarten newsletter composed by the teacher.

K-play

I interviewed Mrs. Collins, and these are the results.

Q: Do you feel nervous about the play you're doing?
A: No, I don't feel nervous. I know their parents love what they do.

Q: What is the play about?
A: It's about night, darkness, and bedtime.

Q: What type of play is it?
A: It's mostly poems and songs.

Q: How many children are in the class?
A: Eighteen children.

Mrs. Collins' theory is: The children learn the songs and stories, although she doesn't ask her children if they want to do the play until a week before the play.

By: Anne-Marie Kratofil!!

Winter Tuesday

This Winter Tuesday there will be 9 people doing computer, art, and guitar; 50 people skating; and 97 people skiing. This year we haven't been able to go skiing enough, we think.

by Graham and James

Movie Reviews
By Vicki Jonkers

This year was an exciting year for the box office. I had the opportunity to see many movies this year.

<u>Dracula:</u> This was a great movie starring Winona Rider and Gary Oldman. This is about a guy named Dracula who buys some land in Carfax and falls in love with a girl. It was exciting and funny, though it is rated "R". I give it a ten.

<u>Leap of Faith:</u> This movie was sort of annoying. Steve Martin was funny, but you have to be in a mood to see it. In this movie Steve Martin pretends to be a man of God. See it once and see if you like it, I give it a seven.

<u>Poison Ivy:</u> This movie is a new release that you can pick up at your local video store. Poison Ivy is wonderful, I loved it! It get's a nine. I wouldn't recommend it for younger audiences. You have to see it.

<u>Home Alone 2:</u> If you liked the first one, don't see the second one. It is the same thing over and over again. It gets a two.

(Because of timing, movies may be gone from movie theater before this paper comes out.)

WINTER TUESDAY
By Morgan Marcani
Please circle one:

1. Do you feel Winter Tuesday should be discontinued? Yes. No.
2. Do you think Winter Tuesday should have more choices? Yes. No.
3. If you don't like any of the choices do you think you should be able to: a. go home b. do a school project

A monthly newsletter written by students in grades six, seven, and eight.

THE STUDENT COUNCIL
by Nate Z.

The Student Council is a group of students from each of the upper school classes who are elected by their classmates into the positions of President, Vice President, Treasurer, and Secretary (the positon I was ironically elected to).

Every Friday possible, the Student Council gathers, along with Mrs. Vance and Mr. Lathrop, to talk about issues currently happening throughout Powhatan. The Student Council also arranges dances, special occasions (such as our mock election), and tries to improve things here to make this school a better place for the students of Powhatan.

Word Find

```
ARBGNATEKJDJDU
NDIENGSARAHBJFK
NAJGUSAMFKDUT
EJFDIRDIANNAKFU
-AKDJASKATIEJKFJ
MLJFAMORGANKMOUJ
ASHANNONDKJFKJEKJJKH
RJHNUJFRYIPUJAMESMUHF
INKGMNJFSTEGRAHAMKJH
EJDJKGISMRSROBBJIJGIR
KJHADVICKIJLHFFTYERCI
```

RULES: One word goes down, the rest go across. Look for these words: NATE SARAH SAM DIANNA KATIE MORGAN SHANNON JAMES GRAHAM MRSROBB VICKI ANNE-MARIE

GOOD LUCK!!!!!!!!
BY:KATIE GOODLOE

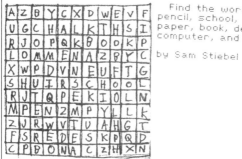

Find the words: pencil, school, pen, paper, book, desk, computer, and chalk.

by Sam Stiebel

SPORTS

I interviewed Mr. Robb (our newest teacher at Powhatan), and this is what I found out.

He was born in Cincinnati, Ohio, and has lived in Virginia for one-and-a-half-years.

Before coming to Powhatan, he taught high school math, and he coached football and baseball in Alexandria, VA. Here he teaches math, problem solving, and language arts. He loves teaching here.

His favorite summer sport is baseball. His favorite winter sport is downhill skiing.

Mr. Robb is married to Mrs. Ann Robb, and they have a son named Kevin, who is two years old.

by Dianna Hoover

The Carol Sing
by Shannon Ghramm

This year's Carol Sing was loaded with great songs to make everyone laugh and feel good. Mrs. Bryant was hurrying to get positions and the songs perfected. But the Carol Sing was wonderful.

It was the first to ever be in the new auditorium. Our pianist was Mrs. Robb. Last year she was our pianist, and she did great. This year she was even better! I thought it was a success!

What was your favorite song?

––––––––––––––––––

(Cut out and put in the box in the 5th grade.)

February Birthdays!!

1 Frances Wood
4 Molly Mcmillen
4 Sally Stiebel
6 Andrew Mayfield
7 Sarah Bandyke
7 Donnie Plumly
7 Kathleen Kennedy
10 Caitlin Shiftlett
11 Whitney Groseclose
14 Mia Biller
21 Charles Pastore
24 Mrs. Fox
24 Mrs. Vance
26 Mrs. Collins
28 Ms. Lacy

By Katie Goodloe

Newsletter, continued.

Powhatan School
Route 2A, Box 177A
Boyce, VA 22620

February 14, 1992

Dear Third Grade Parents,

The children enjoy reading and talking with you and proudly
read their entries to the entire class. Several asked if
they could read ahead and then reread sections with you, and
that is truly exciting. Sharing in the making of the cover
established a coneection that the story now reinforces.

What you write in the journal is your choice, and it doesn't
matter who writes about the chapters first. The children
came up with several suggestions for responding that I will
share, but please don't limit yourselves to those.

1. Draw a picture and write abou it.
2. Comment on your buddy's entry.
3. Write about your favoirte part or character.
4. What does the story remind you of?
5. Is a character like you or different from you?
   How?
6. Did you like or hate this section? Why?
7. Did the story remind you of your own experiences?
8. You can also ask your buddy questions about the
   story and see what s/he thinks.

Your children are thrilled to regularly read and talk about
a book with you.

Sincerely,

Laura Robb

A letter from a teacher offering buddy journal entry suggestions to parents of third graders.

SPELLING

MCGUFFEY READING CENTER
Qualitative Inventory of Word Knowledge
FORM B

LEVEL I	LEVEL II	LEVEL III	LEVEL IV	LEVEL V	LEVEL VI
bump	batted	find	square	enclosed	absence
net	such	paint	hockey	piece	civilize
with	once	crawl	helmet	novel	accomplish
trap	chop	dollar	allow	lecture	prohibition
chin	milk	knife	skipping	pillar	pledge
bell	funny	mouth	ugly	confession	sensibility
shade	start	fought	hurry	aware	official
pig	glasses	comb	bounce	loneliest	inspire
drum	hugging	useful	lodge	service	permission
hid	named	circle	fossil	loyal	irrelevant
father	pool	early	traced	expansion	conclusion
track	stick	letter	lumber	production	invisible
pink	when	weigh	middle	deposited	democratic
drip	easy	real	striped	revenge	responsible
brave	make	tight	bacon	awaiting	accidental
job	went	sock	capture	unskilled	composition
sister	shell	voice	damage	installment	relying
slide	pinned	campfire	nickel	horrible	changeable
box	class	keeper	barber	relate	amusement
white	boat	throat	curve	earl	conference
	story	waving	statement	uniform	advertise
	plain	carried	collar	rifle	opposition
	smoke	scratch	parading	correction	community
	size	tripping	sailor	discovering	advantage
	sleep	nurse	wrinkle	retirement	cooperation
			dinner	salute	spacious
			medal	treasure	carriage
			tanner	homemade	presumption
			dimmed	conviction	appearance
			careful	creature	description

Source: Houghton Mifflin Spelling, Levels 1-VI, 1982

Qualitative Inventory of Word Knowledge, from the McGuffey Reading Center of the University of Virginia.

```
        QUALITATIVE INVENTORY OF WORD KNOWLEDGE
             McGuffey Reading Center


  Level 7                          Level 8

  illiteracy                       meddle
  communicate                      posture
  irresponsible                    knuckle
  succeed                          succumb
  patience                         newsstand
  confident                        permissible
  analyze                          transparent
  tomatoes                         assumption
  necessary                        impurities
  beret                            pennant
  unbearable                       boutique
  hasten                           wooden
  aluminum                         warrant
  miserable                        probable
  subscription                     respiration
  exhibition                       reverse
  device                           olympic
  regretted                        gaseous
  arisen                           subtle
  miniature                        bookkeeping
  monopoly                         fictional
  dissolve                         overrate
  equipped                         granular
  solemn                           endorse
  correspond                       insistent
  emphasize                        snorkie
  scoundrel                        personality
  cubic                            prosperous
  flexible
  arctic
```

Qualitative Inventory of Word Knowledge, continued.

BEGINNERS AND ADVANCED SPELLING FEATURES LIST

STUDENT RESPONSE	LIST WORDS	SCORE

Developmental Stages

Prephonemic_____
Early phonemic_____
Letter-name_____
Transitional_____
Correct_____

Number of Examples

_____
_____
_____
_____
_____

Beginning and advanced spelling features list form.

DIALOGUE JOURNALS

September 1993.

Dear Sarah,

I am so pleased that you and I will be reading together and writing about our reading. This is an opportunity for you to choose the books you want to read and share your thoughts and feelings about your reading with me.

Each week, I'll look for a journal entry from you, and each week I will write back to you. I only ask that you not retell the story or chapters to me. You can write about your personal reactions and feelings to what has happened to certain characters. I'd love to see you make predictions about what will happen and support your predictions with what you've already read. You can also write about the problems characters face, how they solve them, and how you evaluate the way the characters handle their lives. When characters can't solve problems, you might want to suggest solutions. You might want to talk about which characters would make good friends and why, as well as what makes a character change or feel anger, hate or love? Does the book connect you to other texts, movies or experiences? You might also enjoy quoting favorite passages or pointing to a section that moved you or taught you something about writing. If you recognize a literary technique such as foreshadowing, irony, and flashback, consider writing about how the technique enhanced or detracted from the story. Finally, feel free to discuss anything that relates to literature discussions during reading-writing workshop.

Raise questions about parts of the story and things that confuse you, and I'll try to respond. When I write back, I'll be asking you questions and sharing my reactions and thoughts about the book as well as what you've written. Sometimes I'll recommend a book that I believe you might enjoy reading; the choice to read recommended titles will always be yours. Please comment on and question my responses, too.

Finally, I ask that you keep a reading record, in the back of your journal, of each title, author, and the date you completed the book. Please enter all the books you've read, including titles you haven't corresponded about.

I look forward to our writing back and forth, because having someone to share books and stories with means I'll have chances to learn more about books.

Can't wait for your first entry!

Fondly,

Mrs. Robb

A letter of invitation to an eighth-grade class from their teacher.

INVENTORIES AND INTERVIEWS
WRITTEN BY STUDENTS

1. What kind of games do you play?

2. What is your favorite color?

3. Do you like to help other? What do you do?

4. Do you like math.? Why?

5. What subject do you like best? Why?

6. What is your favorite book that you have written?

7. What is the best book you've read? Why?

8. What is your favorite food?

9. What do you like to do in your free time?

10. What is your favorite thing outdoors?

11. What is your hobby?

12. What is your favorite restaurant?

13. Do you like to draw? What?

14. Do you have any sisters or brothers? How do you feel about them?

15. Do you like to write? What do you like to write about?

16. Do you like to read? What kinds of books do you enjoy?

17. What do you like to do with your family?

A third-grade interest interview.

TYPE OF CONFERENCE: Reading

Student's Name Rich - Grade 6   Date Mar. 7, '91

Title Mufaro's Beautiful Daughters Author John Steptoe

Non-Prompted Comments:
I like where he tells about the names and what each means. The meanings matched their personality. I looked up my name and it means strong king. But it doesn't fit me now. aren't the pictures great?

Review Book Log
"I'm into folk tales," and R. points to his last 3 log entries. "Now I'm gonna read as many Cinderella tales I can find - like The Egyptian Cinderella we read last year. Maybe I'll write my own."
I promised R. to bring in any Cinderella tales, which I tell him fall under the "rags to riches" motif.
"I'm also going to read all of Patricia Beatly's Books. I'm in the middle of [he shows me Eben Tyne, Powdermonkey] and its all I want to do. I suggest he read Lupita Manana next and give him my copy to skim through.

Self-Evaluation — I read more than write in my log.
    Goal   I should try to enter more.
Next Conf. — In April — Have a mini-check to discuss what Rich has read in Cinderella tales.

A sixth-grade reading interview.

WRITING INTERVIEW QUESTIONS BY MRS. ROBBS' EIGHTH GRADE

1. How do you feel about writing?

2. Do you write outside of school? What are some of the things you write?

3. Do you keep a journal or notebook outside of school?

4. Do you have a favorite kind of writing?

5. How do you feel about mini-lessons?

6. Do you enjoy conferring with classmates? Explain why or why not.

7. Are you a reader? What do you enjoy reading?

8. Do you write letters? How often?

9. Do you enjoy helping younger students with writing?

10. How do you feel about reading your writing aloud?

11. Do you think revising is important? Give reasons.

12. Do you read any books, authors, genres to help you with your writing? How do you think this helps?

13. Do you ever struggle with writing? Tell about it.

WRITING INTERVIEW QUESTIONS FROM AT-RISK SECOND GRADERS TAUGHT BY MRS. ROBB

1. Do you like writing workshop?

2. Do you want to rewrite parts?

3. How do you feel about studying leads?

4. Does it bother you to make up spellings?

5. Do you like reading stories to everyone?

6. Do you like keeping a writing folder?

7. Do you use the chart we wrote with topics for writing?

Eighth- and second-grade writing interviews.

ASSESSMENT AND EVALUATION

Names of students	Teacher's Observations	Comments by students, parents, other teachers
	Focus:	

Evaluation Notes

Date _____ Grade _____

An anecdotal note form for group observation.

Examples of criteria for student self-evaluation.

I.   Criteria for each student to evaluate his/her role in a
      literature discussion group, grade 5:

      . Did I participate?
      . Did I support my statements with 2 examples from
         the story?
      . Did I listen when others spoke?
      . Did I respect other's views?
      . Did I bring my book and journal to group discussions?

II.   Criteria for each student to evaluate his/her plan and
      drafts of an illustrated book. grade 2.

      . Did I make a "dummy?" Did my "dummy" change in
         my published book? How?
      . Do I have a title, author, copyright, dedication.
      . Do I have illustrations that help make the story
         clearer and more interesting?
      . What genre did I choose? Why did I make that choice?
      . Did I write in complete sentences and make sure my
         spelling is correct?

III. Criteria to evaluate journal notes taken after reading
      and discussing an article on the Civil War, grade 8:

      . Entry has my name, date, title and author of article.
      . My article summary is brief--no more than 1/2 page.
      . I have reacted to statements in the article and given
         my personal opinion.
      . Others can read my entry.

IV.   Criteria to evaluate participation after several physical
      education periods, grade 4.

      . Did I come to class with my uniform and the equipment
         I needed?
      . Did I participate in daily warm-ups?
      . Did I cover my position during soccer practice?
      . Did I support my classmates during practice?
      . Did I help with clean-up and putting equipment back?

      After the teacher and students negotiate the criteria for
self-evaluation, the teacher should demonstrate on chart paper, how
to respond to these standards in a detailed paragraph that contains
specific examples. Such modeling can avoid "yes" and "no"
responses and clearly illustrates the level of reflection you are
seeking.

Criteria for student self-evaluation.

B - because I don't think I
am doing to well.

Barbara Ashwood

Name Tina Ashwood   Date April, 30, 1993

READING AND READING RESPONSE

	MOST OF THE TIME	SOMETIMES	RARELY
1. Uses independent reading time productively.	✓		
2. Retells story with rich details.	✓		
3. Supports responses with the story.	✓		
4. Identifies changes in character throughout the story.		✓ Because I don't understand the stuff.	
5. Identifies problems and solutions within a story.		✓ Because I don't think I'm very good at it	
6. Writes reaction to story in journal.	✓		
7. Understands and uses terms such as protagonist and antagonist.		✓ Because I don't know want they mean.	
8. Keeps a record of reading homework.			✓ Because I like to read and not stop all the time.
9. Participates in book discussions.		✓ Because I think my ideas are stupid and will make people fun of me.	
10. Listens to others' ideas and values others' opinions.	✓		
11. Organizes journal carefully.	✓		

A sixth-grade reading checklist based on expectations for one grading period.

```
        WRITING WORKSHOP:   TEACHER EVALUATION


NAME   D. J.


WRITING BEHAVIORS              MOST OF   SOMETIMES  RARELY
                               TIME
```

WRITING BEHAVIORS	MOST OF TIME	SOMETIMES	RARELY
1. Files writing in folder.		✓	my folder is messy
2. Uses workshop time productively.		✓	I do when no one is talking
3. Elects writing during choice times.		✓	I do this when I have
4. Writes a coherent draft during reasonable time limit.		✓ If I'm not talking	something to write about
5. ~~Makes reading-writing~~ connections.			
6. Revises drafts.	✓		
7. Edits before turning in final draft.	✓		
8. Conferences constructively with peers.		✓	Most of time constant
9. Conferences with teacher.	✓		
10. Offers positive & constructive suggestions.	✓		
11. Considers the suggestions of others.	✓		—
12. ~~Writes in a variety of genres.~~			
13. Free writes Daily		✓	Because of people around me

A sixth-grade writing checklist based on workshop expectations for one grading period.

Class Inventory: Writing Workshop
Abbreviations

C: collecting
R: researching
F: focusing, organizing
M P: making a plan
D: drafting (1,2,3...)
PC: peer conference-
content or edit
Rev.: revising

SGC: small group conference-
content or edit
TC: teacher conference-
content or edit
DD: deadline draft
Self-C: self-conference-
content or edit

Dates

Class List								

Class Inventory: Writing Workshop Abbreviations.

HOLISTIC RATING SCALE FOR WRITING

Here are some criteria to include in your rating scale. The items you and students select to rate will change depending on where individual students are in writing process.

Students can rate their own writing and compare their self-evaluation with their teacher's evaluation.

- collects information
- lead or introduction
- content: rich in specific details
- clairty: presents content to meet needs of audience
- spelling
- paragraphing
- punctuation
- sentence structure
- focuses topic
- takes risks as a writer
- dialogue
- uses time productively
- meets deadlines
- revises according to mini-lessons
- includes title
- name and date on paper
- makes reading-writing connections
- ending or conclusion
- uses active voice
- uses illustrations
- shows instead of tells
- genre structure

Name_____ Date_____

Type of Writing_____

Evaluation Criteria List these on the lines.	Rating Scale				
	Fair	Good		Excellent	
_____	1	2	3	4	5
_____	1	2	3	4	5
_____	1	2	3	4	5
_____	1	2	3	4	5
_____	1	2	3	4	5

Written Comments:

Holistic rating scale for writing.

POWHATAN SCHOOL
TRIMESTER REPORT CARD
FIFTH GRADE

Student: _____ Beginning: _____ Ending: _____

Key: M-Most of the Time   S-Sometimes   R-Rarely   N-Not Yet Observed

READING BEHAVIORS	M	S	R	N
1. Uses free time to read..	☐	☐	☐	☐
2. Reads for pleasure and enjoyment................................	☐	☐	☐	☐
3. Reads at home regularly..	☐	☐	☐	☐
4. Fills in independent reading card................................				
5. Honors the spirit of SSR...				
6. Selects a variety of genres: mystery, poetry, historical and realistic fiction, biography, fantasy, folk and fairy tale............				
7. Attends during book discussions................................				
8. Values the opinions of others......				
9. Waits his/her turn to speak..				

READING COMPREHENSION	M	S	R	N
1. Connects prior to reading..				
2. Uses pre-reading strategies before reading				
3. Makes logical predictions..				
4. Supports predictions with text				
5. Uses facts to draw conclusions and references				
6. Uses narrative to draw conclusions and references....				
7. Understands story structure				
8. Distinguishes between genres				
9. Uses context clues to understand unfamiliar vocabulary				
10. Creates mental images of texts				
11. Participates in class discussions				
12. Connects learning experiences to other texts and contexts				
13. Understands story elements: setting, character, plot, climax ...				
14. Can identify major temes in text				
15. Applies reading strategies modeled by teacher to own reading.				

Signed: _____

A fifth-grade report card designed by Laura Robb and Cecily Haston (through page 341).

POWHATAN SCHOOL
TRIMESTER REPORT CARD
FIFTH GRADE

Student: _____ Beginning: _____ Ending: _____

Key: M-Most of the Time   S-Sometimes   R-Rarely   N-Not Yet Observed

WRITING BEHAVIORS	M	S	R	N
1. Uses writing time productively...	☐	☐	☐	☐
2. Applies demonstrations to own writing................................	☐	☐	☐	☐
3. Organizes writing folder...	☐	☐	☐	☐
4. Places name and date on each paper..				
5. Conferences productively with peers.......................................				
6. Offers positive suggestions...				
7. Revises following pattern of teacher demonstrations...........				
8. Meets writing deadline..				
9. Has developed ability to plan for a long-term writing project				
10. Keeps writing materials neat and organized so others can use them				
11. Self-edits				

Signed: _____

POWHATAN SCHOOL
TRIMESTER REPORT CARD
FIFTH GRADE

Student: _____   Beginning: _____   Ending: _____

Key: M-Most of the Time   S-Sometimes   R-Rarely   N-Not Yet Observed

MATH	M	S	R	N
1. Uses appropriate vocabulary................................	☐	☐	☐	☐
2. Demonstrates proficiency in basic computation: add, subtract, multiply, divide................................	☐	☐	☐	☐
3. Has grasped the concept of place value....................	☐	☐	☐	☐

4. Transfer knowledge of place value to the basic operations..
5. Understands basic properties of numbers: associative, communicative, zero, and the one property of multiplication ....

6. Follows steps, modeled by teacher to solve problems............

7. Can identify the necessary operation(s) involved in problem solving ....

8. Sees the relationships between math and daily living............

9. Understands concepts taught through decimals.......................
    Understands concepts taught through fractions.......................
    Understands concepts taught through geometry.......................
    Understands concepts taught through percent.......................

10. Demonstrates understanding of concepts through math journal writing ....

11. Uses logical reasoning to assess answers...................................

12. Estimates before solving ....

13. Labels answers when solving problems ....

14. Studies and reviews models to understand process ....

Signed: _____

POWHATAN SCHOOL
TRIMESTER REPORT CARD
FIFTH GRADE

Student: _____   Beginning: _____   Ending: _____

Key: M-Most of the Time   S-Sometimes   R-Rarely   N-Not Yet Observed

CONTENT AREA: Science and Social Studies	M	S	R	N
1. Uses new vocabulary appropriately..	☐	☐	☐	☐
2. Transfers new vocabulary to other subjects				
3. Observes and records observations in detail	☐	☐	☐	☐
4. Creates logical hypotheses...				
5. Gathers information and support for hypotheses				
6. Follows one step directions...				
7. Follows muliple step directions				
8. Summarizes information...				
9. Reads sources other than core text..................................				
10. Keeps work neat and organized				
11. Completes assignments on time......................................				
12. Brings materials to class				
13. Listens when others speak				
14. Works cooperatively in a group				
15. Completes fair share of work in a group				
16. Takes home appropriate books and materials				
17. Studies and reviews notes and materials night by night				
18. Understands and identifies various land-forms				
19. Places cities, countries, states, mountains, etc. on map				
20. Connects current events to map work				

Signed: _____

POWHATAN SCHOOL
Boyce, Virginia

PROGRESS REPORT
FOR
FIFTH GRADE

Student _____

TRIMESTER   1   2   3

PHYSICAL EDUCATION
  Skills
  Interacts well with his/her peers

MUSIC
  Class participation
  Displays good effort and attention

ART
  Class participation
  Displays good effort and attention

PROGRESS IN SCHOOL ADJUSTMENT

TRIMESTER	1	2	3
WORK AND STUDY HABITS			
Listens to and follows directions			
Works independently			
Uses time and materials wisely			
Participates in class discussions			
Does neat and careful work			
Classwork completed and turned in			
Homework completed and turned in			
Work area neat and materials well-organized			
CITIZENSHIP			
Accepts responsibility			
Works and plays well with group			
Respects authority			
Is self disciplined			
Is courteous and considerate			

1st Trimester

Head

STUDENT WORK

What makes hair grow?

What happens to blood when you die?

How do you get HIV and AIDS?

How many muscles do we have in our
bodies?

Is blood blue or purple inside?

Why do we have fingernails?

How many veins are in the human body?

How does your heart work?

What does your appendix look like?

What is it like to have a baby?

Why do you loose your hair?

Why doesn't food digest itself?

How hot or cold can your body get
before you die?

What happens to your body when you die?

What 3 things make a girl a woman?

Why does hair get gray?

Is is true if you hold a seashell up to
your ear you will hear the blood go up
to your brain?

Why does your skin become dry?

If one of your veins pop in your brain
will you die?

If you drink water: will it become spit
or blood?

How can the flu get in your muscle?

How do we talk?

What are we made of?

What are our reproductive parts?

A fourth grader's questions about the human body compiled from inquiry notebooks (through page 344).

How many bones are there in the human body?

How many veins is in the human body?

Which bone is the most important?

Which bone is the hardest?

How does hair grow?

What is skin made of?

What are the names of the organs and how many are there?

Why is the body mainly made of water?

How does your brain control your body?

How does your brain think?

What are the most important parts of your body?

How do you get stronger and how do you grow?

How do you dream?

How many cells does a newborn baby have?

How does the body react to fighting?

Why does a certain human die because of bees?

What does Joe Montana have that is hurting him?

How does the body react to football?

Is there air in the leg?

Where are your kidneys?

What do you call the "V" shaped thing that the middle of is close to the beginning of your leg?

What does marrow do?

How are we formed?

How does the nervous system work?

What are the organs in the blood
system?

Why does anger usually make the brain
do strange things?

Why do you have uteruses?

My Brother Sam Is Dead

Emily Caldwell   May 5 1989

There are few things in this world capable of disrupting the natural stages of human life. One of them is war. War not only kills, but also ravages the lives of survivors. War has the capability to force children to grow up and become adults before their time. War was the master force behind every incident that caused Tim to literally "grow up" overnight.

During the war America was in turmult. All of the towns and cities were disorganised and split into basically three sides, The tory, the patriot, and the neutral. No longer could a man trust his neigbor. The loss of familiar securities left Tim to stand alone in the midst of chaos. This rather adrupt change required Tim to confidently make a quick adjustment on his own.

During the course of the war, Tim woke up to the real world. Perhaps one of childhood's greatest fantasies is the belief that everyone is good and kind. As a child you believe that everyone will sacrifice to help others. When the war began Tim was awakened to a harsh and cruel world. He witnessed once, the decapitation of a man, for no other reason other than he was in the wrong place at the wrong time, and his skin was black. It was awakening, an experience that left Tim somewhat dissillusioned but nevertheless wisened, perhaps for the better.

When the war took the lives of his brother and father, Tim truly believed that it was wrong. He did not care who won, only that the bloodshed ended. He was now left with the shock of death on his shoulders. It took great courage and wisdom to put the lost lives of his brother and father behind him. He did do this, and focused on supporting his mother and self.

An eighth grader's essay on My Brother Sam Is Dead, *by James L. Collier and Christopher Collier.*

Taking the technical viewpoint, after the loss of life and soul meeker, Tim was left with triple the responsibilies he had had previously. The extreme pressure and necessity of keeping up with all the work forced Tim to buckle down and manage matters. He was doing all the jobs he had once admired, now void of any feel aside from that of obligation. This showed that he had almost completely adjusted.

Perhaps the most damaging force bearing down upon Tim, was self implied pressure. Tim believed that it was his duty to drive, drive, drive. To provide for his mother and maintain the tavern. He never allowed for playing, or time for being a child once more. He was no longer capable of being a child.

It is tragic that one must be robbed of childhood. It makes for a life with missing pieces. The fact that once an adult your always an adult should say in itself that nothing on this earth, save death alone, should have the right to rob of childhood.

Essay, continued.

Julie of the Wolves

Renee C. Haston   April 2, 1996

Why might an Eskimo girl who has been searching for her father all of her life turn her back on him because he married a gussak (a white person)?

Miyax is a girl that does that. One reason she turns her back on her father, Kapugen is that he killed the chief of the wolves named Amaroq by shooting from his airplane. Amaroq gave Miyax food when she was helpless and hungry in the tundra. Another reason that Miyax left Kapugen is that she felt angry because her father had married a gussak and that was not part of the Eskimo traditions. I think she also felt angry because Kapugen didn't come back after he left even though his canoe had smashed. He got rich and then came back to Miyax. Miyax might of thought that money was more important than her. Miyax left Kapugen because she felt that Kapugen had changed from a traditional person to a more modern person. Kapugen had a telephone, radio

A sixth grader's essay on Julie of the Wolves, *by Jean Craighead George.*

phonograph, china dishes, an electric stove, and a coffee pot. Miyax also left because she wanted to meet her pen pal Amy, who promised her a pink bedroom, curly hair, and a theater with velvet seats.

I think the pack of wolves led to Miyax wanting to live a traditional life. I think Miyax wanted to learn the language of the wolves so that she had somebody to communicate with. I also think the gussak that Kapugen married changed her decision because she did not want to stay with a white woman in a more modern society. Miyax wasn't used to a modern society she was more used to Eskimo traditions.

Miyax has to suffer through life and death threats. She feels that she can live on her own for the rest of her life since she has made it this far. All of this leads to her leaving Kapugen.

Essay, continued.

BIBLIOGRAPHY

Anderson, Richard. "Role of the Reader's Schema in Comprehension, Learning and Memory." In *Learning to Read in American Schools*. Richard Anderson, Jean Osborne, and Robert Tierney, eds. Hillsdale, NJ: Lawrence Erlbaum Associates, 1984.

Ashton-Warner, Sylvia. *Teacher*. New York: Simon and Schuster, 1963.

Atwell, Nancie. *In the Middle: Writing, Reading and Learning with Adolescents*. Portsmouth, NH: Heinemann, 1987.

Barr, Rebecca, Marilyn Sadow, and Camille Blachowicz. *Reading Diagnosis for Teachers: An Instructional Approach*. New York: Longman, 1990.

Bateman, Walter L. *Open to Question*. San Francisco: Jossey-Bass Publishers, 1990.

Bloom, Benjamin S. *Taxonomy of Educational Objectives, Handbook I: Cognitive Domain*. New York: McKay, 1956.

Bromley, Karen D'Angelo. "Buddy Journals Make the Reading-Writing Connection." *The Reading Teacher* 43, no. 2 (November 1989).

Burrows, Alvina T., Doris C. Jackson, and Dorothy O. Saunders. *They All Want to Write*.

Hamden, CT: Library Professional Publication, 1984.

Bynner, Witter, ed. *The Way of Life According to Lao-tzu*. New York: Putnam, 1986.

Calkins, Lucy. *The Art of Teaching Writing*. Portsmouth, NH: Heinemann, 1986.

———, with Shelly Harwayne. *Living Between the Lines*. Portsmouth, NH: Heinemann, 1991.

Cambourne, Brian. *The Whole Story: Natural Learning and the Acquisition of Literacy in the Classroom*. Auckland, New Zealand: Ashton Scholastic, 1988.

Chall, Jeanne S. *Learning to Read: The Great Debate*. New York: McGraw-Hill, 1967.

Chomsky, Carol. "Write Now, Read Later." In *Language in Early Childhood Education*. Association for Education of Young People (1971).

Clay, Marie. *The Early Detection of Reading Difficulties*. 3rd ed. Portsmouth, NH: Heinemann, 1980.

———. *Reading: The Patterning of Complex Behavior*. Portsmouth, NH: Heinemann, 1985.

Coles, Robert. *The Call of Stories: Teaching and the Moral Imagination*. Boston: Houghton Mifflin, 1989.

The Commission on Reading, National Council of Teachers of English. "Basal Readers and the State of American Reading Instruction: A Call for Action." *Language Arts* 66, no. 8 (December 1989).

Crafton, Linda K. *Whole Language: Getting Started . . . Moving Forward*. Katonah, NY: Richard C. Owen, 1991.

Dewey, John. *Experience and Education*. New York: Collier, 1938.

Dillard, Annie. *The Writing Life*. New York: Harper & Row, 1989.

Dillon, J. T. "Research on Questioning and Discussion." *Educational Leadership* 42 (November 1984): 50–56.

Edelsky, Carole, Bess Altwerger, and Barbara Flores. *Whole Language: What's the Difference?* Portsmouth, NH: Heinemann, 1991.

Farrel, Edmund J., and James R. Squire. *Transactions with Literature: A Fifty-Year Perspective*. Urbana, IL: National Council of Teachers of English, 1990.

Feeley, Joan T., Dorothy Strickland, and Shelley B. Wepner. *Process Reading and Writing: A Literature-Based Approach*. New York: Teachers College Press, 1991.

Ferreiro, Emilia, and Ana Teberosky. *Literacy Before Schooling*. Portsmouth, NH: Heinemann, 1982.

Fredericks, Anthony D. "Mental Imagery Activities to Improve Comprehension." *The Reading Teacher* 40, no. 1 (October 1986): 78–81.

Freeman, Judy. *Books Kids Will Sit Still For: A Guide to Using Children's Literature for Librarians, Teachers & Parents*. New York: Bowker, 1990.

Gentry, J. Richard. *Spel . . . Is a Four-Letter Word*. Portsmouth, NH: Heinemann, 1987.

Gillet, Jean Wallace, and Charles Temple. *Understanding Reading Problems: Assessment and Instruction*. 3rd ed. Boston: Little Brown, 1991.

Ginsburg, Herbert, and Sylvia Opper. *Piaget's Theory of Intellectual Development*. Englewood Cliffs, NJ: Prentice-Hall, 1979.

Goodman, Kenneth S. *What's Whole in Whole Language?* Portsmouth, NH: Heinemann, 1987.

———, Lois Bird Bridges, and Yetta M. Goodman, eds. *The Whole Language Catalog*. New York: American School Publishers, Macmillan/McGraw-Hill, 1991.

———, and Frank Smith. "On the Psycholinguistic Method of Teaching Reading." *Elementary School Journal* 41, no. 5.

Goodman, Yetta M., Dorothy J. Watson, and Carolyn L. Burke. *Reading Miscue Inventory*. Katonah, NY: Richard C. Owen, 1987.

Graves, Donald H. *Discover Your Own Literacy*. Portsmouth, NH: Heinemann, 1989.

———. *Writing: Teachers and Children at Work*. Portsmouth, NH: Heinemann, 1983.

Halliday, Michael A. K. *Learning How to Mean: Explorations in the Development of Language*. New York: Elsevier North-Holland, 1975.

Hansen, Jane. "The Manchester Portfolio Project." University of New Hampshire, April 1991.

———. *When Writers Read*. Portsmouth, NH: Heinemann, 1987.

Harste, Jerome, and Kathy Short. *Creating Classrooms for Authors*. Portsmouth, NH: Heinemann, 1988.

Heath, Shirley Brice, and Leslie Mangiola. *Children of Promise: Literate Activity in Linguistically and Culturally Diverse Classrooms*. Washington, D.C.: National Education Association, 1991.

Henderson, Edmund. *Teaching Spelling*. Boston: Houghton Mifflin, 1985.

———, and Shane Templeton. "A Developmental Perspective of Formal Spelling Instruction Through Alphabet, Pattern, and Meaning." *The Elementary School Journal* 86, no. 3 (1986).

Holdaway, Don. *The Foundations of Literacy*. Portsmouth, NH: Heinemann, 1980.

———. *Independence in Reading*. Portsmouth, NH: Heinemann, 1980.

Huck, Charlotte S., Susan Hepler, and Janet Hickman. *Children's Literature in the Elementary School*. New York: Holt, Rinehart and Winston, 1987.

Illich, Ivan. *Deschooling Society*. New York: Harper & Row, 1970.

Jett-Simpson, Mary. "Writing Stories Using Model Structures: The Circle Story." *Language Arts* 58, no. 3 (March 1991): 293–300.

Johnson, Terry D., and Daphne R. Louis. *Literacy Through Literature*. Portsmouth, NH: Heinemann, 1987.

Kukla, Kaila. "David Booth: Drama as a Way of Knowing." *Language Arts* 64, no. 1 (January 1987): 73–78.

Livingston, Myra Cohn. *Poem-Making: Ways to Begin Writing Poetry*. New York: Harper-Collins, 1991.

Lytle, S. L. "Exploring Comprehension Style: A Study of Twelfth Grade Readers' Transactions with Text." Ph.D. diss., University of Pennsylvania, 1982.

Minsky, Marvin. "A Framework for Representing Knowledge." In *The Psychology of Computer Vision*, edited by P. H. Winston. New York: McGraw-Hill, 1975.

Moffet, James. "Liberating Inner Speech." *College Composition and Communication* 36, no. 3 (October 1985): 304–8.

Murray, Donald. *Write to Learn*. New York: Holt, Rinehart and Winston, 1987.

Ogle, Donna M. "K-W-L: A Teaching Model That Develops Active Reading of an Expository Text." *The Reading Teacher* 39 (February 1986): 564–70.

Paterson, Katherine. *Gates of Excellence: On Reading and Writing Books for Children*. New York: Elsevier/Nelson, 1981.

———. *The Spying Heart: More Thoughts on Reading and Writing Books for Children*. New York: Lodestar, 1989.

Read, Charles. "Preschool Children's Knowledge of English Phonology." *Harvard Educational Review* 41 (1971).

Rhodes, Lynn K., and Sally Mejia-Nathenson. "Anecdotal Records: A Powerful Tool for Ongoing Literacy Assessment." *The Reading Teacher* 45, no. 7 (March 1992): 502–8.

Rico, Gabriele L. *Writing the Natural Way: Using Right-Brain Techniques to Release Your Expressive Powers*. Los Angeles: J. P. Tarcher, 1983.

Robb, Laura. "Breaking Through Traditions: Initiating the Writing Workshop." *Reading in Virginia* (Virginia State Reading Association) 14 (Spring 1989).

———. "Building Bridges: Eighth and Third Grade Read Together." *The New Advocate* 4, no. 3 (Summer 1991): 151–60.

———. "A Cause for Celebration: Reading and Writing with At-Risk Children." *The New Advocate* 6, no. 1 (Winter 1993): 25–40.

———. "Mapping the Agonists." *The Reading Teacher* 42, no. 7 (March 1989): 549.

———. "More Poetry, Please." *The New Advocate* 3, no. 3 (Summer 1990): 197–203.

Rosenblatt, Louise M. *Literature as Exploration*. 4th ed. New York: The Modern Language Association of America, 1983.

———. *The Reader, the Text, the Poem: The Transactional Theory of the Literary Work*. Carbondale, IL: Southern Illinois University Press, 1978.

———. "Retrospect." In *Transactions with Literature*. Urbana, IL: National Council of Teachers of English, 1990.

Smith, Frank. *Reading without Nonsense*. New York: Teachers College, Columbia University, 1978.

Stauffer, Russell G. *Directing the Reading-Thinking Process*. New York: Harper & Row, 1975.

———. *The Language-Experience Approach to the Teaching of Reading*. Rev. ed. New York: Harper & Row, 1980.

Sullivan, Anne McCrary. "The Natural Reading Life: A High-School Anomaly." *English Journal* (October 1991): 40–46.

Tannen, Deborah. "Hearing Voices in Conversation, Fiction, and Mixed Genres." In *Linguistics in Context: Connecting Observation and Understanding Lectures from the 1985 LSA/TESOL and NEH Institutes*. Ablex Publishing Company, 1988.

Taylor, Denny, and Dorothy S. Strickland. *Family Storybook Reading*. Portsmouth, NH: Heinemann, 1986.

Templeton, Shane. "New Trends in an Historical Perspective: Old Story, New Resolution—Sound and Meaning in Spelling." *Language Arts* 69 (October 1992): 454–66.

Tierney, Robert J., Mark A. Carter, and Laura E. Desai. *Portfolio Assessment in Reading-Writing Classrooms*. Norwood, MA: Christopher-Gordon Publishers, 1991.

Trelease, Jim. *The New Read-Aloud Handbook*. New York: Viking-Penguin, 1989.

———. *The Read-Aloud Handbook*. New York: Viking-Penguin, 1985.

Valencia, Sheila. "A Portfolio Approach to Classroom Reading Assessment: The Whys, Whats and Hows." *The Reading Teacher* 43, no. 4 (January 1990): 338–40.

Vaughan, Joseph L., and Thomas H. Estes. *Reading and Reasoning Beyond the Primary Grades*. Boston: Allyn and Bacon, 1986.

Vygotsky, Lev S. *Thought and Language*. Translated by A. Kozulin. Cambridge, MA: MIT Press, 1986.

Watson, Dorothy, Carolyn Burke, and Jerome Harste. *Whole Language: Inquiring Voices*. New York: Scholastic, 1989.

Wells, Gordon. *The Meaning Makers: Children Learning Language and Using Language to Learn*. Portsmouth, NH: Heinemann, 1986.

Welty, Eudora. *One Writer's Beginnings*. New York: Warner Books, 1983.

Wigginton, Eliot. *Sometimes a Shining Moment: The Foxfire Experience*. New York: Anchor Press/Doubleday, 1985.

CHILDREN'S BOOKS CITED

Alexander, Lloyd. *The Kestrel*. New York: Dutton, 1982.

Andersen, Hans Christian. *Hans Christian Andersen: The Complete Fairy Tales*. Translated by Erik Haugaard. New York: Doubleday, 1974.

Babbitt, Natalie. *Tuck Everlasting*. New York: Farrar, Straus & Giroux, 1975.

———. "The Very Pretty Lady." In *The Devil's Storybook*. New York: Farrar, Straus & Giroux, 1974.

Baum, L. Frank. *The Wonderful Wizard of Oz*. New York: World, 1972.

Begay, Shonto. *Maii and Cousin Horned Toad: A Traditional Navajo Story*. New York: Scholastic, 1992.

Bennett, Jill. *Teeny Tiny*. Illustrated by Tomie De Paola. New York: Putnam, 1985.

Blanco, Alberto. *The Desert Mermaid*. Illustrated by Patricia Riveh. San Francisco: Children's Book Press, 1992. (Bilingual in English and Spanish.)

Bowden, Joan Chase. *Why the Tides Ebb and Flow*. Illustrated by Marc Brown. Boston: Houghton Mifflin, 1979.

Bradbury, Ray. "The Veldt." In *Saturday Evening Post* under the title "The World the Children Made." 1950.

Brett, Jan. *Annie and the Wild Animals*. Boston: Houghton Mifflin, 1989.

Bryan, Ashley. *Turtle Knows Your Name*. New York: Atheneum, 1989.

Bunting, Eve. *Terrible Things: An Allegory of the Holocaust*. Philadelphia: The Jewish Publication Society, 1989.

———. *The Wall*. Illustrated by Ronald Himler. New York: Clarion, 1990.

Burnett, Frances Hodgson. *The Secret Garden*. Illustrated by Tasha Tudor. New York: Lippincott, 1962.

Byars, Betsy. *Cracker Jackson*. New York: Viking, 1985.

———. *The Pinballs*. New York: Harper & Row, 1987.

Carle, Eric. *The Very Busy Spider*. New York: Philomel, 1989.

———. *The Very Hungry Caterpillar*. New York: Philomel, 1981.

Carroll, Lewis [Charles L. Dodgson]. *Alice's Adventures in Wonderland* and *Through the Looking Glass*. Illustrated by John Tenniel. New York: Macmillan, 1963.

Collier, James Lincoln, and Christopher Collier. *My Brother Sam Is Dead*. New York: Macmillan, 1974.

Collodi, Carlo. *The Adventures of Pinocchio*. Illustrated by Naiad Einsel. New York: Macmillan, 1963.

Conrad, Joseph. *Lord Jim*. New York: Bantam, 1981.

Coolidge, Olivia. *Greek Myths*. Boston: Houghton Mifflin, 1949.

Cooney, Barbara. *Miss Rumphius*. New York: Viking, 1982.

Cormier, Robert. *The Chocolate War*. New York: Pantheon, 1974.

Dahl, Roald. *The Wonderful Story of Henry Sugar and Six More*. New York: Puffin, 1988.

Ehrlich, Amy. *Lucy's Winter Tale*. Illustrated by Troy Howell. New York: Dial, 1992.

Fritz, Jean. *Traitor: The Case of Benedict Arnold*. New York: Putnam, 1981.

Funk, Charles Earle. *Thereby Hangs a Tale: Stories of Curious Word Origins*. New York: Harper & Row, 1985.

Funk, Wilfred. *Word Origins and Their Romantic Stories*. New York: Crown, 1979.

Gág, Wanda. *Millions of Cats*. New York: Coward-McCann, 1977.

Galdone, Paul. *The Gingerbread Boy*. New York: Clarion, 1983.

Gallaz, Christophe, and Roberto Innocenti. *Rose Blanche*. Illustrated by Roberto Innocenti. New York: Stewart, Tabori & Chang, 1990.

George, Jean Craighead. *The Cry of the Crow*. New York: Harper & Row, 1980.

———. *Julie of the Wolves*. New York: Harper & Row, 1972.

———. *My Side of the Mountain*. New York: Dutton, 1988.

———. *The Summer of the Falcon*. New York: Harper & Row, 1979.

———. *The Talking Earth*. New York: Harper & Row, 1983.

———. *Water Sky*. New York: Harper & Row, 1987.

Giblin, James. *The Riddle of the Rosetta Stone: Key to Ancient Egypt*. New York: Harper-Collins, 1990.

———. *The Truth about Santa Claus*. New York: Crowell, 1985.

———. *The Truth about Unicorns*. New York: HarperCollins, 1991.

Grahame, Kenneth. *The Wind in the Willows*. Illustrated by Ernest H. Shepard. New York: Scribner, 1983.

Grimm, Jacob and Wilhelm. *Fairy Tales of the Brothers Grimm*. Illustrated by Kay Nielsen. New York: Viking, 1979.

———. *Grimms' Fairy Tales: Twenty Stories*. Illustrated by Arthur Rackham. New York: Viking, 1973.

Henkes, Kevin. *Chrysanthemum*. New York: Greenwillow, 1991.

Hoberman, Mary Ann. *A House Is a House for Me*. Illustrated by Betty Fraser. New York: Viking, 1978.

Hunt, Irene. *No Promises in the Wind*. New York: Berkley, 1987.

Hutchins, Pat. *Rosie's Walk*. New York: Macmillan, 1968.

Joyce, William. *George Shrinks*. New York: Harper & Row, 1985.

Keats, Ezra Jack. *Over in the Meadow*. New York: Scholastic, 1971.

Kellogg, Steven. *Chicken Little*. New York: Morrow, 1985.

———. *The Island of the Skog*. New York: Dial, 1973.

———. *Mike Fink: A Tall Tale*. New York: Morrow, 1992.

———. *The Mysterious Tadpole*. New York: Dial, 1977.

———. *The Mystery of the Missing Red Mitten*. New York: Dial, 1974.

———. *Pinkerton, Behave!* New York: Dial, 1979.

———. *There Was an Old Woman*. Reissued ed. New York: Four Winds Press, 1984.

Keyes, Daniel. *Flowers for Algernon*. San Diego: Harcourt Brace, 1966.

Lee, Harper. *To Kill a Mockingbird*. New York: Warner Books, 1982.

Little, Jean. *Hey World, Here I Am!* Illustrated by Sue Truesdell. New York: Harper & Row, 1989.

Livingston, Myra Cohn. *Celebrations*. New York: Holiday House, 1985.

———. *There Was a Place and Other Poems*. New York: Margaret K. McElderry, 1988.

Louie, Al-Ling. *Yeh-Shen: A Cinderella Story from China*. New York: Philomel, 1982.

MacLachlan, Patricia, *Sarah, Plain and Tall*. New York: Harper & Row, 1985.

———. *Through Grandpa's Eyes*. Illustrated by Deborah Kogan Ray. New York: Harper & Row, 1980.

Marshall, James. *Fox at School*. New York: Dial, 1983.

———. *Goldilocks and the Three Bears*. New York: Dial, 1988.

———. *The Three Little Pigs*. New York: Dial, 1989.

Marshall, James Vance. *Walkabout*. Littleton, MA: Sundance, 1984.

Martin, Bill, Jr. *Brown Bear, Brown Bear, What Do You See?* Illustrated by Eric Carle. New York: Holt, 1983.

Maruki, Toshi. *Hiroshima No Pika*. New York: Lothrop, Lee & Shepard, 1982.

Mayer, Marianna. *The Unicorn and the Lake*. New York: Dial, 1982.

Meltzer, Milton. *Rescue: The Story of How Gentiles Saved Jews in the Holocaust*. New York: Harper & Row, 1988.

Merriam, Eve. "A Lazy Thought." In *Jamboree*. New York: Dell, 1984.

Milne, A. A. *Winnie-the-Pooh*. Illustrated by Ernest H. Shepard. New York: Dutton, 1926.

Noyes, Alfred. "The Highwayman." In *The Family Book of Verse*. New York: Harper & Row, 1961.

Olsen, Tillie. *Tell Me a Riddle*. New York: Dell, 1956.

Paterson, Katherine. *Bridge to Terabithia*. New York: Crowell, 1977.

———. *The Great Gilly Hopkins*. New York: Crowell, 1978.

———. *Of Nightingales That Weep*. New York: Crowell, 1974.

———. *The Sign of the Chrysanthemum*. New York: Harper & Row, 1973.

———. *The Tale of the Mandarin Ducks*. Illustrated by Leo and Diane Dillon. New York: Lodestar, 1990.

Paulsen, Gary. *Hatchet*. New York: Viking, 1987.

———. *The River*. New York: Dell, 1991.

Peck, Richard. *Dreamland Lake*. New York: Doubleday, 1973.

Pyle, Howard. *The Story of King Arthur and His Knights*. New York: Scribner, 1984.

Rappaport, Doreen. *The Journey of Meng*. Illustrated by Yang Ming-Yi. New York: Dial, 1991.

Roop, Peter. "Keep the Lights Burning, Abbie." In *Silver Burdett & Ginn Reading Series*, level II. New York: Silver Burdett & Ginn, 1989.

Rylant, Cynthia. *Henry and Mudge in the Green Time: The Third Book of Their Adventures.* Illustrated by Suçie Stevenson. New York: Macmillan, 1987.

Sandburg, Carl. "Fog." In *Harvest Poems, 1910–1960*. New York: Harcourt, Brace & World, 1960.

Scieszka, Jon. *The True Story of the Three Little Pigs*. Illustrated by Lane Smith. New York: Viking, 1989.

Sendak, Maurice. *Chicken Soup with Rice.* New York: Harper & Row, 1962.

Sharmat, Marjorie. *Nate the Great.* New York: Coward, 1972.

Showers, Paul. *The Listening Walk.* Illustrated by Aliki. New York: HarperCollins, 1991.

Simon, Seymour. *Big Cats.* New York: HarperCollins, 1991.

Sleator, William. *Interstellar Pig.* New York: Dutton, 1984.

Speare, Elizabeth George. *The Sign of the Beaver*. Boston: Houghton Mifflin, 1983.

Staples, Suzanne Fisher. *Shabanu: Daughter of the Wind.* New York: Knopf, 1989.

Steptoe, John. *Mufaro's Beautiful Daughters.* New York: Lothrop, Lee & Shepard, 1987.

Strasser, Todd. *The Wave*. New York: Dell, 1981.

Strieber, Whitley. *Wolf of Shadows.* New York: Knopf, 1985.

Sutcliff, Rosemary. *Flame-colored Taffeta*. New York: Farrar, Straus & Giroux, 1986.

Swope, Sam. *The Araboolies of Liberty Street.* New York: Clarkson Potter, 1989.

Taylor, Mildred. *Mississippi Bridge.* New York: Dial, 1990.

Terban, Marvin. *Eight Ate: A Feast of Homonym Riddles.* Illustrated by Giulio Maestro. New York: Clarion, 1982.

Travers, P. L. *Mary Poppins.* Illustrated by Mary Shepard. San Diego: Harcourt Brace Jovanovich, 1934.

Tresselt, Alvin. *The Gift of the Tree.* New York: Lothrop, Lee & Shepard, 1992.

Volavkova, H., ed. *I Never Saw Another Butterfly. . . .* New York: McGraw-Hill, 1964.

Wallace, Karen. *Think of an Eel.* Cambridge, MA: Candlewick Press, 1993.

Watanabe, Shigeo. *What a Good Lunch!* Illustrated by Yasuo Ohtomo. New York: Philomel, 1981.

Wells, Rosemary. *Hazel's Amazing Mother.* New York: Dial, 1985.

Winthrop, Elizabeth. *The Castle in the Attic.* New York: Holiday House, 1985.

Worth, Valerie. *More Small Poems.* New York: Farrar, Straus & Giroux, 1976.

———. *Small Poems.* New York: Farrar, Straus & Giroux, 1972.

———. *Still More Small Poems.* New York: Farrar, Straus & Giroux, 1978.

Yorinks, Arthur. *Hey, Al.* Illustrated by Richard Egielski. New York: Farrar, Straus & Giroux, 1986.

Young, Ed. *Lon Po Po: A Red Riding Hood Story from China.* New York: Philomel, 1989.

INDEX

SYNOPSIS

PART ONE: TEACHER AS LEARNER

BEGINNINGS
Author's first teaching experience

BREAKING TRADITIONS
Author's break with traditional curricula
The traditional learning model
The whole language learning model
The challenges of change

A SOLID FOUNDATION
Gordon Wells and active learning
Brian Cambourne's seven conditions for children's literacy learning
Four additional learning conditions
Applying the eleven conditions to teachers and adults
Discover and assess your own teaching model

GETTING STARTED
Making the transition to whole language
Suggestions from teachers
The changes you will experience during transition
Designing curricula
Teaching process: minilessons and demonstrations
Whole class gathering

Self-evaluation

Teacher-student recommendations and goals

The story of James and Robbie: two different readers

WRITING PROCESS IN A WHOLE LANGUAGE CLASSROOM

An overview of the writing process

Collecting

Focusing

Ordering

First drafts

Revising

Editing

Suggestions for writing minilessons

Literary structures and techniques

Writing conferences

Whole group

Miniconferences

One-on-one conferences

Publishing students' writing

List of authentic writing events

PART THREE: THEORY INTO PRACTICE

LITERATURE DISCUSSION GROUPS: TALKING TO REFLECT AND INTERPRET

The value of literature response groups

Diverse membership

Teacher modeling

Choice

Meaningful reading and talking

Groups foster social and individual learning

Some management tips for organizing response groups

Transcriptions of students' discussions

Some strategies that stimulate discussions

Problems characters faced

Events and dialogue

Setting

From beginning to ending

READING TO WRITE

Five conditions that foster reading-writing connections

Collaborative innovations on texts

Individual students' reading-writing connections

Folk- and fairy tales can reclaim memories

Tapping memories for writing

Collecting words for writing

INQUIRY AND CONTENT AREA JOURNALS

Student-made questions

Writing to learn in content subjects

Inquiry notebook

Double-entry journals

Mathematics journals

Fifteen suggestions for writing to learn in math

Critical thinking and analysis

Research: four recursive stages

Deciding

Collecting

Sharing

Selecting

SPELLING AND WORD STUDY

Overview of the five developmental spelling stages

Identifying a child's developmental stage through writing, a word features list, and a qualitative spelling inventory

How to administer and analyze spelling inventories

Word sorting

Changing your spelling program

Learning new vocabulary

AUTHENTIC ASSESSMENT

Authentic assessment defined

Evaluation as conclusions drawn from assessment

Anecdotal records

Tips for taking them

Suggested anecdotal note form

How to use them for evaluation

Portfolios

Holistic portfolios

About the Author

Laura Robb has been a teacher and mentor for the past thirty years. She speaks regularly at the International Reading Association, National Council of Teachers of English, and Virginia State Reading Association conventions. Her articles have appeared in numerous publications, including the *New Advocate* and *Parent and Preschooler,* and she is the compiler of two upcoming poetry anthologies for children. Laura Robb and her husband, Lloyd, are the parents of two grown children, Evan and Anina, and make their home in Winchester, Virginia.